Social-Scientific Old Testament Criticism

The Biblical Seminar
47

edited by
David J. Chalcraft

Sheffield
Academic Press

Copyright © 1997 Sheffield Academic Press

Published by
Sheffield Academic Press Ltd
Mansion House
19 Kingfield Road
Sheffield S11 9AS
England

Typeset by Sheffield Academic Press
and
Printed on acid-free paper in Great Britain
by Cromwell Press
Melksham, Wiltshire

British Library Cataloguing in Publication Data

A catalogue record for this book is available
from the British Library

ISBN 1-85075-813-1

CONTENTS

ABBREVIATIONS

AB	Anchor Bible
AESC	*Annales Économies, Sociétés, Civilisations*
AJS	*American Journal of Sociology*
ASSR	*Archives de Sciences Sociales des Religions*
BA	*Biblical Archaeologist*
BASOR	*Bulletin of the American Schools of Oriental Research*
Bib	*Biblica*
BibB	Biblische Beiträge
BibLeb	*Bibel und Leben*
BKAT	Biblischer Kommentar: Altes Testament
BZAW	Beihefte zur *ZAW*
BZNW	Beihefte zur *ZNW*
CBQ	*Catholic Biblical Quarterly*
ConBOT	Coniectanea biblica, Old Testament
CONCILIUM	N. Greincher, N. Mette and M. Leféure (eds.), *Concilium: Religion in the Eighties-Popular religion* (Edinburgh: T. & T. Clark, 1986)
DBSup	*Dictionnaire de la Bible, Supplément*
HTR	*Harvard Theological Review*
HUCA	*Hebrew Union College Annual*
IEJ	*Israel Exploration Journal*
Int	*Interpretation*
JAAR	*Journal of the American Academy of Religion*
JAOS	*Journal of the American Oriental Society*
JBL	*Journal of Biblical Literature*
JNES	*Journal of Near Eastern Studies*
JNSL	*Journal of Northwest Semitic Languages*
JQR	*Jewish Quarterly Review*
JRAI	*Journal of Royal Anthropological Institute*
JSOT	*Journal for the Study of the Old Testament*
JSOTSup	*Journal for the Study of the Old Testament*, Supplement Series
JSSR	*Journal for the Scientific Study of Religion*
JTS	*Journal of Theological Studies*
LRP	*La religion populaire: Paris 17-19 octobre 1977* (Colloques Internationaux du Centre National de la Recherche Scientifique, 576: Paris: Éditions du Centre National de la Recherche Scientifique, 1979)
NCB	New Century Bible
NTS	*New Testament Studies*

OPRAT	P.H. Vrijhof and J. Waardenburg (eds.), *Official and Popular Religion: Analysis of a Theme for Religious Studies* (The Hague: Mouton, 1979)
OrAnt	*Oriens antiquus*
OT	Old Testament
OTS	*Oudtestamentische Studiën*
PEQ	*Palestine Exploration Quarterly*
ROPFES	E. Badone (ed.), *Religious Orthodoxy and Popular Faith in European Society* (Princeton: Princeton University Press, 1990)
SA	*Sociological Analysis*
SBL	Society of Biblical Literature
SI	*Sociological Inquiry*
SJOT	*Scandinavian Journal of the Old Testament*
SJT	*Scottish Journal of Theology*
TDOT	G.J. Botterweck and H. Ringgren (eds.), *Theological Dictionary of the Old Testament*
TRu	*Theologische Rundschau*
TynBul	*Tyndale Bulletin*
VT	*Vetus Testamentum*
WMANT	Wissenschaftliche Monographien zum Alten und Neuen Testament
ZAW	*Zeitschrift für die alttestamentliche Wissenschaft*
ZNW	*Zeitschrift für die neutestamentliche Wissenschaft*

LIST OF CONTRIBUTORS

Lyn M. Bechtel, Bethlehem, PA, USA

Elizabeth Bellefontaine, Halifax, NS, Canada

J. Berlinerblau, Brooklyn, NY, USA

John L. Berquist, Louisville, KY, USA

Mark B. Brett, Melbourne, Australia

Walter Brueggeman, Decatur, GA, USA

Patricia Dutcher-Walls, Toronto, Canada

David Fiensy, Grayson, KY, USA

James W. Flanagan, Cleveland, OH, USA

Gary A. Herion, Oneonta, NY, USA

David Jobling, Saskatoon, Canada

Thomas W. Overholt, Stevens Point, WI, USA

J David Pleins, Santa Clara, CA, USA

D.N. Premnath, Rochester, NY, USA

Cyril S. Rodd, Havant, UK

J.W. Rogerson, Sheffield, UK

Lori Rowlett, Newport, VA, USA

Keith W. Whitelam, Stirling, UK

INTRODUCTION

In justifying his application of a sociological imagination[1] to Old Testament materials Max Weber (1864–1920) appealed to the fact that his approach was bound to look at old questions in new ways (Weber 1952). The enthusiasm for social science within biblical studies has been growing considerably in the last two decades and one can detect a sharing in Weber's view that social science has an ability, in a discipline normally dominated by philological, theological and humanistic approaches to open new vistas and settle old *crux interpretum*. In the selection made here from some 71 issues of *The Journal of Old Testament Studies* over the last 20 years, the promise of the approach and the dedication to it clearly emerges. Since Weber wrote, what constitutes a social scientific approach to Old Testament times and literature has been further elaborated and in some quarters even rendered fully 'scientific'. Indeed, some of the practitioners in this area can often approach the positivistic confidence expressed by one of the other great founders of sociology, namely, Emile Durkheim (1857–1917), who, in *The Rules of Sociological Method*, managed to carve out a niche for a sociological discipline. Since, he argued, there is a distinct class of phenomena, which he labelled social facts, it was possible to study these external coercive forces scientifically and, moreover, they were readily distinguishable from a whole range of vague ideas and phenomena considered, inaccurately by the non-specialist, to be 'social'. Moreover, these social facts were explainable only by reference to other social facts (Durkheim 1895). I will return to this point

1. The phrase 'a sociological imagination' derives from C.W. Mills (1959) and whilst it betrays my disciplinary context, I use it to subsume the perspectives of historical sociology, cultural anthropology and social theory in this introductory essay. It seems to me that these are the key subjects in Old Testament Social Science Criticism with economics, political science and psychological/psycho-historical approaches being less commonly attested.

when thinking about what constitutes a contribution to social science criticism in Old Testament studies.

The fundamental research strategy for Durkheim was comparative and historical. Weber was equally historical in his approach, but held a healthy scepticism towards the nomothetic tendency. Weber's *verstehende* approach and the causal significance he gave to motives and meaningful orientations to action in his work (e.g. Weber 1920) also distinguishes his sociology from Durkheim's, albeit early, suspicion of non-scientific values and common-sense knowledge in social scientific research. Contemporary social theory has often been accused of retreating 'into the present'; hence one good reason for maintaining a lively interest in the classics of anthropological and sociological theory is their importance for the pursuit of historical research, which is central to the enterprise of biblical studies. Classical theory can also serve to unite diverse practitioners.

There have been some truly inspirational studies in applying social science to Old Testament materials. Indeed, the whole field became an essential one to work in after the publication of Norman Gottwald's path-breaking *Tribes of Yahweh*, which convinced many, including the present author, that interpreting the Hebrew Bible in the (post-, global) modern world was not possible without the assistance of social science. In this volume, one cannot fail to be convinced by the passionate argument of Brueggemann for the necessity of looking at the social dimensions of theodicy. Similarly, Overholt's use of the ethnography of the Ghost Dance of the 1890s, which has been protean for his work, and Premnath's application of insights from the sociology of development, are but two examples of the imaginative use that can be made of comparative materials. Nevertheless, it is perhaps best to describe Old Testament social scientific criticism as a series of (often unrelated) experiments. What the area lacks is a tradition, and a shared language of concepts and methods. One way that this is provided in social science is through the common (though now increasingly questioned and extended/contracted) sharing of key (classical) texts, immersion in which cultivates a disciplinary perspective and imagination which allows for communication and debate even when participants come from totally different theoretical positions. A task remaining in Old Testament studies is the search for more common paradigms in so far as, with the possible exception of the study of early Israel and the formation of the state, most contributions are not written in dialogue with others; rather, we have a series of individual contributions each often utilizing a new or different theorist. Alternatively, certain social scientists are popular within biblical studies to the exclusion of others: for example, Peter Berger, Gerhard Lenski and Mary Douglas are perhaps the most frequently cited, whilst it is often commented that Weber's work, for example, has been unexplainably overlooked (e.g. Berlinerblau in this volume). This selection may well contribute to the development of a comprehensive tradition (which would include Weber, Berger, Douglas and a host of others) by bringing together in one volume a variety of studies and inviting comparison of their theoretical and methodological bases.

Keeping classical disputes in mind is also important in Old Testament circles since it reminds us continually of the need to find a balance, on the one hand, between a rigorous, controlled and systematic approach to the materials and the various theories, concepts and models that are suggestive, with, on the other, a developed sociological imagination which is more attuned to typical questions and issues (e.g. the relation between action and structure, social stability and social change and the social construction of realities and their contestation) than the 'scientific' application of formal procedures and predictive theories. That is, keeping the Durkheimian and Weberian traditions identified above in creative tension.

For example, Cyril Rodd (in this volume)—and others have often repeated the argument since—has a tendency, alongside some otherwise telling criticism, to restrict sociological work to a small range of particular methods of data collection; these tools he sees as incapable of application to historical societies. He is of course correct in the observation that questionnaires can hardly be administered as neither can participant observations be carried out, in the study of historical societies (though of course they are of relevance for the sociological study of contemporary biblical/textual communities). The point is that this does not exhaust social science; neither does it reflect the scepticism with which these particular methods can be viewed by social scientists themselves. Further, it does not encourage looking at those methods in social science that are geared specifically to textual/discourse analysis. In contrast, a growing sophistication is observable in Old Testament criticism which continually asks which social groups are being considered when one is talking of the construct 'Israelite society'. This development is a direct result of social scientific perspectives and is not reducible to any one technique or methodology and is, in effect, far more significant to the field.

One of the principles that guided my selection was this felt need for balance between 'science' and 'imagination'; between positivistic and interpretative strands; between social scientific modelling and 'grounded theory'. There are many fascinating articles in *JSOT* that have for their subject areas of ancient Israelite life and thought that are of concern to social science: roles, power, gender, values, law and the quality of life, for example. What one can frequently find, however, is an under-theorization of those concepts. One impact of social science on Old Testament studies is the acceptance that there are many social assumptions and implicit theories often buried unconsciously in the reconstructions offered of Israelite history, culture and society. It follows therefore that it is good practice at least to attempt to control these prejudgments by recognition of these very assumptions, through grounding in social theory; it also follows that investigating ancient Israelite social worlds requires at least a familiarity with social science discussions. The point here is that, building on the contributions already made, there is great scope for further development in many areas that would benefit from a more thorough articulation and application of a social scientific imagination. In particular, the areas of law and deviance (from the criminal to the stigmatized) seem a rich vein to mine (cf. Chalcraft 1990), as does the extension of social stratification to include gender and age alongside traditional socioeconomic categories, together with a theorization of the sources and nature of power. Alternatively, there are also some examples that are over-theorized: in the enthusiasm for a new approach, and one that seems, as Gary Herion alerts us, to offer the aura of 'science', Old Testament materials are unable, as it were, to fight back against the rigid models and courses of social development postulated in some apparently widely accepted social theory.

The distinguishing features of social science are its conceptual precision, its comparative methodology and its desire to continually revise and expand its theories of societies in general. Since the Old Testament materials are often the case to be examined with the aid of social theory, rather than being just one example among many for the development of generalizations and the comprehension of fascinating social worlds, it is easy for Old Testament scholars to forget that social scientific criticism should not be restricted to the application of models and predictive theories in an effort to reconstruct the world 'behind the texts'; rather, it embraces a whole range of questions, theories, concepts and methodologies. Most importantly it involves sociological and anthropological 'ways of thinking'. These are all used to illuminate the worlds within the texts which, moreover, span the whole breadth of ancient Israelite social forms and productions. I have selected from such a range of interests that is admirably reflected in *JSOT*.

The articles selected and grouped together are wide-ranging, spanning from involved, sceptical (yet helpful and clear-headed) methodological and theoretical overviews, to contributions to the substantive areas of early Israel and the development of the state; the formal and informal regulation of social life and the experience of deviance; the distribution of power and justice and its articulation with stratification systems and various *Weltanschauung*, and, the performance of social roles and the processes of group formation, maintenance, growth, alteration and decline. In these studies we encounter both formal discussions of models of Israelite society and attempts to work closely with the texts less with a particular model or theory in mind, than with an informed social scientific consciousness. I would include under the latter category the contributions of Bechtel, Pleins, Berquist and Rowlett. This Reader provides examples, therefore, of different types of social-scientific Old Testament criticism for examination and comparison.

There is also a section on the sociology of knowledge: given the reflexive nature of social science it is no surprise to learn that Old Testament scholars have not been slow in appreciating that we ourselves are implicated in the approaches we apply to others. Arguably, one of the key impacts of social science on Old Testament studies, which can be clearly gathered from the contributions of Herion and Brett in this volume, is the application of social science to our own practice which then, in turn, allows us to see how knowledge of the social world of ancient Israel is articulated and manipulated in the texts themselves. A focus on social theory *in* the Old Testament rather than the production of a social theory *of* the Old Testament. Rather than social science offering a sharpness to cut through various Gordian knots, the approach helps us appreciate the highly complex nature of the warp and woof not only of our materials and ancient Israelite worlds, but of our own worlds and productions as well. No one was more aware than Weber himself of the complex, multilayered nature of social life and the limits to making categorical and final interpretations of social phenomena and we do well to keep these notions alive (e.g. Weber 1919; Chalcraft 1994) at the same time as we seek to be precise about the social and how we are to interpret it.

Of course, social scientific Old Testament criticism existed prior to the contributions of Durkheim and Weber and is now moving—as recent issues of *JSOT* confirm—swiftly along new, but perhaps still far from fully crystallized, postmodernist and feminist directions. The affinities with cultural studies and the New Historicism grow closer and closer. To date, a range of approaches, including the structural-functionalist, the systemic, the structuralist, the post-structuralist, the social-evolutionist and the cultural-materialist have been explored, even though the traditions have not always been openly acknowledged or theorized by practitioners. We have yet to explore fully the interpretative and ethnomethodological traditions in social science and give equal attention to the micro-dimensions of social life as to the macro- (and how to link them), although developments along these lines are occurring as part of the attempt to answer Jobling's question, in reviewing Gottwald, of how the twain—social scientific and literary approaches—may meet?

When the necessary history of the approach comes to be written it will need to articulate fully the traditions of social science utilized. The time-span involved is also not protracted. It is quite likely that, for the modern period at least, the discussion will begin with the impact of Montesquieu and continue, alongside examination of the important contributions from the likes of William Robertson Smith and Louis Wallis, with concentration on many figures previously overlooked, including the work of Herbert Spencer, born in Derby in 1820 and director of the multi-volume *Descriptive Sociology* which includes the volume *Hebrews and Phoenicians* of 1880. To be sure, a thorough exegesis of the contributions of classical theory, in particular of Durkheim and Weber, will be required.

The history will probably consider future prospects with reference, for example, to the work of Habermas, Foucault, Baudrillard, Bataille and Irigaray, to name but a few. One thing is certain: the contribution of *The Journal of Old Testament Studies* will figure prominently in the account. Indeed, and just to take the contributions to the discussions of early Israel as an example, *JSOT* has carried examination of the amphictyonic hypothesis, was prescient in its publication of key debates surrounding the 'revolt hypothesis' and then blazed a trail of review of this thesis and other reconstructions—chiefdoms, segmentary social systems, processes of highland settlement and the frontier thesis. One can also find examination of the impact of social science on historiographical practice in general, and latterly *JSOT* has taken readers through the encounter with the development of what might be called 'total history'. This debate alone could fill the pages of this Reader and hence I selected as ground-breaking and representative the well-argued work of James Flanagan, the theoretically informed scepticism of John Rogerson about the postulation of Israel as a segmentary society, and rounded off the section with the sober and extensive review of the present situation regarding social scientific and historical reconstructions of early Israel and their limits ably constructed by Keith Whitelam.

In all areas I have had a difficult, while challenging and informative, task to perform in whittling down the selection to those chosen here. My only hope is that readers find the material selected ample encouragement to renew their acquaintance with the whole area, both within and without the pages of *JSOT*, and join the enterprise of developing further a sophisticated social-scientific imagination in Old Testament Studies.

BIBLIOGRAPHY

Chalcraft, D. J.
1990   'Deviance and Legitimate Action in the Book of Judges' in D.J.A.
            Clines *et al.* (eds.), *The Bible in Three Dimensions* (JSOTSup, 87;
            Sheffield: JSOT Press, 1990): 177-201.
1994   'Bringing the Text Back In: On ways of Reading the Iron Cage Meta-
            phor in the Two Editions of *The Protestant Ethic*', in Larry J. Ray and
            Michael Reed (eds.), *Organizing Modernity: New Weberian Perspec-
            tives on Work, Organisation and Society* (London: Routledge): 16-45.
Durkheim, E.
1895   *The Rules of Sociological Method* (London: Macmillan [1982]).
Mills, C.W.
1959   *The Sociological Imagination* (Oxford: Oxford University Press).
Weber, M.
1919   'Science as a Vocation', in H. Gerth and C.W. Mills (eds.), *From Max
            Weber* (London: Routledge [1947]): 129-58.
1920   *The Protestant Ethic and the Spirit of Capitalism* (London: Unwin and
            Hyman [1990]).
1952   *Ancient Judaism* (Glencoe: The Free Press).

THEORY AND METHODOLOGY

JSOT 19 (1981), pp. 95-106

ON APPLYING A SOCIOLOGICAL THEORY TO BIBLICAL STUDIES

Cyril S. Rodd

A rapid survey of writings which contain sociological approaches to the Old and New Testaments shows that they fall into three categories: 1. some scholars are essentially historians who examine the evidence with an awareness of the influence which social forces have upon individuals and groups in society; 2. others utilize explicit sociological concepts such as 'millenarian cult', 'sect', 'class', 'role' or 'charismatic authority', though frequently the terms are used descriptively rather than analytically and are not always given precise content;[1] 3. the third type of study applies a specific sociological theory to a particular problem. It is with this last that I am concerned in this paper. I propose to examine two studies: John G. Gager's *Kingdom and Community* and Robert P. Carroll's *When Prophecy Failed.*[2] The scope of Gager's book is broader than this category and in much of it the other two approaches are dominant. Here I confine myself to a consideration of the chapters in which he considers Festinger's theory of cognitive dissonance and Coser's theory of the functions of social conflict.

By now the theory of cognitive dissonance is probably well enough known. Briefly it states that human beings cannot tolerate conflict between different beliefs or experiences. When such dissonance

---

1. I place the works of Gerd Theissen, David L. Mealand and Howard C. Kee in these two categories, as well as parts of Gager's book. For an overall survey and listing of the literature see R. Scroggs: 'The Sociological Interpretation of the New Testament: The Present State of Research', *NTS* 26 (1979–80), pp. 164-79. It is of interest, and possibly significant, that Max Weber in *Ancient Israel* (Glencoe, 1952) fails to set out the theoretical basis of his work, which is essentially descriptive (see my article 'Max Weber and Ancient Judaism', *SJT* 32 (1979), pp. 457-69.

2. John G. Gager, *Kingdom and Community* (Englewood Cliffs: Prentice–Hall, 1975); Robert P. Carroll, *When Prophecy Failed* (London: SCM Press, 1979).

occurs, for example, with the acquisition of new information or when a prediction is not fulfilled, pressure to resolve the inconsistency will build up and various means of reducing the tension will be adopted. Among these the most common are: avoiding the conflicting evidence; securing group support for the original belief by engaging in increased interaction within the group and securing additional members by proselytizing; and reinterpreting or rationalizing the beliefs. In his study *When Prophecy Fails*,[3] Festinger stresses group support and proselytizing, although he does not ignore the other methods, and Roger Brown points out that in fact there was, in the case studied by Festinger, a massive reinterpretation of the prophecy before the proselytizing was possible.[4]

Festinger sets out five conditions that must be present before one can expect proselytizing to occur: 1. the belief must be held with deep conviction and must have some relevance to action; 2. the person holding the belief must have committed himself to it by taking some important action that is difficult to undo; 3. the belief must be sufficiently specific and sufficiently concerned with the real world that events may unequivocally refute it; 4. such undeniable disconfirmatory evidence must occur and must be recognized by the believer; 5. the believer must have the social support of a group. He suggests that the theory applies to many millenary groups, including the followers of Jesus, but that it cannot be tested with regard to the latter because there is doubt about whether Jesus did proclaim the idea of a suffering messiah and therefore we do not know whether disconfirmation occurred (conditions 3 and 4). This lack of clarity makes the whole episode inconclusive with respect to the hypothesis.[5]

In order to apply the theory to early Christianity Gager has first to refute this last assertion. He argues that the crucifixion clearly constituted a major obstacle to faith among the Jews (cf. 1 Cor. 1.23), and that if the prediction of Jesus' sufferings (Mt. 16.21) was created after the event to lend supportive meaning to the otherwise disconfirmatory events it sustains the theory, while if it was actually spoken by Jesus himself the context shows that it was not accepted or understood by

3. L. Festinger *et al.*, *When Prophecy Fails* (Minneapolis: University of Minneapolis Press, 1956).

4. Roger Brown, *Social Psychology* (New York: The Free Press, 1965), pp. 601-602.

5. Festinger, *Prophecy*, pp. 4, 23-25.

the disciples. The whole incident of Peter's confession in Mk 8.27-33, whether or not it happened, 'conveys the clear sense that the death of Jesus was a problem for his followers from the beginning and that its problematic character persisted thereafter, no doubt reinforced by Jews who maintained that a crucified Messiah was a contradiction in terms'. Thus we have here distress at Jesus' death and the rationalization that normally accompanies proselytizing. Gager concludes: 'It would appear, then, that we are justified in maintaining that the death of Jesus created a sense of cognitive dissonance, in that it seemed to disconfirm the belief that Jesus was the Messiah. Even the event of the resurrection, which the Gospels present as having surprised the disciples every bit as much as the death, seems not to have eradicated these doubts.'[6]

Gager finds a further occasion for dissonance in the delay of the parousia, arguing that whether Jesus prophesied an imminent kingdom or not, there are sufficient New Testament passages to show that the first Christians had a clear and developed parousia hope (e.g. 1 Thess. 4.16f.) and that this was followed by concern at the delay (e.g. 1 Clem. 23.3-5, 2 Pet. 3.3-9, and even 1 Thess. 4.13–5.11, where the death of some Christians before the parousia was being seen as disconfirmatory evidence). His conclusion is that all five conditions are also met in the parousia hope and that the early church 'carried out its mission *in an effort to maintain* its eschatology'.[7]

Before concluding this exposition of Gager's theory we need to note two further points. First, he proposes certain modifications of Festinger's original theory, partly in the light of a study by Jane Hardyck and Marcia Braden, who observed a Pentecostal community known as True Word which did not turn to proselytism after the failure of a prediction of nuclear destruction on a given date, and partly to achieve a closer fit to the New Testament evidence. Gager's modifications are: (1) Proselytism as a means of reducing cognitive dissonance will appear primarily in new groups, like early Christianity, whose existence has been occasioned by or associated with a belief that is subsequently disconfirmed. (2) Public ridicule at the time of disconfirmation may play an important role in turning such a group toward missionary activity. (3) The limit beyond which belief will not withstand disconfirmation is a function of the degree to which

6.   Gager, *Kingdom*, pp. 40-43.
7.   Gager, *Kingdom*, pp. 43-46.

identification with the group supplants the original belief as the basic motivation for adherence to the group.[8]

The second point is that Gager applies dissonance theory to conversion, and in particular to Paul's conversion. Festinger in his second book *A Theory of Cognitive Dissonance*[9] urged that all decision-taking leads to dissonance which is reduced by increasing confidence in the decision itself and by intensifying the attractiveness of the chosen alternative in contrast with the rejected one. Gager suggests that in addition to this, attempts to diminish post-decision dissonance may also lead to or reinforce an inclination to proselytization. Thus Paul played down the status and significance of the law and engaged in active missionary work.[10]

Gager's main aim is to explain the missionary activity of early Christianity and its polemic against Judaism and paganism. He finds it surprising that Harnack failed to consider the motivation of the Christian mission beyond saying that missionary zeal was inherited from Judaism. Later scholars offer a variety of explanation: obedience to Jesus' command (F. Hahn), a sense of responsibility for the unevangelized world, or enthusiastic anticipation of the End (Cullmann). Gager does not wish to claim cognitive dissonance as the sole explanation, and admits that it would not apply to those who did not see the decision for Christianity as a choice between incompatible systems of belief—e.g. Jewish Christians who continued to observe the law, and Gentiles who saw Christianity as the fulfilment of Greek wisdom—although he suggests that hostility to Jewish Christianity and Gnosticism can be viewed as an attempt to emphasize the discrepancy between chosen and rejected alternatives. 'These movements were threatening precisely because they diminished this discrepancy and thereby increased dissonance for those who had made the decision to convert.'[11]

I am prepared to accept that there is evidence that the crucifixion and the delay of the parousia created difficulties for the early Christians and that to sustain the theory it does not matter whether we hold with Grässer that Jesus did prophesy an imminent end or follow

8. Gager, *Kingdom*, p. 47.
9. L. Festinger, *A Theory of Cognitive Dissonance* (Evanston: Row Peterson, 1957).
10. Gager, *Kingdom*, p. 48.
11. Gager, *Kingdom*, pp. 38, 49.

Glasson and Robinson in thinking that apocalyptic hopes sprang from the early church.[12] What concerns me is the logic of the programme. How is Gager using the theory of cognitive dissonance? It is popular nowadays to speak of the theories as a 'heuristic device', and if by this no more is meant than that the theory suggests a fresh set of questions and in this way stimulates further research, few will quarrel with it.[13] As we shall see, Carroll provides a good example of the way the theory of cognitive dissonance can be used to raise important new questions about Israelite prophecy. But Gager goes well beyond this.

Let me start from the status of a hypothesis in sociology. The theory is essentially a prediction of what is likely to happen, other things being equal. The work of the researcher is to test the truth of the hypothesis through experiment or by observation, and in fact this is precisely what Festinger and his colleagues did with regard to the flying saucer group at Lake City and what others have done in laboratory experiments as well as by participant observation. But experiment and participant observation are impossible with historical sociology. This is fully recognized by all who engage in it, but it makes it all too easy to adjust the evidence to fit the theory and makes any conclusions no more than tentative.

Now what are the assumptions behind Gager's application of cognitive dissonance theory to the New Testament? First, that the theory is correct: his study is not an attempt to test the theory but to explain the mechanism behind the historical events of the Christian mission. Secondly, that the cultures are sufficiently similar for direct application of the theory to be meaningful. Both these assumptions are doubtful. Roger Brown's discussion of the theory (to go no further) reveals what searching criticisms can be made against it.[14] And it is certainly far from being immediately apparent what similarities there are between the early church and students who have been given a boring task and then are paid $1 to tell the next experimental group that the

---

12. E. Grässer, *Das Problem der Parusieverzögerung in den synoptischen Evangelien und in der Apostelgeschichte* (BZNW, 22; Berlin: de Gruyter, 2nd edn 1960 [1957]); T.F. Glasson, *The Second Advent: The Origin of the New Testament Doctrine* (London: Epworth Press, 3rd edn, 1963); *Jesus and the End of the World* (Edinburgh: Saint Andrew Press, 1980); J.A.T. Robinson, *Jesus and His Coming* (London: SCM Press, 1957).

13. Cf. Scroggs, *Sociological Interpretation*, p. 166.

14. Brown, *Social Psychology*, pp. 601-604.

work was wildly exciting. Even more remote from the first Christians are the Lake City group who spent the last evening as they waited for the coming of the flying saucer to deliver them from the threatened flood cutting all the metal fastenings from their clothes because they have been told that metal will in some way be harmful to the space-ship. There is a further difficulty in that Gager circumvents the uncer-tainty as to whether Jesus predicted his death and preached an apocalyptic kingdom by picking up beliefs from widely separated parts of the New Testament and the Apostolic Fathers. In this matter, I suggest, the time scale matters. Both the Lake City and the True Word groups faced a definite moment of disconfirmation, they were small-scale, local groups, and their proselytizing (or lack of it) fol-lowed immediately. This might accord with the disciples in Jerusalem (though if Luke is to be relied on, there was an interval even after the reinterpretation of the death of Jesus in the resurrection had been made), but it fits very badly with the delay of the parousia, many fea-tures of the eschatological teaching in the New Testament, and the Gentile mission.

A somewhat different set of problems is raised by Gager's use of Coser's *The Functions of Social Conflict.*[15] Coser takes up theses pro-posed by Georg Simmel's *Conflict*, and after examining them he offers his own reformulations. He adopts a selection of these and applies them to the life of the church in the New Testament period and into the second and third centuries. Having followed Coser in distin-guishing between in-group conflict (with heretics) and out-group conflict (with Jews and pagans) he notes four chief points: (1) conflict serves as a group-binding function, helping to define Christianity more closely; (2) ideology intensifies conflict, increasing the tension in the conflicts between the church and Judaism, its conflict with pagan-ism over the claims to possess true wisdom, and conflicts within Christianity itself over the claim to embody the authentic faith of Jesus and the apostles; (3) the closer the relationship the more intense the conflict, hence the bitterness of the Christian–Jewish conflict and the struggles against the Gnostics; (4) conflict serves to define and streng-then group structures, e.g. the opposition to Marcion led to the defini-tion of the New Testament, the inclusion of the Old Testament in the canon, and the development of an anti-docetic christology, while the

---

15. L. Coser, *The Functions of Social Conflict* (New York and London: Rout-ledge and Kegan Paul, 1956).

works of the apologists were directed less towards those to whom they were ostensibly addressed than to Christians in danger of adopting pagan or Jewish images of Christianity.[16]

This oversimplified outline is sufficient to reveal the general trend of Gager's argument. It stands out immediately that much of this has already been said by historians without the aid of Coser's general theory, and also that Gager follows Coser extremely closely, some of his illustrations coming from this source. My difficulty here concerns Gager's method rather than his conclusions. He adopts a theory which is adumbrated at a fairly high level of generalization and abstraction to explain events in the history of the early church. Not only is this questionable in itself, but Coser's theory has been criticized by other sociologists, John Rex asserting that conflict is far less functional than Coser alleges and is, indeed, an important agent in social change,[17] and Phillipson attacking the production of general theory as such on the ground that it is divorced from empirical studies and distorts research.[18]

From the New Testament we turn to the Old. In *When Prophecy Failed* Robert Carroll utilizes Festinger's theory to interpret the Israelite prophetic traditions. My judgment is that this is a much more impressive study than Gager's. Carroll has thoroughly mastered the literature and gives an excellent critical account of the theory, while he ranges widely across the prophetic writings with the facility of the Old Testament specialist. His interest, however, differs from Gager's in that instead of concentrating on the motivation for proselytizing, he examines three types of resolution of dissonance between what is predicted and the subsequent events: the social support from the group of followers of the prophet and groups of tradents maintaining the traditions, the isolating of the prophet from information that is dissonant from his predictions through the close-knit group of disciples, and the production of explanatory schemes which change the original prophecies or rationalized dissonant cognitions. Indeed, Carroll sets

16. Gager, *Kingdom*, pp. 79-87.

17. John Rex, *Key Problems of Sociological Theory* (London: Routledge & Kegan Paul, 1961), pp. 115-20.

18. Michael Phillipson, 'Theory, Methodology and Conceptualization', in Paul Filmer, Michael Phillipson, David Silverman and David Walsh, *New Directions in Sociological Theory* (London: Collier-Macmillan, 1972).

out as his main thesis that 'dissonance gives rise to hermeneutic'.[19]

Carroll stresses that prophecy was only a small part of a larger cultural movement and since the dissonance experienced by the prophetic group did not affect this larger religious structure, the theology of that structure could provide a hermeneutic system for dealing with the dissonance. Moreover, he uses dissonance theory only as a heuristic device to assist understanding and to uncover non-obvious sources of tension.[20]

The main analysis of traditions containing secondary, interpretative material concentrates upon the books of Isaiah, Haggai and Zechariah. For example, Isa. 8.16-18 reveals the prophet retreating into the company of his disciples after his failure to persuade Ahaz to trust Yahweh. The retirement from public activity is a defence mechanism against dissonance, and the gathering of disciples provided a positive context which would reinforce the prophet's own convictions. The Immanuel oracle (Isa. 7.14) on the other hand had to be reinterpreted. Originally it seems to have been a promise of salvation to the Davidic dynasty, but later editing transformed it into the preface to judgment (Isa. 7.17b-25), and introduced an element of conditionality (v. 9b) which rendered the prediction immune from falsification. Similarly the additions to the confident message of Second Isaiah in Isaiah 56–66 resolve the dissonance produced by the limited and ineffective return.

What makes Carroll's book impressive is his keen awareness of cultural relativity and of the extreme difficulty in transferring a theory from the twentieth century to ancient Israel. He devotes a whole chapter to this problem and makes four points:

(1) There are problems about the actual dissonance. What constituted fulfilment of a specific prophecy? Even more serious, what in prophetic circles counted as awareness of disconfirmation? To what extent were the communities which cherished the prophetic traditions disturbed by the failure of their expectations? Could each failure be simply shrugged off by saying that it was not yet the time? And even if there was such awareness of dissonance that it troubled members of the prophetic circles, how many of their responses remained at an oral level and failed to be incorporated in the written traditions and so are inaccessible to us?

19. Carroll, *Prophecy*, pp. 110, 124.
20. Carroll, *Prophecy*, p. 110.

(2) There is a limitation imposed by the nature of the material. Although the terms and methods used in cognitive dissonance theory can be shown to be applicable to the prophetic books, it is the explanatory schemes and rationalization (= hermeneutic) which has left most traces in the Old Testament documents and so can be explained most readily by the modern scholar.

(3) Further limiting factors arise because of the marked difference between the tests devised by modern social psychologists and ancient Israelite society. Carroll points to the fact that prophecy functioned within a conceptual framework of the transcendence of Yahweh, that Torah became the context for the post-exilic community, and that ancient Israelite religion was a highly complex system so that explanations in terms of, e.g., Yahweh having changed his mind are entailed by the theological system rather than being instances of dissonance resolution.

(4) Finally he points out that while hermeneutic is not inevitably a response to dissonance, in structures vulnerable to dissonance its presence provides powerful support for reducing dissonance.[21] Because of his refusal to adopt a simplistic application of cognitive dissonance theory to the Old Testament and his awareness that 'there can hardly be a straightforward transference of research material from the field of social psychology to that of biblical studies' he avoids the pitfalls into which Gager falls, and his work leads to a genuinely fresh understanding of the Israelite prophets.

Nevertheless, although in *When Prophecy Failed* we probably have an example of the most effective application of a specific sociological theory to the biblical documents, I have two reservations about it. First, I think that Carroll has exaggerated the awareness of dissonance on the part of the prophets and the later editors of the traditions. T.E. Lawrence notes that the way the Arabs among whom he lived thought in black and white led them to pursue 'the logic of several incompatible opinions to absurd ends, without perceiving the incongruity'.[22] D.M. Carstairs in *The Twiceborn*[23] observes that high-caste Indians would frequently juxtapose statements that were in open contradiction without showing any awareness of the fact. It is true that

21. Carroll, *Prophecy*, pp. 121-28.
22. T.E. Lawrence, *The Seven Pillars of Wisdom* (London: Jonathan Cape, 1940), p. 36.
23. D.M. Carstairs, *The Twiceborn* (London: Hogarth Press, 1957).

their manifest unease when the inconsistency was pointed out revealed that they were not without all sense of the law of contradiction, but the fact remains that their attention had to be drawn to it by a Westerner. Ancient Israel is not modern Indian or early twentieth-century Arabia, and it may be that the fierce conflicts seen in the Old Testament and the early church, e.g. at Corinth, prove that the Jews sensed contradiction more than many peoples of the East. On the other hand, the two creation stories and divergent accounts of the flood in Genesis may indicate a high tolerance of inconsistency. If this is so it undermines the thesis. In correspondence Dr Carroll pointed out to me that some glosses and changes between texts (e.g. Goliath in 2 Sam. 21.19 and 1 Chron. 20.5) indicate an awareness of dis-crepancies or of contradictions. He wrote: 'It seems to be the case that where the editors were aware of discrepancies they made changes, but were not overly conscious of problems created by contradictions.' The question may be slightly more complex than this. Whether dissonance is actively experienced will depend on how important logical consistency is relative to other interests. The fundamentalist is not aware of inconsistencies in the Bible and resorts to rationalizing har-monizations when they are pointed out because he holds strongly to the belief in the inerrancy and authority of scripture. Similarly the two creation stories may have been juxtaposed by an editor who had an overriding purpose to preserve all the sacred traditions because they were sacred and traditional. This emphasizes the problems involved in transferring a sociological theory to a different culture.

My second demurrer is simply to say that Carroll provides an excellent example of the way a theory derived from social psychology can be used as a heuristic device, but I wonder whether the detailed theory is needed since it cannot be applied in this developed form. The details of the theory in his second chapter are evidence of diligence, but in the end have little relevance in the resultant study. If these queries have to be raised with regard to Carroll's most cautious study, how much more should we hesitate before proceeding to a more direct application of hypotheses proposed by sociologists.

In conclusion I will draw together the points that I have made and broaden the discussion slightly. It appears to me that the difficulties posed by the nature of the evidence and the differences in culture are greater than the exponents of sociological interpretation of biblical societies recognize, despite the qualifications which they insert into their writings. G. Vermes, commenting on the possibility of recovering the historical Jesus states: 'The real question is this: how much history can be extracted from sources which are not primarily historical.'[24] One does not need to adopt a thoroughgoing canonical criticism approach to see that what we possess are documents written from faith to faith and preserved within the circle of believers. Historians have always had to draw out what we regard as history from sources that were written for quite different purposes and on quite other assumptions. But the nature of the biblical source increases the danger of manipulating the evidence and imposing theory upon it. Similarly one does not need to go the whole way with Dennis Nineham to become aware of the difficulties involved in transferring theories derived from evidence in one kind of society to a very different society. I have already commented sufficiently on this. But the liability to error is increased when theories that operate at a high level of abstraction are applied directly and in their totality to a narrow and highly specific situation. This was my main criticism of Gager's use of Coser's theories about conflict, and it applies equally to the adoption of 'ideal types' such as 'sect', 'millenarian cult', or 'charismatic personality' and the immediate application of them to the Old or New Testaments. This is not what 'ideal types' were designed for.[25]

But even if we discount these difficulties (and it might be argued that if we become obsessed by them we should be landed in complete scepticism), I would claim that the attempt to apply sociological theories to biblical documents is not likely to be fruitful. The chance of testing a hypothesis is so slight as to be negligible. Thus what remains possible is either to accept the theory as valid for the biblical period and then to use it to organize and interpret the evidence, even, if we follow Scroggs, to posit parts of the model for which evidence is missing, on the grounds that the absence of such evidence is accidental and the entire model was a reality in the early church,[26] or else to use the theories entirely heuristically to suggest lines of research, which

24. G. Vermes, *Jesus the Jew* (London: SCM Press, 1973), p. 235.

25. Cf. e.g., Robert Towler, *Homo Religiosus* (London: Constable, 1974), pp. 108-27, for an example of the way there have been shifts even among sociologists between ideal types and typical empirical examples. An ideal type is basically a definition of a term. How closely this corresponds to the real world then becomes the question under discussion.

26. Scroggs, *Sociological Interpretation*, p. 166.

then have to stand or fall on their own merit. The first is illegitimate, the second can be fruitful, but only so long as the researcher does not incorporate in the study assumptions derived from the theory. I would urge further that the utmost rigour needs to be exercised with regard to datings and direction of causation and that due heed should be paid to David Martin's observation that general theory simply states that in given circumstances certain developments tend to occur, other things being equal, but that other things are never equal and the universal process operates differently according to the complex in which it operates. The influence of historical and geographical chance must not be ignored.[27]

It will probably be retorted that my argument undercuts historical research of any kind, since the historian is never a mere collector of 'facts' but in selecting, ordering, interpreting and explaining of those facts works with theories about the use of evidence and the interaction of human beings. With this I would agree. My plea is that there is a world of difference between sociology applied to contemporary society, where the researcher can test theories against evidence which is collected, and historical sociology where there is only fossilized evidence that has been preserved by chance or for purposes very different from that of the sociologist. It is a cardinal error to move promiscuously between the two. Indeed, the weaknesses of sociological studies of historical movements from Max Weber onwards suggest that historical sociology is impossible.[28]

27. David Martin, *A General Theory of Secularization* (Oxford: Basil Blackwell, 1978), pp. 2, 4-5.
28. Cf. my concluding comments in 'Max Weber and Ancient Judaism', p. 469.

JSOT 38 (1987), pp. 85-93

SOCIOLOGICAL AND LITERARY APPROACHES TO THE BIBLE:
HOW SHALL THE TWAIN MEET?*

David Jobling

The announcement of an introduction to the Hebrew Bible by Gottwald aroused high expectations and keen speculation. He holds a unique position in the debate over the Bible in North America, for he is in touch with a wider range of points of view in that debate than anyone else. When some students of mine asked for a course of study which would integrate sophisticated hermeneutical trends with the political commitment found in feminist and materialist readings of the Bible, they summarized all this as 'what Gottwald does'. One is reminded, at a less exalted level, of Michel Foucault's 'initiators of discursive practices', figures like Marx and Freud, whose significance lies not so much in particular works and theories as in the very existence of a certain discourse. The introduction was announced as 'Socio-Literary'. The power of Gottwald's sociological method was well-known from *The Tribes of Yahweh*. Would he develop an equally powerful approach to literature, and achieve some 'articulation' of sociological with literary method? And would he press the political question, raised already in *Tribes*, of the *answerability of biblical scholarship to its various contexts*—religious and academic institutions, culture at large? For this question is especially urgent when it is a matter of 'introducing' people to the Bible. It is now time to assess how far our expectations have been met, and our questions answered. My interest, then, is primarily in the *concept* of introduction. But I should not (especially in a market so glutted with introductions) omit a few comments on *technique*, the myriad issues which determine a

---

*   A review of Norman K. Gottwald, *The Hebrew Bible: A Socio-Literary Introduction* (Philadelphia: Fortress Press, 1985).

book's usability with beginning students—presentation, organization, demands made on the student, treatment of controversial issues, and so on—though I am limited by the fact that, being on sabbatical leave this year, I have not had the opportunity to use the book with students. In fact, the distinction between concept and technique is not to be too sharply drawn; they affect each other, and my discussion of Gottwald's concept will have radical implications for his organization. But, to the extent that technique may be considered autonomously, his book gets high marks.

It is cast in four parts plus a conclusion. Part I, 'The Text in its Contexts', consists of three chapters: the first is on method in biblical studies; the second, 'The World of the Hebrew Bible', deals with geography, archaeology, and ancient Near Eastern history; the third, 'The Literary History of the Hebrew Bible', covers not only the formation and transmission of the canon, but also its relation to other ancient literatures. Parts II–IV then treat the Hebrew Bible in three chronological divisions; pre-monarchy, monarchy, and exile/post-exile (down to the somewhat arbitrary, but practical, terminus of 63 BCE). In connection with the nine chapters in these three parts, the student is to read the whole Bible in literary-chronological fashion. The conclusion returns to issues of method.

Gottwald makes heavy demands on students, for he is not prepared to shield them from complexity and controversy, but he works hard to ease the burden. Great care has been taken for clarity of presentation and organization. Maps, tables, and charts are used extensively and creatively, and there is generous cross-referencing both within the book and to tools like atlases and collections of Near Eastern texts. Attention to the practical needs of students is shown in such ways as the inclusion of an assessment of available English translations of the Bible. And many of the particular sections of the book are models of brief exposition (for example, those on Lamentations and Ezekiel).

As expected, Gottwald has achieved a breakthrough in the areas of sociology and political theory, easily outstripping any other introduction in his insistent pressing of these questions. The names he gives to Parts II–IV, 'Intertribal Confederacy: Israel's Revolutionary Beginnings', 'Monarchy: Israel's Counterrevolutionary Establishment', and 'Home Rule Under Great Empires: Israel's Colonial Recovery', show where his stress will lie. This stress pervades not only the treatment of the biblical books themselves (of many examples, one might single out the issue of oppressed and oppressors in the Psalms), but also the discussions of canon-formation, of archaeology (e.g. the urban bias it gives to our view of Israel), even of geography (e.g. the 'Asiatic mode of production' as linking physical and economic geography). Gottwald blows away vague 'religious' causes of the effects we find in the Bible, and this is an immense gain. On the other hand, the treatment of literature is at first sight such a disappointment, much of it seems so conventional and conservative, that one wonders what 'Literary' is doing in the subtitle. There are two main problems, the first concerning the autonomy of literature, the second concerning its articulation with socio-history.

The first problem, of literary autonomy, arises most obviously for those parts of the Bible which developed over long periods. Within the chronological organization of the book, these come to our attention first in fragments, as sources for one historical period, and later as the finished texts of another period. Gottwald explains in his preface his general strategy for dealing with the issue, but the results are not convincing. Most often, he is ready to make extensive use of a document as source before dealing with it as text; the Deuteronomic History, for example, is not discussed as a whole until long after Joshua and Judges have been dealt with. The problem with this is that it misses the effect which a textual reading might have on our use of the document as a source. But elsewhere we seem to meet the converse problem; for example, Gottwald weakens his treatment of monarchical ideology in Part III by making only brief use of Wisdom and Psalms, perhaps because he is unwilling to do much with them in advance of his literary analyses in Part IV. There is little evidence that Gottwald has tried to find, within the given organization of the book, the best compromise with the demands of literature. Still less does he allow these demands to call in question the given organization. The nemesis of his whole approach may be seen in his asking students to read Genesis 12–50 in connection with Part II, chs. 2–11 with Part III, and ch. 1 with Part IV. Having done so, will the students have read Genesis?

The second problem is that Gottwald does not overcome a naively representational approach to literature. Despite stating that literature 'does not simply directly mirror its society', he still favours the metaphor of 'reflection', and proceeds accordingly in specific cases. He suggests, for example, that the strong role of women in many stories in Genesis points to a corresponding role in the groups contributing these traditions to Israel. But might not the stories be a compensation for the opposite social reality? Incest is a major motif in the folklore of certain American Indians (I am borrowing from unpublished work by Carole R. Fontaine), but anthropological data show that incest is in fact very rare among them. Literature and 'reality' are here related, but not by 'reflection'.

These problems are large, and the disappointment they cause is real. But to concentrate on them alone would be to do Gottwald grave injustice, for he is urgently seeking a deep engagement with recent literary approaches to the Bible. 'Exactly how does social reality inscribe itself in language and in literary creations?'—this question, even if he does not know how to answer it other than representationally, exercises him perhaps more than any other (at least, he presses it harder than do most of us on the literary side!). His methodological discussions, in Chapter 1 and in the conclusion, give great prominence to 'newer literary methods', and it is to his special credit that he includes, in the body of his introduction, accounts of many of the products of these new methods, which he has read with careful attention (even if their radical concern with *text* has been obscured in their subsumption to the organization of his book). Finally, when he has a well-defined literary text before him (for example, Ruth or Jonah), his literary reading is impressive, going beyond merely reporting on the work of others.

The gap between Gottwald's literary intentions and his results points to theoretical inadequacy. Yet there is evidence in the conclusion to his book that he is in touch with much more powerful theory, capable of governing much more satisfactory literary practice. In the conclusion, he defines five 'general socio-political domains' in Israel's history:

1. a socio-religious revolution of confederated Yahweh-worshiping tribes in Canaan (1250–1000);
2. a socio-political counterrevolution of united Israel under monarchic state rule (1000–930);
3. internal division of the united monarchy (930–586);

4. destruction of Judah: subjection to colonial rule and exile (586–38);
5. restoration of Judah: colonial home rule subject to imperial dominion (538–63).

'Domain' is defined as 'the broadest determinative level of social and political organization operative in each temporal phase' (but this seems confusing; it is the recognition of successive socio-political organizations which determines the temporal phases). Within each domain, three 'sectors' are defined, 'social' (specific social forms, within the broad organization), 'literary', and 'theological' (or 'ideological'). On extensive charts, Gottwald summarizes for each domain the specific entities produced in each sector (institutions such as courts, pieces of literature, doctrines).

This conclusion is an enigma. On the one hand, it is the most important part of the book for discerning Gottwald's *concept* of biblical introduction, brilliant in its synthesis, and bold in its implications. On the other hand, it is peculiarly effaced. It appears as a mere summary of, or footnote to, the body of the book, concealing the fact that it is in considerable tension with the rest of the book; and it does not make clear its important links to a much wider theoretical debate. To begin with the last point, Gottwald's conclusion is theoretically related to Marxist analysis of social, including literary, production, as developed especially by Louis Althusser. The 'sectors' are the same as Althusser's 'instances', though the latter are more differentiated, and the 'domains' have a relationship, albeit a much more complicated one, to the concept of historical 'modes of production'. Althusser's analysis gives no privilege to literature; it is one 'instance' among others. But use has been made of it, especially in Fredric Jameson's *The Political Unconscious*, to achieve a theory of literary production, and, even more, a practice of literary analysis. The bibliography attached to Gottwald's conclusion omits both Althusser and Jameson. But Gottwald is aware of the connection I am making; I have heard him refer to Jameson, his bibliography does contain a related work by Terry Eagleton, and his use of 'ideology' belongs within the Althusserian framework.

The conclusion is in tension with the rest of the book in the areas both of theory and of practice. Theoretical discussion is concentrated in Chapter 1, where Gottwald discerns in the present scene 'at least a four-party conversation' over method, the outcome of a long history of interpretation (to the 'Confessional Religious' and 'Historical-Critical' approaches, with their history of interaction, have recently been added 'newer Literary' and 'Social Science' methods). Veering close to a celebration of pluralism, he disclaims any attempt to provide a 'higher-order model' or 'paradigm of paradigms' which will combine these approaches; he does look forward to the synthetic aims of the conclusion, but only in very modest terms. The tone of the conclusion itself is markedly different from the tone of this introductory discussion, and what he sketches in the conclusion is unmistakably a 'higher-order model'!

The conclusion is also in tension with the detailed treatment of the Bible in Parts II–IV. The conclusion does not, as Gottwald suggests, merely summarize the findings of those parts; it provides the structural plan for a book which would be significantly different. The plan would be *first* to identify a series of historical periods as 'domains' and to characterize each socio-politically; *then*, within each domain to analyse the productions in the various sectors (particular social forms, literature, ideology) and to show the logic of their relations to each other in the terms of the domain. While the treatment of sectors need not follow any rigid order, but could vary as each case demanded, it is hard to see how the *prior* characterization of the domain could be dispensed with, since it is the domains which govern the historical periodization, and hence the entire organization.

To what extent do Parts II–IV manifest this plan? Gottwald prefaces each with an enumeration of our sources for the period in question; this, of course, is necessary within his organizational structure, but creates literary problems, as I have already argued. What then follows is different for each part. The first problem is that there are five domains in the conclusion to map onto three parts of the book, and we find that Parts III and IV each correspond to *two* of the domains. Is the monarchy (and likewise the post-586 period) to be thought of as a single domain, or as more?; if more, why does the book not have more parts? The second problem is with the need for *prior* socio-political characterization of the domains. Only in Part IV is this given according to plan. In Part II, we have to wait until the very end to find the socio-political characterization. In fact, the student would have trouble realizing that the pre-monarchic period was being subsumed under a single domain, since different 'socio-historic horizons' are discussed for ancestor, Moses, and Joshua–Judges traditions. And in Part III, Gottwald never, either at the beginning or anywhere else, gives a clear socio-political account of monarchy (though various pieces of such an account appear in various places). The third problem area is the treatment of the sectors, which is too complex to go into here (especially since Gottwald makes no use of 'sector' as an organizing concept in the body of the book), except to make the major point that he fails to clarify the relationship between *the sources for a period* (in the body of the book) and *literary production within a domain* (in the conclusion). Of the three parts, it is Part IV which follows the plan of the conclusion much the most closely, a fact to whose significance I shall return.

The power of Gottwald's conclusion, together with its effacement in relation to the rest of the book, may suggest that he is developing a comprehensive theory which is not quite working, or which he is not quite prepared to carry through in practice. If so, it is surely at the point of literature that the problem lies. In his conclusion Gottwald, like Althusser, makes literature into simply one 'sector' among others. While this is appropriate in Althusser's general theory, it must be inadequate to the specific case of the Hebrew Bible, for it ignores the fact that almost all we know, in all sectors, and even the domain definitions themselves are mediated through literature. In any adequate theoretical approach to ancient Israel, literature will be a privileged sector, which suggests a particular importance for Jameson's development of Althusser.

To return to the final issue in my opening paragraph, Gottwald has been relatively reticent, in the book before us, about the socio-politics of current biblical scholarship; the occasional hint, however, reminds us of the importance of the issue for him (the strongest is this: 'how we assess Jewish statehood and social order in the second century BCE will be greatly influenced by our own class interests and religious affiliations, as will also our views of international politics today, including the claims and policies of Israeli Zionism and Arab nationalism'). No doubt he wants to avoid pointless battles, but above all he rightly believes that the best arena for political engagement is the methodological revolution of which he is a part. But I have a concern here. Up to now, Gottwald's name has been associated chiefly with a single major hypothesis put forward in *The Tribes of Yahweh*, that

Israel had its origin in a retribalizing revolution against the statist Canaanite system; it is this hypothesis above all which has caught the political imagination of our time, and made 'Gottwald' into the name of a vital discourse. In his introduction, he does not so much force this hypothesis on our attention as quietly assume its truth; in Part II, it is less prominent than one might have expected, but the rest of the book explicitly presents Israel's history as the working out of its revolutionary origins. My concern is that the establishing in biblical studies of the kind of theory and practice to which Gottwald is committed, and which I have been discussing, be seen as vastly more important than getting people to believe a particular hypothesis. The *Tribes* hypothesis is eminently attackable from various angles; for all kinds of historical and literary reasons, the origins of Israel is a field peculiarly unsuited for theoretical battles. To put the hypothesis too up-front is to invite rejection of the methodological revolution along with the hypothesis.

In the light of the foregoing discussion, I make two suggestions. The first is that Gottwald, in his articulation of literature with the other sectors, exchange his dominant metaphor of 'reflection' for Jameson's (taken from Althusser) of history as the 'absent cause' in literature. I take this to mean that literature often functions by occluding (or, it is a function of literature to occlude) its own relation to history, and leave it to Jameson's own work to provide further commentary.

The second suggestion is to introduce the Hebrew Bible chronologically backwards, instead of forwards. It does not seem remarkable when an introduction like W. Lee Humphreys's *Crisis and Story* begins with the monarchy, enabling J to be treated first as text, then as source. My suggestion is to treat the whole canon this way, beginning with a reading of it which would be as radically social, political, and historical as Gottwald demands, but also radically *textual* (Jameson providing at present the best paradigms for bringing the two sides together). This would then lead to a similar treatment of the hypothetical stages of the Bible's literary prehistory. I feel sure that such a procedure would not lead merely to doing backwards the same things we have been doing forwards. For all the existing hypotheses about the literary prehistory would be thrust into a new hypothetical marketplace, there to compete with perhaps quite different kinds of proposal for relating literature to history. We have yet to see what the *historical* implications of the 'newer literary methods' may be, for their practitioners have often been so busy defending themselves from old-style historicism as to forget altogether the historicality of their texts.

In fact, Gottwald has laid, in Part IV of his book, an excellent basis for my project. It is the longest and in every way the best of the three historical parts. Only here, as I have already noted, does his work conform to the plan laid out in his conclusion, and this is no accident. The conditions for a socio-literary approach are present here, as they are not for the earlier periods, and everything falls into place. Perhaps Gottwald has seen how much more promising a field for theoretical debate the post-exilic period is than the period of Israel's origins (indeed, it has always seemed to me that the best evidence for his hypothesis is to be found in the persistence of egalitarian ideals into later periods and domains). Not only does Gottwald deal with literature better in Part IV (having well-defined texts before him), but he lays the basis for dealing with the canon itself as text, as a system of internal forces (e.g. 'pollution' system vs. 'debt' system; cf. Fernando Belo, *A Materialist Reading of the Gospel of Mark*) which can be convincingly related to struggles between the 'establishment' and marginalized groups. Basic questions remain, especially the representational approach to literature. But the greater theoretical coherence and practical success of Part IV over Parts II and III make me confident of my suggestion, and when I use Gottwald's book with students next year, it is with Part IV that I intend to start, anticipating great battles over Parts III and II!

JSOT 38 (1987), pp. 73-83

USING THE NUER CULTURE OF AFRICA IN UNDERSTANDING
THE OLD TESTAMENT: AN EVALUATION

David Fiensy

Both Old Testament specialists and anthropologists have in some way or other compared the Old Testament with primitive cultures for at least 200 years,[1] but the modern study of the Old Testament from an anthropological perspective begins around the turn of the century especially with W. Robertson Smith's *Lectures on the Religion of the Semites.*[2] Anthropologists have used the Old Testament as one more collection of data to be used in understanding primitive culture, while Old Testament scholars have used the ethnological theories and ethnographical data from other cultures to aid in understanding the Old Testament.

Methodology among Old Testament specialists has always been a problem. Does one need to accept ethnological theory to use ethnographic material? Which theory is most appropriate? How does one study a text based on observations of a society?[3] How can one explain parallels between the Bible and contemporary primitive cultures, or is

1. See J.W. Rogerson, *Anthropology and the Old Testament* (Oxford: Basil Blackwell, 1978), pp. 1-21, who describes the eighteenth-century work of J.D. Michaelis (*Fragen an eine Gesellschaft gelehrter Männer die auf Befehl Ihres Majestät Königes von Dännemark nach Arabien reisen*, 1662). Another useful discussion of the history of anthropoligical study of the Old Testament is Herbert F. Hahn, *The Old Testament in Modern Research* (Philadelphia: Fortress Press, 1966), pp. 44-82.

2. *Lectures on the Religion of the Semites* (Edinburgh: A. & C. Black, 1889).

3. These and other issues are raised by R.C. Culley, 'Anthropology and Old Testament Studies: An Introductory Comment', in *Anthropological Perspectives on Old Testament Prophecy* (Chico, CA: Scholars Press, 1982), p. 105. See also J.W. Rogerson, *Anthropology and the Old Testament, passim*, and Hahn, *The Old Testament in Modern Research*, pp. 44-82.

it necessary to explain them in order to utilize them exegetically?[4]

R.R. Wilson has, in the interest of methodological clarity, suggested six guidelines, the most important of which, for this study, is the second:

> Comparative material must be properly interpreted in its own context before any attempt is made to apply it to the biblical text... Sociological and anthropological data on a particular phenomenon must be seen in the context of the whole society which produced the phenomenon. Only by doing this is it possible to understand the social function of the phenomenon.[5]

I agree with this statement but wish to add to it. The Old Testament interpreter must be sensitive to anthropologists' ongoing evaluation of ethnological and ethnographic material. If an anthropologist's work is under increasing criticism it must be used with great caution.

To illustrate this point we shall do a methodological sounding into the anthropological study of the Old Testament by investigating the use by Old Testament interpreters of one African people: the Neur of southern Sudan. Exegetes seem especially interested in African society. They have compared the Old Testament with the Tallensi of Ghana, the Tiv of Nigeria, the Karanga and Lemba of Rhodesia, the Masai of Kenya and many others.[6] The Nuer, however, seem to be used as much as any African people in the study of Hebraic society and religion. The comparative use of that culture group should, therefore, provide a good opportunity for our methodological sounding.

Necessarily, when we investigate the appropriation of data and theory

---

4.   See M.J. Buss, 'Anthropological Perspectives upon the Prophetic Call Narratives', in *Anthropological Perspectives on Old Testament Prophecy*, p. 11.

5.   *Prophecy and Society in Ancient Israel* (Philadelphia: Fortress Press, 1980), pp. 15-16, and *Genealogy and History in the Biblical World* (New Haven: Yale University Press, 1977), pp. 11-18. The guidelines are: 1. the ethnographic material must be collected by a 'trained scholar'; 2. the material must be properly interpreted in its own context before applying it to the biblical text; 3. the biblical scholar must survey a wide range of societies in making comparisons; 4. the biblical interpreter must concentrate on the data and avoid if possible the 'interpretive schemata' into which anthropologists and others have placed the data; 5. the biblical scholar must be sure that the comparative material is truly comparable to the biblical material; 6. the biblical text itself must be the controlling factor in the exegetical process.

6.   See the survey of A.E. Jensen, 'Beziehungen zwischen dem Alten Testament und der nilotischen Kultur in Afrika', in A.S. Diamond (ed.), *Culture in History* (New York: Columbia University, 1960), pp. 449-66, and A. Malamat, 'Biblical Genealogies and African Lineages', *Archives Européennes de Sociologie* 14 (1973), pp. 126-36.

on the Nuer by Old Testament interpreters, we also investigate the
works of E.E. Evans-Pritchard who lived with the Nuer for a total of
twelve months in several visits from 1930 to 1936. He described Nuer
social institutions and customs first in a series of articles and finally in
three monographs.[7] Other anthropologists have described the Nuer
but they did so largely from Evans-Pritchard's perspective;[8] he has
shaped the study of this Nilotic people. Therefore conclusions of recent
ethnologists regarding Evans-Pritchard's contribution are significant
for Old Testament studies. These conclusions we shall survey below.

Since several scholars doing comparative work between the Nuer
society and the Old Testament have focused on the concept of segmentation and since the explanation of this concept is one of the significant
achievements of Evans-Pritchard, we shall concentrate on it.[9]

7. See the *Sudan Notes and Records*: 'The Nuer: Tribe and Clan' in 1933,
1934, and 1935; and 'The Economic Life of the Nuer: Cattle' in 1937 and 1938.
Also see: *The Nuer: A Description of the Modes of Livelihood and Political Institutions of a Nilotic People* (Oxford: Clarendon, 1940); *Nuer Religion* (Oxford: Clarendon Press, 1956); and *Kinship and Marriage among the Nuer* (Oxford: Clarendon
Press, 1960).

8. See C.G. Seligman and B.Z. Seligman, *Pagan Tribes of the Nilotic Sudan*
(London: George Routledge, 1932), p. xiii; P.O. Howell, *A Manual of Nuer Law*
(London: Oxford, 1954). (Howell was a student of Evans-Pritchard); and A. Butt,
The Nilotes of the Sudan and Uganda (London: International African Institute,
1952), who merely summarizes Evans-Pritchard's publications.

9. See for other areas of comparison between Nuer and Hebraic culture: Evans-
Pritchard, *Nuer Religion*, pp. vii, 5, 11, 15, 44, 213, 292, and 304; A.E. Jensen,
'Beziehungen zwischen dem Alten Testament und der nilotischen Kultur in Afrika',
Culture in History; E.A. McFall, *Approaching the Nuer of Africa through the Old
Testament* (South Pasadena, CA: William Carey Library, 1970); E.I. Lfesieh, 'Web
of Matrimony in the Bible, Social Anthropology, and African Traditional Religion',
Communio Viatorum 26 (1983), pp. 195-221; I. Schapera, 'The Sin of Cain', *Jour-
nal of the Anthropological Institute* 85 (1955), pp. 33-43, reprinted in B. Lang,
Anthropological Approaches to the Old Testament (Philadelphia: Fortress Press,
1985), pp. 26-42; M. Douglas, 'The Abominations of Leviticus', in *Purity and
Danger: An Analysis of Concepts of Pollution and Taboo* (London: Routledge and
Kegan Paul, 1969, [1966]), pp. 41-57, reprinted in Lang, *Anthropological
Approaches to the Old Testament*, pp. 100-16; J.W. Rogerson, 'Sacrifice in the
Old Testament: Problems of Method and Approach', in M.F.C. Bourdillon and
M. Fortes (ed.), *Sacrifice* (London: Academic Press, 1980), pp. 45-59; T.W.
Overholt, 'Two Nuer Prophets and their Pyramid', *Prophecy in Cross-Cultural
Perspective* (Atlanta: Scholars Press, 1986), pp. 215-30.

The concept of segmentation originated apparently with E. Durkheim,[10] but Evans-Pritchard was the first to apply ethnographic data to the theory. He boasted that his work on the Nuer was 'the first systematic field studies of [segmentary] lineage system...'[11] A. Kuper considers the work of Evans-Pritchard on the Nuer and the subsequent work of M. Fortes on the Tallensi to be the 'central monographs' in explaining segmentation. Kuper states that the works of Evans-Pritchard and Fortes developed a theory of a particular society which then served as an exemplary model that could be applied to other societies, thus making the works of Fortes and Evans-Pritchard foundational. On the whole, however, Kuper regards the contribution of Fortes as 'less influential' than that of Evans-Pritchard.[12] M.D. Sahlins considers Evans-Pritchard's description of the Nuer and P. Bohanan's of the Tiv as foundational for understanding segmentary systems.[13] Thus it would seem that Evans-Pritchard has had the greatest impact in the development of the theory of segmentation in the light of ethnographic application.

Evans-Pritchard wrote[14] that the largest political unit among the Nuer is the tribe, since beyond the tribe the Nuer seem to feel no sense of loyalty. Nuer will fight with other Nuer tribes or steal from them as readily as from non-Nuer people. Moreover, no compensation for homicide could be demanded from anyone outside the tribe.

Tribes are split into political segments which are associated with lineage segments. Both geography and population determine the perimeters of the largest segments, the primary segments, as well as the smaller segments, the secondary and tertiary segments. Geography is a determinate because rivers, uninhabited areas, forests, and swamps divide the territories. Population is a determinate because only the

10. See J. Middleton, 'Segment', in J. Gould and W.L. Kolb (eds.), *A Dictionary of the Social Sciences* (New York: The Free Press of Glencoe, 1964), pp. 627-28.; A. Kuper, "Lineage Theory": A Critical Retrospect', *Annual Review of Anthropology* 11 (1982), p. 75.

11. See the preface (p. 10) in J. Middleton and D. Tait (eds.), *Tribes without Rulers: Studies in African Segmentary Systems* (London: Routledge and Kegan Paul, 1958).

12. Kuper, 'Lineage Theory', pp. 79, 80 and 84.

13. Sahlins, *The Tribesmen* (Englewood Cliffs, NJ: Prentice–Hall, 1968), p. 50; and 'The Segmentary Lineage: An Organization of Predatory Expansion', *American Anthropologist* 63 (1961), p. 322.

14. Evans-Pritchard, *The Nuer*, pp. 117-49.

larger tribes with large primary segments are divided into secondary and in turn tertiary segments.

The political principle that obtains among the Nuer regarding the tribal segments or sections is, according to Evans-Pritchard, the 'principle of contradiction'. A member of a tertiary section sees himself as a member of that section only in relation to the members of another tertiary section within the same secondary section. In regards to members of another secondary section he is a member not of a certain tertiary section, but of a certain secondary section. A segment, Evans-Pritchard maintained, sees itself as independent when in relation to another segment of the same section, but as united with the other segments of the same section when in relation to a segment from another section. Thus the segments could be hostile to one another until threatened by those of another larger section.

Evans-Pritchard concluded:

> We would, therefore, suggest that Nuer political groups be defined, in terms of values, by the relations between their segments and their interrelations as segments of a larger system in an organization of society in certain social situations, and not as parts of a kind of fixed framework within which people live.[15]

Such a system has little place for individuals or groups to gain political ascendency, except for very brief periods of time, for the segments exist in balanced structural opposition to each other. Nuer society since it is segmented is by definition acephalous. Thus Evans-Pritchard observed:

> The lack of governmental organs among the Nuer, the absence of legal institutions, of developed leadership, and, generally, of organized political life is remarkable...The ordered anarchy in which they live accords well with their character, for it is impossible to live among Nuer and conceive of rulers ruling over them.[16]

A. Malamat maintains that the principle of segmentation obtained also in ancient Israel. The tendency toward tribal splitting in Old Testament Israel corresponds closely to the Nuer. Malamat states:

> In the Bible and in Africa this segmentation with its wide range of primary and secondary lineages is the foremost concept in the genealogical positioning of the individual and in ascertaining relations.[17]

15. Evans-Pritchard, *The Nuer*, p. 149.
16. Evans-Pritchard, *The Nuer*, p. 181.
17. Malamat, 'Biblical Genealogies', p. 131.

N. Lohfink argues that the amphictyony model used to describe the tribes of Israel based on ancient Greek and Roman examples is inadequate for understanding pre-monarchic Israel. He follows F. Crüsemann in suggesting as the model the segmentary societies of Africa, especially the Nuer. These societies are mostly leaderless, Lohfink affirms, with leaders only arising in critical situations.[18]

J.W. Rogerson states that the Nuer model of segmentation explains Judges 5 and 12, where the tribes are both united and in opposition to each other.[19] R.R. Wilson says that genealogies of the Old Testament reflect the segmentary lineage structure of the Hebrew society.[20] N. Gottwald uses the principle of segmentation as one of the main ethnological constructs in describing Israelite tribalism.[21]

Most of these authors have relied to a great extent on Evans-Pritchard's work. Malamat, Rogerson and Wilson refer explicitly to his monographs and articles.[22] Gottwald cites mainly Sahlins, but Sahlins has drawn heavily upon Evans-Pritchard.[23] Thus the model of segmentation based to a great extent on Evans-Pritchard's description of the Nuer is having an impact in Old Testament studies.

Yet at the same time, contemporary anthropologists are growing more and more uncomfortable with some of the aspects of this model. In the first place, many anthropologists are beginning to doubt that the Nuer society was without continuous leaders. A corollary to the theory of balanced segmentary opposition is that Nuer society is acephalous, that no segment ever dominates another and that ambitious men seldom attempt and never succeed in raising influence into real political power except for brief, extraordinary periods. Anthropologists appear now to suggest that, among others, the Leopard-Skin Priest commanded both respect and political authority among the Nuer.

18. Lohfink, 'Die segmentären Gesellschaften Afrikas als neue Analogie für das vorstaatliche Israel', *Bibel und Kirche* 38 (1983), pp. 55-58; F. Crüsemann, *Der Widerstand gegen das Königtum* (Neukirchen–Vluyn: Neukirchener Verlag, 1978), pp. 200, 203-204.

19. Rogerson, *Anthropology and the Old Testament*, p. 98.

20. Wilson makes the segmentary system the model of Hebrew society. See *Genealogy and History*, p. 19.

21. *The Tribes of Yahweh* (Maryknoll, NY: Orbis Books, 1979), p. 332.

22. Malamat, 'Biblical Genealogies', pp. 132-36; Rogerson, *Anthropology and the Old Testament*, pp. 95-96; Wilson, *Genealogy and History*, pp. 18-55.

23. Sahlins, *The Tribesmen*, p. 50.

P.J. Greuel argued that the priest based his power not only on his religious functions—settling disputes especially in homicides and offering sacrifices—but on his possession of cattle. Since the priest was paid for his services in cattle he would soon be a wealthy man. Cattle to a Nuer symbolize not only wealth but prestige and power. People hope to receive favors from owners of large herds and so become loyal and obedient followers. Thus, says Greuel, the priest has more authority than is obvious to the western observer.[24]

T.O. Beidelman[25] suggested that the reason Evans-Pritchard played down the authority of the Leopard-Skin Priest was because he observed mostly the eastern Nuer tribes, in which the priest seldom came from a dominant or aristocratic lineage. P.P. Howell, P. Coriat, and B.A. Lewis[26] on the other hand stressed the importance of the priest because they relied on evidence from the western sections of Nuerland. Beidelman concluded that when the chief comes from a dominant lineage he is politically very powerful, but if he does not he is uninfluential. Beidelman also pointed out that some Leopard-Skin Priests have used magic to enhance their power and others—most notably Ngundeng and Gwek—were charismatic prophets as well as priests.

The reflections of F.M. Deng, himself a Dinka—a people who are culturally akin to the Nuer and who border Nuerland—on political authority are interesting. Deng once told a certain Dinka named Chol Adija about the anthropological assertion of the chiefless nature of Dinka society and received an angry rebuke. The man disgustedly related the Dinka myth of the origin of the power of the priests. Deng states that anthropologists, especially Evans-Pritchard, have had a bias to stress the idealized freedom of the Nilotic Africans from the restraints of both law and government. But Evans-Pritchard has misunderstood the politics of the Nuer and their neighbors. The priests have power physically to harm dissenters, not by their own hands but

24. 'A Note on the Leopard-Skin Chief: An Examination of Political Power Among the Nuer', *American Anthropologist* 73 (1971), pp. 115-20.

25. 'Nuer Priests and Prophets: Charisma, Authority, and Power among the Nuer', *The Translation of Culture: Essays to E.E. Evans-Pritchard* (ed. T.O. Beidelman; London: Tavistock, 1971), p. 387.

26. Howell, *A Manual of Nuer Law*, p. 29; P. Coriat, 'Gwek the Witch-Doctor and the Pyramid of Dengkur', *Sudan Notes and Records* 22 (1939), pp. 221-38; B.A. Lewis, 'Nuer Spokesmen: A Note on the Institution of the Ruic', *Sudan Notes and Records* 32 (1951), pp. 77-84.

by their curses. A priest can invoke 'the sanction of his spiritual powers which may inflict a curse and perhaps death on an uncooperative culprit'.[27] Beidelman had also pointed out that priests' curses are greatly feared by Nuer.[28]

To a Westerner such curses may seem insignificant and thus to represent no power base. Consequently, the Westerner concludes that the Leopard-Skin Priest has no political power and is not a leader with enduring authority. But to a Nuer or Dinka, according to Deng, such religious and spiritual authority carries with it a real threat and thus the priest truly possesses political power. In other words Deng seems to be accusing Evans-Pritchard of the worst sin for an anthropologist: ethnocentrism. This ethnocentrism may have made Evans-Pritchard's segmentary tribal model fatally flawed.

Thus recent anthropological studies have seriously questioned the model of an acephalous, segmented Nuer society.

Another criticism of Evans-Pritchard's segmentary tribal model comes from anthropologists using a different theoretical framework. Evans-Pritchard studied and described the Nuer within the perspective of British functionalism. K. Gough has maintained that because of Evans-Pritchard's perspective he '[ascribed] Nuer actions to various structural principles as if they were timeless and [gave] at times the impression of a society in a state of equilibrium'.[29] What happens if one examines the Nuer segmentation diachronically? Ethnologists pursuing such study have focused on the relationship of the Nuer to their neighbors, the Dinka.

The Nuer undoubtedly are an offshoot from their neighbors and cultural kinsmen the Dinka. They share both cultural and racial characteristics. Both peoples are segmented tribally, yet the Dinka segments tend to fragment into absolute independent entities whereas, among the Nuer, the segments are matched 'by fusion with lineage equivalent segments in a higher-order'.[30] The Dinka segments are not genealogically connected and hence tend to break apart. Thus a society

---

27. F.M. Deng, *Africans of Two Worlds: The Dinka in Afro-Arab Sudan* (New Haven: Yale University Press, 1978), p. 120. See also *The Dinka of the Sudan* (New York: Holt, Rinehart, and Winston, 1972).

28. 'Nuer Priests and Prophets', p. 383. See Evans-Pritchard, 'The Nuer: Tribe and Clan', *Sudan Notes and Records* 17 (1934), pp. 46-47.

29. 'Nuer Kinship: A Re-examination', in *The Translation of Culture*, p. 88.

30. Sahlins, 'The Segmentary Lineage', p. 328.

can be segmented and be quite different from Nuer society.

Even more intriguing is to ask why the Nuer segmented society has evolved into its present form as opposed to the Dinka type of segmentation. One of the best answers to that question comes from an examination of ecology. M. Glickman argues that the semi-nomadic life style of the Nuer distinguishes them from the Dinka. Nuerland floods every year, forcing the Nuer to cluster into villages on ridges. In the dry season they are forced to drive their cattle far from their villages to find water. There the men of different segments live in cattle camps and thereby strengthen and renew their lineage ties that cut across political segments. Such lineage ties prevent the Nuer from fragmenting as the Dinka, who do not stay in the cattle camps since plentiful water is always nearby.[31]

A. Southall basically agrees with Glickman but points out that the eastern Nuer—among whom Evans-Pritchard spent most of his time and whom he mainly described—are in some respects quite different from the western Nuer. The Nuer living in the western part of Nuerland share the same environment with their neighbors the Dinka and therefore live politically much the same as the Dinka. Thus the nature of political segmentation can be greatly influenced by ecology.[32]

K. Sacks argues that the difference between segmentation among the Dinka and the Nuer is based in the history of the upper Nile. The Dinka were directly on the trading route and thus were pacified and ruled by the Turks in the nineteenth century. The Dinka therefore became dependent on the Turks for political unity and thus when the Turks left became politically fragmented. The Nuer escaped Turkish domination due to the remote region in which they lived.[33]

Thus the segmentary model of the Nuer which Evans-Pritchard describes and which most Old Testament scholars use either directly or indirectly, based as it is on a sense of structuralist equilibrium, may be flawed. We cannot speak of political segmentation in timeless terms. Ecology or history or both may cause one segmented society to develop in a way quite different from another.

A. Kuper has also advanced a critique of Evans-Pritchard and the

31. 'The Nuer and the Dinka: a Further Note', *Man* 7 (1972), pp. 586-94.

32. 'Nuer and Dinka are People: Ecology, Ethnicity, and Logical Possibility', *Man* 11 (1976), pp. 463-91.

33. 'Causality and Chance on the Upper Nile', *American Ethnologist* 6 (1979), pp. 437-48.

concept of the segmentary political and lineage system on a theoretical level. He believes that Evans-Pritchard revived under a new name the antiquated and discredited clan theory of the nineteenth century without solving the problems the theory had with the empirical data from numerous societies among the North American Indians and Oceania. Secondly, Kuper maintains that Evans-Pritchard's theory does not even correspond to his own ethnographic data acquired from his stay among the Nuer.[34]

Kuper's conclusions should be carefully considered by any Old Testament exegete using segmentation to understand pre-monarchy Israel:

> I see no reason to salvage any part of the Nuer model.[35] It is more reasonable to conclude that the Nuer model provides reliable guidance neither to Nuer social behavior nor to Nuer values.[36]

The segmentary political and lineage theory, especially as developed by Evans-Pritchard, is experiencing serious problems among anthropologists at the same time as it enjoys some popularity among Old Testament scholars as a means of understanding Israelite society. Our sounding into the anthropological investigation of the Old Testament has uncovered one of the problems in such procedure. The Old Testament specialist must follow the current debate in anthropology to ensure that biblical research is not based on discredited ethnological theories.

We do not necessarily as a result of this study suggest, along with some, that Old Testament scholars abandon the use of the concept of segmentation in Hebraic society. We do suggest, however, that more study on this problem needs to be done.

34. Kuper, 'Lineage Theory', pp. 71-95.
35. Kuper, 'Lineage Theory', p. 83.
36. Kuper, 'Lineage Theory', p. 84.

JSOT 60 (1993), pp. 3-26

THE 'POPULAR RELIGION' PARADIGM IN OLD TESTAMENT
RESEARCH: A SOCIOLOGICAL CRITIQUE

J. Berlinerblau

> Il faudra dire d'abord qu'il n'y a pas de *différence qualitative*, pour l'historien, entre la religion savante et la religion populaire. L'étude de l'une et de l'autre contribue également à une compréhension totale de la réalité humaine et de la vie concrète (Raoul Manselli, *La religion populaire au moyen âge*).

The nascent and fertile field of 'popular religion' is perched at the confluence of various streams of sociological, anthropological and historical research. In this paper I will argue that biblical scholarship must venture into these waters in order to engage the issue of 'Israelite popular religion'. As we shall see, the current discourse on this subject is predicated on a variety of assumptions that need to be critically re-evaluated in light of recent theoretical and methodological advances in social-scientific and historical research.

'Popular Religion': What is it?

Tacit Consensus

The study of 'Israelite popular religion' has generally garnered two distinct treatments in Old Testament scholarship.[1] In the first, the researcher's conceptual blueprint of 'Israelite Religion' accords only the most limited space to issues of popular religiosity.

In Julius Wellhausen's *Prolegomena to the History of Israel* (1885), for example, one is wont to encounter sporadic references to 'the

---

1. I will not discuss the other types of treatment which the 'popular religion' construct has received. For a fuller examination see Berlinerblau 1991a: 12-29; Berlinerblau 1996.

popular recollection' (18), 'the popular fancy' (326), 'popular legends' (336), or simply, 'the people'. Nowhere in this masterful work, however, do issues of popular religiosity figure prominently in Wellhausen's discussions of ancient Israel's religious institutions. Nor will one find any significant analysis of the religious life or historical trajectory of 'the people'; the bulk of Wellhausen's scrutiny is focused on—to borrow a term from Hegel—'world-historical men' (1956: 30).[2]

Or perhaps one thinks of the methodology adumbrated on the opening pages of Roland de Vaux's *Ancient Israel*. Here, the author intentionally eschews an analysis of 'how in fact the Israelites practised their religion' in favor of an examination of those cultic institutions which the Old Testament presents as 'legitimate institutions of *true Yahwism*' (1965: 273 [emphasis mine]).[3]

In more recent work on Israelite religion, issues of popular religiosity are also likely to be only briefly engaged. In the recent compilation *Ancient Israelite Religion: Essays in Honor of Frank Moore Cross*, for example, one may encounter occasional references to 'popular religion'. Yet here again, most of this volume's distinguished contributors have paid little attention to the subject in question.[4]

By way of contrast, we will place in our second category those

2.   For an excellent critique of biblical scholarship's obsession with 'the great figures of the past', see Whitelam 1986; also see Gottwald 1985: 11 and Gelb 1967: 1. For articulations of the desire to study non-world-historical men, see Le Roy Ladurie 1984: 24 or the first paragraph of Natalie Zemon Davis's *Culture in Early Modern France* (1975a: xv).

3.   In the same paragraph de Vaux draws a connection between non-official religion and such 'deviations' as 'syncretist' or 'purely pagan' cults (1965: 273). This association is by no means rare (Albright 1957: 247; 1968: 199) and see, revealingly, Albright's views on 'official religion' (1940: 112); also see Wellhausen 1973; Fohrer 1972: 152, 155, 159; Guillaume 1938: 233-89; Hooke 1938: 57; Patai 1987: 379; Mensching 1964: 256. At the other end of the spectrum, Y. Kaufmann attempts to depict 'Israelite popular religion' as essentially monotheistic, albeit a bit misdirected (1972 and see below).

4.   Most notable perhaps, is the contribution of J. Tigay, 'Israelite Religions: The Onomastic and Epigraphic Evidence' (1987). In light of his conclusion, 'After the united monarchy, perhaps even earlier, the evidence currently available makes it very difficult to suppose that many Israelites worshipped gods other than YHWH' (p. 180), it would seem that 'popular religion' has been negated before it was ever posited. As we shall see below, a society as homogeneous as the one presented by Tigay cannot really be said to possess a 'popular religion' (for brief reviews of Tigay's hypothesis see Miller 1985: 216; Smith 1990: xxi).

studies in which 'Israelite popular religion' stands as the specific object of inquiry. The early decades of the twentieth century produced a few contributions of this nature—ranging from Eduard Meyer's intriguing chapter 'Die jüdische Volksreligion in Jerusalem und in Elephantine' (1912) to Anton Jirku's somewhat eclectic *Materialien zur Volksreligion Israels* (1914), to Yehezkel Kaufmann's important section 'The Religion of the People' in his *The Religion of Israel: From its Beginnings to the Babylonian Exile* (1972 [1953]).

After a few fallow decades, the seventies and eighties witnessed the publication of several studies on 'popular religion', many bearing this term in their titles.[5] What is most surprising about biblical scholarship's appropriation of the 'popular religion' construct—among works of the first *and the second category*—has been its reluctance to proffer any theoretical analysis, precise definitions or even conscious consideration of this term. Accordingly, one receives the distinct impression that a sort of tacit consensus exists as to what is meant by 'Israelite popular religion'.

'Popular Religion' in Non-Biblical Research
As the reader might have noticed, I have persistently surrounded the term 'popular religion' with a pair of cautionary quotation marks. This usage is owing to the fact that, in social-scientific and historical research, little or no consensus exists as to what 'popular religion' actually means. Accordingly, the last quarter-century of work in this area has evinced an explosion of definitional activity, as well as a vigorous process of conceptual rechristening.

Terms such as 'common religion' (Towler 1974: 148), 'folk religion' (Mensching 1964: 254; also see Bock 1966), 'subaltern religion' (e.g. de Martino 1975; Prandi 1977: 31), 'religion vécue', 'nonofficial religion' (Vrijhof 1979b: 688), 'extra-ecclesiastical religion' (Williams 1989: 5), 'local religion' (Christian 1981), 'popular faith' (Brandes 1990: 186) among others, have served to recast, refine, and, in some cases, reject outright the traditional typology of 'popular' (and 'official')[6] religion.[7]

---

5. See Miller 1985: 215.
6. It should be noted that the term 'official religion' is equally problematic in Old Testament research. In Berlinerblau 1996 and Berlinerblau 1998 (forthcoming) I re-evaluate critically the status of this term in modern biblical scholarship. In this article—only so that massive theoretical confusion may be avoided—I will abide by

Advocates of the latter position include sociologist Robert Towler, who writes: 'The term "popular religion" is really too vague to signify anything at all...' (1974: 148).[8] J.C. Schmitt proposes 'd'éviter ce terme ambigu' (1976: 942), and Enzo Pace refers to it as a 'blurred category' (1979: 72).[9] Peter Williams, however, opines that '"popular religion" is too useful as an heuristic, if not a classificatory, device to be done away with' (1989: 18).[10]

Regardless of the status of this term in modern research, it would seem that the establishment of a universally valid, ahistorical classificatory scheme of 'popular religion' is neither tremendously important nor immediately forthcoming. For, as many have noted, any definition or theoretical statement regarding 'popular religion' must first corres-pond to the particular social facts observed in the society in question. Vittorio Lanternari writes:

> La seule réalité que l'on puisse raisonnablement tenter de saisir et de comprendre au moyen d'analyses appropriées est celle de formes variées et concrètes que peut assumer la religiosité populaire au sein des diverses civilisations—Européennes, occidentales et non occidentales, antiques et modernes—tout au long de leur évolution historique propre (1982: 140).[11]

> The only reality one can reasonably try to grasp and comprehend by means of the appropriate analyses is that of the forms, various and concrete, which popular religion can assume within the diverse civilizations— European, Western and non-Western, ancient and modern—throughout the whole of their own historical evolution.

This remark reminds us of the importance of respecting the unique temperament of the sociological time and space we are examining; what may hold true for thirteenth-century Sicily may not for thirteenth-century Canaan.

---

the traditional, albeit unproven, conception that views the words of the Old Testament as synonymous with the 'official religion' of ancient Israel.

7.   On the multiplicity of approaches as well as the difficulties inherent in defining this term see Scribner 1984; Pace 1979; Pace 1987; Staples 1979: 260; Orsi 1985: xiv; Badone 1990: 4; Isambert 1979: 219-92; Isambert 1982: 7-39. Additionally, I have not cited the many studies that retain the term 'popular religion' and offer precise definitions of its nature.

8.   For a critique of Towler see Vrijhof 1979a.

9.   Also see Christian 1981: 168; Roebroeck 1979: 188, 190 and Platvoet 1979: 545. Elsewhere, Pace attempts to revalue the usefulness of this term (1987).

10.   Also see Isambert 1977: 184.

11.   Also see Hilaire 1979: 194; Van Beek 1979: 539; and Bouritius 1979: 156.

'Israelite Popular Religion': A Definition Deconstructed

In a brief 1986 article, 'Aspects of Popular Religion in the Old Testament', Hermann Vorländer offers one of the few definitions to date of 'Israelite popular religion'.[12] I would like to use Vorländer's clearly stated definition as a means of identifying certain common-denominator assumptions that many biblical scholars share regarding 'popular religion'. He writes: *'the term "popular religion" refers to the popular ideas entertained by the Israelites concerning God's action in the life of the individual, the community, and in nature'* (1986: 63).

'Popular Religion'

One of the major drawbacks of the term 'popular religion' in general is that it fosters the impression of one religious movement, one 'popular religion', which stands as a unified antithesis of an 'official religion'. Yet as historians and social scientists have pointed out, there need not be homogeneity among the heterodox.[13] Thus, inaccuracies may arise when we structure our inquiries around the study of *the* 'popular religion' of an entire society. For this latter term tends to conceal the fact that numerous religious *groups*—each with their own distinct political and metaphysical agendas—may all exist contemporaneously.

Anthropologist Stanley Brandes offers an important analogy of no small relevance for students of 'Israelite religion':

> No matter where we go in Europe, no matter how large or small our unit of analysis, we inevitably discover *the coexistence of several competing, mutually derivative systems of religious beliefs and practices*. If it would be oversimplifying matters to speak of Australian aboriginal religion, Trobriand religion, or Ife religion, then it is an even graver injustice to refer to Roman Catholicism or Eastern Orthodoxy as if these each

12. On this account, it should be noted that Rainer Albertz has also discussed this term and deemed it inadequate for his inquiry (1978: 18 and see below). T.J. Lewis has offered a definition of 'popular religion' within the context of his study of cults of the dead (1989: 2).

13. An interesting example of this phenomenon is touched upon in historian Brenda Bolton's study of the relation between Pope Innocent III and a curious Middle-Age sect known as the *humiliati*. Bolton focuses on a letter in which the Pontiff mentions that the *humiliati*, whose status as heretics was being debated, 'were being indiscriminately excommunicated and classed with Cathars, Arnaldists and Poor Men of Lyons' (1972: 75).

reflected homogeneous, undifferentiated cosmologies, world views and
sets of ritual behavior (1990: 185 [emphasis mine]).

Whereas nearly all studies of our first and second category have
spoken of one 'Israelite popular religion', none has as of yet envisioned
the possibility that considerable differences may have existed within
this putative non-official religion.[14] Yet, what basis do we have for
supposing that Baal worshippers, devotees of the Queen of Heaven,
those who worshipped under trees and the rest, were part of a consolidated anti-Yahweh coalition? Unless a scholar can point to conclu-
sive evidence demonstrating the existence of political and/or religious
solidarity among those who did what was offensive to 'the Lord', it
would seem that the term 'popular religion' is inappro-priately con-
stricting vis-à-vis the manifold religious orientations known to the
biblical literati.

Old Testament research has also been inclined to speak of this
'popular religion' as if it were the very antithesis of 'official religion'.
The following remark from J.B. Segal's article 'Popular Religion in
Ancient Israel' epitomizes this particular approach:

> There were two levels of Israelite religion. The one... is that of estab-
> lished sanctuaries and of established dates, a formal religion, in short,
> which followed lines clearly defined and precise in detail. The other is less
> easy to characterize... Outside the borders of the established cult lies the
> shadowy region of popular superstition, of actions that arise from the
> vague, half-conscious feelings of fear and anticipation that have been
> summed up in the not ill-chosen term of 'Nature religion' (1976: 1).

In many works, 'popular' and 'official' spheres are imagined to be
exact opposites. The 'truths' of the 'official' doctrine of monotheistic
Yahwism were apparently scorned by what T. Vriezen calls 'the great
mass of people' (1967: 20). The psychological constitution of the laity
stands in rigorous contrast to that of the litterateur.[15] And the possibility that 'official' and 'popular' religion exerted a reciprocal
influence upon one another is only rarely addressed.[16]

In non-biblical research, however, this monadic conception of
'popular' and 'official' religion has been re-evaluated. As Ellen Badone

14. However, see Lewis who observes, 'In the past *the* "popular religion" was
looked upon as if it was a clearly identifiable homogeneous entity which was merely
a corruption of "true Yahwism"' (1989: 1).

15. See in particular Greenberg 1983: 51.

16. For example, see Albright 1968: 199.

points out, 'Rather than viewing official and popular religion as monolithic entities, immutable and distinct, it is more fruitful to focus on the dialectical character of their interrelationship' (1990: 6).[17] Donald Weinstein and Rudolph Bell note that recent research has demonstrated the existence of a 'multidirectional' flow 'between elite and popular culture' (1986: 12).[18]

What emerges from these studies is the sense that a *nexus* must exist among various religious groups in a society. No matter how dissimilar, how antagonistic 'popular' and 'official' religion actually are, it is conceded that they must exist in some sort of a relation. Whether this relation is belligerent,[19] ambivalent[20] or symbiotic,[21] we must always recognize that religious groups sharing a common social space mutually affect one another. The traditional division of ancient Israel into 'popular' and 'official' domains, however, makes it almost impossible to conceptualize any form of interaction between these two spheres.[22]

Popular Ideas ('Popular Religion')

In this section I would like to examine the ways in which scholars have attempted to extract 'popular ideas' from the Old Testament. Let

17. The interactive nature of 'popular' and 'official' religion, the fact that they influence one another in a variety of subtle and not so subtle ways, constitutes one of the most widespread and consistent findings in modern 'popular religion' research. See in particular Jill Dubisch's study of pilgrimages to modern Greek shrines (1990: 135) or Caroline Brettell's work on a Portuguese community in which she examines 'the way in which priest and parishioners negotiate the practice of religion...' (1990: 55; also see Chaline 1979: 173; Carpenter 1963: 310; Manselli 1975: 20, 27; Huisman 1979: 66-67; Bouritius 1979: 156; Vrijhof 1979a: 239-40).

18. Also see Ginzburg 1980: 126.

19. As that observed between the Cathars and the Catholic Church in Emmanuel Le Roy Ladurie's *Montaillou: The Promised Land of Error* (1979) or Ginzburg's *The Cheese and the Worms: The Cosmos of a Sixteenth-Century Miller* (1980), Ginzburg 1985 and countless other studies.

20. See, for example, Orsi 1985: 55-56.

21. See van den Broeck 1979: 40; Rousseau 1979: 356; Semporé 1986: 50.

22. Vorländer, one of the few biblical scholars to avoid this sort of approach, notes, 'Even the official cult of Jahwe was permeated by elements of popular religion right into the time of the monarchy' (1986: 67). Nor should we exclude the very real possibility that alternative forms of religiosity absorbed many aspects of the 'official religion' (for this point see John Holladay Jr's remarks on 'dissenting groups' in his invigorating, 'purely archaeological', study of Israelite religion [1987: 267]).

us begin this discussion with the restatement of a question posed by
Y. Kaufmann: 'To what extent is this [the Bible] a portrayal of the
religion—not of individual thinkers—but of the people at large?'.[23]

For Kaufmann, the Old Testament does not merely convey the religious ideas of 'the people', but it is predicated on their very beliefs:

> Biblical faith is thus based on the popular legends. It draws on them even
> when it battles the people's backslidings into idolatry. The popular leg-
> ends and the beliefs they imply are the common property of the folk and
> the authors of the Bible... Biblical religion is therefore not an esoteric
> religion of a spiritual elite like the higher pagan religions, but is a growth
> that is rooted in and nourished by the popular religion of Israel (1972:
> 132, 133).[24]

The assumption that popular ideas may be *directly*, even effort-
lessly, reaped from the witness can also be detected in other works of
biblical scholarship. J.B. Segal's aforementioned article begins with
the sober methodological contention that biblical references to religious practices 'are sometimes didactic or aetiological, and frequently
fortuitous rather than deliberate...the picture that they present is
incomplete' (1976: 1). Curiously, however, Segal continues to offer a
rather confident analysis of Old Testament 'popular religion' based
exclusively on a blizzard of biblical citations.[25]

This approach is quite comparable to that of Vorländer, who also
uses the reports of the literati as a means of extracting various popular
ideas. Vorländer's study of the sacred text leads him to conclusions
such as the following:

> Israelite popular religion makes a close connection between what a person
> does and what happens to him, between one's attitude and one's fate in
> life (1986: 65).

It is essential to recall that this inference (among others) is based
solely on the words of the Old Testament. If a methodology may be
identified here, it would consist of collating all biblical references to

23. Kaufmann 1972: 122; Moshe Greenberg poses a similar question (1983: 18).

24. As such, the Psalms are held to originate in the hands of popular poets, and
the Torah is regarded as a 'folk literature' (1972: 223). It must be recalled that Kaufmann's main interest lies not in discerning the nature of 'popular religion', but in
demonstrating its non-pagan disposition. For a critique of Kaufmann's position see
Sperling 1986.

25. For example, observe Segal's use of biblical quotes in proving his observations about 'birth' (1976: 3).

'popular'—that is, heterodox or 'deviant'—religious activity, and then summating them so as to produce a basic statement regarding the way 'Israelite popular religion' was practised.[26]

A different type of strategy for deriving popular ideas can be detected in the works of Moshe Greenberg and James Crenshaw. These researchers are much more discriminating in their selection of literary sources that illuminate popular ideas. In order to reach 'unmediated, direct forms of popular piety', Moshe Greenberg, in *Biblical Prose Prayer as a Window to the Popular Religion of Ancient Israel*, argues that we must avoid using the 'stock compositions of trained liturgical poets' (1983: 6-7). Temple-ritual texts and Psalms then 'are thus deficient as mirrors of the *commoners' religion*; both are prescriptions of the schooled; they belong to a class of experts' (pp. 6-7 [emphasis mine]).

Greenberg's justifiable misgivings about using such texts to illuminate popular piety lead him to concentrate on what he labels 'prayers embedded in the narratives of Scriptures' (1983: 7). It is Greenberg's opinion that the great similarity which these prayers of confession, petition and gratitude share with instances of inter-human speech in the Bible proves that they accurately reflect popular supplication, as opposed to the intellectual wares of the literati.[27]

James Crenshaw's monograph, *Prophetic Conflict: Its Effect upon Israelite Religion*, features a section entitled '*Vox Populi* in Ancient Israel'. Here, it is argued that the voice of the people may be dis-covered when we examine the prophetic denunciations of the so-called 'false prophets' and 'the people'. When, for example, Micah disparagingly regurgitates the words 'Then my enemy will see, and shame will cover her who said to me, "where is the Lord your God"' (7.10), it is asserted that a normative pattern of popular behavior has been identified. The person Micah is referring to—the one who allegedly said 'where is the Lord your God'—is taken by Crenshaw as representative of a general pattern of popular 'defiance' (1971: 28).[28]

---

26. For similar instances of the 'direct' approach in 'popular religion' studies, see Kraeling 1928: 159; Jirku 1914; Meyer 1912 and Patai 1987.

27. For a critique of Greenberg's hypothesis, see Berlinerblau 1995; Berlinerblau 1998 (forthcoming).

28. After noting that some of the prophetic quotations which he has cited may be 'creations of the prophets', Crenshaw concludes that 'most of the quotations have a *ring of authenticity* that justifies their acceptance as genuine popular response to

The Verisimilitude of Popular Ideas

The common and easily identifiable thread that runs throughout all of these works is knotted around the contention that the Old Testament provides veridical information regarding 'popular religion'. The text is viewed as a sort of literary omphalos, an intersection where, to varying degrees and through differing means, the diverse social elements of ancient Israel manage to express themselves.

This assumption finds its most characteristic illustration in Kaufmann, Vorländer and Segal's *direct* extraction of textual references referring to heterodox activity. Crenshaw and Greenberg read the sacred text more selectively; they employ *indirect* methods for accessing authentic popular religious ideas.

None of these researchers, however, has yet begun to grapple with argu-ments made by sociologists, historians and biblical scholars alike, regarding the possibility that the words of 'official' texts may be at best slightly biased, and at worst so thoroughly misrepresentative as to be of little value for the elucidation of popular religiosity.

William Dever, in his *Recent Archaeological Discoveries and Biblical Research*, labels biblical texts 'elitist', and goes on to note: 'the Hebrew Bible is a highly sophisticated literary creation which was written by and for the intelligentsia, who preserved, transmitted, and finally edited it into its final form' (1990: 123). Claudia Camp asks, 'how do we know when literary sources are giving a reasonably accurate picture of *historical reality* and when, for reasons ideological or esthetic, this picture has been distorted?' (1990: 185).[29]

These remarks provide us with two conceptual buzzwords, 'elitism' and 'ideology', which are of tremendous importance for a discussion regarding the reliability of our textual sources. In beginning with the notion of 'elitism', we would suppose that a certain class, 'an elite', is primarily responsible for the authorship of the Old Testament.

---

prophetic faith' (1971: 34) (emphasis mine). In a recent article Crenshaw writes, 'The Book of Proverbs expresses the views of countless individuals ranging from simple rural folk to a Queen Mother' (1990: 205). The belief that popular wisdom surfaces in Proverbs can also be identified in Lemaire 1990: 175 and McKane 1970: 2-3.

29. Sentiments of this order are by no means rare in biblical scholarship. As Keith Whitelam notes, 'The text is not a witness to historical reality... It is a witness to a particular perception of reality' (1986: 52; also see Coogan 1987: 115; Dever 1987: 220; Smith 1971: 19; McCarter 1987: 137; Sperling 1986: 7; Ackerman 1989: 109; Holladay Jr 1987: 249; Garbini 1988: 14).

Accordingly, we might infer that members of this elite class retain their own particular understanding and interpretation of their world, a 'world vision'[30]—what some Marxian scholars might refer to as 'a class-consciousness'. Georg Lukács writes:

> [...] class consciousness consists in fact of the appropriate and rational reactions 'imputed' [zugerechnet] to a particular typical position in the process of production... the historically significant actions of the class as a whole are determined in the last resort by this consciousness... and these actions can be understood only by reference to this consciousness (1986: 51).

If we assume that the 'historically significant' activity of this 'elite' was the actual writing, compilation, redaction and maintenance of the Old Testament, and if we accept R.N. Whybray's recent conclusion that 'much of the literature composed during the period of the Monarchy was the work of either the royal or the priestly scribes' (1990: 137), then we must begin to wonder to what extent the class-consciousness of this group impacted upon their literary production.

It must be recalled that such a consciousness precludes the capacity for objective (historical) assessment. The proletariat notwithstanding, class-consciousness is inextricably bound with beclouded social vision. Lukács refers to class-consciousness as 'a class-conditioned *unconsciousness* of ones [*sic*] own socio-historical and economic condition' (1986: 52). Karl Mannheim, in defining the term 'ideology', writes:

> ... ruling groups can in their thinking become so intensely interest-bound to a situation that they are simply no longer able to see certain facts which would undermine their sense of domination... the collective unconscious of certain groups obscures the real condition of society both to itself and to others... (1985: 40).[31]

Students of 'popular religion', then, have two basic concerns when it comes to assessing a text's capacity to relinquish popular ideas. First, we are fearful that an elitist literati may *intentionally misrepresent* the religious beliefs of all other groups. Thus, the particular ideology of the literati may have been so 'interest-bound' with the hegemonic perpetuation of monotheistic Yahwism, that their views on the religion of other classes and groups will inevitably be pejorative

---

30. See Goldmann 1964.

31. For a discussion of the differences between Mannheim and Critical Theorists see Bailey 1994. Or as Raymond Aron notes, Marx 'was inclined to think that a class cannot see the world except in terms of its own situation' (1968: 218).

and misleading. It is this incredulity as regards the witness, which is so lacking in the *direct* methods espoused by Kaufmann, Vorländer and Segal. For there, the possibility that the Old Testament may intentionally mislead us, may offer us less than judicious and balanced accounts of 'heterodox' religiosity, is not adequately explored.

Yet ideologies and class-consciousness present us with an even greater—and subtler—methodological danger. For the possibility exists that the literati *unintentionally misrepresent* the religious life of other classes and groups. In this instance we conjecture that, regardless of whether they were inimical toward alternative forms of religiosity, their own particular class-consciousness prevented them from accurately understanding them.

Can highly educated litterateurs interested in chronicling the 'truths' of monotheistic Yahwism truly hear the '*vox populi*', or is it articulated in a dialect which, to them, is socially incomprehensible? Can the scribes really understand the religion of the agriculturalist, or the meaning of the Baal worshipper's rituals—what they signify *to the Baalist* and what they are really intended to do?

Now if unintentional misrepresentation is a valid concern, then the 'interhuman speech' identified by Greenberg may only be an instance of how the literati thought members of other groups addressed one another. Crenshaw's *vox populi* may be a conjectured *vox*—the manner in which the literati imagined that their 'impious' compatriots thought and spoke.[32]

In leaving the realm of class-consciousness, we must never forget that a great number of facts are simply not accessible to the consciousness of the modern historian. W.T.M. Frijhoff, in an article on 'popular religion' in the Middle Ages, identifies the shortcomings of using historical texts to illuminate either 'popular' or 'official' religion:

> ...one can only measure that which has been conserved, i.e. has been *transmitted* in measurable form. This means in fact only the written (or printed) word, pictorial material, and fixed physical arrangements, but *not* the spoken word, the rumor, the mental structure, fear, sickness, immediate events, hidden practices, ignored movements, public opinion etc... (1979: 73).[33]

---

32. It should be noted that the tendency of the ecclesiastical authorities to decide what heterodox groups are 'really' saying, is a major dynamic of the interaction between 'official' and powerless non-official religions (see Ginzburg 1985: 88).

33. David Sperling has remarked, 'Unfortunately, the best biblical criticism can

Herein lies one of the most disheartening verities of 'popular religion' research. The student of 'popular religion' probes in the interstices of history, and it is precisely these mundane quotidian activities and fleeting cognitions—not a register of great battles and royal coronations—which are of paramount significance.[34] Hence, regardless of the intentions of our authors, our ancient documents often obscure the very type of information which is of such importance to the study of this subject.[35]

Israelites

In his definition of 'popular religion', Vorländer speaks of 'the popular ideas entertained by Israelites'. It seems to me that the use of the term 'Israelites' as a heuristic morpheme for the study of 'popular religion' is also highly problematic. For, in employing this adjectiveless designation, we run the risk of obscuring the fact that *certain groups of Israelites* may have maintained distinct religious orientations.

The examination of groups is of great importance to both the sociology of religion and the sub-field of 'popular religion' studies.[36] To study the latter is *de facto* to assume that within a given society complete similarity of religious belief does not exist. As Peter Williams has observed, 'The notion of popular religion makes no sense in the context of homogeneous and undifferentiated societies...' (1989: 9).

tell us only about the texts studied. The world outside those texts remains unknown' (1986: 7). One of the most radical suggestions regarding the insufficiency of our textual canon has been made by Giovanni Garbini, who raises the possibility of 'the *damnatio memoriae* of the monarchy and all the documents relating to it' (1988: 18).

34. See Robert Orsi's remark in his *The Madonna of 115th Street: Faith and Community in Italian Harlem, 1880–1950* (1985) regarding the significance of seemingly trivial aspects of the Madonna celebration (p. xix). Or, one thinks of Carolo Ginzburg's comment in a recent issue of the *New York Times Magazine* that his was the study of 'peripheral phenomena' (Kandell 1991: 45).

35. I do not believe that the arguments presented above categorically exclude the prospect that authentic popular ideas may be located. I would strongly suggest, however, that future researchers more directly incorporate the aforementioned difficulties into their methodological designs for studying 'popular religion' in northwest Semitic antiquity.

36. For an excellent introductory discussion on the use and importance of 'groups' as an analytical tool in the sociology of religion, see Joachim Wach's chapter, 'Religion and Natural Groups', in his *Sociology of Religion* (1967).

Rather, the researcher begins with the supposition that some group(s) will espouse a system of religious beliefs which—to varying degrees—stand in tension with those of the ecclesiastical authorities.

Sociological examinations of religion often attempt to identify the interrelations between the economic and social attributes of the group and the religious ideas that it embraces. The most eloquent, and for our purposes pertinent, treatment of this issue may be identified in the sociology of Max Weber. As Reinhard Bendix has pointed out, 'Weber's approach conceived of society as an arena of competing status groups, each with its own economic interests, status honor, and orientation toward the world and man' (1977: 262).

In Weber's inexplicably overlooked[37] *Ancient Judaism*, this approach is constantly employed as 'Weber deals...with a great variety of concrete groups' (Eisenstadt 1981: 61). The demarcation of these groups is the prelude to an analysis that emphasizes a society's con-siderable capacity for internecine group conflict. What emerges from Weber's *Ancient Judaism*, then, is the delineation of an inexorable sociology of (group) self-interest, whereby the urban patrician exploits the peasant (1967: 21), the aristocracy disdains the 'undignified plebs' (p. 98) or the priestly class seeks 'to monopolize the regular management of Yahweh worship and all related activities' (p. 168).[38]

Scholars who study 'popular religion' however, have rarely engaged in the practice of 1. identifying distinct groups or 2. searching for their potentially antagonistic interrelations. Throughout this article we have seen the adherents of 'Israelite popular religion' referred to as 'the people',[39] 'commoners', 'Israelites', and 'the great mass of people'.

In Rainer Albertz's *Persönliche Frömmigkeit und offizielle Religion: Religionsinterner Pluralismus in Israel und Babylon* (1978), such general terms are eschewed. In fact, Albertz begins by discarding the term 'Volksfrömmigkeit' (p. 18) in favor of a fruitful bifurcation of the religion of the community and a type of family-centered religion of the individual. It is argued that certain individually and family-

37. As many have noted, with varying degrees of bewilderment, Weber's *Ancient Judaism* has received very little critical attention both among biblical exegetes and sociologists (Holstein 1975: 160; Petersen 1979: 137; Eisenstadt 1981: 54; Fahey 1982: 62).

38. Also see Weber 1988: 140-41.

39. For a discussion of the difficulties inherent in the term 'the people', see Maldonado 1986: 4-5; Davis 1975b: 190.

experienced situations, such as death, birth, marriage and the like, have served to channel the individual's relation to the deity in a manner distinct from that experienced by the Israelite community (1978: 37).[40]

As intriguing as Albertz's theory is, it would seem that a discussion of *religionsinterner Pluralismus* should focus a bit more on the sociological aspects of the individuals being studied. It is certainly not erroneous to maintain that an individual's relation to a deity may be distinct from a community's. Yet insofar as not all individuals and families are the same, insofar as some are indigent, some embrace Chemosh and some—such as women—find their gender status prohibiting them from participating in the cult as would their male coreligionists, it would seem that other aspects of the individual's identity may have a more profound influence on this relation.[41]

As a methodological *Ausgangspunkt*, I would suggest that it would be best to structure future investigations around 'adjectived' Israelites—bearers of precise economic, social, gender and geographic attributes.

Conclusion

There is great irony in the fact that those who have impugned the historical validity of the Old Testament generally acknowledge that it remains the single most valuable source for the study of ancient Israelite religion. This dialectic of disdain and reliance results in an oft-encountered concession: it is maintained that the witness, as unsatisfactory a historical document as it might be, must nevertheless have been witness to something.

My own particular methodological approach begins with the rule that no matter what this something is, it is invariably bound up with the perceptions of the biblical literati.[42] Our future task, then, lies in

40. See W. Brueggemann's review (1980: 86).

41. This is a recurring difficulty with explorations of 'personal religion' (e.g. Jacobsen 1963; 1976: 147-64) which often reduce the individual to a purely psychological entity. Yet it must not be forgotten that, as a member of a society, this individual retains manifold sociological attributes that cannot be ignored.

42. It must be recalled that the forthcoming methodology is proffered solely with the intention of stimulating further discussion. These suggestions are offered not as an anchor, but as a raft; let them serve whatever purpose they can and then be discarded.

the creation of a methodology that manages persistently to incorporate this inconvenient fact into its general design. Any study that does otherwise runs the risk of reading the text in exactly the way that its authors would have wanted it to be read; Baal worshippers will be predictably judged 'abominable', worshippers of the Queen of Heaven will inevitably be labeled 'deviants'.

With this in mind, I will make the recommendation that we lessen our reliance on the term 'popular religion'. Earlier, I called attention to the fact that ancient Israel may have accommodated more than one non-official religious movement. Thus, instead of speaking of '*the* popular religion', or 'popular religion' among 'the people' or 'the masses', I believe a more sociologically precise methodology would undertake to delineate religiosity among *particular Israelite groups*.

As such, I would like to suggest that we endeavor to study what I call 'popular religious groups' and 'requisite groups'. My definition of the former is based on the fact that the authors of the Old Testament perceive the existence of alternative religious communities in ancient Israel. Since we have so little else to go on outside of these perceptions, and since their accuracy and impartiality are always in question, we must come to the following conclusion: the 'popular religious group', as far as we are presently able to study it, is a construction of the biblical literati. Accordingly, I would define a 'popular religious group' as *any association of individuals living within the borders of ancient Israel who by dint of their religious beliefs, political beliefs, rituals, symbols and so on, are denigrated by the authors of the Old Testament*.

For the time being, when I speak of a 'requisite group', I am referring to women and the non-privileged classes. I use the word 'requisite' to suggest that, even though information about such groups is scarce, the fact that they existed is indisputable.[43] They are to be distinguished from popular religious groups insofar as they are not categorically derided by the authors of the Old Testament. While the literati's portrayal of women's religious activity is by no means appreciative, they nevertheless occasionally concede that a woman is capable of being an exemplary Yahwist.[44] This, of course, is a

43. Though it is hoped that researchers will delineate other requisite groups for future study.

44. For some studies of 'popular religion' which discuss women's religiosity see Radford Ruether 1986; Bolton 1972: 73; Hilaire 1979: 197; Orsi 1985: 129-49;

courtesy that they do not routinely extend to Baal worshippers.

In closing, I would like to suggest that we retain the term 'popular religion' only as a disciplinary logo. Let the field of 'popular religion studies' in Old Testament research refer to a type of discourse that abnegates the study of 'world-historical men'. This term, then, would serve as a sort of conceptual umbrella under which the investigation of women, heterodox elements, the non-privileged classes, what Clifford Geertz once called 'the personally idiosyncratic' (1972: 17), among others, would serve as the primary objects of scholarly scrutiny.[45]

BIBLIOGRAPHY

Ackerman, S.
1989   '"And the Women Knead Dough": The Worship of the Queen of Heaven in Sixth-Century Judah', in P. Day (ed.), *Gender and Difference in Ancient Israel* (Minneapolis: Fortress Press): 109-24.

Albertz, R.
1978   *Persönliche Frömmigkeit und offizielle Religion: Religionsinterner Pluralismus in Israel und Babylon* (Calwer Theologische Monographien, 9; Stuttgart: Calwer Verlag).

Albright, W.F.
1940   'The Ancient Near East and the Religion of Israel', *JBL* 59: 85-112.
1957   *From the Stone Age to Christianity: Monotheism and the Historical Process* (AB; Garden City, NY: Doubleday, 2nd edn).
1968   *Yahweh and the Gods of Canaan: A Historical Analysis of Two Contrasting Faiths* (Garden City, NY: Doubleday).

Aron, R.
1968   *Main Currents in Sociological Thought Volume. I. Montesquieu, Comte, Marx, Tocqueville and The Sociologists and the Revolution of 1848* (trans. by H. and H. Weaver; Garden City, NY: Anchor Books).

Badone, E.
1990a   'Introduction', in Badone 1990 (below): 3-23.

Badone, E. (ed.)
1990   *Religious Orthodoxy and Popular Faith in European Society* (Princeton: Princeton University Press).

Manselli 1975: 117-24. I would call the interested reader's attention to de Ste. Croix's *The Class Struggle in the Ancient Greek World: From the Archaic Age to the Arab Conquests*, where for purposes of analysis it is proposed that women be regarded as a class (1981: 99).

45. I wish to thank Dr José Casanova and Dr Mustafa Emirbayer of the Department of Sociology of the New School for Social Research and Dr Juan Corradi of the New York University Department of Sociology for their helpful suggestions and intellectual assistance throughout this project.

Bailey, L.
1994   *Critical Theory and the Sociology of Knowledge: A Comparative Study in the Theory of Ideology* (New York: Peter Lang).

Bendix, R.
1977   *Max Weber: An Intellectual Portrait* (with an Introduction by G. Roth; Berkeley: University of California Press).

Berlinerblau, J.
1991a   *The Israelite Vow and the So-Called 'Popular Religion': A Sociological and Philological Investigation* (Ann Arbor, MI: University Microfilms International).
1991b   'The Israelite Vow: Distress or Daily Life', *Bib* 72: 548-55.
1995   'Some Sociological Observations on Moshe Greenberg's *Biblical Prose Prayer as a Window to the Popular Religion of Ancient Israel*', *JNWSL* 21: 1-14.
1996   *The Vow and the 'Popular Religious Groups' of Ancient Israel: A Philological and Sociological Inquiry* (Sheffield: Sheffield Academic Press).
1998   'Preliminary Remarks for the Sociological Study of "Israelite Official
(forthcoming)   Religion"', in *Baruch Levine Festschrift* (Winona Lake: Eisenbrauns).

Bock, E.W.
1966   'Symbols in Conflict: Official versus Folk Religion', *JSSR* 5: 204-12.

Bolton, B.
1972   'Innocent III's Treatment of the *Humiliati*', in G.J. Cuming and D. Baker (eds.), *Popular Belief and Practice: Papers Read at the Ninth Summer Meeting and the Tenth Winter Meeting of the Ecclesiastical History Society* (Cambridge: Cambridge University Press): 73-82.

Bouritius, G.J.F.
1979   'Popular and Official Religion in Christianity: Three Cases in Nineteenth Century Europe', in Vrijhof and Waardenburg 1979: 117-65.

Brandes, S.
1990   'Conclusion: Reflections on the Study of Religious Orthodoxy and Popular Faith in Europe', in Badone 1990: 185-200.

Brettell, C.
1990   'The Priest and his People: The Contractual Basis for Religious Practice in Rural Portugal', in Badone 1990: 55-75.

Brueggemann, W.
1980   Review of *Persönliche Frömmigkeit und offizielle Religion: Religionsinterner Pluralismus in Israel und Babylon*, by R. Albertz, *CBQ* 42: 86-87.

Camp, C.
1990   'The Female Sage in Ancient Israel and in the Biblical Wisdom Literature', in Gammie and Perdue 1990: 185-204.

Carpenter, H.J.
1963   'Popular Christianity and the Theologians in the Early Centuries', *JTS* 14: 294-310.

Chaline, N.J.
1979   'La religion populaire en Normandie au XIXe siècle', in *LRP*, 171-78.

Christian, W.
1981   *Local Religion in Sixteenth-Century Spain* (Princeton: Princeton University Press).
Coogan, M.D.
1987   'Canaanite Origins and Lineage: Reflections on the Religion of Ancient Israel', in Miller, Hanson and McBride (eds.), 1987: 115-24.
Crenshaw, J.L.
1970   'Popular Questioning of the Justice of God in Ancient Israel', *ZAW* 82: 380-95.
1971   *Prophetic Conflict: Its Effect upon Israelite Religion* (BZAW, 124; Berlin: de Gruyter).
1990   'The Sage in Proverbs', in Gammie and Perdue 1990: 205-16.
Davis, N.
1975a   'Introduction', in *Society and Culture in Early Modern France* (Stanford: Stanford University Press).
1975b   'Printing and the People', in *Society and Culture in Early Modern France* (Stanford: Stanford University Press).
Dever, W.
1987   'The Contribution of Archaeology to the Study of Canaanite and Early Israelite Religion', in Miller, Hanson and McBride (eds.), 1987: 209-48.
1990   *Recent Archaeological Discoveries and Biblical Research* (Seattle, WA: University of Washington Press).
Dubisch, J.
1990   'Pilgrimage and Popular Religion at a Greek Holy Shrine', in Badone 1990: 113-39.
Eisenstadt, S.N.
1981   'The Format of Jewish History—Some Reflections on Weber's Ancient Judaism', *Modern Judaism* 1: 54-73.
Fahey, T.
1982   'Max Weber's *Ancient Judaism*', *AJS* 88: 62-87.
Fohrer, G.
1972   *History of Israelite Religion* (trans. D. Green; Nashville: Abingdon Press).
Frijhoff, W.T.M.
1979   'Official and Popular Religion in Christianity: The Late Middle-Ages and Early Modern Times (13th–18th Centuries)', in Vrijhof and Waardenburg 1979: 71-116.
Gammie, J., and L. Perdue (eds.)
1990   *The Sage in Israel and the Ancient Near East* (Winona Lake, IN: Eisenbrauns).
Garbini, G.
1988   *History and Ideology in Ancient Israel* (trans. J. Bowden; New York: Crossroad).
Geertz, C.
1972   'Deep Play: Notes on the Balinese Cockfight', *Daedalus* 19 (Winter): 1-37.

Gelb, I.
1967   'Approaches to the Study of Ancient Society', *JAOS* 87: 1-8.
Ginzburg, C.
1980   *The Cheese and the Worms: The Cosmos of a Sixteenth-Century Miller* (trans. J. and A. Tedeschi; New York: Penguin Books).
1985   *Night Battles: Witchcraft and Agrarian Cults in the Sixteenth and Seventeenth Centuries* (trans. J. and A. Tedeschi; New York: Penguin Books).
Goldmann, L.
1964   *The Hidden God: A Study of Tragic Vision in the Pensées of Pascal and the Tragedies of Racine* (trans. P. Thody; New York: The Humanities Press).
Gottwald, N.
1985   *The Tribes of Yahweh: A Sociology of the Religion of Liberated Israel, 1250–1050 BCE* (Maryknoll, NY: Orbis Books).
Greenberg, M.
1983   *Biblical Prose Prayer as a Window to the Popular Religion of Ancient Israel* (Berkeley: University of California Press).
Guillaume, A.
1938   *Prophecy and Divination among the Hebrews and Other Semites* (London: Hodder & Stoughton).
Hegel, G.W.F.
1956   *The Philosophy of History* (trans. J. Sibree; prefaces by C. Hegel and J. Sibree; introduction by C.J. Friedrich; New York: Dover).
Hilaire, Y.M.
1979   'Notes Sur La Religion Populaire au XIXe Siècle', in *LRP*, 193-98.
Holladay, J.S., Jr
1987   'Religion in Israel and Judah under the Monarchy: An Explicitly Archaeological Approach', in Miller, Hanson and McBride 1987: 249-302.
Holstein, J.
1975   'Max Weber and Biblical Scholarship', *HUCA* 46: 159-79.
Hooke, S.H.
1938   *The Origins of Early Semitic Ritual* (London: Oxford University Press).
Huisman, J.A.
1979   'Christianity and Germanic Religion', in Vrijhof and Waardenburg 1979: 55-70.
Isambert, F.A.
1977   'Religion Populaire, Sociologie, Histoire et Folklore', *ASSR* 43: 161-84.
1979   'L'aujourd'hui', in *LRP*, 283-92.
1982   *Le sens du sacré: Fête et religion populaire* (Paris: Les Editions du Minuit).
Jacobsen, T.
1963   'Ancient Mesopotamian Religion: The Central Concerns', *Proceedings of the American Philosophical Society* 107: 473-84.
1976   *The Treasures of Darkness: A History of Mesopotamian Religion* (New Haven: Yale University Press).

Jirku, A.
1914   *Materialen zur Volksreligion Israels* (Leipzig: A. Deichert'sche Ver-
           lagsbuchhandlung Werner Scholl).

Kandell, J.
1991   'Was the World Made out of Cheese? Historian Carlo Ginzburg is
           Fascinated by the Questions that Others Ignore', *New York Times
           Magazine*, 17 November: 45-50.

Kaufmann, Y.
1972   *The Religion of Israel: From its Beginnings to the Babylonian Exile*
           (trans. M. Greenberg; New York: Schocken Books [1953]).

Kraeling, E.G.
1928   'The Real Religion of Ancient Israel', *JBL* 47: 133-59.

Lanternari, V.
1982   'La religion populaire: Prospective historique et anthropologique',
           ASSR 53: 121-43.

Lemaire, A.
1990   'The Sage in School and Temple', in Gammie and Perdue 1990: 165-
           84.

Le Roy Ladurie, E.
1979   *Montaillou: The Promised Land of Error* (trans. B. Bray; New York:
           Vintage Books).
1984   'History That Stands Still', in *The Mind and Method of the Historian*
           (trans. S. and B. Reynolds; Chicago: University of Chicago Press).

Lewis, T.J.
1989   *Cults of the Dead in Ancient Israel and Ugarit* (HSM, 39; Atlanta:
           Scholars Press).

Lukács, G.
1986   *History and Class Consciousness: Studies in Marxist Dialectics* (trans.
           R. Livingstone; Cambridge: MIT Press).

Maldonado, L.
1986   'Popular Religion: Its Dimensions, Levels and Types', in *CONCILIUM*,
           3-11.

Mannheim, K.
1985   *Ideology and Utopia: An Introduction to the Sociology of Knowledge*
           (trans. L. Wirth and E. Shils; New York: Harcourt Brace Jovanovich).

Manselli, R.
1975   *La religion populaire au moyen âge: Problèmes de méthode et d'his-
           toire* (Paris: Institut D'Etudes Médiévales Albert Le-Grand).

Martino, E. de
1975   *Mondo Popolare e Magia in Luciana* (preface by R. Brienza; Rome:
           Basilicata Editrice).

McCarter, P.
1987   'Aspects of the Religion of the Israelite Monarchy: Biblical and Epi-
           graphic Data', in Miller, Hanson and McBride (eds.) 1987: 137-56.

McKane, W.
1970   *Proverbs: A New Approach* (OTL; Philadelphia: Westminster Press).

Mensching, G.
1964   'Folk and Universal Religion', in L. Schneider (ed.), *Religion, Culture and Society: A Reader in the Sociology of Religion* (New York: John Wiley).

Meyer, E.
1912   *Der Papyrusfund von Elephantine: Dokumente einer jüdischen Gemeinde aus der Perserzeit und das älteste erhaltene Buch der Weltliteratur* (Leipzig: J.C. Hinrichs, 2nd edn).

Miller, P.D.
1985   'Israelite Religion', in D. Knight and G. Tucker (eds.), *The Hebrew Bible and its Modern Interpreters* (Chico, CA: Scholars Press): 201-38.

Miller, P.D., Jr, P. Hanson and S. McBride (eds.)
1987   *Ancient Israelite Religion: Essays in Honor of Frank Moore Cross* (Philadelphia: Fortress Press).

Orsi, R.
1985   *The Madonna of 115 Street: Faith and Community in Italian Harlem, 1880–1950* (New Haven: Yale University Press).

Pace, E.
1979   'The Debate on Popular Religion in Italy', *Sociological Analysis* 40: 71-75.
1987   'New Paradigms on Popular Religion', *ASSR* 64: 7-14.

Patai, R.
1987   'Folk Religion: Folk Judaism', *The Encyclopedia of Religion*, V.

Petersen, D.
1979   'Max Weber and the Sociological Study of Ancient Israel', *Sociological Inquiry* 49: 117-49.

Platvoet, J.G.
1979   'The Akan Believer and his Religions', in Vrijhof and Waardenburg 1979: 544-606.

Prandi, C.
1977   'Religion et classes subalternes en Italie: Trente années des recherches Italiennes', *ASSR* 43: 93-139.

Radford Ruether, R.
1986   'Women–Church: Emerging Feminist Liturgical Communities', in *CONCILIUM*, 52-62.

Roebroeck, E.J.M.G.
1979   'A Problem for Sociology: Contemporary Developments in the Roman-Catholic Church', in Vrijhof and Waardenburg 1979: 166-99.

Rousseau, A.
1979   'Sur la "religion populaire": Une perspective sociologique', in *LRP*, 355-60.

Schmitt, J.C.
1976   ' "Religion populaire" et culture folklorique', *AESC* (September): 941-53.

Scribner, R.W.
1984   'Ritual and Popular Religion in Catholic Germany at the Time of the Reformation', *JEH* 35: 47-77.

Segal, J.B.
1976   'Popular Religion in Ancient Israel', *JJS* 27: 1-22.
Semporé, S.
1986   'Popular Religion in Africa: Benin as Typical Instance' in *CONCIL-
            IUM*, 44-51.
Smith, Mark
1990   *The Early History of God: Yahweh and the Other Deities in Ancient
            Israel* (San Francisco: Harper & Row).
Smith, Morton
1971   *Palestinian Parties and Politics that Shaped the Old Testament* (New
            York: Columbia University Press).
Sperling, D.
1986   'Israel's Religion in the Ancient Near East', in A. Green (ed.), *Jewish
            Spirituality* (New York: Crossroad): 5-31.
Staples, P.
1979   'Official and Popular Religion in an Ecumenical Perspective', in Vrij-
            hof and Waardenburg 1979: 244-93.
Ste. Croix, G.E.M. de
1981   *The Class Struggle in the Ancient Greek World: From the Archaic Age
            to the Arab Conquests* (New York: Cornell University Press).
Tigay, J.
1987   'Israelite Religion: The Onomastic and Epigraphic Evidence', in
            Miller, Hanson and McBride 1987: 157-94.
Towler, R.
1974   *Homo Religiosus: Sociological Problems in the Study of Religion*
            (New York: St Martin's Press).
Van Beek, W.E.A.
1979   'Traditional Religion as a Locus of Change', in Vrijhof and Waarden-
            burg 1979: 514-43.
Van Den Broeck, R.
1979   'Popular Religious Practices and Ecclesiastical Policies in the Early
            Church', in Vrijhof and Waardenburg 1979: 11-54.
Vaux, R. de
1965   *Ancient Israel. II. Religious Institutions* (ET; New York: McGraw–Hill
            Book Company).
Vorländer, H.
1986   'Aspects of Popular Religion in the Old Testament' (trans.
            G. Harrison), in *CONCILIUM*, 63-70.
Vriezen, T.
1967   *The Religion of Ancient Israel* (trans. H. Hoskins; Philadelphia: West-
            minster Press).
Vrijhof, P.H.
1979a   'Official and Popular Religion in Twentieth Century Western Christ-
            ianity', in Vrijhof and Waardenburg 1979: 217-43.
1979b   'Conclusion', in Vrijhof and Waardenburg 1979: 668-99.
Vrijhof, P.H., and J. Waardenburg
1979   *Official and Popular Religion: Analysis of a Theme for Religious
            Studies* (The Hague: Mouton).

Wach, J.
1967   *Sociology of Religion* (Chicago: Phoenix Books).
Weber, M.
1967   *Ancient Judaism* (trans. and ed. H. Gerth and D. Martindale; New York: The Free Press).
1988   *The Agrarian Sociology of Ancient Civilizations* (trans. R.I. Frank; London: Verso).
Weinstein, D., and R. Bell
1982   *Saints and Society: The Two Worlds of Western Christendom, 1000–1700* (Chicago: University of Chicago Press).
Wellhausen, J.
1885   *Prolegomena to the History of Israel* (Preface by W.R. Smith; Edinburgh: A. & C. Black).
Whitelam, K.
1986   'Recreating the History of Israel', *JSOT* 35: 45-70.
Whybray, R.N.
1990   'The Sage in the Israelite Royal Court', in Gammie and Perdue 1990: 133-40.
Williams, P.
1989   *Popular Religion in America: Symbolic Change and the Modernization Process in Historical Perspective* (Urbana: University of Illinois Press).

Sociology of Knowledge

JSOT 34 (1986), pp. 3-33

THE IMPACT OF MODERN AND SOCIAL SCIENCE ASSUMPTIONS ON
THE RECONSTRUCTION OF ISRAELITE HISTORY*

Gary A. Herion

The past few years have witnessed an increasing interest in using the
social-sciences to elucidate the history of ancient Israel. This interest is
typically expressed in the biblical scholar who re-examines the historical data in terms of particular models or theories borrowed from this
or that social-science discipline. The results of this cross-disciplinary
activity generally have been positive, if for no other reason than because
they sensitize biblical historians to the nomothetic aspects (as opposed to
the idiographic features) of ancient Israel,[1] and because they force them
to confront the social dimension of Israelite religion (see the important
statement of Gottwald 1979: 8-17).

However, there are also some problems inherent in this cross-disciplinary activity, problems related to what is commonly labelled 'the
sociology of knowledge'. Most biblical scholars have become increasingly aware of the subtle ways in which scholars' backgrounds and
training, heritage, social-class position and even gender influence their
views about ancient Israel. Yet there is at least one other factor that

*   The author wishes to thank the James A. Gray Endowment, whose post-doc-
toral fellowship at the University of North Carolina at Chapel Hill provided him with
both the opportunity and the resources to prepare this paper. He also wishes particularly to thank University of North Carolina professors Gerhard Lenski (Sociology)
and Jack Sasson (Religious Studies) for their very helpful comments and criticisms
of earlier drafts of this manuscript. The author assumes full responsibility for all the
inadequacies that remain, as well as for all opinions expressed in this paper.

1.   Wilhelm Windelband formulated the classic distinction between the idiographic
aims of the historian and the nomothetic objectives of the sciences; the former being a
concern for specific or unique traits while the latter is an interest in observed regularities and explanatory generalizations. Cf. Mandelbaum 1977, pp. 4-14.

plays a crucial role in shaping the sociology of their knowledge: modernism. This paper will focus on the ways in which scholars' distinctively modern social contexts and experiences of society help to shape the 'pre-understandings' they have about what is generally 'true' of human social life, and about what is particularly 'true' of ancient Israelite society.[2]

This has an important bearing on biblical studies' interest in social science, since in many respects the assumptions of the social sciences and those of the modern social context are similar:

> They came into existence together and are indissolubly interlinked. A critique of social science cannot but be a critique of modern society, and vice versa (Bellah 1981: 8).

These modern assumptions or perspectives that helped to bring the social sciences into existence may be listed as positivism, reductionism, relativism and determinism. By viewing the 'social-scientizing' of biblical studies in terms of these four assumptions, this paper will exhibit a superficial dependency upon Robert Bellah's somewhat polemical and oversimplified article 'Biblical Religion and Social Science in the Modern World' (1981). However, it must be pointed out that Bellah's description there of the nature of the social sciences is hardly an accurate portrayal of the current state of social-science inquiry since each of these four assumptions has fallen under critical review and has been rejected by large portions of the social-science community. Nevertheless, he has identified certain tendencies that come to play powerful roles when students of biblical religion begin utilizing the social sciences (cf. the very useful introduction in Wilson 1984: 1-29).

Modern Assumptions and the Scholarly Perspective

An important part of scholars' modernism is the extent to which they live in a complex society and are thereby thoroughly accustomed to the vital and seemingly natural social roles played by formal institutions.

---

2.   Cf. Sasson 1981, who provides a succinct statement about the relationship between modernism and the scholar's pre-understandings: 'Thus whenever a scholar compares kingship, democracy, absolutism, etc., in the Ancient Near East and in the Old Testament, his comparison is understood by his audience—and by him, for that matter—not so much because he has recreated the political realities in Israel and in the Ancient Near East, but because he is using currently understood models as frames of reference' (p. 8).

A consequence of this is that sometimes the modern person tends to assume that social organization should typically proceed through such formally organized, collective bodies or institutions (Wirth 1938: 23), taking for granted what economist Kenneth Boulding has called 'the organizational revolution'.[3] Sometimes, however, this can lead even some scholars to assume that formal, organizational or institutional structure is a universal prerequisite in all other societies as well, including ancient Near Eastern and village-based societies. Thus, the experiences of society built into the modern context can sometimes operate to limit the number of understandable options available to historians when they reconstruct the past.[4]

The past eighty years of inquiry into the Hebrew prophets may well be called as illustration. The old nineteenth-century view of the prophet as 'inspired individual' has given over to the twentieth-century view of the prophet as 'organizational spokesman', a view that reached an extreme forty years ago with the thesis that every prophet held an 'office' or was a member of some 'guild' or 'cult association'. The current interest in the prophets' 'support groups' or 'followings' is yet a more recent illustration of how modern, scholarly understandings of 'social organization' can sometimes be confused with

3. 'The past fifty or a hundred years have seen a remarkable growth in the number, size and power of organizations of many kinds, ranging through all areas of life... Yet this revolution has received little study, and it is not something of which we are particularly conscious. It has crept upon us silently. It is something we accept as "natural" almost without thinking' (Boulding 1953: 3-4).

4. While kinship is the organizational basis of most simple societies, it is rare these days to find it discussed as a significant aspect of Israelite social organization. In part this is the consequence of kinship's close tie a century ago to now-discredited hypotheses about Israel's nomadic origins; in part its neglect may also stem from a belief that its impact on Israelite society was negligible compared to the impact of formally organized institutions (military, priesthood, bureaucracy, etc.), on the assumption that Israel was a relatively complex society like our own. No one can deny that certain segments of Israelite society indeed resemble modern society (cf. Rosenbloom 1972), but other segments undoubtedly were simpler, and functioned as such. The point is: Can we understand these simpler functions? For example, to what extent can we fully appreciate the social function of kinship systems as long as we experience kinship in a modern setting that has translated many of its traditional functions into formal institutional structures (e.g. daycare centers for children, formal schooling for youths, government assistance for impoverished relatives, nursing homes for the elderly)?

distinctively different concepts such as 'political organization' or 'professional organization', all of which are more familiar to the scholar living in the modern world.

As one example of such a modernist view of social organization one may cite Odil Steck's article on 'Theological Streams of Tradition' (1977), noting especially his assumption that the prophetic stream (like the wisdom stream of the royal court and the cultic stream of the temple) must have had some kind of institutional 'centers' associated with formally organized, collective bodies:

> Distinctive, long-lasting intellectual movements of this kind are not borne by individuals but only by groups in which the tradition streams are kept in flux through transmission, learned discussion, and development of new witnesses to the tradition. For carrying out their activities and training their successors these groups need fixed meeting places and durable, more or less established institutions (Steck 1977: 197-98).

Although Steck admits that 'we do not have a concrete historical picture of these centers of prophetic tradition' (1977: 201-202), this notable lack of evidence does not prompt him to re-evaluate his assumptions or to consider alternative hypotheses. In fact, his assumptions appear specifically to rule out other possibilities—e.g. that 'prophetic' traditions may have been nurtured and transmitted outside such institutional settings and without official maintenance, perhaps being part of the more loosely structured 'cultural repertoire' of peasant villages. Steck's assumption might be attributed in part to a modern context that naturally associates religious (and political) expression with formally organized, institutional settings, groups and activities. Thus, a modern tendency to assume society's prerequisite need for formal institutions may interfere when reconstructing the tradition-process behind the Hebrew prophets by limiting scholars' pre-understanding (and therefore limiting the number of intelligible options available to them).[5]

---

5.   We also tend to retroject modern notions of 'authority' into the past where they do not belong (cf. Arendt 1958). While we have a tendency to institutionalize authority and associate it with the political monopoly of force, this is not at all how authority operates in the more folk-like setting of simple societies. Authority there has nothing to do with coercive force, persuasive argumentation or institutional organization. Because it is so prevalent, so absolute and yet so diffuse as to defy anthropological attempts to 'locate' it, authority in these settings is unlike anything with which we 'politicized' moderns are familiar. Perhaps the closest we in biblical studies have

Social-Science Assumptions and the Scholarly Perspective

In order to demonstrate more precisely the variety of ways in which distinctively modern social contexts and experiences can shape one's pre-understandings of what was 'true' (or at least possible) in ancient Israel, one must examine in more detail the four assumptions that sometimes play powerful roles when social science is used—positivism, reductionism, relativism and determinism. It is important to keep in mind that these four basic assumptions are usually interwoven with one another, often making it difficult to isolate clearly the unadulterated influence of any one of them. Nevertheless, it is possible to view these four in terms of two pairs of influences: 1. the way in which positivism and reductionism combine to influence cross-disciplinary methodology; and 2. the way in which relativism and determinism combine to shape a more 'scientific' view of Israelite religion.

Positivism, Reductionism and the Cross-Disciplinary Method
Positivism may be defined broadly as the desire to emulate the empirical methods of natural science in the quest for knowledge. At best, positivism encourages methodological and intellectual rigor while stressing the central role that reason must play in scholarship. However, positivism can sometimes degenerate into a form of 'scientism' in which science is no longer understood as one form of knowledge but where the nomothetic character of science comes to be viewed as the only valid terms in which any 'knowledge' can be achieved (Habermas 1972: 4). In such an intellectual climate, many scholars trained in the more 'subjective' approaches of the humanities (history, theology and philosophy) may come to believe that the 'more objective' social sciences *per se* can render a more accurate picture of what was 'real' in ancient Israel. Consequently there may arise certain inhibitions about

come to recognizing this general type of authority in ancient Israel was in our rather imprecise references to the authority of the judges as being 'charismatic'. Initially there was never any doubt that the word 'charismatic' cautioned against any association of authority with institutional organization; similarly it was understood to refer to something quite different than a judge's ability to coerce or persuade others rationally. Subsequently, however, some scholars have begun to coin qualifying terms such as 'institutional charisma' or 'office charisma', which have not necessarily provided a more accurate picture of the judges, only one that is more easily comprehended in modern terms.

criticizing the more 'prestigious' social sciences.[6]

Ideally, responsible interdisciplinary activity is a 'two-way street', meaning that the historical and the social-scientific approaches to knowledge inevitably affect and alter one another when they are brought together. Most social scientists concede this, viewing the tasks of the social sciences and history (as well as the humanities in general) as being complementary. However, it seems that sometimes in the appeal to the social sciences positivist inclinations may operate in such a way that the interdisciplinary 'two-way street' carries mainly 'one-way traffic' from the social sciences into historical studies, but not vice versa. As a result, biblical studies sometimes witnesses the uncritical (not necessarily inaccurate always, but unquestioning) use of social-science models and theories.

It is impossible to appreciate fully this impact of positivism without simultaneously appreciating the impact of reductionism. *Reductionism* generally is the tendency to explain as much of the complex as possible in terms of the simple. This means that if one is to handle complex phenomena, one has little choice but to 'chunk' or abstract similarities, thereby reducing the number of items being considered (Malina 1982: 231-32). Such abstractions of similarities are called 'models' or 'typologies' in the social sciences. While no model has yet been devised that can explain 100% of the variance, the study of any real social phenomena would be difficult if not altogether impossible without the aid of models. Yet models or typologies must be used with a conscientious regard for their limitations; the reduction of complexity always entails a certain methodological risk since the line separating the enlightening epitome from the vulgarized distortion can sometimes be very fine.

Since the construction and use of models have been integral parts of the 'social-scientizing' of biblical studies, a few remarks about the nature of models seem in order. All societies are alike in some respects, and each differs from others in other respects. Yet some social phenomena have certain features in common enabling us to designate them as a 'type' of phenomenon. This 'type' or 'model' is constructed by assembling and listing only those common features, temporarily ignoring the existing differences, divergences, inconsistencies and

---

6. As Robert Bellah has noted, what often guarantees the authority and even the power of professional social scientists is 'the theoretical and methodological prestige of social science as science' (1982: 36).

irregularities. For this reason it must never be forgotten that a 'type' is not 'real':

> The type is an imagined entity, created only because through it we may hope to understand reality. Its function is to suggest aspects of real societies which deserve further study, and especially to suggest hypotheses as to what, under certain defined conditions, may be generally true about society (Redfield 1947: 295).

Three important points emerge: 1. models are hypothetical entities, not real descriptions; 2. they are to be used to analyze existing data, not to serve as substitutions in the absence of data; and 3. they do not conclude a study or provide definitive answers, but rather they (a) summarize current thought, or (b) help to raise new questions for study, suggest fresh lines of inquiry, and expose relevant topics for research when used as a basis of comparison with real phenomena. It is suggested here that positivist and reductionist tendencies sometimes combine in such a way that these three important points become lost, and that consequently the application of social-science models and theories to biblical studies sometimes lacks proper methodological rigor and balance.

Relativism, Determinism and the Scientific Study of Religion
In focusing on the remaining two assumptions, it should be noted that relativism and determinism have dovetailed to shape an empirical approach to the study of religion that is often associated with the social sciences, and that in this respect they can influence scholarly pre-understandings and reconstructions of ancient Israel. *Relativism* is here defined as the assumption that issues of morality and religion can never be considered truly right or wrong in any 'absolute' sense, rather that they vary with (or are 'relative' to) persons, societies and cultures. In conjunction with this, *determinism* may be defined as the general tendency to think that human values, choices and actions are caused (or 'determined') by certain variables in the social and cultural environment.[7]

---

7.   Both relativism and determinism have been subjects of debate within the social sciences, and most social scientists probably would no longer accept my admittedly reductionistic definitions of these two tendencies. However, there are noticeable traces of these tendencies still lingering in the social sciences, and some social scientists still feel compelled to criticize the ways in which these assumptions dominate some social-science studies. Cf. Haes 1980 and McGehee 1982.

These assumptions can combine to produce a general view of human values that denies the individual any genuine claim to socially autonomous or 'transcendent' beliefs. In this view, it is characteristically assumed that human values—including religious beliefs—are not held independently or actively but rather that they result from socialization. In other words, values are not seen as reflecting any deep-seated, personal belief in anything truly universal; instead, they become indications of one's acquiescence to a particular set of norms prevalent in the immediate social environment. If a person should claim to possess a deep-seated, autonomous belief in certain transcendent 'things', this is typically dismissed as simply an example of the extent to which 'superstructural' social concerns and interests have successfully been internalized by the individual.[8]

This general view of human values is in some respects similar to certain social-science theories of religion. From its inception in the French enlightenment, sociology was committed to the positivist view that religion is institutionalized ignorance, a vestige of man's primitive past doomed to disappear in an era of scientific rationalism. This view was laid to rest when Emile Durkheim's celebrated study of totemism (1912) demonstrated that religion often functions in a very sophisticated manner to help control, stabilize and legitimize social systems. Ever since, the social sciences have tended to consider 'religion' primarily as a public, not a private phenomenon, and they have tended to find beneath it particular social control interests, but not more transcendent values or beliefs.

This view of passive man and ideological religion may be associated generally with the rise of modernism and urbanism, wherein 'the juxtaposition of divergent personalities and modes of life tends to produce a relativistic perspective and a sense of toleration of differences which... lead toward the secularization of life' (Wirth 1938: 15). The modern, urban context requires religious groups and individuals to interact with others on the basis of some 'relative moral minimum'

---

8.   It is important for biblical scholars to appreciate that social-science consensus on these matters has disappeared. There is now significant dissatisfaction within the social sciences over such a one-sided appeal to the passive conception of man as implied in Marxian historical materialism. Many—even many neo-Marxists—are trying to strike a more reasonable and accurate balance by supplementing it with the view of active, autonomous man implied in Kantian transcendental idealism (Habermas 1971, 1973, 1976; Dawe 1970; Haes 1980).

rather than a 'transcendent moral absolute', compromising internally held values and beliefs for the rational pursuit of shared social, economic and political interests (Lenski 1961: 9; Wirth 1938: 18).

This truism of modern, urban society has been summed up by the theologian Harvey Cox, who notes that 'in the secular city, it is not religion but politics that brings unity and meaning to human life and thought' (1965: 254). There is a two-part corollary to this statement: 1. religion remains meaningful in such an environment only to the extent that it, too, is secularized and 'politicized' (relativism); and 2. when religious views are expressed in this milieu, it is likely that certain (sometimes latent) social, economic or political interests underlie and prompt them (determinism—more specifically, social or economic determinism).

It is interesting to note what might result if this modern truism were read into the ancient past. One might assume a priori that ancient persons were not individuals actively motivated by or autonomously voicing their deep-seated private beliefs and values. Guided by these relativist and determinist assumptions, one might be more inclined to view the ancients as being influenced by and giving expression to the social, economic and political interests of the immediate social group of which they were a part. Consequently, the religious mindset of the ancient Near Easterner could be portrayed as being every bit as secular in its orientation as is the modern mindset.[9] It is important to note that when this happens one is not necessarily rendering a picture of the past that is more accurate (or more erroneous), only one that is more understandable, meaningful or 'relevant' to a modern audience.

Example A: The Impact of These Assumptions on Reconstructions of the Hebrew Prophets

Robert Wilson's *Prophecy and Society in Ancient Israel* (1980) provides a useful illustration of how these modern, social-science assumptions can sometimes play a decisive role in shaping reconstructions of the past. In this important work, Wilson examines the entire range of phenomena associated with Hebrew prophecy in terms of I.M. Lewis's

9.   Given the fact that most 'religious' texts recovered from the ancient Near East originally were public and ideological in nature, this view would not be at all improper when applied to such texts. The question is: is it proper to extend this view into a generalization about every 'religious' expression originating in the ancient Near East?

anthropological model of central/peripheral intermediation. In many cases the model clarifies quite clearly certain instances of prophecy recorded in the Hebrew Bible, and if biblical scholars possessed a complete record of all 'prophetic' activity occurring in Palestine during the Old Testament period (including especially the activities of the so-called 'false prophets'), Wilson's study probably would describe very well the aggregate of such activities.[10]

Yet even a brief review of Wilson's study reveals the unmistakable impact that relativism and determinism have had upon his view of prophetic religion, and that positivism and reductionism have had upon his cross-disciplinary method. The issue at hand concerns the extent to which Wilson's reconstruction might have been unduly determined by these assumptions.

The Impact of Relativism and Determinism
At the heart of Wilson's study lies the suggestion that the anthropological model of intermediation provides a close parallel to biblical 'prophecy'. Wilson points out that:

> Intermediaries do not operate in a vacuum. They are integral parts of their societies and cannot exist without social guidance and support (1980: 51).

and that consequently:

> On the basis of the comparative evidence, we may expect Israelite society to have been involved in every phase of prophetic activity, from the prophet's 'call' to the delivery of his message (1980: 86).

His description of how external group processes shape or determine the content of an intermediary's/prophet's message is quite detailed (1980: 51-62). He notes that the 'candidate is frequently trained at the request of the society and is encouraged in his attempts to bring about the expected intermediation' (1980: 53).[11] His study then proceeds to

---

10. In noting that Wilson's thesis may very well describe what was typical of prophetic phenomena, we must remember that it might not apply at all to those prophets who were not typical. Were Amos, Hosea, Micah, Isaiah or Jeremiah 'typical' pre-exilic prophets? If so, why were their words initially remembered, valued and preserved while those of countless others were not? See Heschel 1962, 2.252-53, who argues that these individuals represent a type *sui generis*.

11. Wilson's use of the word 'expected' is quite revealing: the intermediary's/ prophet's message can be predicted once we know which group he represents. Wilson's actual method is the reverse of this: since we know the prophet's message from the biblical text, we can predict the group to which he belonged. The potential

promote the view that every prophet in Israel (writing and non-writing, 'true' and 'false', cultic and non-cultic, court and non-court, Yahwist and non-Yahwist) should be approached less as an individual auto-nomously voicing his inner convictions and more as a group spokes-man whose message has been shaped by some external social forces and interests.

By tying the prophet so closely to group processes, Wilson has appreciably limited the range within which one is now permitted to understand the historical nature of the prophet and his message. The religious 'tone' of a prophet's message may now be explained, at best, as indicative of the extent to which he had internalized the interests of his support group or, at worst, as mere ideological 'forms of speech' under which may be found a particular sociopolitical or socioeconomic agenda. In this view, the prophet's autonomy and individuality essen-tially have been stripped from him: his personal convictions, values and beliefs are either non-existent (which makes him a hypocrite) or more simply they are reflective of his particular (central or periph-eral) group's interests (which makes him a spokesman). The prophet's genuine sense of any 'good' transcending his social group's interests has been effectively denied.

The point here is not to deny that Hebrew prophets could be group spokesmen, even though Wilson's blanket application of this conclu-sion to every single prophet is arguable (cf. Herion 1982: 245-53). Rather it is to note that Wilson's reconstruction of this ancient Israel-ite phenomenon amounts to a classic description of modern, urban relativism and social determinism.[12] The diminished capacity of the individual to believe autonomously in absolutes—which is charac-teristic of the secular, modern world—has been projected on to the world of the ancient Near East. The result is the view that in ancient Israel, as in the modern 'secular city', it was not any socially tran-scendent religious values or convictions but relative (and partisan) sociopolitical goals or socioeconomic interests that brought unity and meaning to the life and thought of the Hebrew prophet.

for circular reasoning here should be obvious.

12. 'The individual counts for little, but the voice of the representative is heard with a deference roughly proportional to the numbers for whom he speaks.' Interest-ingly, this statement was not made by Wilson with respect to the ancient Hebrew prophets (although it seems to apply quite well to his thesis); rather it was made by a sociologist with respect to modern, urban society (Wirth 1938: 14).

The Impact of Positivism and Reductionism

It was noted above that at the heart of Wilson's study lies the assumption that there can be no socially isolated intermediaries. Wilson's reconstruction concludes that in ancient Israel there indeed were no socially isolated prophets. There is a perfect correlation here between assumption and conclusion. The issue is whether there might be something in Wilson's cross-disciplinary methodology that accounts for such neat symmetry.

Perhaps a good place to begin is with the observation that there exists some evidence which could easily be interpreted in such a way as to challenge the validity of the assumption and the accuracy of the conclusion, and thereby to disturb the symmetry of the reconstruction (cf. Heschel 1962, 1.3-26, especially pp. 17-19). As one important example one may note Jeremiah's lament to Yahweh: 'I sat alone because your hand was upon me' (15.17). While it would be possible simply to reinterpret this passage (e.g. as a mere figure of speech that should not be taken literally), Wilson ignores it altogether. This is significant because it provides a useful glimpse into how the cross-disciplinary method often operates: data are consistently manipulated to the distinct advantage of the model, although the reverse is never attempted. In order to fit the historical data into the central/peripheral scheme of the model that necessarily ties prophets to support groups, some evidence is omitted (e.g. Jer. 15.17; 1 Kgs 19.10, 14) and a great deal is simply explained away—e.g. Micaiah had a 'weak' support group in 1 Kings 22 (p. 211), or Jer. 20.10 refers to the prophet being rejected by 'portions' of his support group (p. 246).

When Wilson does attempt to reinterpret the evidence, this often involves questionable and sweeping re-creations of entire prophetic biographies and careers. In short, the methodological stance toward the historical data seems highly critical (even revisionist at times), while the stance toward the social-science model seems credulous. Wilson has permitted the model to interpret the data for him—in fact, he seems improperly to have permitted it to fill in gaps existing in the data—but he has not permitted the data reciprocally to address, much less to challenge the model. This is not an appropriate method for using models since basic to all models is their falsifiability (cf. the critique by Long 1982: 251).

It is here suggested that this methodological oversight may, in part, result from a positivist bias about the supremacy of more 'scientific' approaches to knowledge, a bias that inhibits one from critically reviewing those approaches—e.g. passive acceptance of the more 'scientific' definitions (of religion) or the more 'scientific' models (of intermediation). Another part of the oversight might well be attributed to a reductionism that leads one to confuse a simple, abstract model with an actual description of complex reality. Despite these problems, however, it must be underscored that Wilson has provided biblical scholars with an important aid for the study of the Hebrew prophets. His model of intermediation is an extremely useful one, but not because it necessarily fills in any gaps in data or serves as a possible description of what was 'real' in ancient Israel. It is important because, when used properly and critically, it can point scholars to potentially fruitful areas for further study.

The model performs this service only to the extent that one permits it and the data to go their separate ways. Unfortunately, in the quest for precise and definitive (not to mention publishable) results, many biblical scholars utilizing social science seem reluctant to permit this, perhaps believing incorrectly that unless there is a direct and consistent correlation between model and data their theses were wrong and their research was a waste of time and effort. Thus scholars may be found overlooking data (probably subconsciously) that do not mesh with their models or else straining them in such a way that they do mesh. Yet the point where the social-science model and the historical data diverge is precisely the area where further study should be directed. Without the model there could be no such divergence, and without the divergence it would be much more difficult to ascertain what are the truly exceptional (and therefore important) historical features of ancient Israel. Social-science models, therefore, have great heuristic value. One must then seek not to gloss over or to downplay the divergences between data and model but rather to recognize them, to underscore them for colleagues, and to invite those colleagues to join in the task of trying to account for the divergences.

Thus, for example, Wilson's study now invites scholars to raise important questions about the nature of a prophet's 'support group'. What does it mean to say that these groups were *socially* organized, as opposed to being politically, professionally, religiously or culturally organized? What does it mean to say that they were socially *organized*, as opposed simply to 'being present' in society? In what sense did 'support groups' provide the impulse behind a prophet's outspokenness, and in what sense did they coalesce as a response to his message? More fundamentally, however, the divergence between the model of intermediation and the data about Hebrew prophecy suggests that Wilson may have initiated his study with too narrow a concept of 'support group' in mind. In the future, it might be more appropriate (as well as less relativistic and deterministic) to begin more generally with references to a prophet's 'support structure', noting that in some instances this may indeed have been a tangible (central or peripheral) social group, but that in other instances a prophet's 'support structure' may have been something more intangible and internalized such as a cultural heritage or a religious tradition. These things also exist in society, although they do not necessarily manifest themselves as an identifiable, socially organized 'group'.[13] To the extent that cultural and religious values (not just social solidarities) can give an individual both vision and resolve, it seems fair to consider them important potential elements in a prophet's 'support structure'.

Example B: The Impact of These Assumptions
on Reconstructions of Premonarchic Israel

Norman Gottwald's *Tribes of Yahweh* (1979) provides another useful illustration of how modern, social-science assumptions can sometimes play a decisive role in shaping reconstructions of the past. In this extensive re-examination of the nature of premonarchic Israel, Gottwald introduces a wealth of social-science material presented against the backdrop of the macro-sociological theories of Durkheim, Weber and Marx. The cumulative effect of this is to underscore in a most convincing manner the importance of the social dimension in ancient Israel—more specifically, the relationship between Israelite religion and society.

A brief review of Gottwald's study also reveals the impact that relativism and determinism have had upon his view of premonarchic religion, and that positivism and reductionism have had upon his sociological method. Once again, the issue at hand concerns the extent to which Gottwald's reconstruction might have been unduly determined by these assumptions.

13. Jack Sasson has reminded me furthermore that one must be very cautious when undertaking 'scientific' inquiries dependent on evidence found in literary pieces (e.g. the non-writing prophets who appear in Deuteronomistic literature). One would somehow feel it inappropriate to apply anthopological models to gain scientific information about the 'seers' found in Homer or in the plays of Sophocles.

The Impact of Relativism and Determinism

At the core of Gottwald's study lies the assumption that 'only as the full *materiality* of ancient Israel is more securely grasped will we be able to make proper sense of its *spirituality*' (1979: xxv). In light of this assumption, it is not surprising that Gottwald tends to locate causality as low as possible on the 'conceptual pyramid of culture',[14] with technological innovations (iron, waterproof plaster, agricultural terracing) providing a new basis for social relations among now-relative equals; and this, in turn, engendering an 'egalitarian' ethic in early Israel that became ideologically enshrined in Yahwist religion (1979: 650-63). Thus, in premonarchic Israel religion (Yahwism) was essentially a projection of the economic and political interests of the social organization (tribal confederacy).

This hypothesis draws heavily upon relativist and determinist notions about religion, and perhaps nowhere does this surface more clearly than in Gottwald's critique of John Bright and George Mendenhall (1979: 592-602), both of whom generally share his view of the social process while disagreeing with his views about the accompanying religious process.

Religion Related to Society: Contra John Bright

According to Gottwald, Bright improperly severs religion from society by claiming that the religion of early Israel was unique and that its socio-political origins, while revolutionary, were not. The issue here seems to be the applicability of relativism—the assumption that religion must necessarily be tied to the social sphere.

Gottwald counters Bright first with a questionable testimony to the

---

14. The anthropological 'pyramidization' of culture conceives of a culture's economic institutions as the base of a conceptual, three-tiered 'pyramid' anchored to the ecosystem by a technology that can exploit and capitalize upon existing resources, both natural and human. Above this economic base is the middle tier representing the social structures that exist to insure orderly (although not necessarily equitable) economic activity—chief among these is the political monopoly of force (i.e. instruments of government). At the peak of the 'pyramid' are the ideological symbols, including religion and morality, which work to provide a sense of legitimacy and stability for everything underneath. Economic determinism conceives of causation as being from the bottom up (materialism), and religion thus comes to be viewed as the ultimate 'effect'. This has reinforced the relativist tendency to view religion as a public phenomenon related to social control interests, not as a private phenomenon related to personal experience.

uniqueness of Israel's sociopolitical origins,[15] and secondly with an imaginative (and admittedly caricatured) reconstruction of how unexceptional Israel's rituals and beliefs in God must have seemed to Israel's neighbors (1979: 595-96). From this it logically follows that if Israel's religion was unique it was so only because it was tied to its unique sociopolitical existence.

However, this conclusion is sustained only by misconstruing or ignoring Bright's understanding and use of the word 'religion'. One does not have to read much that Bright had written to realize that he characteristically uses the word 'religion' as it is often used in the humanities, to refer to constitutive factors of human cognitive existence. For him 'religion' is largely synonymous with 'world view' or 'faith'; it is a process whereby people attempt to make sense out of their experiences of existence. It might be fair to say that Bright presumes a 'religion-experience' nexus, with the understanding that many human experiences come from outside the 'conceptual pyramid of culture'—i.e. beyond a given society's range of control. It seems that it is in this 'area beyond' that Bright presumes the existence of a Truly Other, and hence he feels one is justified in talking about a God 'acting' and 'being revealed' in history (i.e. in human experience).

Gottwald, however, characteristically uses the word 'religion' as it is often used in the social sciences, to refer to symbolic elements of human social existence. He tends to presume a 'religion-society' nexus wherein it is proper to speak of religion narrowly in terms of organized 'belief systems' (doctrines) and 'cult practices' (rituals). By imposing this definition on Bright's use of the word 'religion', Gottwald effectively sidesteps Bright's claim that the uniqueness of Israel's religion is to be found in its peculiar way of discovering meaning and coherence in human existence (cf. Bright 1972: 140-56), and thus he is able to rule out any possible connection between religion and factors outside the social domain. By substituting his narrow social-science definition of religion ('set of beliefs and cult practices',

---

15. 'Gottwald claims that there is no parallel for this development in the Middle East, and I cannot suggest one. I am not persuaded, however, that the dynamics of the process by which Israel came into existence are quite as unique as Gottwald sometimes implies' (Lenski 1980: 275). One wonders if an enterprising Egyptologist could argue a 'peasant revolt' hypothesis to describe the First (or Second) Intermediate period at least as plausibly as Gottwald had done for ancient Israel. Perhaps an enterprising Assyriologist could do the same for the end of the Ur III period.

1979: 595), he is able to view religion in such a way that it must be linked to the social process. Thus, Gottwald's ability to demonstrate that relativism was as pervasive in ancient Israel as it is in modern society (and as it is in the theories of Durkheim, Weber and Marx) hinges on little more than the way he has chosen to define the word 'religion'.

Religion Determined by Society: Contra George Mendenhall

Having thereby demonstrated the exclusive connection between religion and social processes, Gottwald moves on to address the ways in which one influences the other. His concern here seems to be one of priority: which came first, the religion or the society? According to Gottwald, Mendenhall improperly derives early Israelite society from its religion instead of vice versa. The issue here, of course, is the applicability of social determinism—the assumption that social processes influence or determine religious ideas and values.

One does not have to read Mendenhall too deeply to appreciate that he characteristically makes two basic connections when he writes about the relationship of religion to social processes. First, like Bright, he uses the word 'religion' in a much broader sense than doctrines and rituals. It may be fair to say that Mendenhall presumes a 'religion–ethical values' nexus (with these values understood to originate in historical experiences). Thus Mendenhall concludes that since human values influence human choices, and since the sum of these choices patterns the character of social relations and structure, then one correctly may assert that 'religion' (i.e. ethical values) shapes society. Secondly, Mendenhall tends to contrast his 'religion–ethics' nexus with a 'politics–power' nexus, thereby drawing a sharp distinction between ethical values ('religion') and social control interests ('politics'; cf. esp. Mendenhall 1975 and 1973: 198ff.).[16]

---

16. Mendenhall seems to agree with the social sciences (and with Gottwald) that doctrines and rituals play important roles in social control (cf. 1973: 72-73); but for that reason he tends to think of them in terms of political (power) functions, not religious (ethical) ones. To some extent the differences here between Mendenhall and Gottwald are primarily semantic and emphatic. However, there are very sharp confessional differences in their personal evaluations of political power. Mendenhall, apparently employing a Lutheran 'two-kingdom' concept, seems to concede the necessity of social control interests while secularizing them. Gottwald, apparently employing a Marxist-style liberation theology, seems to regard upper-class power as illegitimate (even 'evil'?) while lower-class power is justified (even 'righteous'?).

In his response to this, Gottwald again either misconstrues or ignores how Mendenhall uses the word 'religion', and again substitutes his narrower social-science definition (doctrines and rituals). It is at this point that Gottwald introduces the concept of 'politics' in order to demonstrate 'religion's' dependence upon social processes. Moreover, he avoids a precise, analytical, social-science definition of the word in order to embrace a more intuitive, Christian, theological view of politics as 'ethics' (1979: 601)—the substance of both in early Israel being 'egalitarianism'.[17] This semantic 'twist' serves Gottwald's thesis well since it enables him to co-opt all of Mendenhall's categories by rearranging all the connections. Thus, Mendenhall's 'religion–ethics' and 'politics–power' connections (and all the issues Mendenhall raised through those connections) are replaced with Gottwald's connections of 'religion' to 'cult' and 'ethics' to 'politics'.

By connecting 'ethics' to 'politics', Gottwald has appreciably limited our options in trying to identify the prime factors of causation. First, he can now agree with Mendenhall in principle that 'ethical values' are the primary determinants, but in practice he can identify these with 'political interests', not with 'religion', and therefore he can locate them lower on the 'conceptual pyramid of culture'. Second, he can agree with Mendenhall that there are certain ways in which 'religion' can be regarded as a cause, but he identifies these with the ways in which the cult provides secondary, ideological legitimation and

17. One is reminded of theologian Paul Lehmann's definition of politics as 'activity, and reflection on activity, which aims at and analyzes what it takes to make and keep human life human in the world' (1963: 85), or Harvey Cox's statement that politics is what makes human life and thought meaningful (1965: 254), or Miguez Bonino's contention that politics is the outward form of love (1983), or John Howard Yoder's *The Politics of Jesus* (1972), which is really about the ethics of Jesus. Certainly this confusion of 'politics' with 'ethics' is the consequence of commendable efforts to encourage Christians to act out their values rather than passively to pay them lip-service; the use of the word 'politics' underscoring this call to act. But such naive definitions (conveniently?) avoid the ethically troublesome problem of power—i.e. 'playing to win' instead of 'playing with integrity'. No social-scientific study of political phenomena can hope to be taken seriously if it refuses to recognize that politics refers to the manipulation of coercive force in an orderly and prescribed manner. It necessarily assumes a highly utilitarian view of humans as manipulable objects. Thus, the paradox of 'politics' in Gottwald's (and the others') ingenuous sense of the word is that at times it must be somewhat dehumanizing, unloving and unethical if it is to promote humanity, love and ethics. Cf. Mendenhall 1973: 196-97.

reinforcement of existing social, political and economic norms (Yah-wism as a 'societal "feedback" servomechanism', 1979: 642-49). Once again, Gottwald's ability to demonstrate that social determinism was as pervasive in ancient Israel as it is in modern society (or in Durkheim, Weber and Marx) hinges on little more than the way he has chosen to define such key words as 'religion' and 'politics'. The result is an historical reconstruction unable to concede the Israelite peasants' ability to possess any genuine sense of 'good' transcending their own socio-political goals and socioeconomic interests.

The point here is not to assert that early Israel was an exceptional time and place wherein self-interest largely disappeared (not even the Bible makes that statement!); nor is it to deny that premonarchic Yahwism may indeed have come to serve as an ideological projection of social, political and economic interests for a majority of Palestinian peasants (although one may debate Gottwald's assertion that this was the unique aspect of Yahwism from its inception). Rather it is to note that Gottwald's reconstruction amounts to a classic description of modern, urban relativism and social determinism. The result is the view that in premonarchic Israel, as in the modern 'secular city' (or in modern radical political movements, whether of the left or the right), it was not any socially transcendent ethical values or convictions but relative political interests and economic goals that brought unity and meaning to premonarchic Yahwism. Gottwald has not necessarily rendered a picture of ancient Israel that is more accurate (or erroneous), only one that is more intelligible, meaningful and 'relevant' to a modern audience whose perspective is similarly imbued with relativist and determinist assumptions.

The Impact of Positivism and Reductionism

In summarizing his critique of Mendenhall, Gottwald offers a statement reflecting the relativism and determinism that inform his assumptions and that are confirmed by his conclusions. Despite this, the following statement will probably strike most modern scholars as self-evidently true:

> Yet to grant that the religion of the state serves the interests of the state, but to deny that the religion of the tribe or of the intertribal confederacy serves the interests of the tribe or intertribal community, is to desert socio-logical method at a decisive juncture (1979: 601).

As with Wilson, there is almost a perfect correlation between Gottwald's assumption that religion serves the interests of the social organization and his conclusion that in premonarchic times Yahwism served the political and economic interests of the Israelite tribal organization. Early Israel obeys all the rules laid out in the macro-sociological theories of Durkheim, Weber and Marx. The issue here is whether there might be something in Gottwald's sociological methodology that accounts for this neat symmetry.

eavily upon the macro-socio-
nd Marx. All 'theories' are
constitute summaries of cur-
th-century) thought and that
which 'reality' may be mea-
ticular exhibit a much higher
, do micro-sociological theo-
cal entities that are falsifiable
ces to result when abstract
ght together.
ed the application of these
, concrete social phenomena,
cientists (more so than non-
to the shortcomings and inad-
h-century confidence in rela-
helped to fuel these theories
study) has noticeably drained
n fact, almost all social scien-
ves 'materialists' but rather
s and beliefs—including eco-
ng forces in society. Thus,
t social scientists themselves
that they no longer depend
inist (much less materialist)
result of a number of related
s, an increasing number of
l to the sometimes powerful

influences arising outside the 'conceptual pyramid of culture', and have challenged the truism that religion necessarily serves the interests of society.

In the first place, even classical nineteenth-century studies of the different bases of social solidarity (Durkheim 1893) suggest that religion functions quite differently in folk (or tribal) and urban (or state) types of societies. For example, the notion of religion serving the material interests of the social or political organization makes very little sense when applied to the ideal-typical folk society (Redfield 1947). This does not deny that religion functions to sustain society by promoting the solidarity of its members, but it points out that a wide range of possible relations between religion and society may be found beneath such simple truisms as 'religion serves the interests of society', especially when those interests can be so radically different typologically. The truism only serves to obviate further study and to encourage modern and ethnocentric views about religion's 'social utility' (cf. the comments in Malina 1982: 240-41).

Secondly, several prominent social-science theorists from Tönnies (1887) to Parsons (1960) have hinted at the initial autonomy and independence of inner values by basing their respective social typologies (dependent variables) upon underlying typologies of personal values and volitional processes (independent variables). While few have considered such values and processes under the rubric of 'religion', the important works of Weber (1930) and Lenski (1961) have demonstrated that distinctively 'religious' factors can inform these values and processes in profound ways, helping to shape the 'moral ecology' upon which social relations, institutions and organizations are established.[18]

Thirdly, recent sociological inquiry into the nature and origin of human values has demonstrated that values ultimately arise not from social structures/economic interests per se (as social and economic determinists maintain) but rather from human experiences (Rokeach 1979). This insight is significant because it no longer limits one to looking for causation exclusively within the 'conceptual pyramid of

18. The very important concept of 'moral ecology' is analogous to the biological concept of 'gene pool'; it refers to the *pre-existing* 'raw material' out of which selections can be made so as to produce a unique and viable social (or biological) organism (cf. Sullivan 1982). The values constituting the 'moral ecology' are not created by the social organization but rather are presupposed by it. To be sure, all social organizations inevitably turn around and actively promote an ideology to bolster those select values upon which its existence absolutely depends; but many values thus remain untouched or unincorporated by the social organization, and are still capable of inspiring individual and mass divergences from the social norm.

culture'. To the extent that social, economic and even technological factors are parts of those experiences, and to the extent that social organizations can control and meaningfully integrate both its constituents and their experiences, they can all determine human values. Causation can indeed exist within the pyramid of culture, and Gottwald has provided a necessary reinforcement of this important point. However, no social system exists that can completely control this process of integration, no matter how 'totalitarian' it strives to be. Therefore, the potential for new values (or for the resurgence of older, dormant values) is forever present, constantly presenting a challenge or even threat to the social organization (cf. Heirich 1976). Thus, to the extent that experiences lie outside the 'cultural domain' and beyond human personal or social control, the resultant values likewise originate outside the human consciousness. No person or society 'plans' what its values will be. This is the significant element of truth underlying Bright's and Mendenhall's understanding of the potential 'transcendence' of religion.[19]

The above three areas of development within the social sciences reflect if not an abandonment at least a critical revision of nineteenth-century macro-sociology's comfortable dependence upon neat relativist and determinist assumptions. Yet these very important advancements and revisions seem not to have been significantly incorporated into Gottwald's study. While a number of factors may account for this,[20] it seems also that positivism and reductionism may have played decisive roles in bringing about this methodological omission. Positivism may have had a hand to the extent that the more scholars are convinced of the validity of the 'scientific' nature of the theories being used, the less they may be inclined to appreciate their falsifiability. Simultaneously, reductionism may have worked to blur the distinction between abstract theories about general social tendencies and concrete descriptions of actual social realities.[21] Under the influence of these

19. This also helps to clarify something that historians take for granted but that social scientists often tend to be confounded by: change.

20. One factor undoubtedly is the inevitable 'interdisciplinary lag' and 'academic specialization' that make it impossible to keep abreast of developments in other fields. Another factor may be certain personal ideological or partisan political reasons that make these theoretical abstractions attractive and useful in their unrevised nineteenth-century forms (see excursus).

21. The temptation to rely heavily upon theories (or upon intuition) is perhaps especially strong for historians of the ancient past who often have very little 'concrete

two factors, it is relatively easy to see why one might avoid dealing with those more recent developments that would only serve to complicate matters further.

The solution to the methodological problems in *The Tribes of Yahweh* seems to be not so much a matter of recognizing the inevitable divergences between social-science theories and historical data but rather the demanding task of incorporating the subsequent criticisms, modifications, qualifications and even the affirmations of the basic social-science theories being used. Even though Gottwald seems not to have done this, it must be underscored that he has nevertheless introduced into the discussion a very important theoretical framework from which it is possible to explore a whole new range of issues related to early Israel. The theories of Durkheim, Weber and Marx are extremely important ones, but not because they provide a definitive statement about the 'religion–society' nexus in ancient Israel (or anywhere else for that matter). They are important because they continue to raise issues for scholars subsequently to test, and for this reason these theories must be used with respect to the subsequent qualifications that have resulted from those tests.

When viewed in light of these more recent developments in sociology, Gottwald's study now urges biblical scholars to be much more cautious in making sweeping statements about the necessary 'religion–society' nexus in early Israel. There is still much to understand about how religion may have been related to values, and more specifically about how values in ancient Israel were tied to human experiences. It might well be that experiences such as the collapse of Late Bronze Age civilization (1225–1175 BC) loom large in accounting for the expression of certain 'religious' values or concepts in early Israel; perhaps they may even loom larger as 'value determinants' (particularly for the first generation or so) than do particular social structures (such as an 'egalitarian' confederation of tribes).[22] But even

reality' (i.e. data) to begin with. It is perhaps in this light that we should try to understand Gottwald's appeal to 'imagination' in lieu of evidence. Thus we must appreciate that some of his confident remarks about the state of our knowledge (e.g. 'We know very well what these contemporaries noticed in Israel…', 1979: 596) are really highly subjective intuitions. In fact, on a number of occasions Gottwald seems to recommend as proper methodology the reading of such modern intuitions into the ancient past (1979: xxv and 801 n. 644).

22. We might also apply these insights to Wilson's *Prophecy and Society in Ancient Israel*. It might well be that experiences such as the westward march of the

if they do not, the narrow view of religion serving the interests of the social structure can no longer be sustained as an unequivocal, 'scientific' truism.

Finally, Gottwald's study also encourages biblical scholars to be more truly interdisciplinary when using the word 'religion'. He is correct in noting that one cannot continue to use the word exclusively in a humanities sense that overlooks the cult and how it comes to function systemically to symbolize and legitimize the social order and its interests. Conversely, it must now also be recognized that one cannot use the word 'religion' in such a restricted social-science sense that values become linked narrowly to social interests instead of more properly (and more broadly) to human experiences. Religion is not entirely a subset or an extension of society; it is a subset and an extension of human experience (a part of which is the experience of society). This suggests that in order fully to ascertain the historical nature and impact of religion in early Israel (or among the Hebrew prophets), biblical scholars must utilize an interdisciplinary method wherein they can prevent positivist and reductionist assumptions from leading them to embrace the more 'scientific' theories of religion without first criticizing them or without appreciating that they still remain just theories.

Conclusion

Hopefully, this focus on *Prophecy and Society in Ancient Israel* and *The Tribes of Yahweh* has illustrated that even in the best studies utilizing the social sciences a special set of modern assumptions can come to play a pronounced role in shaping the sociology of knowledge in biblical studies and, therefore, in shaping conclusions about ancient Israel. This paper has not intended to suggest that positivism, reductionism, relativism and determinism are wholly 'bad' influences on scholarship, for they certainly are not. Rather, it has been suggested that these modern assumptions often work to restrict historical reconstruction by imposing limits on the range of understandable options available to historians even prior to an examination of the evidence.

Assyrian army in the second half of the eighth century BC loom large in accounting for the outburst of prophetic activity in Israel at the time. Perhaps such experiences were more significant in stimulating their religious values than were specific central or peripheral support groups.

Such 'problems' related to the sociology of knowledge can never be eliminated, but at least they can be acknowledged, and at most one can hope that some ways may be found to compensate for their restrictive influences and to broaden the base of scholarly pre-understandings about society.

It is also hoped that this paper will help to stimulate efforts to discover those ways in which biblical scholars can acquire this greater range of options for reconstructing the historical nature of Israelite religion and society. The present writers feels that four such ways of improving cross-disciplinary research seem to follow naturally from everything that has been said above. They are offered here as tentative suggestions to help biblical scholarship more responsibly refine its use of social-science models and theories.

First, there seems to be a crucial need for a truly interdisciplinary understanding of what is meant by the words 'religion' and 'religious values' (see above). Distortions seem to result when either the definitions current in the humanities or those current in the social sciences begin to dominate historical reconstructions. This suggests that biblical scholars ought to exercise special care when using models and theories in a 'social-anthropological' perspective. 'Social anthropology' is that branch of the social sciences that seeks the social and political interpretation of essentially non-political, symbolic expressions and activities (cf. Cohen 1969). This discipline can tend to rely heavily upon relativist and determinist assumptions that religious expressions and activities have sociopolitical interpretations. Scholars must first have a reasonable level of certainty that religion indeed has a sociopolitical function in a given historical context before attempting to interpret the nature of that function. Admittedly, this is a somewhat circular approach to the material; nevertheless, this seems preferable to an uncritical positing of sociopolitical functions in areas where such might not exist.

For example, this suggests that for the moment scholars avoid the popular temptation of examining premonarchic Israel and the Hebrew prophets in social-anthropological terms. While these arguably are the most important, unique and interesting aspects of ancient Israel, the social and political realities associated with them are notoriously ill-defined. (In fact, we have seen that both Gottwald and Wilson for the most part had to 'create' these realities.) Perhaps biblical scholars' social-anthropological skills first ought to be sharpened against the wisdom texts of the monarchic period or the pre-exilic psalms (cf. Herion 1982: 110-92) since in both these cases scholars have better (even cross-cultural) control of the data, fairly straightforward symbolic and/or religious expressions, and a relatively well-defined sociopolitical context within which to place the data.

Secondly, the need for scholars to expand their pre-understandings beyond their own modern experiences of complex, urban society suggests that scholars need to acquire a more sympathetic awareness of the simple, 'folk' or primitive types of societies that are typologically contrary to modern society. An informed appreciation of these types of societies should help to counterbalance or nullify the influences of modernism (a) by sensitizing biblical scholars to their own modern tempocentrism and urban ethnocentrism, and (b) by enabling them to recognize a conceptual 'continuum' of societal typologies against which specific features of ancient Israel may be viewed.

Thirdly, because historians of ancient Israel cannot observe first-hand the object of their study as can most scientists, they are always searching for possible analogies to ancient Israelite phenomena. Thus, in addition to studying other texts recovered from the ancient Near Eastern (and Mediterranean) world, biblical scholars may look for possible analogies in that specific branch of the social sciences known as cultural anthropology—more specifically, ethnography. Ethnographic studies of Arab peasant village life may be particularly beneficial to those ancient Near Eastern and biblical scholars who have few occasions to travel the backroads of the Middle East. The conservative aspects of village life there may provide revealing glimpses into the ancient past, and it is curious that more biblical scholars have not sought for analogies in this corpus of material. In many pockets of the Middle East, modernism and industrialism have had little impact, and consequently these cultures can still be comparatively close to those of the ancient Near East both geographically and culturally—although due consideration must be given to the historical variables (notably Islam). Ethnographic studies of more recent non-Semitic societies (e.g. medieval European, Latin American, sub-Saharan African, Far Eastern) will probably yield less convincing analogies to ancient Israel since they are so widely separated historically, geographically and culturally.[23] The least convincing analogies of all will probably be

23. In utilizing contemporary Third World ethnography, biblical scholars must appreciate that extensive and sometimes intensive colonialism, Protestant and

those drawn between ancient Israel and the modern, industrial (and post-industrial) West. Thus, to the extent that the specific branch of the social sciences known as sociology derives its models and theories from the study and observation of this type of society, one may seriously question what it has to contribute to our understanding of ancient Israel.

Fourthly, biblical scholars need to adopt a more rigorous method of using social-science models and theories. Perhaps this means that every social-science study of ancient Israel should begin not simply with a description of a particular model or theory but also with a critical evaluation of it, especially noting how subsequent social-science study has qualified, modified or revised that model or theory. It follows from this that every social-science study of ancient Israel should be committed to pointing out not only the parallels but more importantly the inevitable divergences that will result whenever social-science models or theories are brought together with historical data. This heuristic value of social-science models and theories finally suggests that every social-science study of ancient Israel should conclude with a directive for the continued investigation of the phenomenon in question. In short, those who engage in this cross-disciplinary study should be as committed to pointing out new and often more subtle questions and lines of investigation as they are committed to answering and clarifying the old ones.

Excursus on 'Genre-Confusion'

I hope that the preceding comments will not be construed either as a general assault on interdisciplinary study or as an attack centering on the works of Robert Wilson and Norman Gottwald. Whatever sharpness one may detect in my criticisms of these works is probably due to the uncertainty and frustration I felt when reading *Prophecy and Society* and *The Tribes of Yahweh*: I was never sure what I was supposed to read those books 'as'.

I have gradually begun to suspect that one of the casualties of interdisciplinary study is clarity about 'genre'. For example, I had no

Catholic evangelism, industrialism and more recently Marxism have all helped to modernize and westernize even the peasant villages there. Significantly, the Arab Third World has most successfully resisted these influences, although even that has begun to change in the past twenty years.

doubt that I was supposed to read both these books generally 'as' historiography, but the difficulty I still experienced in trying to determine what the respective authors were intending to accomplish sensitized me to the wide range of sub-genres associated with history-writing. What 'type' of historiography are these books?

For example, all biblical scholars are familiar with academic historiography. But even within this sub-genre, distinctions must be made between a work that tests an hypothesis and one that more fundamentally proposes a reconstruction of the past. These distinctions easily become confused in an interdisciplinary study when the researcher fails to note the inevitable divergences between social-science models and theories and the historical data. This was the confusion I had in reading *Prophecy and Society in Ancient Israel*. Had Wilson looked for and pointed out the divergences then it would have been more obvious that he was testing an hypothesis rather than proposing a (sweeping) reconstruction. I believe this would have made it easier to respond more fairly to his study since I would then have been more sensitive to what he was trying to accomplish.

Also, when an interdisciplinary study fails to include a critique of the social-science theories being applied, the careful reader begins to question how 'realistic' is the resulting picture of the past. In fact, the reader may no longer be certain that the writer is primarily motivated by a 'dispassionate', academic quest for the 'reality' of the past in its own terms. This suggests another type of history writing: ideological historiography. Here the past becomes an authoritative vehicle for expressing and legitimizing contemporary concerns (Plumb 1971; B. Lewis 1975). In fact, the use of social science can actually facilitate such history-writing, since social science can also be highly ideological in its own right.[24] When the authority of 'the past' is combined with the authority of 'science'—not to mention the additional sense of authority that in certain religious circles adheres to any statement made about the Bible or ancient Israel—an interdisciplinary study combining history, social science and biblical studies becomes ripe for ideological

---

24. Over thirty years ago Reinhold Niebuhr commented that 'While the ideological taint upon all social judgments is most apparent in the practical conflicts of politics, it is equally discernible, upon close scrutiny, in even the most scientific observations of social scientists' (1953: 75). Even in America today sociologists are often viewed as progenitors of social vision and political directions (cf. Bellah 1982: 35).

exploitation. One is no longer certain whether the study is an objective accounting of the 'real' past or a partisan advocacy of a desirable future. This was the confusion I had in reading *The Tribes of Yahweh*. Had Gottwald criticized the nineteenth-century macro-sociological theories he used, the resulting picture of premonarchic Israel would certainly have been more 'realistic' and less 'utopian'; it would then have been more obvious that Gottwald was indeed writing academically about ancient Israel instead of ideologically about (legitimate) contemporary political concerns, and it would have been easier for me to know how to respond to his study.

Hopefully a more rigorous methodological use of social-science models and theories will help clear up much of the historiographic 'genre-confusion' that has accompanied the social-scientific study of ancient Israel.

BIBLIOGRAPHY

Arendt, H.
1958   'What Was Authority?', in C.F. Friedrich (ed.), *Authority* (Nomos II) (Cambridge, MA: Harvard University): 81-112.

Bellah, R.
1981   'Biblical Religion and Social Science in the Modern World', *The National Institute for Campus Ministries Journal* 6.3: 8-22.
1982   'Social Science as Practical Reason', *The Hastings Center Report* 12.5: 32-39.

Bonino, J.M.
1983   *Toward a Christian Political Ethics* (Philadelphia: Fortress Press).

Boulding, K.
1983   *The Organizational Revolution* (New York: Harper & Brothers).

Bright, J.
1972   *A History of Israel* (Philadelphia: Westminster, 2nd edn). In the 3rd edn (1981) Bright responds to Gottwald (1979).

Cohen, A.
1969   'Political Anthropology: The Analysis of the Symbolism of Power Relations', *Man* 4: 217-35.

Cox, H.
1965   *The Secular City: Secularization and Urbanization in Theological Perspective* (New York: Macmillan).

Dawe, A.
1970   'The Two Sociologies', *British Journal of Sociology* 21.2: 207-18.

Durkheim, E.
1893   *De la division du travail social* (5th edn; Paris: Alcan, 1926 [ET *The Division of Labor in Society*, New York: Macmillan, 1933]; repr. Glencoe, IL: Free Press, 1949).

1912   *Les formes élémentaires de la vie religieuse* (Paris: Alcan).

Gottwald, N.
1979   *The Tribes of Yahweh* (Maryknoll, NY: Orbis Books).

Habermas, J.
1971   *Towards a Rational Society* (London: Heinemann).
1972   *Knowledge and Human Interests* (London: Heinemann).
1973   *Theory and Practice* (Boston: Beacon Press).
1976   *Legitimation Crisis* (London: Heinemann).

Haes, J.
1980   'The Problem of Cultural Relativism', *Sociological Review* 28.4: 717-
            43.

Heirich, M.
1976   'Cultural Breakthroughs', *American Behavioral Scientist* 19.6: 685-
            702.

Herion, G.
1982   *The Social Organization of Tradition in Monarchic Judah* (PhD dis-
            sertation, University of Michigan, Ann Arbor: University Microfilms).

Heschel, A.
1962   *The Prophets: An Introduction*, I–II (New York: Harper & Row).

Lehmann, P.
1963   *Ethics in a Christian Context* (New York: Harper & Row).

Lenski, G.
1961   *The Religious Factor* (Garden City, NY: Doubleday).
1980   Review of Gottwald's *The Tribes of Yahweh, Religious Studies Review*
            6.4: 275-78.

Long, B.
1982   'The Social World of Ancient Israel', *Int* 37.3: 243-55.

Malina, B.
1982   'The Social Sciences and Biblical Interpretation', *Int* 37.3: 229-42.

Mendelbaum, M.
1977   *The Anatomy of Historical Knowledge* (Baltimore: The Johns Hopkins
            University Press).

McGehee, C.
1982   'Spiritual Values and Sociology: When We Have Debunked Everything
            What Then', *The American Sociologist* 17: 40-46.

Mendenhall, G.
1973   *The Tenth Generation* (Baltimore: The Johns Hopkins University
            Press).
1975   'The Conflict Between Value Systems and Social Control', in
            H. Goedicke and J.J.M. Roberts (eds.), *Unity and Diversity* (Baltimore:
            The Johns Hopkins University Press): 169-80.

Niebuhr, R.
1953   *Christian Realism and Political Problems* (New York: Charles
            Scribner's Sons).

Parsons, T.
1960   'Pattern Variables Revisited', *American Sociological Review* 25: 467-
            83.

Redfield, R.
    1947   'The Folk Society', *American Journal of Sociology* 52: 293-308.
Rokeach, M.
    1979   *Understanding Human Values* (New York: Free Press).
Rosenbloom, J.
    1972   'Social Science Concepts of Modernization and Biblical History', *JAAR* 40: 437-44.
Sasson, J.
    1981   'On Choosing Models for Recreating Israelite Pre-Monarchic History', *JSOT* 21: 3-24.
Steck, O.
    1977   'Theological Streams of Tradition', in D. Knight (ed.), *Tradition and Theology in the Old Testament* (Philadelphia: Fortress Press): 183-214.
Sullivan, W.
    1982   *Reconstructing Public Philosophy* (Berkeley: University of California Press).
Tönnies, F.
    1887   *Gemeinschaft und Gesellschaft* (Leipzig: Reisland).
Weber, M.
    1930   *The Protestant Ethic and the Spirit of Capitalism* (trans. T. Parsons; London; Allen & Unwin).
Wilson, R.
    1980   *Prophecy and Society in Ancient Israel* (Philadelphia: Fortress Press).
    1984   *Sociological Approaches to the Old Testament* (Philadelphia: Fortress Press).
Wirth, L.
    1938   'Urbanism as a Way of Life', *American Journal of Sociology* 44: 1-24.
Yoder, J.
    1972   *The Politics of Jesus* (Grand Rapids: Eerdmans).

JSOT 37 (1987), pp. 15-40

LITERACY AND DOMINATION:
G.A. HERION'S SOCIOLOGY OF HISTORY WRITING

Mark G. Brett

1. *Introduction*

G.A. Herion has presented two studies in this journal which have dealt primarily with issues in the sociology of knowledge. The most recent contribution (*JSOT* 34, 1986) urges us to reflect on our own social location within complex, modern societies and argues that this location has influenced our perception of ancient Israelite history. In the earlier paper (*JSOT* 21, 1981), Herion urges us to consider the social location of historians in ancient Israel and argues that this location has influenced their perception of the past. The discussion that follows will focus primarily on the earlier paper, and in particular on Herion's treatment of literacy, domination, and the nature of sociological models. We shall attempt to show that these issues are somewhat more complex than Herion seems to think.

Both of Herion's essays reflect and develop some of the views expressed by his teacher George Mendenhall. Some time ago, Mendenhall maintained that modern scholarship had been slow to appreciate the difference between authentic Yahwism and city-state political ideology, because we ourselves are 'increasingly conditioned by political power concerns' (Mendenhall 1976: 146). Even Norman Gottwald, who holds ostensibly similar views to Mendenhall on pre-monarchic Israel, has incurred a similar criticism for his preoccupation with politics (Mendenhall 1983). Herion (1986) has followed suit by arguing that religion has been politicized in some recent Old Testament studies and that Gottwald's work, for example, might easily be understood as the advocacy of a desirable future rather than as a description of the past. More importantly, Herion thinks that our participation in complex, modern societies leads us to interpret the history of Israel by means of sociological categories that are only appropriate for the modern period or for complex social organizations. For example, since we are accustomed to societies being uneasy conglomerations of disparate social groups, we tend to view a prophet as the representative of a particular social group (Herion 1986: 11).

As one remedy for this kind of distortion, Herion encourages us to study the different functions of religion in 'folk' as opposed to 'urban' types of societies. He suggests, for example, that in folk or tribal settings authority has 'nothing to do with coercive force'. Hence if we appreciate that 'politics' refers to the manipulation of coercive force, it becomes clear that folk or tribal societies will not be susceptible to *political* analysis (Herion 1986: 23, 27, 30). Similarly, Mendenhall carefully distinguished between authentic religion and political, coercive force (Mendenhall 1973: xv, 69-104, 195, 200). Moreover, he thought that the term 'social organization' could be highly misleading if used in connection with premonarchic Israel. He reluctantly used the term with the proviso that it did not imply 'power structure' or 'particularistic interests' (Mendenhall 1976: 132). This is the necessary conceptual background to his thesis that the Iron Age Israelite Federation

> ... was an oath-bound unity of the village populations of ancient Palestine that was oriented first toward the realization of the ethical rule of Yahweh as the only Suzerain, and secondly toward the avoidance of the reimposition of the... Palestinian power structures—the city states (Mendenhall 1976: 136).

Mendenhall's description of premonarchic Israel rests on a basic distinction between authentic religion and ethics on the one hand and politics and power on the other. Herion adopted a similar distinction in his earlier article on historiography (1981), but he applied it to the whole of Israelite history. He argued that folk communities have primarily *ethical* social concerns while urban societies have primarily *political* social concerns. On the basis of this divergence, he suggested that we can find two distinctive types of historiography in ancient Israel—one characterized by 'folk' ethics and the other characterized by 'urban' politics.

Herion has used this 'folk versus urban' contrast to make two different claims. First, he wants to distinguish between modern, urban politics and ancient, folk religion. This allows him to criticize the use of modern sociological methods (1986). Secondly, he wants to distinguish between folk ethics and urban politics. This distinction informs his view of Israelite historiography (1981). He has not made clear how these two claims are to be related, but we can infer that they dovetail together in so far as modern sociology is shot through with urban politics. It is also unclear whether he thinks there are important differences between modern urban societies and ancient urban societies; he has been more concerned to clarify the 'ideal type' of urban society over against the ideal type of folk community.

Insofar as Mendenhall's opposition of city-states and village communities rests upon comparative anthropology, he drew in particular from the work of E.R. Service. Herion, however, has had recourse to a 'folk versus urban' typology developed by Robert Redfield (1947) and his student Horace Miner (1952). Herion made passing references to Redfield in his most recent *JSOT* article, but the typology was developed in detail in his earlier paper on Israelite historiography. In section 2 we shall present some of the background of the folk–urban typology and explain how Herion forged the link between Redfield and Miner's anthropological work and his own account of Israelite historiography. In the sections that follow we shall critically examine the premisses of Herion's argument. We shall suggest that the link between folk communities and historiography cannot be forged as easily as Herion seems to think. In addition, we shall have cause to question whether any clear sense can be made of Herion's claim that the folk–urban typology is a 'heuristic' model. We shall argue that his idea of heuristic models is confused. This will lead us to doubt whether some of the problems in sociological studies recently identified by Herion (viz. positivism, reductionism and determinism) can be resolved by thinking of all sociological models as 'heuristic'. If Herion's notion of heuristic models is confused, then we cannot reasonably expect it to resolve these problems.

2. 'Folk' and 'Urban' Tendencies

Most of the characteristics of ideal 'folk' and 'urban' societies have been discussed in a long tradition of sociology under the rubrics of *Gemeinschaft* and *Gesellschaft*. In this tradition of social theory different types of social organization have been conceptualized as fitting along a spectrum or continuum with 'communities' at one end and 'societies' at the other (cf. Miner 1968). It would be a mistake, however, to regard this tradition as homogeneous. In his classic work *Gemeinschaft und Gesellschaft* (1887) Ferdinand Tönnies suggested that one of the highest cultural expressions of *Gemeinschaft* may be found in the city-states of ancient Greece (1887: 226). This view would seem to conflict with a folk-urban model which draws a clear distinction between ancient Palestinian villages and city-states.

In his original statement of the theory, Tönnies conceived of *Gemeinschaft* largely in historical terms as an earlier stage in the evolutionary development of social organization. But in his later work he laid more stress on *Gemeinschaft* and *Gesellschaft* as 'pure concepts of sociology'. This allowed him to ascribe the qualities of *Gemeinschaft* to his own contemporary German state, while *Gesellschaft* was seen as a fitting description of the English 'contractual' state. Organic German society was opposed to the non-integrated English society described by Thomas Hobbes and later liberal political theory. The polarity was applied to national cultures as well as to historical stages.[1]

Max Weber's version of the opposition was also articulated in more conceptual terms, more specifically, in terms of his theory of 'ideal types'. Redfield followed suit in his folk-urban typology: an ideal folk community was precisely that, an ideal type, a heuristic model which may have no empirical counterpart. Its function was to assist the development of empirical studies. Herion's account of heuristic models, and in particular his account of the folk-urban model, follows closely on the heels of Redfield.

According to Redfield, a folk society is 'small, isolated, non-literate, and homogeneous, with a strong sense of group solidarity' (1947: 293, 297). It will often have fictive kinship ties which may be associated with an equitable distribution of resources and a lack of social stratification. Minimal division of labour leads to a minimal divergence of interests. Moral values are traditional, unchanging and held in common

---

1.   Cf. for example, the illuminating preface to the third edition of *Gemeinschaft und Gesellschaft* (1919) reprinted in F. Tönnies, *Soziologische Studien und Kritiken*, vol. 1 (Jena: Gustav Fischer, 1925): 58-64. The development of Tönnies' thought has been traced by Mitzman (1971) in relation to contemporary sociopolitical developments in Germany. The opposition between organic German society and contractual English society was also expressed by the theologian Ernst Troeltsch. Cf. his essay, 'The Ideas of Natural Law and Humanity in World Politics' (1923), in O. Gierke, *Natural Law and the Theory of Society* (Boston: Beacon, 1957): 201-22.

by the whole community. They are not justified by formalized law but by conceptions of the supernatural. Communication is personal and face-to-face (Redfield 1947; Herion 1981: 34-36). These characteristics are systematically negated in urban societies. Communication is impersonal, transitory or literary. Division of labour leads to diversity of interests. Urban cosmopolitanism encourages tolerance, secularism and the 'lowest common denominator' in moral norms. Urban stratification of society brings with it privileged strata with interests in social control and domination. The privileged strata tend to formalize legal processes and command the monopoly of force (Herion 1981: 29-33).

In his earlier study, Herion's object is to describe the various social functions of historiography in ancient Israel. On the basis of the model described above he posits a divergence of Israelite social concerns. On the one hand there were folk 'grassroots' interests, and on the other hand there were urban 'official' interests. These different social interests each produced a distinctive style of historiography which may be related back to their sociological *Sitz im Leben*. His key examples of the dichotomy are Psalm 105 and Mic. 6.1-8. Psalm 105 is taken to be 'blatantly official' and the product of the temple cult. It recounts the past in order to enjoin the observance of formal religious and civil norms, thereby legitimating the state and the cult itself. On the other hand, the Micah text is critical of the temple cult; it is 'blatantly grassroots' and the product of a rural villager. It recounts the saving acts of Yahweh in order to enjoin 'internalized' values that are to be sharply distinguished from the formal and official norms which are at home in urban contexts of social control (Herion 1981: 41-42).

The major problem that Herion faces in the use of the folk-urban model is that the ideal folk community lacks a 'sense of history' (Herion 1971: 37). This is not an insurmountable problem since the model is actually a continuum; Herion can speak of folk-like 'tendencies'. What were the factors that made non-urban Israelites *unlike* their ideal folk counterparts? Herion argues that 'the crucial influence leading to the rise of "historical sense" in ancient Israel is to be found in the pre-monarchic (hence pre-urban as well) structure of Hebrew covenant ideology'. In defending this thesis he draws on those studies which have emphasized the affinities between Israelite and Hittite historical narrative. It is particularly the prologues of Hittite suzerainty treaties that interest Herion. These are taken to be models or parallels for the Israelite covenant with Yahweh as its suzerain. 'Only a genuine (i.e. historical) experience of the suzerain's past favor could even hope to instill in the vassal a compelling sense of gratitude, obligation, and loyalty'. The origin of Israelite historical sense is said to be located in a genuine event of liberation, the liberation from bondage to Egypt, interpreted by means of covenant ideology. The Hittite prologues and the Israelite covenant may well be 'interpreted' history, but they are not 'fabricated' history (Herion 1981: 37-40).[2]

It should now be clear how Herion accounts for the rise of 'historical sense' in ancient non-urban Israel. Since, according to the model, folk communities are traditional and unchanging we can see that these communities will be more likely to preserve the original features of this historical sense. Now the question arises of how later urban historiography diverged from covenant ethics and 'genuine' history. We need to remember that the model ascribes a dominant interest in social control to the privileged strata of urban societies. They will therefore be willing to sacrifice genuine history for almost any fabrication that will legitimate their position. Hence, Herion describes the official history writing of the urban monarchy and priesthood as 'mythic'. He uses the term 'myth' both to connote 'fabrication'[3] as well as to connote a sacred story that legitimates a social group:

> A myth is, after all, a conscious portrayal of the past (or of the divine) world in ways that satisfy and reflect the subjective values, interests and needs of the present mythmaker and his audience (Herion 1981: 31).[4]

2.   More recent studies have begun to express doubts about this Hittite connection insofar as it rests upon H. Cancik's *Grundzüge der hethitischen und alttesta-mentlichen Geschichtsschreibung*. For a review of these studies and a reformulation of the issues cf. Van Seters 1983: ch. 4. Especially noteworthy in this context is Van Seters's discussion of mythological material in the treaty prologues and his claim that the Hittite treaties with kingless states contain no historical prologue (1983: 117).

3.   A more subtle and differentiated view of 'fabrication' has been presented by Oeming 1984: 254-66.

4.   A curious feature of this definition is that it seems to make one of the nineteenth-century fathers of critical history writing into a mythmaker: recent editors of Leopold von Ranke's works have concluded that he saw history as a process 'in which spiritual forces assumed concrete reality in social and political institutions' and that he used his historiography to serve conservative political ends. Cf. von Ranke 1983: xxx and lii.

We shall examine the issue of myth in more detail, but first we need to discuss some anthropological studies that might cast doubt on the usefulness of a folk model for historiography.[5]

3. *Literacy and History*

Jack Goody has described Redfield's model of an ideal folk or 'little' community as 'not so much an abstraction as a distraction' which 'has led to a dialogue of little moment' (Goody 1968: 7). This might be excessively critical and it would not apply to the broad *Gemeinschaft–Gesellschaft* tradition. But at the root of Goody's criticism lies a key issue for Herion's view of historiography. Goody has argued, and even his critics tend to agree, that literacy is a necessary (but not sufficient) factor in the development of 'historical consciousness'.[6] The argument, first presented by Goody and Ian Watt in 1963, has been much discussed (e.g., Goody 1968; Horton Finnegan 1973) and refined by Goody himself in *The Domestication of the Savage Mind* (1977). It should be remembered that Redfield described the folk community as non-literate, a point that is connected with the face to face nature of folk communication. That is, the culture of folk societies is transmitted orally. If it can be shown that the lack of an historical sense is directly connected with the oral model of cultural production, and conversely that historical consciousness is connected with a literary mode of cultural production, then Herion's view becomes problematic. This is indeed the implication of Goody's work. (The issue is also interesting insofar as it brings a new significance to the form-critical view of Gunkel and Noth that the Israelite sagas arose in

---

5.   A strong tradition of scholarship, especially in Germany, has tended to see only the nation state as the proper object of history writing, a view which underlies many Old Testament studies on historiography. Given such a view, there could never be a folk history since 'history proper' is national history. But it would be inadvisable to reject the idea of folk history for such *a priori* reasons. This 'national' tradition has been rejected by many contemporary historians. Its rise and fall have been chronicled by George Iggers in *The German Conception of History* (Middletown: Wesleyan University Press, 1968).

6.   Historical 'consciousness' should not be understood here as a structure of the mind that excludes the possibility of also using cyclical or magical concepts of time alongside a linear one. Cf. Gough 1968: 76, 84.

the context of oral tradition while the genre 'history writing' was from the first a literary product.)[7]

Goody is one among a growing number of anthropologists who are suspicious of some of the older strategies used to isolate the area of interest peculiar to the discipline of anthropology. What makes 'primitive' or traditional societies a separable area of interest? More important for us is Goody's criticism of the great dichotomies like 'primitive versus advanced' and 'mythopoeic versus logico-empirical': theories built on these dichotomies rarely propose any substantive reasons for the difference or mechanisms for change. Scholars have tended to think of these great dichotomies as in themselves a form of explanation (Goody 1977: 147-48). In addressing this problem Goody has focused on the issue of literacy.

Goody argues that the invention of writing brought with it qualitatively new possibilities for critical attention. Changes in the means of communication created a new potential for cognition. 'Writing is critical not simply because it preserves speech over time and space, but because it transforms speech, by abstracting its components, by assisting backward scanning' (1977: 127). According to Goody, the early effects of literacy can be illuminated by study of ancient administrative and economic lists and tables. This leads to his discussion of the large amounts of such material from Sumer, Assyria, Egypt and Ugarit (1977: ch. 5):

> For writing is no mere phonograph recording of speech... depending on social as well as technological conditions, it encourages special forms of linguistic activity associated with developments in particular kinds of problem-raising and problem-solving, in which the list, the formula and the table played a seminal part. If we wish to speak of the 'savage mind', these were some of the instruments of its domestication (1977: 162).

---

7.   Cf. Noth (1958) who reiterates the view of Gunkel expressed in earlier editions of *Die Religion in Geschichte und Gegenwart*. Cf. also Gunkel, 1906/1963: 3, 16, 24. Noth did not exclude the possibility that Israelite historians used oral sources, and he accepted the fact that we only know the sages in their written form. The distinction seems to be at least partly founded on hypotheses about the length of oral transmission. It should perhaps be stressed that the views of Gunkel and Noth on this point were form-critical. Such claims about the genre 'history writing' were not primarily directed at the issue of historical consciousness. Von Rad, for example, thought that historical sense had arisen in Israel 'long before there was any real historical writing' (1966: 168).

The observation that writing preserves speech over time and space leads in to the issue of historical consciousness. Goody takes up the view expressed by Lévi-Strauss that there is no history without archives (so also Redfield 1947: 296). Documentary records of the past allow a type of critical attention, a precision, that does not apply to accounts of the past which are transmitted orally. Societies with no enduring records have nothing substantial to set beside their present views for the purposes of critical checking.[8] (A potentially relevant biblical example of this critical process is Josiah's reform, which was apparently stimulated by the discovery of the 'Book of the Law'.) A cumulative repository of written records allows the possibility for the past to persist in all its difference to the present. Anthropologists have been impressed by the enormous capacity of memory in oral cultures, but closer studies over long periods have shown that folk legends, genealogies and myths which purport to be unchanging are in fact flexible. In oral cultures, 'the unobtrusive adaptation of past tradition to present needs' means that 'myth and history merge into one' (Goody 1968: 34, 48).[9] Historical consciousness, according to Goody, was one of the new modes of critical thought that were made possible by literacy. At the level of genre, he regards king lists, annals, and chronicles as the preliminary steps to history writing (1977: 90).

This analysis of historiography and historical sense as dependent upon writing is closely linked with an account of non-literate culture as well. Goody has no fundamental objection to Redfield's picture of a small community characterized by face-to-face (oral) communication

8.   Goody is, of course, aware of the studies of oral tradition which show that audiences sometimes 'correct' reciters. Cf. Goody 1977: 117-19. Even Goody's critic Ruth Finnegan accepts the 'profound' importance of the 'yardstick of accuracy' provided by writing. Cf. 'Literacy versus Non-literacy: The Great Divide', in R. Horton and R. Finnegan (eds.) 1973: 125, 140.

9.   Douglas Knight (1975: 389, 391) follows Ivan Engnell in assuming that a connection with the cult assures the greater reliability of ancient Israelite oral tradition. This assumption is not substantiated by comparative studies of oral ritual that purports to be unchanging (cf. e.g. Van Baaren 1984: 218-20). Nor does Knight consider the interests at work in cultic roles that might compete with the pure preservation of historical information. Oral tradition may at times be quite reliable, but only corroborative evidence will tell. (It may be indirectly reliable as a reflection of the contemporary situation of performance, but this raises a complex set of issues that are separable from the question of historicity. Historicity involves the apparent claim of the text to describe the past).

and cultural homogeneity. But he goes beyond Redfield by arguing that the mechanism for this homogeneity is to be found in the oral mode of communication; there is an important causal connection between face-to-face communication and cultural homogeneity. In an exclusively oral culture, tradition is in an important sense non-cumulative, or more accurately, it is 'homeostatic': 'something new gets incorporated all the time, just as something old gets dropped' (Goody 1977: 27). Since whatever is remembered by a community will be related to the interests or needs of each generation, those parts of the cultural heritage which have become ill-fitting or have ceased to be of contemporary relevance are likely to be forgotten and thus eliminated from the cultural repertoire. Goody draws an analogy between this process of digestion and elimination and the homeostatic organization of the human body. Given this kind of homeostatic process oral culture would naturally maintain a close connection to the experience of the community; criticism or scepticism would be generally unsystematic or unlikely to lead to radical reinterpretations of social dogma (Goody and Watt 1968: 48). Redfield himself seems to assent to this kind of view when he claims that folk communities were 'uncritical' (Redfield 1947: 293, 300). The process of critique may move so slowly, or in such a piecemeal fashion, that the content of tradition seems unchanging; there is no sure means of making the past appear in its difference from the present.

The observation that writing preserves speech over time and space led Goody to a plausible hypothesis for the rise of historical consciousness. But there are other implications to be considered as well. Building on Goody's discussion of ancient economic and administrative lists, Anthony Giddens has presented an argument that is relevant to Herion's theme of social control:

> All modes of information storage are simultaneously forms of communication, cutting across the face-to-face communication that is exhaustive of human interaction in oral cultures... Writing provides a means of coding information, which can be used to expand the range of administrative control... [it] makes possible the stretching of social relations across broader spans of time and space than can be accomplished in oral cultures (Giddens 1985: 14, 44-45).

A biblical example of literate administration would be the census (Exod. 30.11-16; Num. 1; 26; 2 Sam. 24), a practice connected particularly with military organization and the distribution of land.

Giddens's main point in this context is that administration and surveillance associated with such listing is 'necessarily rudimentary in terms of the power it can generate' (1985: 45). This leads him to distinguish carefully between the non-modern state and the modern nation-state: non-modern or traditional states have 'frontiers', while nation-states have 'boundaries'. Only in the modern period have states successfully laid claim to the monopoly of force within an administrative realm defined by precise territorial boundaries (1985: 18, 38, 52). This view of traditional states is connected with our folk-urban theme: in traditional states, 'city' and 'countryside' had 'a contrasting and distinctive character'. Given the increased powers of administration, the modern nation-state brings with it, in a sense, the elimination of the 'countryside' (1985: 21-22).

This discussion of the modern nation-state brings us to the extremities of complex social organization. The urban pole in Redfield's model, we should remember, was also *modern* urban society (Redfield 1947: 297). We have noted that there are good reasons to think that literacy was a necessary condition of historical consciousness as well as of more complex and comprehensive forms of administration. These are just two of the probable consequences of literacy in ancient societies.[10] But now we need to draw this discussion together and state the implications for Herion's case more explicitly.

Goody's work not only suggests that historical sense rests upon literacy but also that literacy will tend to break down the cultural homogeneity of a folk society. Cumulative records of a past that is different from the present will work against the homeostatic mechanism which allows cultural homogeneity. Giddens has developed Goody's work on literate administration to make explicit the implications for social control. The recent studies of Goody and Giddens in some respects

10. Goody and Watt also argue that the alphabet brought potentially 'democratic' effects which were especially realized in ancient Greece after the adoption of the Semitic alphabet. The relative economy of the Semitic alphabet was a significant innovation but its potentially radical effects were probably diminished in Israel by a continuing respect for memory and oral communication (1968: 36-40). In his article on the diffusion of the alphabet, P.K. McCarter (1974: 58) rejected the idea that the origin of the Semitic alphabet can be traced to an 'egalitarian impulse'. The alphabet was more 'a make-shift device of inconspicuous genius'. It should be clear, however, that Goody's argument is not directed at the *intentions* of those who invented the alphabet. It is directed at the *effects* of the invention, which could not possibly be foreseen, even by the most conspicuous genius.

concur with the earlier folk-urban studies devoted to the issue of literacy which came to the following conclusion:

> Written languages seem to appear... only in societies which also had complex systems of exchange, law, religion, education and government (Miner 1968: 178).

Thus it seems that one may not be able to discuss historiography without attracting all the characteristics relevant to the 'urban' type of society. A folk historiography seems difficult to account for. Most societies have no doubt formulated accounts of their past, but whether these accounts should count as 'historiographical' might well depend at least in part on whether they have made use of written records. With the homeostatic organization of oral tradition, real differences between the present and the past are forgotten or unnoticed. Herion's addition of historical sense to Redfield's folk model seems a small adjustment, but it has far-reaching ramifications.

Having considered some of the difficulties with Herion's account of folk historiography we may now turn to examine his account of urban, mythic historiography.

4. *Myth and Domination*

Urban interests, according to Herion, promote 'the mythical sacrosanctity of the present'; the over-riding concern is to legitimate the status quo. But folk societies seem to promote their own version of the mythical sacrosanctity of the present: the present is legitimated because the homeostatic process allows things in the present to appear as if they derive from the past. Etiological myths, legends and genealogies legitimate the present beliefs, practices and social structure. Herion cuts through a long and complex discussion of myth in Old Testament studies by simply stating that urban myths 'satisfy and reflect the subjective values, interests and needs of the present mythmaker and his audience'. This thesis fits equally well with Goody's description of the homeostatic oral process; each generation makes the tradition relevant. Ironically enough, Herion's thesis fits particularly well with the folk model since it seems to imply that the mythmaker and the audience have homogeneous values and interests. In short, the problem is this: the properties of myth which Herion wishes to restrict to the urban context seem equally at home in the sphere of folk tradition. It may be useful at this point to trace back a genealogy of ideas in Old

Testament myth studies to see whether we can discover some of the factors that may have contributed to this confusion.

In Jonathan Z. Smith's view, the proclivity to locate myth in urban settings goes back to the nineteenth-century 'Pan-Babylonian School' (Smith 1978: 293). But for our purposes a more interesting segment of the genealogy of ideas on urban myth is to be found in twentieth-century 'myth and ritual' research. One of the factors behind the rise of this movement was the publication in 1926 of S.A. Pallis's work on *The Babylonian Akitu Festival*. This study was drawn on extensively by S.H. Hooke (1927) in arguing for the intimate connection between myth and ritual. But Hooke parted company with Pallis in at least one important respect: he rejected Pallis's 'purely anthropological view' that followed V. Grønbech in understanding 'primitive' religion as non-urban (Hooke 1927: 29). For Pallis, urban culture weakened the connection between cult and myth, and since the Akitu festival was urban, there was a real possibility that it had deviated from its primitive roots. The urban manifestation of the myth was in all likelihood a degeneration from its pure form. Clearly, this 'anthropological' view was ill-suited to serve in Hooke's attempt to find the most intimate connections between myth and ritual.[11] Hooke was not the only one to reject Grønbech's lead on this issue. After acknowledging a deep debt to Grønbech and giving him the highest praise, Sigmund Mowinckel finally smudged the urban versus non-urban distinction by calling the whole ancient Orient 'primitive'—including Egypt at the highest point of its civilization (Mowinckel, 1966: vol. 1, Vorbemerkung; vol. 2: 22, 25, 225-26).

In outlining this segment of the 'urban myth' genealogy of ideas in Old Testament studies I am not suggesting that Herion's case rests on the authority of Hooke or Mowinckel. The point is rather that the idea of urban 'mythic history writing' is lent implicit plausibility by a long tradition in biblical studies of blurring the distinction between urban and non-urban myth. The vitality of this 'urban myth' tradition was, at least in one phase of study, dependent upon those who stressed the

---

11. Thorkild Jacobsen (1975) proposed that the original 'agricultural' Akitu festival was later transformed into a 'national' festival. He did not, however, question the extent to which such 'nationalism' was diffused through the society. For a detailed discussion of the urban versus non-urban issue in Hooke's work, see Rogerson 1974: ch. 6. I am grateful to Professor Rogerson for his critique of an earlier draft of this paper.

non-urban roots of myth (Grønbech and Pallis). Herion seems to have remade the 'anthropological distinction', this time restricting myth to the urban setting and withdrawing it from the non-urban realm so that history can take its place. The irony in this 'genealogical amnesia' is not itself an argument against Herion's position; it may well be defended on other grounds. What is important however is that Herion can gain little support from Redfield.

Redfield studied festivals in isolated villages in Central America and compared them with festivals in less isolated villages. His conclusion cannot but provoke comparison with Grøbech and Pallis: the festival in less isolated villages is 'less well integrated with the social organization of the community, is less sacred, and allows for more individual enterprise' (Redfield 1947: 307). This suggests that the purer form of myth-ritual found in folk communities starts to break down as societies move toward the urban pole. Redfield also attributed a peculiar mentality to folk societies which has long been an element in myth studies: these societies were not only characterized by personal contact between people, but nature was also treated 'personally' and given human characteristics.

Herion may still, however, be able to reconstruct a defensible account of mythic historiography. He might argue that the urban mythic tendency reinforces only the common values of the dominant strata of urban society; the lack of homogeneous culture in the urban setting would allow the lower strata to hold a different set of values. This seems to be the direction of his argument when he claims that the urban 'disenfranchized' should be thought of as closer to the rural peasantry than to the urban privileged (Herion 1981: 32).

This kind of argument could indeed find some support in recent studies of ideological patterns in feudal societies. After surveying these studies, Abercrombie, Hill and Turner (1980) have argued that the ideology of the privileged strata can be best understood as reinforcing the social coherence of the dominant classes rather than controlling the subordinate classes (the term 'ideology' here means any set of beliefs regardless of their truth or falsity). They also argue, in a manner suggestive of the folk-urban model, that the rural peasantry were especially resistant to such control (Abercrombie *et al.* 1980: 69-72). Social control exercised by means of administration, brute force and economic coercion was probably much more effective.

We should stress that Abercrombie, Hill and Turner are not

proclaiming a general theory of ideology. They are interested in how ideology functions in different types of societies, and more specifically, in the mechanism or apparatus by which beliefs are transmitted:

> Historical evidence on feudal societies does not allow us to claim that religion was a dominant ideology which had the consequence of successfully incorporating the peasantry... In feudalism and early capitalism there are indeed identifiable dominant ideologies. These are held by the members of the dominant classes but not by those in subordinate classes. One reason why lower classes do not hold these ideologies is the weakness of the mechanisms of transmission (Abercrombie *et al.* 1980: 94, 128).

One of the most notable weaknesses of the medieval apparatus of transmission was the very high level of *illiteracy* (Abercrombie *et al.*: 76). And thus the question arises: is the ideological split in medieval feudalism comparable to the situation in ancient Israel?

Assuming for the moment that literacy is a key mechanism of ideological transmission (there are other mechanisms, like socialization), what can we say about the extent of literacy in ancient Israel? Was it widespread enough to allow the possibility of ideological incorporation? Considering the paucity of evidence, it is not surprising to find that the issue of literacy is problematic. On the basis of paleographic evidence Joseph Naveh (1968 and 1982: 76) stretches his claim for literacy outside the court and temple only as far back as the late seventh century BCE. Roland de Vaux (1961: 49) came to a similar conclusion on the basis of Deut. 6.9 and 11.20—these texts assume a relatively widespread literacy. There seems to be little archeological evidence for writing during the premonarchic period.[12] Frank Frick (1985: 45-47, 71) associates this point with a systematic model of 'state collapse' that encompasses the wide collapse of civilization in the Late Bronze Age. For example, Minoan–Mycenaean writing seems to have died out with the decline of the palaces during 1200–1100 BCE. This seems to indicate that Minoan–Mycenaean writing was not widely diffused. The sheer complexity of the Mesopotamian, Egyptian and Hittite writing systems also apparently preserved elite literate groups which were no doubt strongly conservative forces (Goody 1968: 36-40; Herion, 1981: 44-45).

---

12. Alan Millard (1972) mentions only isolated examples before 750 BCE, for example, the inscribed copper arrowheads found near Bethlehem and dated to the twelfth century BCE.

On the other hand, there are good reasons for being suspicious about close comparisons with these other ancient Near Eastern writing systems. W.F. Albright (1960: 122-23) and Jack Goody (1968 and 1977: 76) both stressed the simplicity and economy of the Semitic alphabet. This greatly reduced the time needed to learn the script, and makes writing potentially more accessible to larger numbers of people (although Israel still had, of course, professional scribes). Norman Gottwald extended the implications of this idea with specific reference to the so-called 'proto-Sinaitic' inscriptions, found at Serabit el-Khadem on the Sinai peninsula and dated between 1800 and 1500 BCE. These texts provide evidence for the use of a Semitic alphabet by mining workers, i.e. by lower strata of society (Gottwald 1979: 781). Gottwald therefore endorses Alan Millard's view that 'writing was theoretically within the competence of any ancient Israelite, not the prerogative of an elite professional class alone...it was, in fact, quite widely practised' (Millard 1972: 111).

Given this discussion about the extent of literacy in ancient Israel, what can we say about the possibility of urban 'mythic historiography' being an agent of upper class social control (Herion 1981: 33)? Since we have good grounds to think that literacy was relatively widespread in the monarchic period this might suggest that, unlike the situation in medieval feudalism, the mechanisms of ideological domination were at least potentially adequate. But were they actually effective?

We have a strong prophetic tradition suggesting that the king's word was not always respected. This implies a relatively weak control over lower-strata beliefs. It may also suggest that any social control exercised by the monarchy should be attributed more to administration, law or coercion than to ideological strategies like mythic historiography. If literacy was not restricted to the court, then it would have been difficult to produce outright fabrications of events recorded in widely diffused sources. The degree of diffusion need not, in fact, have been so great; even two or three dissenting prophets could have provided a checking effect.

It may be that monarchic history writing served simply to reinforce the dominant social strata ideologically. Consider for example the so-called Succession Narrative or Court History. Von Rad thought that this text was concerned primarily with the political question of David's successor (1966). Later writers have described it as political propaganda. But who exactly was the target of this (rather subtle) propaganda? The royal family certainly had a much higher stake in the question of David's successor than the population at large. If the successor had turned out to be a king like the oppressive Rehoboam of 1 Kgs 12.14, then we can imagine that more people would have been vitally interested. (Von Rad's reading of the Succession Narrative provides some indirect support for the folk-urban model, since he took it to be the product of an urban cosmopolitanism, and of a secularized spirituality. But even if this is true, we could not infer anything about the power of the narrative to incorporate the lower social strata ideologically.)

Within the dominant social strata the issue of priestly social control presents a different problem. The 'ruling classes' cannot be made into a single block with a homogeneous set of interests. The Hebrew Bible was in all likelihood preserved by professional religious people, and quite apart from the material customarily considered 'priestly' their influence may have been so subtle as to be undetectable. But once again we have a strong prophetic tradition of criticizing the cult. The priestly control seems to have been limited to some extent. Apart from prophetic material, Deut. 31.24-29 is a particularly relevant text. This passage suggests that the Book of the Law was to function as a 'witness' against all those who were in authority, including the Levites, since these authorities were sure to become corrupt. The written word has become a critical 'check' to be set against later beliefs and practices. Writing has been endowed with the potential function of critique. Critique is made possible by the 'external' and public measure of the law being written down. In Herion's view, only social control interests use 'external' law. (Interestingly, he cites a written text, Exodus 21–23, as an example of 'internalized' folk norms [Herion 1981: 361]). We may guess that the critical potential of writing was only occasionally exercised, for example, by Josiah. Nevertheless, Goody's theory has a kind of biblical precedent. Even if urban priests did manipulate the past, we can doubt whether this was an effective means of controlling the beliefs of the lower social strata.

We can sum up the problem in Herion's account of mythic historiography and social control in the form of a dilemma: (1) either there were basically two streams of culture in ancient Israel, in which case the dominant ideology probably only consolidated the ruling classes, or (2) there was basically one stream of culture in Israel, in which case it would seem difficult to posit two trajectories of historiography.

5. *Heuristic and Empirical Models*

What is striking about all the preceding discussion is that it cannot falsify Herion's theory. He can simply reply that mythic historiography *intends* to dominate the lower classes ideologically but as a matter of contingent fact, other strategies like administration and coercive force turn out to be more effective means of social control. The folk-urban model can also explain why ideological domination fails: there are basically two types of social interest and not much ideological traffic passes between them. (Although Herion does provide at least one example of ideological traffic: the concept of the Messiah, 'which probably had its origins in royal propaganda', was used by Micah the village prophet.) With respect to the folk model, Herion might concede that if literacy turns out to be necessary for historiography, then the Israelite villages need only be moved a few more points away from the folk pole towards the urban pole of his model. They had in any case left the ideal folk society behind by acquiring 'historical sense', and they would still be a long way away from the modern nation-state.

In spite of his account of the two tendencies in Israelite historiography Herion is well aware of the complexity of the actual biblical documents. He concedes that the biblical traditions reflect in various ways a spectrum of ideological concerns (1981: 46). He suggests, for example, that if a court document like Deuteronomy seems to depict 'external' law restraining priests and officials then the book is simply a 'hybrid'. It probably originated in a non-official context and was adapted in order to legitimate king and cult (1981: 47). The transmission of the Messiah concept from an urban to a folk context also suggests that there are ironical twists in Israelite tradition. We might suggest to Herion that if the vast bulk of Israelite material falls in the middle sections of the folk-urban continuum, then surely we need more sophisticated ways of discussing hybrid tradition. But he would no doubt remind us that the continuum is an ideal type, a heuristic 'mental construct' designed to suggest hypotheses for further study. It is not a mirror image of reality (1981: 28).

But there is a basic problem here which Redfield touched on when he claimed that an ideal type has most heuristic value when it depends on a knowledge of real folk societies (Redfield 1947: 295). The problem became clearer later when Miner responded to objections concerning the 'problem of fit' between the ideal folk society and real folk societies: he stressed that the model should be understood as 'heuristic' rather than 'empirical' (Miner 1952) implying that empirical falsification did not strictly affect the value of the model. The problem emerges most sharply when we put together Herion's two claims that (a) all models are ideal types (1981: 28), and (b) all models are falsifiable (1986: 12). These claims neglect some important distinctions that social scientists have made between 'heuristic' and 'instrumentalist' models on the one hand and 'empirical' models on the other (cf. Topolski 1972). Unlike an empirical model, which is falsifiable, a heuristic one has only a greater or lesser degree of utility. The basic sense of 'utility' here is the capacity to generate empirical hypotheses and models which are more strictly falsifiable. Specifically addressing heuristic continua like the folk-urban model, Wilbert Moore argued persuasively that 'such modes of analysis present problems of operational identification in research and of mensuration when mixed situations of empirical reality are approached' (in Miner 1968: 180).

We now have a whole repertoire of empirical models which can replace the ideal folk society: these have been discussed in the anthropological literature under the rubrics of 'acephalous' or 'segmentary' social organization. These societies may be loosely defined in terms of their lack of centralized political authority. They are usually organized by means of genealogies subdivided or segmented into smaller groups politically of equal rank. Group size and cultural homogeneity can vary considerably (cf. Middleton and Tait 1958).

In their highly differentiated account of authority and power types, M. Hennen and W.-U. Prigge note how the study of acephalous communities led initially to the enthusiastic claim (echoed by Mendenhall and Herion) that these groups provided proof of the possibility of political relations unstructured by patterns of power (1977: 87). This enthusiasm was unjustified. Closer examination of these groups revealed distinct patterns of authority, an authority, however, that was invested only temporarily and by means of non-hierarchical patterns of legitimation. These consensual and participatory processes of legitimation were dominated by tradition (1977: 91). The authority type associated with this form of social organization is 'leadership' or 'chieftainship' (1977: 81-95). Some writers have so stressed the point that 'power weaves the cloth of every reality' that its individual manifestations have become almost irrelevant, but chieftains, corporate heads, grandmothers and professors all exercise power in different ways (Hennen and Prigge's study is especially important for showing how power is extremely diverse in its structural forms). There seems to be little gained by following Herion's tendency to seal off the folk society from questions of power.

A further feature of these acephalous groups is that their territorial or lineage segments are nested within each other. The segments have a kind of organic interrelationship, a 'complementary opposition', so that a unit cannot simply be lopped off without social effects reverberating throughout the other segments (Middleton and Tait 1958: 7-8). This implies a shifting and complex pattern of social solidarity similar to that of the Israelite premonarchic 'tribes':

> A segment that is significant as an autonomous unit in one situation is merged with others in other situations, and there occurs the interlocking of groups and statuses...Former competitors may be merged together as subordinate segments in the internal administrative organization of a wider overall segment that includes them both (Middleton and Tait 1958: 6, 11).

Social coherence will change depending on the concrete situation at hand or upon broader types of situation like ritual, marriage, war or markets. This pattern seems to resemble the social organization of the premonarchic period. The comparison becomes even more plausible when one considers the style of temporary leadership that characterizes the 'judges'. Instead of a vague heuristic reference to the social solidarity of folk communities, studies of segmentary societies offer a whole range of empirical models for comparison with premonarchic Israel.

We do, in fact, have a growing number of studies devoted to such a comparison. Gottwald, for example, argued that the premonarchic period had a segmentary structure, but in so doing he stressed its historical peculiarity; it differed from other segmentary societies in that it was a 'politically conscious and deliberate social revolution', an intentional 'retribalization' (1979: 323-27).[13] Frank Frick has recently

---

13. Those still interested in the uniqueness of ancient Israel might find this claim intriguing. But from the perspective of Gottwald's overall approach, it is not particularly significant. It is a claim about the conscious 'intention' of retribalization. But Gottwald's historical method is 'etic': it assigns only relative value to 'what cultural actors think about their action'. From an etic perspective, a historical explanation based on the conscious intentions of cultural actors would be pseudo-explanation, even if that intention was revolutionary (cf. Gottwald 1979: 337, 638, 665, 785 n. 558, 786 n. 564).

gone a step further by arguing that there is another type of social organization in ancient Israel that came between the premonarchic segmentary society and the 'statehood' of the tenth century BCE. He claims that in the mid-to late eleventh century the social organization can best be described as a 'chiefdom', a term that implies 'permanent political structures and ranked segments' (Frick 1985: 65).[14] Some form of segmentation persists even into his idea of Israelite statehood: 'A minimal definition of the state is simply that entity that puts the brakes on the process of fissioning that is everywhere the hallmark of segmentary societies' (1985: 57-58). Frick's model of the emergence of the Israelite state might also be construed as implying a kind of folk-urban continuum, but as against Herion's ideal type its empirical precision offers more footholds for falsification.[15] (The sociology of knowledge suggests, of course, that we should not be surprised if empirical falsification does not always work.)

As a final concession to Herion we should perhaps note that ambiguity can also be found in one of the classic statements of the theory of ideal types. In his essay '"Objectivity" in Social Science and Social Policy', Max Weber treated all social 'laws', 'factors' and 'ideal types' as heuristic. The ideal type was not itself an hypothesis, but it offers guidance to the construction of hypotheses (Weber 1977: 34). It cannot be a mirror of reality since even the smallest slice of reality cannot be exhaustively described (1977: 29). Rather, it offers a consistent conceptual pattern which can guide the selection of characteristic features and regularities and organize them into a coherent mental construct (1977: 34-35). But coherent ideas of regularities, factors and laws are only a means and not an end: 'For the knowledge of historical phenomena in their concreteness, the most general laws, because they are most devoid of content are also the least valuable'. The more comprehensive the model, the more it abstracts from reality. 'Knowledge of the universal or general is never valuable in itself' (1977: 30, 31).

> The determination of those (hypothetical) 'laws' and 'factors' would in any case only be the first of the many operations which would lead us to the desired type of knowledge. The analysis of the historically given

---

14. In this connection the three-part division of Genesis 36 is intriguing: the chapter first lists Esau's offspring as a family, then there follows a list of the chiefs of Edom and lastly of the kings of Edom.

15. For one attempt to falsify the claim that premonarchic Israel was segmentary in its social organization, see Rogerson 1986: 17-26.

individual configuration of those 'factors' and their significant concrete interaction... would be the next task to be achieved (Weber 1977: 27).

This aspect of Weber's argument seems to invoke a distinction between abstract sociological laws, factors and ideal types on the one hand and the concrete empirical hypotheses of historical study on the other. Sociology becomes the heuristic handmaid of empirical history. So far, this seems to be a coherent view.

Difficulties begin to arise as soon as Weber starts (as does Herion) to treat ideal types as falsifiable empirical hypotheses. Not only do these mental constructs guide the construction of hypotheses, they begin to behave as hypotheses: 'Historical research faces the task of determining in each individual case the extent to which this ideal construct approximates to or diverges from reality'. Ideal types are described as 'attempts, on the basis of the present state of our knowledge and the available conceptual patterns, to bring order into the chaos of those facts which we have drawn into the field circumscribed by our interest' (1977: 34-35). Weber would need to forgive those later sociologists who thought that the theory of ideal types was unnecessary; revisable empirical hypotheses can apparently do the job attributed to heuristic models. For example, hypotheses concerning 'social systems' like family, corporation, church, or state might be similar to heuristic models insofar as they are not mirrors of reality; they do not describe social realities which are directly observable in one time and place. But social systems can be conceived of as hypotheses that select and combine a mass of direct observations from different times and places. They can be thought of as falsifiable empirical inferences rather than heuristic mental constructs.

More importantly, even those positivists who think that all valid historical explanation requires the subsumption of individual events under general laws could agree with Weber's argument that historical study is concerned with 'individual configurations' of historical factors. The most notable exponent of this view is Karl Popper, a 'positivist'[16]

16. Those familiar with Popper's rejection of the Logical Positivism stemming from the Vienna Circle might find this label for his work questionable. But with respect to his views on social science and historical explanation Popper's work reveals the characteristic tents of positivism: (1) the unity of scientific method; (2) the exact natural sciences provide a standard for all other sciences; (3) a monistic view of scientific explanation as the subsumption of individual cases under general laws. Cf. von Wright 1971: 4, 175.

who nevertheless stressed the multiplicity of factors at work in human history and the shifting patterns in the combination of these factors. Part of Weber's view of historical study (we are neglecting his theory of values) was that it was concerned with 'individual consequences' produced by laws working in 'unique configurations'. Accordingly, his historical explanations often focused on unintended consequences like the role of Calvinism in the rise of capitalism.[17] But in Popper's view, the kind of historical sociology which attends to concrete consequences rather than 'trends' or 'tendencies' is entirely appropriate. His interest in unique configurations led him to stress that a scientific historical explanation not only requires a knowledge of the relevant general laws but also a knowledge of the concrete initial conditions of the phenomena to be explained (Popper 1957: 120-30, 143-47). He also claimed that one of the main tasks of social science was to trace the unintended repercussions of intentional human action (Popper 1959: 281; 1957: 64-70). A Popperian social science cannot be prevented from taking an interest in the individual and concrete configurations of historical phenomena. Nor can it be easily domesticated as simply a heuristic tool.

It is therefore difficult to endorse Herion's view (1986) that his theory of heuristic ideal types can deal with such social-scientific evils as positivism, reductionism or determinism. If a sociological explanation is to be properly falsifiable it will need to be constructed in empirical terms. But empirical hypotheses cannot be protected from the dangers of positivism, reductionism or determinism by simultaneously claiming only a heuristic status.

Conclusion

We have pursued the logic of the folk-urban model to show that its application to historiography is problematic. Herion neglected the probable connection between literacy and 'historical sense'. As a

---

17. Some contemporary historians express their interest in unintended consequences by means of the concept of irony. 'Ironic' historians characteristically present the consequences of action as escaping the control or intentions of those who possess power. Cf. Reinitz 1978: 95, 117; Wise 1973: chs. 8 and 9. Although these historians are not generally interested in historical 'laws', they might contradict Frick's view of political history as 'the story of deliberate human action' (Frick 1985: 13).

consequence, he has over-estimated the utility of his folk model. He also treated the issue of ideological domination without carefully distinguishing it from other forms of domination like administration, brute force and economic coercion. Even if there was a divergence of social concerns in ancient Israel we may doubt whether historiography was an effective instrument of social control. Finally, his attempt to overcome some of the contemporary evils of social science by means of a theory of heuristic models must be considered questionable insofar as he has not clarified the relationship between these models and empirical historical explanations.

BIBLIOGRAPHY

Abercrombie, N., S. Hill, and B.S. Turner
    1980   *The Dominant Ideology Thesis* (London: Allen & Unwin).
Albright, W.F., *et al.*
    1960   'The Development of Culture in the National States', in C.H. Kraeling
        and R.M. Adams (eds.), *City Invincible* (Chicago: Chicago University
        Press): 102-23.
Canary, R.H., and Konicki, M. (eds.)
    1978   *The Writing of History* (Madison: Wisconsin University Press).
Frick, F.
    1985   *The Formation of the State in Ancient Israel* (Sheffield: Almond Press).
Giddens, A.
    1985   *The Nation State and Violence* (Cambridge: Polity).
Goody, J., and I. Watt
    1963   'The Consequence of Literacy', *Comparative Studies in Society and
        History* 5.3: 304-45 (repr. in Goody 1968: 27-68).
Goody, J. (ed.)
    1968   *Literacy in Traditional Societies* (Cambridge: Cambridge University
        Press).
    1977   *The Domestication of the Savage Mind* (Cambridge: Cambridge University Press).
Gottwald, N.
    1979   *The Tribes of Yahweh* (Maryknoll: Orbis Books).
Gough, K.
    1968   'Implications of Literacy in Traditional China and India', in J. Goody
        (ed.) 1968: 76, 78.
Gunkel, H.
    1906–63   *Die israelitische Literatur* (Darmstadt: Wissenschaftliche Buchgesellschaft).
Hennen, M., and W.U. Prigge
    1979   *Autorität und Herrschaft* (Erträge der Forschung, 75; Darmstadt: Wissenschaftliche Buchgesellschaft).

Herion, G.A.
1981   'The Role of Historical Narrative in Biblical Thought', *JSOT* 21: 25-57.
1986   'The Impact of Modern and Social Science Assumptions on the Reconstruction of Israelite History', *JSOT* 34: 3-33.

Hooke, S.H.
1927   'The Babylonian New Year Festival', *Journal of the Manchester Egyptian and Oriental Society* 13: 29-38.

Horton, R., and R. Finnegan (eds.)
1973   *Modes of Thought* (London: Faber & Faber).

Jacobson, T.
1975   'Religious Drama in Ancient Mesopotamia', in H. Goedicke and J.J.M. Roberts (eds.), *Unity and Diversity* (London: The Johns Hopkins University Press): 65-97.

Knight, D.A.
1975   *Rediscovering the Traditions of Israel* (Missoula, MT: SBL).

Mendenhall, G.
1973   *The Tenth Generation* (Baltimore: The Johns Hopkins University Press).
1976   'Social Organization in Early Israel', in F.M. Cross (ed.), *Magnalia Dei* (Garden City, NY: Doubleday): 132-51.
1983   'Ancient Israel's Hyphenated History', in D.N. Freedman and D.F. Graf (eds.), *Palestine in Transition* (Sheffield: Almond Press).

McCarter, P.K.
1974   'The Early Diffusion of the Alphabet', *BA* 37: 54-68.

Middleton J., and D. Tait
1958   *Tribes Without Rulers* (London: Routledge & Kegan Paul).

Millard, A.R.
1972   'The Practice of Writing in Ancient Israel', *BA* 35: 98-111.

Miner, H.
1952   'The Folk-Urban Continuum', *American Sociological Review* 17: 529-37.
1968   'Community–Society Continua', in D. Sills (ed.), *International Encyclopedia of the Social Sciences* (New York: Macmillan), III: 174-80.

Mitzman, A.
1971   'Tönnies and German Society 1887–1914', *Journal of the History of Ideas* 32: 507-24.

Mowinckel, S.
1966   *Psalmenstudien* (Amsterdam: Schippers).

Naveh, J.
1968   'A Palaeographic Note on the Distribution of the Hebrew Script', *HTR* 61: 68-74.
1982   *The Early History of the Alphabet* (Jerusalem: Magnes).

Noth, M.
1958   'Geschichtsschreibung, Im AT', *Die Religion in Geschichte und Gegenwart* (3rd edn; Tübingen: Mohr/Siebeck), cols. 1498-1501.

Oeming, M.
  1984   'Bedeutung und Funktionen von Fiktionen in der altestamentlichen
              Geschichtsschreibung', *Evangelische Theologie* 44: 254-66.
Popper, K.
  1957   *The Poverty of Historicism* (London: Routledge & Kegan Paul).
  1959   'Prediction and Prophecy in the Social Sciences', in P. Gardiner (ed.),
              Theories of History (London: Allen & Unwin).
Rad, G. von
  1966   'The Beginnings of Historical Writing in Ancient Israel', in *The
              Problem of the Hexateuch and Other Essays* (Edinburgh: Oliver &
              Boyd): 166-204.
Ranke, L. von
  1983   The Theory and Practice of History (K. Igge and K. Moltke [eds.],;
              New York: Irrington).
Redfield, R.
  1947   'The Folk Society', *American Journal of Sociology* 52.4: 293-308.
Reinitz, R.
  1978   'Niebuhrian Irony and Historical Interpretation', in Canary and
              Konicki (eds.), 1978.
Rogerson, J.W.
  1974   *Myth in Old Testament Interpretation* (BZAW, 134; Berlin: Walter de
              Gruyter).
  1986   'Was Early Israel a Segmentary Society?', *JSOT* 36: 17-26.
Smith, J.Z.
  1968   'Map is not Territory', in *Map is not Territory* (Leiden: Brill): 289-
              307.
Tönnies, F.
  1887   *Gemeinschaft und Gesellschaft* (Leipzig: O.R. Reisland).
Topolski, J.
  1972   'The Model Method in Economic History', *Journal of European
              Economic History* 1: 713-26.
Van Baaren, T.P.
  1984   'The Flexibility of Myth', in A. Dundes (ed.), *Sacred Narrative*
              (Berkeley: University of California Press): 217-24.
Van Seters, J.
  1983   *In Search of History* (New Haven: Yale University Press).
Vaux, R. de
  1961   *Ancient Israel* (London: Darton, Longman & Todd).
Weber, M.
  1977   ' "Objectivity" in Social Science and Social Policy', in F.R. Dallmary
              and T.A. McCarthy (eds.), *Understanding and Social Science* (Notre
              Dame: University of Notre Dame Press): 24-37.
Wise, G.
  1973   *American Historical Explanations* (Homewood: Dorsey).
Wright, G.H.
  1971   *Explanation and Understanding* (Routledge and Kegan Paul).

EARLY ISRAEL IN SOCIOLOGICAL
AND ANTHROPOLOGICAL PERSPECTIVE

JSOT 20 (1981), pp. 47-73

CHIEFS IN ISRAEL*

James W. Flanagan

I

In 1962 Elman Service delineated four stages through which societies evolve as their socio-political organization develops from simpler toward more complex forms. Although drawing comparisons among societies which are spatially and temporarily separated as Service has done does not enable complete and flawless reconstruction of a single society's history, his conclusions have proved useful for analyzing a variety of primitive and archaic civilizations. Ancient Egypt and Mesopotamia have been tested, but neither he nor others have used the cultural evolutionary hypothesis for studying a secondary society such as Israel. The fact that Israel developed under the influence of foreign polities, however, need not prevent comparing its evolution to that of other groups. To exclude Israel would isolate the nation from cross-cultural comparisons, a practice which has proven to be counter-productive in the past.

In this essay, I propose to make the comparisons previously avoided.

---

* I first presented evidence regarding chiefs in Israel in a paper delivered before the Pacific Northwest Region of the Society of Biblical Literature in April 1979. A second draft was delivered in the Israelite History Section of the SBL meeting in November of the same year. I am grateful to colleagues who offered encouragement and suggestions at those sessions. (Author's note: between the time this article first appeared [1981] and this reprinting [1997, 97], Service's stages have been challenged for their seeming rigidity. Because the stages provided only a heuristic aid for my reading of the biblical materials, the challenges need not directly affect the argument or conclusions presented here. For further references see pp. 49-50 [and bibliography] in my 'Finding the Arrows of Time', *Currents in Research: Biblical Studies* 3 [1995]: 37-80.)

Israel's evolution from tribal organization toward full kingship will be reviewed in the light of cultural evolutionary theory, such as that of Service, and in comparison with the processes of succession to high office outlined and described by social anthropologists (Goody 1966). The comparisons will aid not only in outlining the stages of evolution, but also in identifying the principal prime movers that affected the nation's changing social organization (see Vogt 1968: 555) and in explaining the origins of hereditary inequality that eventually led to monarchy (see Flannery 1972). The patterns in Israel, however, cannot be constructed solely on the basis of comparisons supported by isolated bits of information. Such a mosaic would be little more than conjectural history. Rather, the pattern of evolution must truly be in Israel, and the comparisons must be used as a heuristic device which helps us understand and describe the processes that were at work in the ancient society. In sum, we must be careful to discover the evolutionary pattern rather than anxious to create it.

Service's analysis of bands, tribes, chiefdoms, and states, and his description of the factors which move a society along its evolutionary trajectory have been so compelling and the cross-cultural comparisons so strikingly consistent that scholars from many schools of thought within several disciplines have adopted his summary with little or no modification. Sahlins (1968), Sanders and Price (1968), Flannery (1972), and E.O. Wilson (1978) adopted the paradigm in their analyses of varied and scattered civilizations. Fried (1967), while agreeing with a four-part division in the evolutionary process, has differed with Service over the description of the stages and the role which stratification plays in bringing about a centralized monopoly of force (Fried 1968; Service 1978; see Redman 1978: 201-13). Like Fried, others have disagreed with portions of Service's description while accepting the general outline of his four stages (Renfrew 1974; Peebles and Kus 1977; see Cohen 1978a; 1978b; and Claessen and Skalnik 1978a).

The impact of the 1962 study has overshadowed modifications Service introduced in 1975. By distinguishing primitive societies known through ethnographic studies from ancient societies that can be retrieved only by prehistoric archaeology, he reduced the discernible phases in the latter to three by combining bands with tribes in a single stage (1975: 303-305). For ancient, prehistoric societies, Service now prefers a new classification with different nomenclature, namely, a tripartite division of segmental (i.e. egalitarian) society, chiefdom, and archaic civilization. Even in the new division, however, he has left his description of chiefdom intact and has continued to insist upon its universality in the evolutionary schema of both primitive and archaic societies (1975: 87). He now admits that, while chiefdoms can be distinguished from segmented societies with relative ease, discriminating between them and the archaic civilizations is a more difficult task (Service 1975: 305; Sanders and Marino 1970: 9; Claessen and Skalnik 1978b: 629).

Because of the universal claims that have accompanied the discussion of chiefdoms, it is well to note several limitations which cultural evolutionists place upon their assertions. First, a predictable evolutionary schema does not guarantee that every human society has evolved to full statehood. This is an obvious but easily forgotten limitation, especially when one is attempting to discern the boundaries between chiefdoms and kingdoms. Second, not all archaic civilizations and states reflect the same patterns of social organization (i.e. not all were monarchies). And finally, evolutionary schemata do not imply that every developing society changes at the same rate or exhibits all the characteristics which another society exhibits at its parallel stage of development. Human societies are not so easily typed, and thus the factors interrelating processual phenomena militate against facile generalizing (Vogt 1968: 535; Leach 1968: 344).

Secondary societies whose development is influenced by polities outside their borders call for additional caution beyond that needed when studying primary or pristine civilizations (Price 1978). In them, the developments already achieved in the alien influential group affect the formation of the subordinate or neighboring society, especially if the secondary group is caught in the throes of tumultuous and unstable conditions.

Caveats such as these explain why few scholars have considered the possibility of chiefs in ancient Israel. Anthropologists have chosen to ignore the Syro-Palestine region even when considering Egypt and Mesopotamia because they prefer to draw evidence from primary societies where the 'natural' processes of development can be tested without concern for acculturation from the outside.[1] Biblical scholars, on the other hand, have accepted the dominant view of the biblical tradition, namely, that Israel moved immediately from tribal confederation

---

1. Professor R.A. Rappaport, The Chair of the Department of Anthropology at the University of Michigan, first suggested this reason to me.

to monarchy. Only recently have they begun to analyze the socio-political forces that accompanied the change.[2]

II

Our investigation of Israel's steps toward monarchy may begin with the statement of Service's thesis on the origins of states:

> [The thesis] locates the origins of government in the institutionalization of centralized leadership. That leadership, in developing its administrative functions for the maintenance of the society, grew into a hereditary aristocracy. The nascent bureaucracy's economic and religious functions developed as the extent of its services, its autonomy, and its size increased, Thus the earliest government worked to protect, not another class or stratum of society, but itself. It legitimized itself in its role of maintaining the whole society (1975: 8).

Here Service argued that the prominence and success of a leader contributes directly to his authority so that, in effect, the community creates its own leadership by becoming dependent upon an individual's charismatic talents. A reciprocal and spiraling relationship is established in which a leader's traits inspire the group's dependence. The dependency in turn enhances the role of the leader so that his success guarantees even greater dependence, and so on, until the role becomes institutionalized in an office.

The gradually ascending authority invested in leadership makes it difficult to draw definite boundary lines between the organizational stages. 'Big man' leadership characteristic of segmental society embodies traits of an embryonic chieftaincy (Service 1975: 75), and a chief is himself an initiatory 'king' whose office may develop into the centralized monopoly of force typically found in the subsequent stage of early state and archaic civilization (Service 1975: 86). So, while a chiefdom stands between segmental society and coercive state, it exemplifies traits of both.

Describing chiefdoms in this fashion introduces a problem which Service sought to avoid. Inherent in discussions of evolutionary processes is the implication that intermediate stages do not have a status of

---

2. Norman Gottwald made occasional references to Israel's tendency toward chiefdom in his study of Yahwistic tribes even though the subject fell outside the scope of his work (1979: 297-98, 322-23). Frank Frick (1979) has drawn attention to evidence, literary and archaeological, supporting a chiefdom hypothesis.

their own, that is, that they are only intermediate and cannot be examined in their own right. But to assume this about chiefdoms would be a fallacy and would jeopardize understanding the nature and role of chiefs in society (Renfrew 1974: 71; Earle 1978: 1).

Still, descriptions of chiefdoms in anthropological literature tend to be lists of similarities and differences comparing and contrasting them with preceding and succeeding phases. Unlike tribes, chiefdoms exhibit sumptuary rules and taboos surrounding the chief (Service 1962: 145). They have ranking systems which add a new structural principle to kinship ties whereby those nearest the chief assume the status of nobility (Service 1962: 141). An emphasis is placed upon the leader as redistributor or, in Harris's terminology, as warrior-intensifier-redistributor (1979: 94). Theocratic claims which are lacking in tribal societies are made on behalf of the chief, and a dichotomy between the chief's center and the dependent settlements develops (Sahlins 1968: 7).

In contrast with states, chiefdoms lack social stratification into classes based upon occupational specialization. They also lack the ability to impose coercive physical sanctions and have to rely upon non-legal enforcement (Flannery 1972: 403). The government of a state is more highly centralized, with a professional ruling class including priests and bureaucrats who function as substitutes for the king in his many expanded roles (Sahlins 1968: 9). In chiefdoms, such tasks are shared by the chief personally.

The character of chiefdoms has been conveniently summarized by Renfrew (1974: 73) who listed twenty traits which distinguish chiefdoms from egalitarian societies:

1. ranked society

2. redistribution of produce organized by the chief

3. greater population density

4. increase in the total number in the society

5. increase in the size of individual residence groups

6. greater productivity

7. more clearly defined territorial boundaries or borders

8. more integrated society with a greater number of socio-centric statuses

9. centers which coordinate social and religious as well as economic activity

10. frequent ceremonies and rituals serving wide social purposes

11. rise of priesthood

12. relation to a total environment (and hence redistribution)—i.e. to some ecological diversity

13. specialization, not only regional or ecological, but also through the pooling of individual skills in large co-operative endeavors

14. organization and deployment of public labor, sometimes for agricultural work (e.g. irrigation) and/or for building temples, temple mounds, or pyramids

15. improvement of craft specialization

16. potential for territorial expansion— associated with the 'rise' and 'fall' of chiefdoms

17. reduction of internal strife

18. pervasive inequality of persons or groups in the society associated with permanent leadership, effective in fields other than the economic

19. distinctive dress or ornament for those of high status

20. no true government to back up decisions by legalized force

Chiefly authority, therefore, is rooted in skills of warfare, dancing, solidifying allegiances, and redistributing goods. These exhibit the chief's charisma and inspire confidence and a sense of solidarity among his followers (Service 1975: 74). Eventually, the people begin to expect and hope that the chief's exceptional qualities will be passed on to his sons so that, over time, a system of succession gradually develops with devolution of office to the chief's offspring, usually to the eldest male. Successful and successive handing on of leadership within the chief's family (dynasty) eventually leads to primogeniture as a binding custom (Service 1962: 293).

Studies on succession have demonstrated that in spite of the stability which presumption of primogeniture brings to the transmission of office, no system of succession is completely automatic even where next-of-kin procedures are thought to be in force (Goody 1966: 13). Succession to chieftaincy is often a highly competitive process with contenders vying for the paramount role both during and after the incumbent's reign (Robertson 1976). Struggles for power often leave a string of assassinations, frustrated pretenders, and exiled losers in their wake so that turbulence rather than tranquility governs the transferral of office in these cultures (Barth 1961: 84).

The competition and tension surrounding high office affects the relationship not only of incumbent to potential successors, but also of competing rivals to each other. The encroachment and usurpation that competing chiefs and successors perpetrate upon one another is so extreme at times that in monadic societies groups often migrate in order to find a strong chief who can bring a modicum of peace to their lives (Barth 1961: 85).

Goody (1966: 5-37) has identified four principal variables affecting the tranquility of successions: uniqueness of the office, time of succession, means of selecting a successor, and relationship between successive office holders. He has found that it is typical for societies to manipulate these in order to cope with disruptions that accompany the transferral of office.

The combined options available to a society are many. When a unique office is open to a number of potential successors, the tension among the eligibles can be reduced by restricting the pool of eligibles or by dividing the office or territory. Tension both between incumbent and successors and among successors can be regulated by adjusting the time of succession making it either pre-mortem or post-mortem in order to bring a strong leader to power at a convenient time. Interregnums, stand-ins, stake holders, and co-regencies are typical forms of partial transfer of office which are employed in order to stabilize government and to insure continuity of mature leadership.

Even when the pre-mortem traumas of dethronement, abdication, and usurpation are not factors, the means of selecting successors is often not left to chance. Procedures vary according to the needs of the office. Where special qualities are required, the selection is apt to be highly regulated so that even where primogeniture plays a major role, divination, appointment, and force—always the final arbiter (Goody 1966: 18)—are also used. The time of selection (not to be confused with the time of accession) can also be adjusted as a ploy for decreasing indeterminancy and diminishing competition among rival successors.

The relationship between successive office holders impinges upon other aspects of indeterminate succession. For example, the larger the pool of eligible successors, the greater the distance between the incumbent and his successor and, therefore, the less the tension within the organization itself (Goody 1966: 23). On the other hand, the greater the indeterminacy of succession, the greater the tension among eligibles and the more frequent the struggles for power.

Seen in the light of such variables, the customs and practices which societies including Israel have adopted assume new meaning. For instance, dynastic shedding can be recognized as a common practice whereby a dynasty or group of eligibles is reduced. This can be accomplished in several ways. In some systems females are automatically excluded from office while distant males are not, or in others sons of a ruler's siblings are excluded so that the system limits succession to the lineal (vertical) line by transferring rights from father to son to grandson, and so on. In lateral systems, however, office is passed along within a single generation before being transferred to the next generation, making it highly unlikely that all males in each generation will survive long enough to assume office. In either system, rather than determining the priority of the sons themselves, elimination among a sibling group may be accomplished by designating a favored mother whose son will succeed. This practice, reminiscent of Bathsheba's choosing Solomon, arises where polygamous marriages make seniority by birth hard to determine or where office is restricted to sons born after the father assumed office (Goody 1966: 33; 1976: 86-98; Cuisenier 1980: 13-14).

A general movement in history from hereditary toward appointive office has accompanied the growing complexity of society and the consequent need for technical competence (Goody 1966: 44). But because appointment is seldom the sole means of selection for high office, in systems where hereditary practices are deeply rooted, appointive (or elective) procedures usually modify rather than replace them. In most cases, however, a candidate's economic and military resources affect his chances more than his access to royal ancestors (Goody 1970: 637).

Although the conditions described here apply to other high offices as well as to chiefdoms, they illustrate forces by which limited access to office can transform the kinship structures of a society in ways that affect succession (Service 1962: 155). Two principal effects which are important for understanding the affairs of Saul and David can be noted: the formation of conical clans and the emergence of ramage descent groups (Service 1975: 79). The former are unilineal kin groups in which, because of primogeniture, certain members are considered closer to the central line and have greater status and access to common property than do others (Alland and McCay 1973: 165). Since unequal access to property and office is a characteristic of ranked society, conical clans signal a move away from segmental social organization.

A ramage descent group is one type of kinship structure caused by limited access. Where first-born sons are expected to succeed their fathers, other sons splinter off to begin their own lineages with themselves as heads of the ramages or 'branches' (Service 1962: 158). Although they retain rights in the central line, the sons' inheritance and office are passed on to their own sons rather than reverting to the father's line. However, if the first-born's line is truncated by the death of all heirs, a childless marriage, or other causes, the right of succession moves laterally to the second son's lineage, or as necessary, to the third and so on. An individual's relative position in this structure is ranked and regulated by genealogy (Earle 1978: 168). Shifts in genealogies therefore reflect shifts in the relative position of eligibles. Fluctuations in the priority list can be frequent and complex because of polygamous marriages and power struggles which can change the eligibility of individuals rapidly.

Optative affiliation can also affect kinship patterns by placing an exogamous male in line for succession, even in an unilineal descent group (Service 1962: 162; Earle 1978: 175). This is a strategy societies employ in order to insure heirs and successors where male descendants are lacking (Goody 1976: 93-96). The phenomenon, first identified by Firth, combines traits of the epiclerate (substitution of a daughter for a son) and adoption. It allows newly married couples to choose affiliation with either parental group, and usually includes a choice of residence as well (Service 1962: 153). The couple generally elects the family that will bestow the higher status upon them. If it is the wife's family, her husband may be taken into her kin group and eventually inherit the title and name of her father. Through this form of adoption, the children of the couple fall in line of succession with the maternal grandfather's line, so descent technically remains patrilineal. The practice will be recalled below when discussing David's marriage to Michal and the latter's barrenness.

III

This brief summary of the circumstances accompanying the development of chiefdoms and the transferral of high office in chiefly societies provides the background for examining premonarchic Israel. To compare the development of chiefdoms in other societies with the evolution of Israelite leadership, we need not delay to defend the existence of an egalitarian, segmental phase among the Yahwists. This stage has been amply documented by the biblical writers and has been extensively analyzed in studies by Noth (1966) and Gottwald (1979).

The end of the Israelite tribal period coincided with a series of events that brought the Yahwists under Philistine domination and initiated the rise of a centralized leadership. For our purposes we may assume that the end of the segmental stage is symbolized in the Bible by the loss of the ark reported in 1 Samuel 4.

The literary record portrays the period following the loss of the ark in terms that can only be read as tumultuous and chaotic, an atmosphere which seems to have persisted until the completion of Solomon's succession and the slayings of Adonijah, Shimei, and Joab in 1 Kings 1–2. Beginning with Samuel's vacillation between legitimating the growing pressures toward centralized rule and refusing to sanction them, deeply felt tensions divided the communities of his, Saul's, and David's days (1 Samuel 5–8).

Saul's election and rule did little to stabilize the situation or to reassure the people. Even when we allow for intentional discrediting by later anti-Saul biblical writers, we are left with a picture of a tragic individual (Gunn 1980: 23-31). A tall, handsome agriculturalist who emerged as a leader because of his military prowess, Saul enjoyed some ability to evoke support of a militia (1 Sam. 9.2; 11), but he eventually failed and stood defenseless before his enemies and slayers, the Philistines (1 Samuel 31). He was a warrior and an intensifier who apparently performed rituals, a duty he shared with the priests (1 Sam. 13.8-15), and who took part in ecstatic religious movements (1 Sam. 10.9-14), although he eventually was chastised for cultic violations (1 Sam. 14.31-35).

In retrospect his leadership can be recognized as having been handicapped from the start. Unlike the Philistines, Saul seems to have lacked the Iron-Age technology needed to exploit the potential of the cattle and plough agriculture of his day or to wage effective war (1 Sam. 13.19-22). He also suffered from periods of depression and jealousy so severe that a musician's service was required to calm him (1 Sam. 15.23). Although history eventually confirmed that Saul's fear of those around him was justified, it prevented him from gaining a useful perspective upon his situation and crippled him when he was forced to compete. His personal weakness contributed directly to David's success, a situation which is typical of chiefs competing for the paramount power.

By comparison, David was a much stronger person and an obvious potential successor. He was handsome, prudent, well-spoken, and one

who made a good first impression (1 Sam. 16.12-19). He was a
musician and poet (1 Sam. 16.16; 2 Sam. 1.22). He was a successful
warrior as well as a popular leader of armies and of the oppressed
(1 Sam. 22.1-2; 27; 30). He created solidarity by his personal traits
and by redistribution, and he enhanced his popularity on many
occasions by sharing his booty with friends, allies, neighbors, and
suzerains (1 Sam. 21; 25; 27.9; 30).

David's life was closely identified with Saul's house even though his
personal relationship with Saul eventually deteriorated to the point of
open hostility. He married Saul's daughter Michal after having been
refused the hand of Merab and after paying the agreed bride-price
(1 Samuel 18); he struck a covenant with Jonathan, Saul's eldest son
(1 Samuel 18). On separate occasions, both Michal and Jonathan helped
David escape from their father's wrath (1 Samuel 19; 20). Later,
although David retained affection for Jonathan and his son (2 Samuel 9),
he appears to have reduced Michal to a pawn who could be used in
whatever manner he found advantageous (2 Sam. 3.12-16; 6.20-23).

As would be expected of competing chiefs, the animosity between
Saul and David spilled over into their houses and their entourages.
After Saul died at the hands of an enemy David served, a long war
was waged between their two houses (2 Sam. 3.1). The conflict led to
the treasonous negotiations between David and Abner, who bargained
away the crown of Ishbosheth, Saul's son and successor (2 Samuel 3).

The rift between the factions deepened when David permitted the
wholesale slaughter of Saul's family in a blood feud with the
Gibeonites. The massacre cost the lives of all surviving male heirs in
Saul's house except for Jonathan's son, the crippled Mephibosheth, and
his son Micah (2 Samuel 21; 9). The consequences were widespread.
Shimei, a supporter of Saul's house, cursed David for his complicity
in the deaths, and the long-standing feud fed the imaginations of
Absalom and Sheba who organized rebellions to topple David (2 Sam.
15; 16.5-8; 20).

Although the attempted pre-mortem succession by rebellion failed
for Absalom and Sheba, Adonijah, presumably the eldest survivor
among David's sons, tried again when his father became incapacitated
by old age (1 Kings 1). His efforts were quashed, however, by the
appointment of Solomon, the son of the favored wife Bathsheba. With
Nathan, she arranged for her son to be named successor-designate.

This survey illustrates the competitiveness which characterized the emergence of centralized leadership in Israel and demonstrates how eligibles were pitted against incumbents and against each other: Saul feared David and warned Jonathan that his rights of inheritance were in danger; Ishbosheth's succession was challenged by the betrayal of his strong man and cousin, Abner; David's accession in Hebron after Ziklag was during a time of instability in the North and must have had the tacit approval of the Philistines. Absalom's revolt, Sheba's rebellion, and Adonijah's accession, linked with the murder of all the principal actors in the drama of succession except David, fit with other events to form a long chain of intrigues which reached from the early years of Saul down to the appointment of Solomon. When the murders of Joab (son of David's sister), Shimei, and Adonijah had been accomplished, a monopoly of force finally replaced chiefly rule in ancient Israel.

IV

This summary derived from the narrative portions of the books of Samuel can be tested against information retained in the genealogical sections of Ruth, Samuel, and Chronicles. There the counters in the chiefly games can be seen: kinship, politics, economics, and religion, the four rubrics anthropologists use to organize their discussions of primitive and archaic societies. Since narratives and genealogies are not subjected to the same reinterpretations at the hand of traditional scribes, parallels and agreements between the two types of literature make a particularly compelling case for the stages of development in an ancient society.

I have examined several of the genealogies elsewhere (Flanagan 1983) and have found that their function in Israel parallels genealogies in other cultures. A. Malamat (1973) and R. Wilson (1977) have demonstrated similar parallels for other sections of the Yahwistic tradition. Here, I rely heavily upon these earlier studies, and my own, for what I have to say about genealogical evidence.

It is important to understand the function of genealogies in early preliterate and literate societies and to be familiar with several of their most common traits. Genealogies typically exhibit a characteristic called 'fluidity', that is, a moving of names within, onto, or off genealogical lists when the relationship of the named individuals or groups changes. Since genealogies record and regulate relationships in the domestic, politico-jural, and religious spheres of life, fluidity is demanded in order for a genealogy to remain functional. If genealogies were not adjusted as relationships changed, they would lose their meaning and would soon be lost (Wilson 1977: 27-54). As groups migrate, individuals die, or persons' statuses change, the effects of each are reflected in the genealogical record.

A comparison of 1 Sam. 14.49-51, 1 Sam. 31.2 (= 1 Chron. 10.2), 2 Sam. 21.7-8, 1 Chron. 8.33-40, and 1 Chron. 9.39-43 illustrates how Israel's records were adjusted in order to keep them abreast of the rapidly changing alliances outlined above. Consequently, the genealogies serve as guides for reconstructing the history of the period and for tracing the fate of Saul's house. In diagram form, the genealogies appear in Table 1.

In the diagrams, we see that when Abner lost his life, and consequently neither he nor his lineage continued to figure prominently in the affairs of Israel, his name was dropped from the genealogy (compare 1 Sam. 14 with 1 Chron. 8 and 9). Ner, on the other hand, was elevated to the vertical line above Kish and Saul, probably because his importance had already been deeply implanted in the consciousness of the community. Even though the reasons for his prominence are no longer evident to us, we might conjecture that as head of a ramage, Ner had been 'ranked' because he stood high among the pool of eligibles if all male successors to Saul in the vertical line should have been eliminated. Unlikely as this may have seemed in the early days of Saul's reign, the eventual violent deaths of Saul's sons and grandsons made the possibility of lateral succession much less remote. Indeed, it appears as if Abner might have succeeded Ishbosheth if he (Abner) had been successful in the intrigues he initiated.

The order in the birth sequence of Saul's sons changed over time as their rank fluctuated (cf. 1 Samuel 14, 31; 1 Chronicles 8, 9). The elusive Ishvi/Eshbaal (elsewhere Ishbosheth/Ishbaal) moved between fourth- and second-born position, and Abinadab and Malchishua traded positions several times. It is important to observe, however, that Jonathan was consistently ranked as first-born, even after his death and the succession of Ishbosheth. His unwavering prominence demonstrates that the genealogists remembered that Jonathan's line had continued through Meribaal/Mephibosheth, Micah, etc. (cf. 1 Chronicles 8 and 9). Because of his physical handicap, Mephibosheth did not succeed Saul, and as a result his name was not firmly set nor his generation clearly remembered (compare 2 Samuel 21 with

Table 1

GENEALOGIES OF SAUL'S HOUSE

1 Samuel 14.49-51

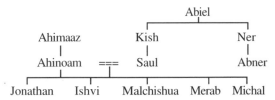

1 Samuel 31.2 (= 1 Chronicles 10.2)

```
                Saul
        ┌────────┼────────┐
    Jonathan  Abinadab  Malchishua
```

2 Samuel 21.7-8

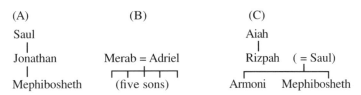

1 Chronicles 8.33-40 and 9.39-43

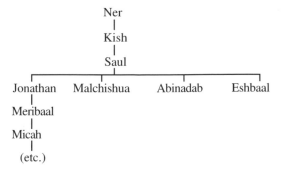

1 Chronicles 8 and 9). Nevertheless, after the Gibeonite massacre of Saul's house, his name was retained as an important link between Saul and later eligibles in Saul's lineage. The retention of the records of Jonathan's descendants explains why Mephibosheth expected the house

of Israel to give him back the kingdom of his father when David was forced into exile by Absalom's coup (2 Sam. 16.3). He assumed that David had been a stand-in who led in place of his wife Michal perhaps for one generation or until Micah achieved majority. Michal's barrenness was connected to Mephibosheth's fortunes because it contributed to the uncertainty of whether the office would pass on in her father's line or in David's through a son born of another wife. If Michal had had a son, the competitors might have chosen different sides.

David's marriage to Michal and his insistence that she be returned before negotiations with Abner could begin must be viewed in the light of the intrigue and indeterminacy that was caused by the deaths and disabilities in Saul's house. The daughter's importance for David's rise within the North can hardly be overestimated. In ways similar to the case of Zelophehad's daughters in Numbers 27 and 36, the issue was inheritance and succession rights of brotherless daughters (cf. Jobling 1980: 203-204). In David's case, he cleverly employed optative affiliation as one ground upon which he could appeal to northern support.

Political factors also figured prominently in David's competition for the paramount chief's role. For instance, when Saul forced him to withdraw to a remote outlying area, he used the distance to build a personal powerbase and to begin his own lineage while waiting for another chance at the chieftaincy. The circumstances were typical of a losing contender. David's rise in Ziklag was as vassal to the Philistines, the arch-enemy of Israel, and his accession in Hebron must have been with Philistine support or acquiescence. Because the biblical writers spent no time trying to connect these successes with David's affinity to the house of Saul, we must conclude that his rise in the South was predicated on different grounds than his succession in the North where optative affiliation played a part that it did not in the affairs of Judah. This may explain why there is no genealogy in the Samuel material connecting the house of Jesse to the house of Saul even though there is narrative evidence of Jesse's sons serving Saul (1 Samuel 17–18). As a losing contender, David had begun his own ramage with its own rights. When the North was finally forced to turn to him for leadership, he accepted their charge from a position of strength and made no effort to subvert Judah to the primacy of Israel. Instead he maintained two bases of power (centred in a 'neutral'

Jerusalem) which he could juggle to his own advantage. In effect, he laid the foundation for the tortuous days that were to follow in the history of Israel and Judah.

The economic as well as the political manoeuvres which took place in David's house are evident in the genealogical records of his family. These are found in lists preserved in Ruth 4.18-23, 1 Chron. 2.9-17, 2 Sam. 17.24, 2 Sam. 3.2-5, 2 Sam. 5.13-16, 1 Chron. 3.1-9, 1 Chron. 14.3-7, and 2 Samuel 11 (see Table 2).

Here again, we must point out several characteristics of genealogies, even though we must limit our remarks to those traits which show the chiefly nature of the early Davidic reign. Foremost is the difference between linear and segmental genealogies. Linear genealogies such as found in Ruth 4 serve to legitimate the last name by connecting it with the names of individuals, groups, or places (sometimes mixed together in the same list) which stand above it. Unlike segmental genealogies, the linear do not rank in priority a pool of eligibles who might all be competing for office simultaneously.

This difference has several causes, but here we may concentrate upon the different sociopolitical situation reflected in the two types. Segmented genealogies belong to segmented societies where kinship ties are stressed, while linear genealogies belong to societies where inheritance and succession are not determined completely by familistic concerns. Since chiefdoms hang in the betwixt and the between, we must avoid making universal claims about this difference, but we can expect to find linear genealogies in ranked societies and segmental ones in egalitarian communities. A shift from one dominant form to the other, therefore, suggests a change in the sociopolitical organization of the time.

In David's case, we find both segmented and linear genealogies. For instance, in 1 Chron. 2.9-17, which is similar to the linear genealogy in Ruth 4, segmented and linear genealogies are combined to trace David's lineage from Hezron (from Perez in Ruth) and to record his position as youngest male among seven sons and two daughters of Jesse. In 2 Samuel 17, however, a segmented genealogy has been used to list his sister Zeruiah as mother of Joab, and Abigail as wife of Jether/Ithra, father of Amasa.

Table 2

GENEALOGIES OF DAVID'S HOUSE

Ruth 4.18-23   *2 Samuel 17.24*

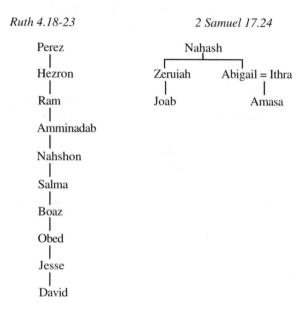

1 Chronicles 2.9-17

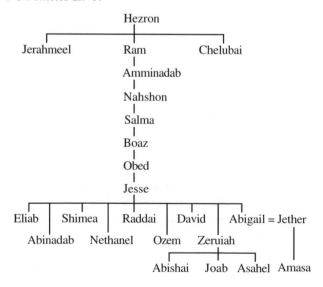

Table 2 (continued)

2 Samuel 11

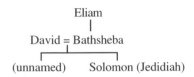

Eliam
|
David = Bathsheba
|
(unnamed)   Solomon (Jedidiah)

2 Samuel 3.2-5		*1 Chronicles 3.1-9*	
(Hebron)		(Hebron-Jerusalem)	
son	*mother*	*son*	*mother*
Amnon	Ahinoam	Amnon	Ahinoam
Chileab	Abigail	Daniel	Abigail
Absalom	Maacah	Absalom	Maacah
Adonijah	Haggith	Adonijah	Haggith
Shephatiah	Abital	Shephatiah	Abital
Ithream	Eglah	Ithream	Eglah

2 Samuel 5.13-16		*1 Chron. 14.3-7*
(Jerusalem)		(Jerusalem)
Shammua	Shimea	Shammua
Shobab	Shobab	Shobab
Nathan	Nathan	Nathan
Solomon	Solomon (4 by Bathshua)	Solomon
Ibhar	Ibhar	Ibhar
Elishua	Elishama	Elishua
	Eliphelet	Elpelet
	Nogah	Nogah
Nepheg	Nepheg	Nepheg
Japhia	Japhia	Japhia
Elishama	Elishama	Elishama
Eliada	Eliada	Beelida
Eliphelet	Eliphelet	Eliphelet

In other lists (2 Samuel 3 and 5; 1 Chronicles 3 and 14) the names of David's children have been recorded, but not without some discrepancies. The variations, however, are strikingly consistent. The sons born at Hebron were listed with their mothers' names, whereas those born in Jerusalem are listed without mothers. The dropping of mothers' names indicates that David was a chief at Hebron where the order within his ramage, ranked according to mothers because of polygamous marriages, had to be maintained for determining statuses and succession rights; but once the bureaucracy of a monarchy in Jerusalem made primogeniture less relevant for succession, the mothers' names were no longer remembered. Here Israel's genealogies functioned in the same manner as those in other societies. The only mother from Jerusalem who was named was Bathshua/Bathsheba, identified as mother of four sons, one of whom was Solomon (2 Samuel 11 and 1 Chronicles 3). In the Court History even Solomon's name was confused with a variant, Jedidiah.

Dropping the mothers' names when the capital moved from Hebron to Jerusalem is typical of transitions from chiefdoms to archaic states. But the continuing competition for David's office after the relocation indicates that full statehood was not achieved at once. During the transitional period, succession remained indeterminate even though the growing complexity of the leader's tasks required candidates who were capable of administering the expanding bureaucracy of an empire. By the time Solomon had succeeded David, pre-mortem, appointive measures complemented heredity as a means of stabilizing the situation. Solomon was chosen from among Bathsheba's sons, and almost as an echo from the past, her name was recorded because of his prominence.

V

Service and others stressed the role which redistributing, organizing, and military leadership play in a chief's rise. Although we have no record of Saul's generosity, the narratives suggest that he was a solidifier who finally failed to knit firm alliances between the village populations and his central administration (Mendenhall 1975: 162). This factor contributed to the decline in his popularity and to the growth of David's public favor. As a result, Saul was unable to establish a state of dependency through redistribution, which otherwise might have stabilized his leadership. The fact that Ishbosheth was forced to lead from afar, probably with only a fraction of Saul's following, also indicates the extent of Saul's failure. He was too weak to rout the Philistines, and they rather than he controlled many of the economic resources.

In contrast, David's rise was closely identified with his role as warrior-intensifier-redistributor. He distributed booty from his raids to his own followers, to the oppressed, to Achish of Gath, and to the elders of Judah—in effect, to those whom he depended upon for his rise. Yet in spite of this record, the difference between such earlier acts of generosity and the later parasitical dependency of his Jerusalem administration upon the resources of the people is striking. The lists of his Jerusalem court officers included commanders of armies and of the forced labor (2 Sam. 20.23-26), and the census he ordered must have been intended as a basis for the taxation and conscription needed to staff and support these forces. The list and the census both reflect a dramatic shift in the values and organization of the Yahwistic community. David the chief had begun to act like a king.

As we would expect in chiefdoms, the religious functions mentioned in the biblical narratives also indicate that Saul's and David's reigns were theocracies. Both individuals were anointed by Samuel; both performed cultic rites; both used priests and prophets. In short, religion was used by both to legitimate their authority and to help maintain social control.

This is especially obvious in David's case where the role of religion was displayed at every major step in his rise. He consulted Yahweh when considering the move to Hebron; he transferred the ark to Jerusalem; he took part in a ritual dance in order to legitimate his new center; and he relied upon a dynastic oracle to assure the continuation of his line. But do these religious functions suggest a chiefdom or a monarchy? Two episodes demonstrate that the people's religious feelings restrained a rapid, total transition to kingship during David's Jerusalem years. The first of these was the prohibition against building a temple (2 Sam. 7). The second was the punishment meted out to David for his taking the census (2 Sam. 24). Each episode was a limitation upon David's power, the likes of which were not evident later when Solomon completed the evolution to full monopoly of force. They suggest that David stood on the boundary line between chiefdom and kingdom.

VI

A review of the royal terminology associated with Saul's and David's reigns reveals a pattern of usage that parallels the stages of cultural evolution outlined here. Although the term is still under study and open to debate, we may suggest that *nāgîd* stands for the chiefly role of Saul and David.

A great deal of ambiguity has accompanied recent studies of the term. Since Albrecht Alt's classic study of the formation of the Israelite state, most scholars have followed him in assuming that *nāgîd* described the religious calling to leadership while *melek* designated the office conferred by the peoples' acclaim (Alt 1968: 274-80). The distinction according to Alt was between religious and political functions which were present simultaneously in a leader's reign.

Studies made since Alt have helped to clarify the meaning of the term, but they have not completely resolved the confusion between *nāgîd* and *melek*. Evidence from the Sefire treaties (Fitzmyer 1958: 459; 1967: 112-13) and the Nora stele (Peckham 1972: 457-68) have influenced Cross's translation of *nāgîd* as 'commander' (Cross 1973: 220-21). For Cross, the term emphasized both the continuity with leadership in the time of the judges and the covenantal character of appointment to leadership roles. He distinguished its use from that of the later term, *melek*, which he believed was used to describe the 'routinized' or dynastic kingship of David and Solomon.

Richter (1965) distinguished three phases in the development of the term. *Nāgîd* in the pre-Davidic period meant a type of military leader specially chosen and installed. During the Davidic monarchy, the title was applied to the king and was equated with *melek*. In the post-Davidic age, it became a title for religious functionaries and administrative officials.

A more recent examination of the term in 1 Samuel by McCarter takes up Mettinger's suggestion that a reigning king could designate a crown prince, a *nāgîd*, to be his successor (Mettinger 1976: 151-84). McCarter's preference is for 'king-designate' because 'In every case the *nāgîd* is an individual singled out from among others as leader' and because the term is usually applied to a king before he begins to reign (McCarter 1980: 178-79).

As a group these studies have shown that *nāgîd* underwent its own evolution corresponding to stages in the overall development of Israel's sociopolitical organization. They have agreed upon the need for a distinction between *nāgîd* and *melek*, but they have also claimed that the terms cannot be completely separated. For these scholars, the words apply either to different aspects of a leader's authority or to different times in the office holder's reign. This confusion can be explained by the gradual evolution in the role of the *nāgîd* as chiefdom gave way to monarchy.

The case for chiefs in Israel does not stand or fall with the meaning of *nāgîd*, but its use in the books of Samuel fits the developmental scheme I have outlined for chiefdom in the North. One of the earliest narrative traditions in the Samuel material is that of Samuel the seer in 1 Sam. 9.1–10.16 which systematically avoided the use of *melek* in favor of *nāgîd* whenever referring to Saul. McKenzie (1962) suggested that the usage reflected the pro-Davidic prejudice of the biblical scribes who reserved *melek* for David who was for them the first true king. The explanation ignores Saul's historical role as chief and overlooks the fact that the term was used when Yahweh rejected Saul (1 Sam. 13.14) and when the tribes of Israel selected David to be their *nāgîd* (2 Sam. 5.2) as Abigail, wife of Nabal, had predicted (1 Sam. 25.30). Each is an early use describing the historical role of Saul and David as chiefs.

David's role as *nāgîd* was also recalled when he chastised Michal (2 Sam. 6.21) and in the Davidic oracle (2 Sam. 7.8). Both references were made in connection with David's relationship to the house of Saul or with his humble pastoral origins. The passages recall David's early role before going on to celebrate and to symbolize his movement toward kingship. The ritualistic quality of these passages makes them especially important for analyzing the social structure of the period, but it also makes them exceptionally complex. Although they require more investigation than can be given here, we may emphasize that at the point of transition between Hebron and Jerusalem, between chief and king, between house of Saul and house of David, the ritualistic transfer of the ark and the utterance of the dynastic oracle were recalled. As in other societies, ritual was used to mediate the transitions and developments which were played out on the stage of history.

VII

To summarize and conclude: the literary record of the reigns of Saul and David reports a period of trauma and uncertainty when individuals competed forcefully for the paramount role. Murders, broken and restored alliances, marriages and separations, sharing of booty, unifying and leading militia, kinship ties, redistribution, and appeals to religious legitimacy all figured as strands in the warp and woof of the social, political, economic, and religious fabric of the day. Studies of the cultural evolutionary and succession patterns of other societies have described similar transitional circumstances and have concluded that such times were periods when the society was led by chiefs. The descriptions drawn from those non-Yahwistic and primary societies fit the evidence found in the literature of Yahwistic, secondary Israel. In fact, most of the elements on Renfrew's list of twenty characteristics of chiefdoms cited above can be documented in Israel. These indicate both the presence of chiefs and the absence of a strong centralized monopoly of force equipped with laws during the time of Saul and the early years of David. Since the parallels between Renfrew's list and the biblical evidence are not random, and because the evolutionary process outlined by Service is clearly evident in Israel, the cross-cultural comparisons are valid and productive. They have helped us understand the processes at work in ancient Israel and have aided in dismissing conjectures about the immediate transition from tribal league to full-blown monarchy.

In retrospect, we can see that Michal's childlessness left the future of Saul's house unclear, and it raised a question which optative affiliation usually did not raise: Should David's successor be from his house or Michal's? As would be expected, two views prevailed, one perhaps northern and pro-Saulide, the other southern and pro-Davidic. The appointment of Solomon temporarily resolved the question in favor of David by shifting the line of succession away from its northern Yahwistic roots. The outcome has left us to wonder what difference a male child born to David and Michal would have made for the history of Israel. But perhaps we do not have to conjecture. Solomon solidified kingship and a schism was avoided, but only for a generation.

BIBLIOGRAPHY

Achteimer, P.J. (ed)
　1974　　　*Society of Biblical Literature 1979 Seminar Papers* (Missoula, MT: Scholars Press).
Alland, A., and B. McCay
　1973　　　'The Concept of Adaption in Biological and Cultural Evolution', in J.J. Honigmann (ed.), *Handbook of Social and Cultural Anthropology* (Chicago: Rand McNally): 143-78.
Alt, A.
　1968 [1930] 'The Formation of the Israelite State in Palestine', in *Essays on Old Testament Religion* (trans. R.A. Wilson; Garden City, NY: Doubleday): 223-310.
Barth, F.
　1961　　　*Nomads of Southern Persia* (Boston: Little, Brown).

Claessen, H.J.M., and P. Skalnik

1978a   'The Early State: Theories and Hypotheses', in *idem, The Early State* (The Hague: Mouton): 3-29.

1978b   'Limits: Beginning and End of the Early State', in *idem, The Early State* (The Hague: Mouton): 619-35.

Cohen, R.

1978a   'Introduction', in R. Cohen and E.R. Service (eds.), *Origins of the State* (Philadelphia: Institute for the Study of Human Issues): 1-20.

1978b   'State Origins: A Reappraisal', in H.J.M. Claesser and P. Stalnit (eds.), *The Early State* (The Hague: Mouton): 31-75.

Cohen, R., and E.R. Service

1978   *Origins of the State* (Philedelphia: Institute for the Study of Human Issues).

Cross, F.M.

1973   *Canaanite Myth and Hebrew Epic* (Cambridge, MA: Harvard University Press).

Cuisenier, J.

1980   'Structural Anthropology and Historical Anthropology', mimeographed.

Earle, T.

1978   *Economic and Social Organization of a Complex Chiefdom* (Ann Arbor: Museum of Anthropology, University of Michigan).

Fitzmyer, J.

1958   'The Aramaic Suzerainty Treaty from Sefire in the Museum of Beirut', *CBQ* 20: 444-76.

1967   *The Aramaic Inscription of Sefire* (Rome: Pontifical Biblical Institute).

Flanagan, J.W.

1983   'Succession and Genealogy in the Davidic Dynasty', in Herbert B. Huffmon *et al.* (eds.), *The Quest for the Kingdom of God* (Winona Lake, IN: Eisenbrauns): 35-55.

Flannery, K.V.

1972   'The Cultural Evolution of Civilizations', *Annual Review of Ecology and Systematics* 3: 399-426.

Frick, F.S.

1979   'Religion and Sociopolitical Structure in Early Israel: An Ethno-Archaeological Approach', in P.J. Achtemeier (ed.), *Society of Biblical Literature 1979 Seminar Papers* (Missoula, MT: Scholars Press): 233-53.

Fried, M.H.

1967   *The Evolution of Political Society* (New York: Random House).

1968   'The State, the Chicken, and the Egg; or What Came First?', in Cohen and Service (eds.), *Origins of the State*: 35-47.

Goody, J.R. (ed.)

1966   *Succession to High Office* (Cambridge: Cambridge University Press).

Goody, J.R.

1970   'Sideways or Downwards?', *Man* 5: 627-38.

1976   *Production and Reproduction* (Cambridge: Cambridge University Press).

Gottwald, N.K.
1979   *The Tribes of Yahweh* (Maryknoll, NY: Orbis).

Gunn, D.M.
1980   *The Fate of King Saul: An Interpretation of a Biblical Story* (JSOTSup, 14; Sheffield: JSOT Press).

Harris, M.
1979   *Cultural Materialism* (New York: Random House).

Jobling, D.
1980   'The Jordan A Boundary', in P.J.Achtemeier (ed.), *Society of Biblical Literature 1980 Seminar Papers* (Chico, CA: Scholars Press): 183-207.

Leach, E.
1968   'VI. The Comparative Method in Anthropology', in *International Encyclopedia of the Social Sciences* 1: 339-45.

McCarter, P.K., Jr
1980   *1 Samuel* (AB, 8; Garden City, NY: Doubleday).

McKenzie, J.L.
1962   'The Four Samuels', *BR* 7: 3-18.

Malamat, A.
1973   'Tribal Societies: Biblical Genealogies and African Lineage Systems', *Archives européennes de sociologie* 14: 126-36.

Mendenhall, G.E.
1975   'The Monarchy', *Int* 29: 155-70.
1978   'Between Theology and Archaeology', *JSOT* 7: 28-34.

Mettinger, T.N.D.
1976   *King and Messiah: The Civil and Sacral Legitimation of the Israelite Kings* (Lund: Gleerup).

Noth, M.
1966 [1930] *Das System der zwölf Stamme Israels* (Darmstadt: Wissenschaftliche Buchgesellschaft).

Peckham
1972   'The Nora Inscription', *Orientalia* 41: 457-68.

Peebles, C., and S. Kus
1977   'Some Archaeological Correlates of Ranked Societies', *American Antiquity* 42: 421-48.

Price, B.J.
1978   'Secondary State Formation: An Explanatory Model', in R. Cohen and E.R. Service (eds.), *Origins of the State* (Philadelphia: Institute for the Study of Human Issues): 161-86.

Redman, C.L.
1978   *The Rise of Civilization* (San Francisco: W.H. Freeman).

Renfrew, C.
1974   'Beyond a Subsistence Economy: The Evolution of Social Organization in Prehistoric Europe', in C.B. Moore (ed.), *Reconstructing Complex Societies* (Cambridge, MA: American Schools of Oriental Research): 69-88.

Richter, W.
1965   'Die *nāgîd*-Formel', *BZ* 9: 71-84.
Robertson A.F.
1976   'Ousting the Chief: Deposition Charges in Ashanti', *Man* 11: 410-27.
Sahlins, M.D.
1968   *Tribesmen* (Englewood Cliffs, NJ: Prentice–Hall).
Sanders, W.T., and J. Marino
1970   *New World Prehistory* (Englewood Cliffs, NJ: Prentice–Hall).
Sanders, W.T., and B.J. Price
1968   *Mesoamerica* (Englewood Cliffs, NJ: Prentice–Hall).
Service, E.R.
1962   *Primitive Social Organization* (New York: Random House, 2nd edn).
1975   *Origins of the State and Civilization* (New York: Norton).
1978   'Classical and Modern Theories of the Origins of Government', in Cohen and Service (eds.), *Origins of the State*: 21-34.
Vogt, E.Z.
1968   'Cultural Change', *International Encyclopedia of the Social Sciences* 3: 555-58.
Wilson, E.O.
1978   *On Human Nature* (Cambridge, MA: Harvard University Press).
Wilson, R.R.
1977   *Genealogy and History in the Biblical World* (New Haven: Yale University Press).

JSOT 36 (1986), pp. 17-26

WAS EARLY ISRAEL A SEGMENTARY SOCIETY?*

J.W. Rogerson

The social organization of Israel in the period 1250 to 1050 BC has received considerable attention in recent years. In particular, Norman Gottwald's *The Tribes of Yahweh* has presented a powerful case for regarding Israel in this period as an egalitarian society throwing off the oppressive rule of Canaanite city states.[1] From a different perspective Frank Crüsemann, in his examination of anti-monarchic passages in Judges and elsewhere, has suggested that opposition to monarchy resulted from the fact that in the premonarchic period political power in Israel had been distributed among the people by means of their membership of groups which had equal political status.[2] Both Crüsemann and Gottwald draw attention to segmentary lineage systems. These are best known from anthropological studies of African peoples, and provide examples of societies in which there is no centralized power, but a distribution of power through groups with equal status.

So persuasive does the analogy between ancient Israel before the monarchy and segmentary lineage societies seem to be, that it is rapidly becoming received opinion in Old Testament studies that premonarchic

---

*   This article is a revised form of a guest lecture delivered in the University of Paderborn in May 1985 under the title 'Das frühe Israel als segmentäre Gesellschaft? Zu einem Versuch, die soziale Organisation des frühen biblischen Israel zu verstehen'. My thanks are due to Professor Bernhard Lang for the invitation to deliver the lecture.

1.   Norman K. Gottwald, *The Tribes of Yahweh: A Sociology of the Religion of Liberated Israel. 1250–1050 BCE* (London: SCM Press, 1980).

2.   Frank Crüsemann, *Der Widerstand gegen das Königtum: Die antiköniglichen Texte des Alten Testaments und der Kampf um den frühen israelitischen Staat* (WMANT, 49; Neukirchen; Neukirchener Verlag, 1978), pp. 201-208.

Israel was indeed a segmentary society. This view is expressed in Robert Wilson's investigation of the biblical genealogies,[3] in the first part of Herbert Donner's *History of Israel*[4] and in Christa Schäfer-Lichtenberger's thesis on citizenship in the Old Testament.[5] The aim of this article is to show that premonarchic Israel could not have been a segmentary lineage society. More likely, it was an association of small chiefdoms. If this is correct, the emergence of the monarchy can be seen as the eventual dominance of one chief over the rest, rather than as a shift from the horizontal to the vertical distribution of power.

Fundamental to the sociological side of the discussion are the collections of essays *African Political Systems* (1940) and *Tribes without Rulers* ((1958)[6] as well as the monographs on individual peoples, such as those by Evans-Pritchard on the Nuer, and Fortes on the Tallensi. There must also be added to the list Christian Sigrist's *Regulierte Anarchie*, which was first published in 1967.[7] This latter book is especially important because Sigrist has attempted to bring some precision to the discussion of segmentary societies. He regards it as necessary to attempt an analysis of the term on a broad basis so as to remove tautological expressions and to be able to judge the explanatory value of the various contributions that he reviews.[8] Wilson and Gottwald did not, apparently, make use of Sigrist. Crüsemann refers

3. Robert R. Wilson, *Genealogy and History in the Biblical World* (New Haven: Yale University Press, 1977), pp. 18-36.

4. Herbert Donner, *Geschichte des Volkes Israel und seiner Nachbarn in Grundzügen* (ATD Ergänzungsreihe 4.1; Göttingen: Vandenhoeck & Ruprecht, 1984), p. 154: 'Der neuerdings in die Debatte gebrachte Begriff der "segmentären Gesellschaft" erscheint sehr gut geeignet, die Struktur des vorstaatlichen Israels zuzuschreiben.'

5. Christa Schäfer-Lichtenberger, *Stadt und Eidgenossenschaft im Alten Testament: Eine Auseinandersetzung mit Max Webers Studie 'Das antike Judentum'* (BZAW, 156; Berlin: de Gruyter, 1983), pp. 333-67. See p. 342: 'Die Übereinstimmungen zwischen dem Typus "Segmentäre Gesellschaft" und der vorstaatlichen Gesellschaft Israels sind unübersehbar'.

6. M. Fortes and E.E. Evans-Pritchard (eds.), *African Political Systems* (Oxford: Oxford University Press, 1940); J. Middleton and D. Tait (eds.), *Tribes without Rulers: Studies in African Segmentary Systems* (London: Routledge & Kegan Paul, 1958).

7. Christian Sigrist, *Regulierte Anarchie: Untersuchungen zum Fehlen und zur Entstehung politischer Herrschaft in segmentären Gesellschaften Afrikas* (Frankfurt/M.: Syndikat, 2nd edn. 1979[1967]).

8. Sigrist, *Regulierte Anarchie*, p. 21.

to Sigrist's work at the end of his book, and sees in it a confirmation of his view that opposition to monarchy in Israel came from the imposition of an alien power structure upon a basically egalitarian society.[9] Schäfer-Lichtenberger, on the other hand, draws heavily upon Sigrist in my opinion quite uncritically, in her attempt to present pre-monarchic Israel as a segmentary society.[10]

According to Sigrist, the term 'segmentary society' was first used by Durkheim in his 'De la division du travail social' (1873).[11] Examining how work was distributed in various societies, Durkheim distinguished between those societies which were centrally organized and those which were not. The latter consisted of a number of autonomous and politically equal groups that were not differentiated by particular roles or specializations, yet which were integrated into a single society. Such societies he called segmentary, that is consisting of a number of autonomous groups or segments.

African Political Systems was concerned less with the division of work, and more with the distribution of power. The contributors concentrated upon unilineal descent groups and upon the processes of fragmentation and segmentation which characterized the groups. For the editors of *African Political Systems* segmentary societies were made up of unilineal descent groups that stood in a relation of political equality to each other. However, by the time that Sigrist published the first edition of *Regulierte Anarchie* in 1967 it had become clear that segmentary societies could not be so easily characterized as had earlier been supposed. Sigrist quotes Audrey Richards as follows: 'the more we learn of segmentary societies, the more we realize that it is the exception rather than the rule for clans and lineages to have an exactly equal status'.[12] Sigrist also noted that in most of the societies labelled as segmentary by Evans-Pritchard and Fortes the constituent unilineal descent groups in fact exhibit differences of rank and function.[13] While fully aware that the notion of a segmentary society was not free

9. Crüsemann, *Der Widerstand gegen das Königtum*, pp. 201-22.

10. Schäfer-Lichtenberger, *Stadt und Eidgenossenschaft im Alten Testament*, pp. 333-67.

11. Sigrist, *Regulierte Anarchie*, p. 21. Schäfer-Lichtenberger, p. 335 n. 27, adds that in the second edition of his book (1902, p. 151) Durkheim described Israel as a segmentary society.

12. Sigrist, *Regulierte Anarchie*, p. 29.

13. Sigrist, *Regulierte Anarchie*, p. 29.

from difficulty, Sigrist proposed the following definition: an acephalous society (i.e. lacking a central political organ) whose political organization operates through politically equal groups which have similar internal hierarchies.[14] I now propose to examine two questions: is the term segmentary society of any use at all, and is its application to Old Testament study based upon a syllogism with an undistributed middle term?

I

From Sigrist's book it becomes immediately clear that there are many differences among segmentary societies.[15] They are of different sizes. The smallest are 35,000 strong while the largest number 800,000.[16] The size factor is significant. In small segmentary societies the segments (the unilineal descent groups) are the minimal political units.[17] In large segmentary societies this is not the case, and the minimal political unit is often defined on the basis of territorial closeness. Many unilinear descent groups are exogamous; Nuer unilineal descent groups, however, are endogamous.[18] Some segmentary societies have age-set systems which cut across the descent groups; others have no age sets.[19] If one examines the processes by which segments are integrated to form the society as a whole, there are again important differences. For the Tallensi, integration is achieved by a series of harvest celebrations; they are a cultic society.[20] The Konkomba base their political units on their territorial possessions.[21] The Nuer, on the other hand, are united by war against a common enemy.[22] If one

14. Sigrist, *Regulierte Anarchie*, p. 30: 'eine akephale (d.h. politisch nicht durch eine Zentralinstanz organisierte) Gesellschaft, deren politische Organisation durch politisch gleichrangige und gleichartig unterteilte mehr- oder vielstufige Gruppen vermittelt ist'.

15. See also *Tribes Without Rulers*, pp. 1-31, where segmentary societies are divided into three main groups which differ significantly at some points (e.g. Group 3 have specialized chiefships).

16. Sigrist, *Regulierte Anarchie*, p. 64.

17. For what follows, see the descriptions of the various peoples in Sigrist, pp. 64-87.

18. Sigrist, *Regulierte Anarchie*, p. 84.

19. Sigrist, *Regulierte Anarchie*, pp. 72, 85.

20. Sigrist, *Regulierte Anarchie*, p. 75.

21. Sigrist, *Regulierte Anarchie*, pp. 81-82.

22. Sigrist, *Regulierte Anarchie*, p. 83.

examines the social roles in segmentary societies it is noteworthy that the Nyabingi have a priestly case with a monopoly of religious power.[23] The Tiv have no priests, and 'elders' perform ritual functions.[24]

In view of such divergences, it is worth asking whether the term segmentary society serves any useful function at all, and Sigrist in fact quotes from *Tribes Without Rulers* the opinion that 'segmentary lineage systems (are) a somewhat arbitrarily defined category'.[25] Sigrist also considers fully the view of M.G. Smith who thinks that it is an error to draw a contrast between centralized and uncentralized societies.[26] In my opinion, Sigrist makes out a satisfactory case for retaining the term segmentary society. It seems that a number of African societies share characteristics which make it reasonable to group them under the heading of segmentary societies. Whether these characteristics entitle us to include premonarchic Israel under the definition is another matter.

On the face of it, many parallels between segmentary societies and premonarchic Israel can be found (assuming that texts such as Judges and 1 Samuel can be used as evidence for premonarchic social organization). Some can be listed as follows:

1.   *Confederations and amphictyonies.* Units with territorial proximity can combine together, particularly against common enemies. Both permanent and occasional confederations are found. In cases of war, leaders emerge, but they have no lasting influence. Amphictyonies are confederations that constitute a cultic community. There are similarities here to Israel as portrayed in the book of Judges, ignoring the deuteronomic framework and ideology.[27]

2.   *Administration of justice.* Because segmentary societies have no central coercive legal institutions, individuals or kin groups must protect their own rights and deal with breaches of norms.[28] The book of Ruth portrays Boaz as assembling a

23. Sigrist, *Regulierte Anarchie*, p. 208.

24. Sigrist, *Regulierte Anarchie*, p. 133.

25. See *Tribes Without Rulers*, p. 3.

26. M.G. Smith, 'On Segmentary Lineage Systems', *JRAI* 86 (1956), pp. 39-80.

27. See Sigrist, *Regulierte Anarchie*, pp. 51, 62, 72, 76, for amphictyonies, and pp. 213-17 for 'charismatic' leaders.

28. Sigrist, *Regulierte Anarchie*, pp. 102-103.

council of ten men to hear the matter of the inheritance of Elimelech, while Joab avenged the blood of his brother Asahel by killing Abner at the gate of Hebron, where councils were convened.[29]

3. *Pollution of the land by shedding blood.* The belief that the unlawful shedding of blood pollutes the land is well attested in the Old Testament.[30]

4. *The rise of centralizing power through recruiting of people without status.* In 1 Sam. 22.2 David is said to have been joined by a group of people who were discontented and in distress and debt. In segmentary societies there are cases where people seek to gain power by recruiting followers of low or no status. In this way, the leader can break free of the kinship networks that normally regulate political relationships, and exercise power through a group with total allegiance to him.[31]

5. *Consciousness of equality, and opposition to prominent people.* Segmentary societies seem to be informed by a consciousness of equality that directs itself against any attempt to establish power.[32] The book of Judges indicates that there was opposition to the idea that 'judges' should establish dynasties and retain any sort of permanent power.

Given these, and other parallels that can be brought between segmentary societies and premonarchic Israel, it is not surprising that the opinion has gained wide approval that early Israel was a segmentary society. Wilson reaches this conclusion by understanding the biblical genealogies in terms of unilineal descent groups.[33] Gottwald is interested in the consciousness of equality in segmentary societies, since this supports his view that premonarchic Israel was essentially an egalitarian society over against the centralized power of the Canaanite city states.[34] (It needs to be asked, however, how Gottwald can base his approach upon Noth's amphictyony theory, one of the points of which is to argue for centralized political and judicial authority in Israel in the time of the Judges, and use the model of segmentary

29. Ruth 4.1-12; 2 Sam. 3.27.
30. See Sigrist, *Regulierte Anarchie*, p. 110 and Deut. 19.
31. Sigrist, *Regulierte Anarchie*, pp. 255-56.
32. Sigrist, *Regulierte Anarchie*, pp. 185-87.
33. Wilson, *Genealogy and History*, pp. 18-21.
34. Gottwald, *The Tribes of Yahweh*, pp. 612-14.

societies where such centralized power is, by definition, lacking.)[35] Crüsemann draws attention to the opposition in segmentary societies to the establishment of permanent power, and explains opposition to the monarchy in Israel as the result of the imposition of an alien power structure upon a system characterized by consciousness of equality (*Gleichheitsbewusstsein*).[36] Schäfer-Lichtenberger offers the fullest comparison to date between segmentary societies and pre-monarchic Israel, discussing in detailed fashion several of the parallels to which I have drawn attention above.[37]

II

I now turn to ask whether, in concluding from such parallels that pre-monarchic Israel was a segmentary society, the scholars concerned have made the mistake of using a false syllogism with an undistributed middle term. Is it the case that those features of segmentary societies which are thought to be paralleled in premonarchic Israel are peculiar to segmentary societies and found nowhere else, so that the conclusion is secure that premonarchic Israel was a segmentary society? The answer must be no. The fact that a society has unilineal descent groups in which can be seen the processes of fission and segmentation does not make it a segmentary society.[38] The descent group may be that of a chief who wields considerable power. The establishment of power by recruiting from people without status is attested among the Kimbu

---

35. See Crüsemann, *Der Widerstand gegen das Königtum*, pp. 201-203, who rightly sees that the segmentary society theory must be an alternative to the Nothian form of the amphictyony theory.

36. Crüsemann, *Der Widerstand gegen das Königtum*, pp. 215ff.

37. On pp. 338-42, Schäfer-Lichtenberger brings Josh. 22.10-34 as an example of a conflict 'der typisch für eine segmentäre Gesellschaft ist'. Josh. 22.10-34 is the dispute about the building of an altar 'by the Jordan' by the east-Jordan tribes. The alleged parallel with segmentary societies appears to be that by setting up a new shrine a group claims to constitute a new segment; or a new shrine is set up if new territory is occupied. This seems, however, to hold for societies where minimal political units are defined in terms of territorial possession (cp. the essay on the Konkomba in Sigrista, *Tribes Without Rulers*, pp. 167-202). Whether it holds true for all segmentary societies, and whether the parallel satisfactorily explains Josh. 22.10-34, is to be doubted.

38. Cp. Patrick Vinton Kirch, *The Evolution of the Polynesian Kingdoms* (Cambridge: Cambridge University Press, 1984), pp. 28-33.

in the case of the nineteenth-century chief Nyung-ya-wame.[39] It is noteworthy that Shorter, in his account of Kimbu political organization, describes it as somewhere between segmentary societies and the so-called segmentary state.[40] Sigrist himself points out that there are four types of acephalous societies, including autonomous acephalous villages without politically significant unilineal descent groups, and societies in which age sets as well as unilineal descent groups have political functions.[41] These societies share some of the features identified as parallels to premonarchic Israel.[42]

It is necessary to proceed by a different logical path and to draw attention to features of segmentary societies which are fundamental and which, if they were not present in premonarchic Israel, point to the conclusion that Israel was not a segmentary society before the monarchy.

1. *Lack of primogeniture or ultimo-geniture.* According to Sigrist, segmentary societies lack the normative precedence of a particular son, whether according to the status of his mother or according to seniority of birth.[43] When a head of a household dies, the eldest son takes over the role of the deceased but also the obligation to treat his brothers equally. Equal treatment of all brothers is not only a well-served norm, it is an *essential mechanism* for maintaining the distinctive features of a segmentary society. It prevents the accumulation of wealth and thus of power by a particular individual or a particular generation.

2. *Lack of parental authority and legal power within small groups.* Segmentary societies differ in the amount of power possessed by a father. It is at its weakest among the Amba, where a father can only advise his adult sons where there are disputes.[44] In Kiga society, a father can threaten his sons with 'psychic' sanctions such as a death-bed curse, but can exercise

39. A. Shorter, *Chiefship in Western Tanzania: A Political History of the Kimbu* (Oxford: Clarendon Press, 1972), p. 276.

40. Shorter, *Chiefship in Western Tanzania*, pp. xxii-xxiii.

41. Sigrist, *Regulierte Anarchie*, p. 59.

42. See Sigrist's discussion of the definition of segmentary societies in relation to 'centralized' and other acephalous societies (*Regulierte Anarchie*, pp. 52-59).

43. Sigrist, *Regulierte Anarchie*, pp. 181-85.

44. Sigrist, *Regulierte Anarchie*, p. 151.

no physical compulsion.[45] The authority of a Tallensi father is confined to such matters as giving permission for his children to marry.[46]

Breaches of norms in small groups are not punished. The Tallensi regard fratricide as a misfortune.[47] The Luiya regard homicide within a group as fratricide, to be ritually purged.[48] The killing of a wife by her husband is regarded as an injury inflicted on the killer by himself.[49] A segment carries out legal sanctions only against other segments that are genealogically distant or unrelated.[50] These characteristics are fundamental for the maintenance of the segmentary mechanisms.

Do these characteristics correspond to what we find in the Old Testament? Surely not. In the patriarchal narratives we find primogeniture. Isaac, not Ishmael, inherits from Abraham, presumably on the basis of his mother's status.[51] Esau sells his birthright to Jacob.[52] In Deut. 21.15 it is forbidden for a man to arrange for his heir to be the son of a beloved wife rather than the son of a disliked wife, if the latter son is the first-born. The power of a father over his sons is mirrored in the story of the binding of Isaac (Genesis 22) and in the command in Deut. 21.18 to kill a disobedient son. In Exod. 21.12-14 homicide is not regarded as fratricide or a misfortune, but as a capital offence. Even manslaughter is treated so seriously that the man-slayer must seek sanctuary if he wishes to escape punishment. In Judges 19–21, the outrage at Gibeah, it is not just distant and unrelated 'tribes', but all the tribes that unite to punish the guilty city.

The use of the biblical passages cited above raises, of course, the question of their reliability for information about premonarchic Israel, but even if it is accepted that all the texts cited reflect the social conditions of the monarchy, it has to be asked how the premonarchic

45. Sigrist, *Regulierte Anarchie*, p. 153.

46. Sigrist, *Regulierte Anarchie*, pp. 154-55.

47. Sigrist, *Regulierte Anarchie*, p. 119.

48. Sigrist, *Regulierte Anarchie*, p. 119. It is to be noted that the Kiga do regard fratricide as a capital offence. It is not always easy to generalize about segmentary societies!

49. Sigrist, *Regulierte Anarchie*, p. 120.

50. Sigrist, *Regulierte Anarchie*, p. 118.

51. Although it is nowhere stated that Isaac inherited from Abraham on the principle of primogeniture this is the implication of the description of Isaac as Abraham's 'son' (e.g. Gen. 24.3-4).

52. Gen. 25.29-34.

conditions were so radically altered by the advent of monarchy, especially if, with Crüsemann, it is asserted that the segmentary organization survived the transition to monarchy and was responsible for opposition to monarchy.

In my view, Israel in the premonarchic period was much closer to a segmentary state than a segmentary lineage society. It may well have been an association of chiefdoms, the genealogies of whose ruling families are to be found in the Old Testament.[53] Such a social structure, in which chiefs exercised political power in conjunction with elders, was better suited to the hilly and forested environment in which the Israelites lived than the quite different environment of the segmentary societies of Africa. The suggestion, to be found in the nineteenth century if not earlier, that the name 'tribe' (*šbṭ/maṭṭeh*) derives from the symbol of authority carried by the chief, is probably correct.[54] The chiefs were able to make pacts with each other, and they also fought against each other. David, before he became king, and was a roving chief with his personal band of followers, had made pacts with the kings of Moab and Ammon, and was even possibly related by marriage to the Ammonite royal house.[55]

All this requires to be worked out in much greater detail. Although the negative direction of this article is much greater than its positive suggestions, it will have succeeded if it serves to warn all those interested in the sociological study of the Old Testament against an over-hasty and superficial equation of premonarchic Israel with segmentary lineage societies. Although parallels can indeed be found between aspects of segmentary societies and passages in the Old Testament it is necessary to relate those aspects of the segmentary societies to their structure and function as a whole. If this is done, the analogy with the Old Testament is hardly persuasive.

53. In small chiefdoms, primogeniture *is* important, as it helps to maintain wealth and power in the hands of the chiefly lineage; cp. Kirch, pp. 28, 34.

54. Cp. Brown, Driver and Briggs, *Hebrew and English Lexicon* (Oxford: Clarendon Press, 1907), p. 641, under *maṭṭeh—tribe*, orig. company led by chief with staff.

55. 2 Sam. 17.25.

JSOT 44 (1989), pp. 19-42

THE IDENTITY OF EARLY ISRAEL:
THE REALIGNMENT AND TRANSFORMATION
OF LATE BRONZE–IRON AGE PALESTINE*

Keith W. Whitelam

Introduction

The publication of research on the emergence of early Israel in Palestine, which reached a climax in the latter half of the 1980s, seems to have subsided into a new phase of assessment, critique and reformulation. The appearance of monographs by Halpern (1983), Lemche (1985), Ahlström (1986), Coote and Whitelam (1987), and Finkelstein (1988) marked the culmination of a period of intensive study arising out of growing dissatisfaction with the ability of the three major models of Israel's origins to cope with the increasing archaeological information or the growing impact of new literary studies on the Hebrew Bible. Trenchant criticisms of some of these views have been raised by Miller (1991a), Bimson (1989; 1991), M. and H. Weippert (1991), and Thompson (1992b), for example, which provoke important questions requiring further discussion and clarification. Coote (1990: viii), by contrast, goes so far as to say that 'recent research on early Israel has brought us to a new understanding', which he terms 'a new horizon', signalling a growing set of shared assumptions despite continuing important differences.[1] Just as we find recurrent patterns

---

* This paper contains some material or ideas that were originally presented in a joint paper with Robert Coote at the SBL/ASOR symposium in Boston, December 1987. I am grateful to Robert Coote for allowing me to include this material here and for his helpful criticisms of an earlier draft of this paper. I remain responsible for the final views expressed here.

1. There are, of course, numerous other specialist works that need to be taken into account in any review of current understandings. H. and M. Weippert (1991)

in the study of long-term trends in history, so we can trace interesting recurrent patterns in the history of scholarship. The present attempts at critique, reformulation, and synthesis at the beginning of the 1990s, following an intense period of research and publication in the 1980s, are not unlike the 1930s when the classic formulations of the infiltration and conquest models were produced by Alt and Albright, to be followed from the 1940s onwards by critique and debate.[2] The present essay is an attempt to explore some of the implications of questions raised by the recent debate on the emergence of early Israel for our understanding of ancient Palestine at the beginning of the early Iron Age and the broader issue of a Palestinian regional history.

It is now generally recognized that the convergence of so-called sociological approaches to the study of Israelite history and literary approaches to the study of the Hebrew Bible has resulted in a major paradigm shift in biblical studies.[3] However, this paradigm shift has largely been understood in terms of its implications for the study of the Hebrew Bible. It is now becoming clearer that such a shift has very profound implications for historical studies. There is now a recognition by a growing number of scholars of the emergence of Palestinian history as a subject in its own right. The study of the history of Israel and in particular the so-called emergence of Israel is

provide an excellent and careful review of literature on the subject. Coote (1990) has a very good up-to-date bibliography. He also summarizes the implications of recent research by stressing the areas of agreement rather than difference, thereby identifying what he calls a 'new horizon' in a synthesis of the most recent scholarship of the last decade or so. The various essays in *SJOT* 2 (1991), which were presented at the SBL/ASOR symposium in New Orleans, November 1990, also highlight areas of convergence as well as very significant differences and unanswered questions. See Thompson 1992b for a comprehensive review of scholarship which is particularly critical of the so-called 'sociological approach'. I provide a response (Whitelam 1995) to some of Thompson's representations and criticisms of this approach.

2.   It will be interesting to see if the trend is continued. The dynamism of the 1930s subsided into an impasse between the two competing models which was only broken by Mendenhall's innovative proposal (1962) and Gottwald's (1979) subsequent formulation of the revolt hypothesis. These in turn, of course, have become the subject of intense debate. It remains to be seen how far the new promise of a regional history of Palestine and its implications for understanding Israelite history will be fulfilled.

3.   Davies (1992) provides the most recent assessment of this paradigm shift and tries to draw out its implications for our understanding of the Hebrew Bible and the society that produced it. See also, now, Whitelam (1996).

a part of this larger regional history. Thompson (1992a: 2) talks in terms of a 'new historiographical paradigm'[4] and certainly the shift towards Palestinian history has been signalled most clearly by the recent publications of H. Weippert (1988), T.L. Thompson (1992b), and G.W. Ahlström (1993). Thompson (1992b: 107) sees a new and promising direction emerging from the studies of the mid-1980s away from biblical and archaeological syntheses towards what he terms an 'independent' history of Israel.[5] His study is a sustained argument for the development of a 'history of "Israel" within the context of a comprehensive regional and historical geography of *Palestine*' (Thompson 1992b: 401). It is the various successes, confusions and failures in the discussions of the mid to late 1980s of the 'emergence of Israel' that have led to a clearer conception of the need for the definition of a history of Palestine.

It is one of the ironies of scholarship that the works of Ahlström, Lemche, and Coote and Whitelam, in particular, which appeal so strongly to the interpretation of archaeological evidence in their reconstructions of the emergence of early Israel in Palestine, were all published before the appearance of Finkelstein's important work. The translation and publication of Finkelstein's monograph mark a significant point in the discussion, since it provides a quantity and quality of archaeological data on early Iron Age Palestine not available since the work of Albright and others in the 1930s. The promise of further publications of survey and site data will ensure that the debate will continue for some time. However, the paradoxical result of recent investigations, and particularly the accumulating archaeological data, appear to lead us even further from an understanding of the nature and organization of early Israel at the beginning of the early Iron Age. This expansion of archaeological data, ironically, just as it

4.   Thompson (1992a: 2-3) sees a strong connection with Chicago and Tübingen. However, it might be argued that the paradigm shift is inspired more by the crisis of the European nation-state and is associated particularly with European scholarship or scholars who have close connections with Europe.

5.   Thompson's use of the term 'independent' is meant to signify a history of Israel independent of later biblical historiography, which he dates to the Persian and Hellenistic periods. The problem of an archaeologically-based history of Israel as distinct from a history of Palestine will be addressed below. Ahlström 1993 is an important work in terms of its conceptualization of a regional history of Palestine. Unfortunately, it was completed in 1986 and therefore does not include a detailed discussion of more recent developments.

undermined Albright's conquest model, has led to many more questions than it has solved.

It is testimony to the tenacity of particular ideas that they have managed to survive in a period in which so many of the basic assumptions that have underpinned biblical scholarship for much of this century have been brought into question or abandoned. Although there has been increasing acceptance in recent years that the emergence of early Israel in Palestine was largely the result of indigenous responses to significant external stimuli, as evidenced in the recent monographs, it remains a domain assumption within biblical studies that Israel in the pre-monarchic period was a unified tribal society. Yet how Israel is to be identified in the archaeological record of the Late Bronze–Iron Age transition or how it might have been organized are moot points. The implications of recent work on tribal organization seem to have had little effect on assumptions prevalent in biblical studies that derive from the work of Noth and others in the 1930s. Although the amphictyonic hypothesis was dramatically overturned two decades or more ago, there remains an underlying assumption of much research that Israel was organized as some form of supratribal *confederation* in the pre-monarchic period which was also an ethnic and religious unity.

Much of the current debate has focused upon the difficulties of differentiating Israelite material culture within the Late Bronze–Early Iron Age remains in Palestine. Even among those who argue that such a distinction is not possible on the basis of the archaeological evidence, the terms 'Israel' or 'Israelite' have been retained in their reconstructions of the period. Clearly a basic assumption of virtually all recent scholarship has been that the proliferation of highland villages during the early Iron Age is to be identified with 'Israel'. Thompson (1992b) has traced the development of this assumption from Alt and Albright through recent scholarship, illustrating how it has influenced almost all subsequent interpretations of the evidence. Equally as pervasive has been the notion that this entity was 'tribal'. Yet the most pressing question remains: How can we identify Israel and its organization? The usual appeal is to two important bodies of information: recent archaeological and survey data alongside the Merneptah stela, in conjunction with the biblical traditions. Although the increase in archaeological data has had a dramatic effect upon the discussion, it is questionable if the far-reaching consequences of this information have been fully recognized or admitted.

The Identity of Israel and Recent Archaeology

The publication of Finkelstein's monograph represents, to use his own words, 'a veritable revolution' in research (1988: 20). It is important to consider the implications of his publication of archaeological data, since it provides a body of data that will be at the centre of a continuing debate on the emergence of Israel for some time to come. This work, along with his numerous important reports in archaeological journals, is a model of clarity in the presentation of vital archaeological data, particularly from the Land of Israel Survey and his own important excavations, which will be the starting point for historians for the foreseeable future. One of the most noticeable trends in recent research, especially by some biblical specialists, has been the questioning of the reliability of the biblical narratives as sources for the history of early Israel in the pre-monarchic period and an appeal to archaeological evidence for an understanding of this period. Yet once again this debate and Finkelstein's interpretation of the data have demonstrated how difficult it is to free the debate from the constraints imposed by the Hebrew Bible.

Finkelstein's interpretation of the archaeological data and his overall reconstruction of what he terms 'Israelite Settlement' is heavily coloured by the picture presented in the Hebrew Bible. His working methodology (1988: 22), briefly set out in the opening chapter, is presented as being primarily concerned with archaeology and settlement, which

> will hardly touch upon the biblical evidence at all (except for site identifications etc.). Without in any way minimizing the singular importance of the Bible for the study of the history of Israel, attempts to reconstruct the process of Israelite Settlement by means of traditional biblical archaeology—by seeking direct correspondences between excavated finds and the biblical text—have been notoriously unsuccessful.

This would appear to be in line with the methodologies professed by Ahlström, Lemche, and Coote and Whitelam, among others. Finkelstein (1988: 22; see also 1991: 56) understands what he terms 'the primary biblical source', the book of Joshua, as being redacted centuries later and as reflecting the understanding of Israelite Settlement at the end of the period of the monarchy. Thus he too advocates trying to reconstruct the process on the basis of new archaeological research, after which it will be possible to return to the question of the implications of archaeological research for understanding the biblical narratives.

However, this strategy of investigating the archaeological evidence independently of the biblical text is not carried through in his attempt to identify 'Israel' and what constituted 'Israelite identity'. Finkelstein (1988: 27) believes that 'the formation of Israelite identity was a long, intricate and complex process which, in our opinion, was completed only at the beginning of the monarchy'. Yet, the presentation and interpretation of archaeological evidence is prefaced by a controlling assumption about Israelite identity which rests upon his understanding of biblical texts. He goes on to say (1988: 27),

> An important intermediate phase of this crystallization is connected with the establishment of supratribal sacral centers during the period of the Judges. The most important of these centers was the one at Shiloh, whose special role at the time is elucidated in 1 Samuel—*a historical work, as all agree*... (emphasis added).

The designation 'the period of the Judges' is, of course, derived from the categories and chronology of the Hebrew Bible rather than archaeological periodizations. Equally striking is his assumption that Shiloh was one of the 'supratribal sacral centers'.[6] This claim clearly embodies an explicit assumption that 'Israel' was some form of tribal organization and religious unity. It hardly needs to be pointed out that it is by no means the case that all agree on the categorization of 1 Samuel as a historical work reflecting the social reality of pre-monarchic and early monarchic Israel, as the proliferation of literary studies makes abundantly clear. Miller (1991a: 97-99) similarly draws attention to Finkelstein's use of biblical traditions such as the so-called Ark Narrative (1 Sam. 4–6; 2 Sam. 6) for controlling the interpretation of archaeological data (see also Dever 1991: 79).

The difficulties of trying to identify and define 'Israel' during the

---

6.   The archaeological evidence presented in his preliminary report of the excavations at Shiloh (1988: 205-34) hardly supports such a claim. He describes (1988: 234) the terraced structures in area C as 'no ordinary houses', representing the only public buildings ever discovered at an 'Israelite' settlement site, 'which hint at the physical character of the sanctuary itself' (cf. also 1985: 168-70). This is rejected by Dever (1991: 82) as 'nothing but wishful thinking, hardly worthy of the hard-headed realism Finkelstein exhibits elsewhere'. Even if it were possible to interpret the archaeological data as evidence for some cultic installation at Shiloh, it goes far beyond the evidence to suggest that this was a 'supratribal sacral centre'.

Iron I period are highlighted by Finkelstein's discussion. He admits (1988: 27) that it is difficult because, he believes, distinctions between ethnic groups at that time were 'apparently still vague'. He goes on to say that it is doubtful whether a twelfth-century BCE inhabitant of Giloh would have described herself or himself as an 'Israelite'. However, despite these reservations, he is still prepared to refer to this site and its material culture with precisely this ethnic label on the justification that

> an Israelite during the Iron I period was anyone whose descendants—as early as the days of Shiloh (first half of the 11th century BCE) or as late as the beginning of the Monarchy—described themselves as Israelites (1988: 27).

This is a claim that can only be advanced on the basis of an acceptance of the essential historicity of the narratives in 1 Samuel, as Miller (1991a: 97-99) points out. In essence the term 'Israelite' is applied to anyone residing in what is thought to have been the territorial framework of the early monarchy, whether they considered themselves to be Israelite or not.

The weakness of this argument is highlighted by his own admission that Galilee poses a particular problem for this definition (1988: 28), especially since it was not part of the territorial jurisdiction of the early monarchy.[7] Furthermore, he illustrates (1988: 323-30) that Iron I settlement in the area was later than previously thought: settlement in Galilee belongs to a later or secondary phase rather than being part of the first phase of settlement as Aharoni believed. Even though it falls outside the territory of the monarchy, Finkelstein still insists, without giving precise reasons, that the population should be considered Israelite. He then offers a definition of 'Israelite' in the following terms:

> Israelites in the Iron I are those people who were in a process of sedentarization in those parts of the country that were part of Saul's monarchy, and in Galilee. The term 'Israelite' is used therefore in this book, when discussing the Iron I period, as no more than a *terminus technicus* for 'hill country people in the process of settling down' (1988: 28).

---

7.   Thompson (1992b: 159-60, 239-50) also criticizes Finkelstein's understanding of the Galilee as being 'Israelite' while excluding the Jezreel valley. He argues that Finkelstein's assertion that these settlements are 'Israelite' is based on his reading of later biblical traditions.

Essentially the term 'Israelite' is nothing more than a designation for those individuals and groups settling in the hill country during the Iron I period. In fact, Finkelstein (1991: 53) has stated more recently that he might be willing to omit the term 'Israelite' from the discussion of Iron I settlement and refer instead to 'hill country settlers' until the period of the monarchy. As many have argued and, I believe, Finkelstein's own presentation of his archaeological findings makes clear, it is not possible to attach ethnic labels to the various sites at the end of the Late Bronze Age and beginning of the early Iron Age. Thus Finkelstein's adoption of the more neutral term 'hill country settlers' is much more prudent. If we cannot attach precise ethnic labels, then the settlement shift should be discussed in broader regional terms of the settlement distribution of the Palestinian highlands and margins in comparison with lowland and coastal areas. The terms 'Israelite' and 'Canaanite' are misleading and carry too many implications which the evidence at present does not support.[8]

It is important to note that a key element of Finkelstein's interpretation of what he terms 'Israelite Settlement' throughout his monograph is the priority of the biblical text for historical reconstruction. Thus he states,

> The starting point of a discussion about the characteristics of Israelite Settlement sites is the historical biblical text (*the only source available*), which specifies the location of the Israelite population at the end of the period of the Judges and at the beginning of the Monarchy. Israelite cultural traits must therefore be deduced from the Iron I sites in the central hill country, especially the southern sector, *where the identity of the population is not disputed* (1988: 28, emphasis added).

The view set out by Finkelstein here begs a whole series of questions. It is clear that his understanding of particular biblical texts has priority in the interpretative strategy which then acts as a controlling factor in understanding the archaeological evidence. The location of 'Israelite' sites depends upon an acceptance of the historical reliability

---

8. See Lemche 1991 for a study of the term 'Canaanite' and a late dating of biblical texts that use this term. Thompson (1992b: 311) also recognizes that 'the sharp boundaries, which the use of the terms "Canaanite" and "Israelite" make possible, are wholly unwarranted and inapplicable'. M. and H. Weippert (1991: 382) remark that Finkelstein's catalogue of criteria for distinguishing Israelite sites 'fällt freilich wie ein Kartenhaus in sich zusammen' when the evidence from Jordan is taken into consideration.

of certain biblical texts that pertain to the so-called 'period of the Judges' immediately prior to the inauguration of an Israelite monarchy. The difficulty of identifying the inhabitants of Iron I villages on the basis of known archaeological data has been overcome by an appeal to these texts which are recognized as having priority. Once again, however, it is far from the case that the identity of the population of the central hill country sites of this period is undisputed. Equally questionable is his contention (1988: 29) that 'it is clear, then, that the Iron I sites in the southern and central sectors of the hill country can be defined as "Israelite" even if at that time certain older or foreign elements were present...' The question raised is what does such a term as 'Israelite' designate, and how are groups identified by this term understood in relation to 'older' or 'foreign' elements? The implication seems to be that Israelites are somehow 'younger' but 'not foreign'. Sites should not be labelled as Israelite solely on the basis that they were located in an area that became part of later monarchic Israel.[9] As we shall see, one of the most puzzling elements in the discussion is the precise relationship between the entity termed 'Israel' in the Merneptah stela, the highland settlements of the early Iron Age, and the later formation of an Israelite state.

The whole focus of our discussion of this period changes once it is accepted that a term such as 'Israelite identity' is much too restrictive when applied to the highland settlements of the Late Bronze–Iron I transition.[10] The ambiguities and lacunae in our current evidence

---

9. Recent studies have raised serious questions about reconstructions of the monarchy or its extent. In particular, Jamieson-Duke (1991) has produced a very stimulating study of scribes and schools in monarchic Judah which raises doubts, on the basis of archaeological evidence, of standard interpretations of the formation of an Israelite state. He finds (1991: 138-39) little evidence that Judah functioned as a state prior to the eighth-century increase in population, building, production, centralization and specialization. Even then it was only a relatively small state. Garbini (1988: 21-32) questions the historicity of the traditions about the early monarchy from a different perspective. Wightman (1990) provides an interesting critique of attempts to identify 'Solomonic' structures in the archaeological record on the basis of the biblical records. See Miller 1991b for a brief discussion of some of the methodological problems in attempts to assess the historical reliability of the biblical traditions for reconstructing the reign of Solomon; this is a response to the more positive approach of Millard (1991).

10. As long argued by Ahlström (1993) and Thompson (1992b) and made explicit in their recent major studies.

demand that a much broader term has to be used to designate the inhabitants of Iron I villages, as Finkelstein (1991: 53) has now recognized. Thompson (1992b: 160) makes a similar point in relation to Finkelstein's earlier use of the term 'Israelite' when he asks, 'Is he not rather and perhaps better dealing with the archaeology of the early Iron Age settlements of central *Palestine*, leaving for others the question of Israel's origin?'[11] This means that any attempt to explain this settlement shift can no longer be concerned solely with trying to identify or explain the origins or emergence of Israel. Rather the historian needs to try to identify and account for the *processes* involved in the settlement shift that took place in Palestine at the end of the Late Bronze Age and the beginning of the early Iron Age. The focus of concern becomes the transformation and realignment of Palestinian settlement. The concern with Israel has been a distraction which has obscured an understanding of the complex processes at work during this period. The socio-economic setting of Iron I sites, which Finkelstein does much to illuminate and confirm, is of considerably more relevance for our understanding than supposed ethnic labels.

This distraction is evident in the other works on the emergence of Israel which appeared in the mid to late 1980s. It has become a commonplace, following the work of Alt and Albright, to identify Israel

---

11. It is puzzling therefore that Thompson (1992b: 161) goes on to argue that Finkelstein's book 'establishes a firm foundation for all of us to begin building an accurate, detailed, and methodologically sound history of Israel'. Thompson (1992b: 162) acknowledges the problems of archaeology, not least the problem of ethnicity, but asserts that 'this book has demonstrated that we must and can use primary historical evidence in writing a history of Israel'. It is difficult to see how this can be achieved without being able to attach ethnic labels to the material culture. The essential value of the data presented in Finkelstein's book, I would have thought, is that it provides primary data for exploring settlement patterns and societal changes in Palestine during the Late Bronze–Iron Age transition. What part 'Israel' plays in this is hidden from our view. The history we are writing, as Thompson argues elsewhere in his study, is a broad regional history of Palestine rather than a history of Israel. In fact he later makes this very point (Thompson 1992b: 311): 'If the distinction between Canaanite and Israelite cannot be made when we speak of the variant cultural traditions of Iron I, have we really sufficient grounds for seeing this period as uniquely the period of emergent Israel? Is the question of Israel's origin a question about events of the Late Bronze–Iron I transition, or is that transition rather only one among many factors relating to the prehistory of people some of whose descendants later formed part of Israel?'

with the growth in early Iron Age rural sites in the highlands and steppes of Palestine.[12] However, one of the major points that Ahlström, Lemche, and Coote and Whitelam emphasize, again in line with many other recent studies, is that it is no longer possible to distinguish an 'Israelite' material culture from an indigenous material culture in terms of the archaeological data. The implication of this is that the term 'Israelite' becomes unusable in the context of the discussion once it is accepted that the biblical traditions do not bear upon the problem. Even though Coote and Whitelam, for the most part, concentrated on trying to understand and account for the processes that led to this switch in settlement during the Late Bronze–Iron Age transition, the term 'Israel' was retained throughout the discussion despite reservations (1987: 179 n. 3):

> We do not assume that by referring to the early Iron Age highland settlement as 'Israel' that anything qualitative has been said about 'early Israel'. We focus our history of 'Israel' on this highland settlement because it is the clearest archaeological datum that precedes the eventual emergence of the kingdoms of Israel and Judah.[13]

The analysis has not been carried through radically enough by those who discount the evidence of the biblical traditions for this period on methodological grounds.[14] However, in the absence of convincing

---

12. Thompson (1992b) is particularly critical of this scholarly trend.

13. It is now apparent that there is a considerable assumption in the last sentence about our knowledge of the Israelite monarchy, its extent, and organization. See n. 5 above. Of more significance, however, is the question of the relationship between the emergence of Israel and the settlement of the highlands. Coote (1991: 45) has pointed out quite clearly that these are not the same issue. 'How and why Israel emerged and how and why village settlement extended in the highland are two different questions.' He acknowledges that this was not stated clearly enough in Coote and Whitelam 1987.

14. Miller (1991a: 95) has made this point in his forceful criticism of what he sees as 'a methodological confusion' in recent studies: 'Any time historians, archaeologists, sociologists, or whoever speak of Israelite tribes in the central Palestinian hill country at the beginning of the Iron Age I, or about the Davidic–Solomonic monarchy, or about two contemporary kingdoms emerging from this early monarchy, they are presupposing information that comes from, and only from, the Hebrew Bible.' Miller (1991a: 95) is particularly critical of Coote and Whitelam 1987 and Whitelam 1986 for claiming to write a history of Israel without recourse to the Hebrew Bible while in effect assuming the basic outline of the biblical account. Although Miller highlights an important and difficult methodological problem, the

evidence, either from the archaeological record or corroborative literary materials, it is better to leave aside the distraction of the supposed ethnic labels and to concentrate on trying to explain the settlement shift in broader regional terms. Or, as Thompson (1992b: 310) puts it, 'It has become exceedingly misleading to speak of the term "Israelite" in an archaeological context of Iron I *Palestine*'. Thus an irony of the increase in archaeological data, such as that provided by Finkelstein, is that it has resulted in a situation where, far from placing discussions of Israel's emergence in Palestine on surer ground, it has led to a position in which it is possible to say very little about 'Israel' at all during the Late Bronze–Iron Age transition. The pre-occupation with Israel has drawn attention away from the most immediate task facing the historian: the task of trying to explain the shifts in regional settlement and society during the Late Bronze–Iron Age transition.

The Identity and Organization of Israel in the Merneptah Stela

The most obvious objection to the above argument is that such an entity is referred to in the Merneptah stela toward the end of the thirteenth century BCE. It is well known that the Merneptah stela represents the earliest reference to Israel outside of the biblical texts. Yet despite the fact that this information has been available since 1896, when the stela was discovered, there is still considerable debate as to its meaning or significance.[15] The mention of 'Israel' in the stela raises

major concern is with trying to free research from the constraints of the picture presented in the Hebrew Bible. The construction of the past presented in the Hebrew Bible has to be understood in the context of its social construction: it is important evidence for the historian in relation to the time at which it was composed. Clearly there are major disagreements on how to date or utilize the narratives and the information they contain. However, it is misleading to speak in terms of trying to write a history of Israel without recourse to the Hebrew Bible. It is a primary source for the period and groups that produced it. It is an entirely different matter whether or not the construction of the past in terms of the history of early Israel corresponds to historical reality. See Davies 1992 for an exploration of the implications of such an approach.

15. Serious questions have been raised about the historical reliability of the stela as representing a Palestinian campaign by Merneptah (see Redford 1986: 196-99). However, even if the description of the campaign is not authentic, it is still the case that the scribes of Merneptah knew of some entity which they termed 'Israel'.

three major questions which are important for the present investigation: what was the entity called 'Israel', how was it organized, and
what was its relationship to the settlement shift at the end of the Late
Bronze Age and beginning of the Iron Age?

The first question as to the identity of 'Israel' in the stela has
received considerable attention. It is not necessary to review recent
theories in detail, but only to mention the salient points which bear
upon the present discussion.[16] The significance and meaning of the
determinative attached to Israel in comparison with the determinative
used for Ashkelon, Gezer and Yano'am and the other entities mentioned in the stela is the most tantalizing feature. Obviously such a
contrast invites speculation, but it has to be admitted that we are
hardly in a position to solve the puzzle. Evidently there appears to be
some differentiation in the minds of the Egyptian scribes but the
reference is so ambiguous and tantalizing that the historian can only
proceed with the utmost caution. It seems reasonable to conclude that
this entity must have been a *relatively* significant political force in the
region for it to be mentioned by the Egyptian scribes. But again
caution is required here since we are dealing with a political and

Finkelstein's (1991: 56) insistence that 'there was no political entity named Israel
before the late-11th century' is puzzling in the light of the reference to Israel in the
stela.

16. Yurco's (1986) understanding of the stela in comparison with his reinterpretation of the battle reliefs at Karnak as coming from the reign of Merneptah rather
than Rameses II suggests that 'Israel' is indigenous to Palestine. He asserts (1986:
210) that 'one thing is clear, *the Israelites* (Scene 4) *were not depicted as Shasu, but
as Canaanites*' (his italics). Here he cites Stager's view (1985: 60) that the Shasu are
pictorially and textually Shasu, whereas the Israelites in Scene 4 are pictorially
Canaanites, and also textually by inference in the Israel stela where it is linked with
Ashkelon, Gezer and Yano'am. This, he claims, refutes suggestions that Israel
emerged out of a Shasu milieu (*contra* Giveon 1971 and Weippert). Redford (1986:
199-200) rejects this claim and states that 'All the names in the poem appear in the
relief sequence except for Israel. Thus the ethnic group depicted and named "Shasu"
by the scribes of Seti I and Ramesses II at the beginning of the thirteenth century BCE
was known to the poet of Merneptah two generations later as "Israel".'

See further Redford 1992: 257-80. Interestingly, the assumption always seems to
be that each of the terms designates an ethnic distinction rather than a sociopolitical
differentiation. As Coote (1990: 178 n. 5) points out, Israelites could have been both
Shasu and non-*Shasu*.

ideological presentation of the achievements of the pharaoh. The scribes are hardly likely to imply that the pharaoh's victory was insignificant, hence it is proclaimed in such categorical terms: 'Israel is laid waste, his seed is not'.

Moreover, the stela offers us precious little information on the precise location or organization of this entity and certainly tells us nothing of its origins. The northern location of Israel in the stela has been asserted on the basis of a supposed south–north arrangement within the text. However, once again the evidence is ambiguous. The location of Yano'am is unknown, undermining attempts to correlate the literary arrangement with precise geographical information. Taking into account the dispute over whether or not Canaan is referred to before Ashkelon or whether this ought to be translated as Gaza, the existence of a south–north orientation rests upon the citation of two (or possibly three) towns and a third (or fourth) unidentified site. The few place names cited, even assuming a positive identification for Yano'am, are too small a statistical sample to confirm or deny their perceived geographical arrangement. If Gaza is not mentioned, but is a reference to Canaan as a whole, as some argue, then the attempt to find a south–north orientation is even more questionable. By contrast, Ahlström (1991: 32; 1986; see also Ahlström and Edelman 1985) believes that a perceived literary structure of the text in terms of a ring structure equates Israel with Canaan as making up Hurru: Canaan represents the well-populated lowlands while Israel refers to the central highlands. Emerton (1988: 372-73) illustrates the problems of such an approach in his critique of Ahlström's attempts to discover a ring structure in the text.[17] Even if it is possible to demonstrate that the stela, or, more accurately, this brief reference at the end of a victory hymn over Libya, has a recognizable literary structure, it is still a major shift in argumentation to conclude that it provides precise geographical information for the location of Israel on the basis of such an arrangement.

Bimson (1991) has drawn some significant conclusions from the stela in his critique of recent discussions of the emergence of early

---

17. Emerton (1988) also makes the telling point that there is no explanation as to why the last few lines of the text are omitted from the proposed ring structure. Bimson (1991: 21-22) argues for a different understanding of the ring structure which does take into account the following lines except the list of royal titles that completes the inscription.

Israel. An important assumption embodied in the work of Bimson is that there is a clear relationship between Israel of the Merneptah stela and the inhabitants of the highland villages at the beginning of the Iron Age. He subscribes to the general scholarly assumption that the inhabitants of these villages were 'Israelites': he refers (1991: 6) to an 'Israelite occupation' at Shiloh separated from a Late Bronze stratum, but he does not spell out the reasons for such an assertion. The existence of some entity called 'Israel' as early as the end of the thirteenth century BCE is considered to be of prime importance in the discussion of this settlement shift. However, in the absence of more precise information, it is difficult to know how this entity referred to by Egyptian scribes relates to the settlement shift at the beginning of the Iron Age. Bimson (1991: 14) is certain that 'there is no reason at all to doubt that the Israel of the stela is biblical Israel of the pre-monarchic period' and that 'it is quite unreasonable to deny that the Merenptah's inscription refers to biblical Israel'. He admits that we cannot be sure what form Israel took in Merenptah's day. Nevertheless, he is 'reasonably sure that Merenptah's Israel was a tribal confederation, such as we find reflected in the Song of Deborah' (1991: 14). Such a view begs a host of questions: what is 'biblical Israel', what is our evidence for 'premonarchic Israel', what is the relationship with Merneptah's Israel, and how do we know that it was organized tribally? Does 'biblical Israel' refer to Israel as pictured in biblical texts? If so, which texts are being considered and why? The question remains whether the representation of Israel in Joshua, Judges and Samuel conforms to historical reality or portrays an important ideological and political presentation of the past from the perspective of the later monarchy or Second Temple period.[18] However, Bimson draws a further important conclusion from the Merneptah stela: 'We may conclude that in Merenptah's reign Israel was a geographically extensive tribal coalition with considerable significance in Egyptian eyes' (1991: 22-23). It has been pointed out above that although it is a reasonable conclusion that Israel is being cited as a relatively significant political entity in the region, it is difficult to see how it can be concluded on the basis of the evidence of the inscription that it was 'geographically extensive' or that it was

18. See Davies 1992 for a devastating critique of attempts to equate 'biblical Israel' with historical reality.

necessarily tribal. The view that Israel of the stela was a 'tribal coalition' can only be maintained on the basis of biblical and extrabiblical evidence and parallels, since the stela itself provides no direct evidence for such a conclusion.[19]

The notion of the existence of a pan-Israelite tribal structure prior to the period of the monarchy is still influential in much biblical scholarship despite the demise of Noth's amphictyonic hypothesis.[20] This notion is evident in Finkelstein's discussion of the results of his archaeological investigation of Shiloh, as we have seen, when he concludes that this site was one of the 'supratribal sacral centers'. As noted above, this is a conclusion based upon an understanding of the biblical traditions and their applicability to historical reconstruction for this period, rather than an analysis of the archaeological data alone. Similarly, Bimson states (1991: 25) that there were 'cultic centres which seem to have served non-sedentary groups, e.g. at Shechem and Shiloh, places that feature as important centres for Israel in biblical traditions concerning the settlement and judges periods (Josh. 24; Judg. 21; etc.)'. In his discussion of the work of Finkelstein, he states that 'since Merenptah's inscription predates the sedentarization process, the Israel to which it refers was presumably nomadic'

19. Lemche (1985: 430-31), whom Bimson cites in support, also refers to 'a fully developed tribal organization' on the basis of the reference to Israel in the Merneptah stela. Ahlström (1991: 33-34) is categorical in his denial that such information can be deduced from the stela: 'There is no way of knowing the social organization of the people who lived in the territory of Israel; one cannot deduce from the Merneptah stele that Israel was a tribe, a tribal league or confederation, as J.J. Bimson, A. Mazar, and L.E. Stager do, even if this could have been the case. The Egyptian text does not give any clue about the social structure of the people of Israel. To draw the conclusion that Israel refers to a tribal league is an inference from another kind of material.'

Redford (1992: 260) holds a similar view—all that can be known for certain is that Egyptian scribes knew of some entity called Israel somewhere in Palestine. Coote (1991: 39-42) understands Merneptah's Israel to be tribal in a political sense as part of 'a complex network of relations of power'.

20. The idea that early Israel was tribal or a tribal confederation has been challenged by Rogerson (1986), who is particularly concerned with the notion of segmentary organization. See Martin 1989 for a recent summary of some of the problems involved in this discussion. Lemche (1985: 84-163, 202-44) provides a detailed treatment of the complexities of nomadic organization and structure and the problems involved in using particular models or parallels to describe the organization of early Israel.

(1991: 19). In his conclusion, he states that 'before the beginning of the Iron Age, Israel must have been chiefly a semi-nomadic people' (1991: 24) and then adds that 'archaeological evidence for the existence of a semi-nomadic population in the highlands during LBA (Finkelstein 1988: 343-45) is probably of relevance to Israel's presedentary stage'. It is not entirely clear from this discussion whether or not he is drawing a clear distinction between nomadism and sedentarization that entails a view of nomadism as some kind of evolutionary stage that is prior to sedentarization.[21]

By contrast, we might compare the recent discussion of the nature of Israel in the Merneptah stela by Coote (1990: 72-83), which superficially seems to be very much in line with Bimson's reading. Although Coote concludes that 'Israel' of the stela was a major political and military power in the region in the thirteenth century BCE and that it was a 'tribe or tribal confederation', his understanding is significantly different from that of Bimson. Coote (1990: 71) concludes that Israel was not a 'single religious group, family, nation, race, nor ethnic group' but as a tribe or tribal confederation during the New Kingdom period 'it was a name for power'. His view is that the biblical texts do not describe the origin of Israel but what some later court writers thought was the origin of Israel on the basis of ideas and experiences of their own time and place.[22] His understanding of the nature of tribal Israel is based upon a wide body of evidence including parallels drawn from similar periods in the history of Palestine. Coote recognizes that the reference to Israel in the Merneptah stela predates the highland settlement by 'at least one generation, and probably several' (1990: 72). However, he also draws a direct link between this entity and the inhabitants of the highland settlements: 'In the twelfth and eleventh centuries, people named Israel inhabited recently founded villages in the highland' (1990: 72). Yet it is difficult to see what archaeological evidence or information on the stela would justify such a link. The root of the problem again appears to be the distraction of the term 'Israel' and the search for the identity of the inhabitants of Iron I highland settlements.

21. Bimson (1991: 24 n. 1) does refer in a footnote to the work of Lemche in making the point that some wealthy individuals in nomadic societies make the transition to a settled existence.

22. Coote places the biblical traditions of Israel's origins at the court of David. See Coote and Ord 1989 and Coote and Coote 1990.

Coote's discussion (1990: 75-93) of the nature of tribal organization in Palestine, on the basis of better-known parallels, and his concentration upon the *political* conditions of highland settlement in the early Iron Age are particularly valuable. He points out that such organization was essentially a concept of political identity and relationship among individuals and families, and between their chiefs and the state. The shifting nature of tribal structures and membership, invariably in response to political and economic conditions, is an important factor that needs to be borne in mind in the discussion of Palestinian history and settlement. It is misleading to think of tribal organizations as necessarily expressions of ethnic or religious unity. It is well known that genealogies in traditional societies constantly change to reflect political and social relationships rather than biological descent. As Coote (1990: 78) notes, 'It continues to beg the question of the nature of Israel, particularly its variability, by implying a singularity and continuity with later Israel, which are commonly presumed but improbable and misleading'.

The historical study of this period is a prime example of the way in which the concerns and categories of the Hebrew Bible have dominated the discussion. The overriding concern with the origins or emergence of Israel has obscured the need to understand and account for the political and economic conditions that influenced the highland settlement shift during the Late Bronze–Iron Age transition. If we think of a realignment of Palestinian society in broad regional terms in response to the disruption of local and regional economies rather than trying to identify highland settlements with 'Israel', then Coote's discussion has a great deal to contribute to our understanding of this settlement shift. Nomadism, with its heavy emphasis on the pastoral element, is a form of specialization that many in the indigenous population adopt under particular political and economic conditions. It forms part of the social continuum rather than being a discrete system (cf. Cribb 1991: 16). The political and economic conditions provide the stimulus for an amalgamation of diverse groups, ethnically and tribally, which is then presented in terms of a lineage system. As Cribb (1991: 53) points out, notions of a perceived lineage system are often products of conscious rationalizations by provincial administrators or tribal leaders. He notes (1991: 54) that many tribal groupings in the Near East involve nomadism only marginally, if at all, ranging from sedentary Kurdish mountain villagers, Berber citrus cultivators, to Marsh Arabs. Importantly, the common denominator appears to be a fluid territorial system and intense competition for scarce land or water resources: 'The inherent instability of the pastoral mode of subsistence, accompanied by constant changes of residence and fluctuations in the size and composition of co-resident groups, both demands and facilitates a territorial system of great complexity and maximum flexibility'. His emphasis (1991: 54) on the notion of the tribe as the sociopolitical structure that is able to secure access to scarce resources is relevant to the sociopolitical situation in Palestine during the Late Bronze–Iron Age transition when the social and political upheavals caused by the disruption of urban-based trade required flexibility of response in order to secure resources for survival.[23]

It is these aspects of tribal organization that undermine the easy assumption that there is a direct and demonstrable link between the 'Israel' of the Merneptah stela, the inhabitants of the highland

23. Cribb offers some instructive examples of the importance of the pastoral element of Middle Eastern society in his dismissal of long-held assumptions that population change is the result of nomadic invasions, particularly during periods of weak state control, and the replacement of the indigenous population. He points out that 'This is not what happened on the Syrian steppe in the last century, nor in western Iran during World War II and only a few years ago after the fall of the Shah. What would a migrationist make of the dozens of abandoned and burned villages? What of the nomad camps that replaced them? Yet in both cases—certainly in the latter—the departed villagers and the newly arrived nomads were in fact the same people! The collapse of state authority, instead of opening the way for a nomad 'invasion', simply permitted large numbers of people to resume a preferred migratory lifestyle more consistent with their unstable mode of subsistence' (1991: 153).

He goes on to add that the widespread desolation of northern Mesopotamia recorded by nineteenth-century travellers, with numerous deserted villages interspersed or overlapping with tent camps, is consistent with weak Ottoman rule and mounting disorder. But the nomads themselves may well have been the former inhabitants of the villages who had become too mobile to maintain a permanent village base. He notes that 'It is curious that the period during which major nomad invasions are known to have occured throughout the Near East—the eleventh and twelfth century—was one of general prosperity and flourishing trade with little hint in the historical or archaeological settlement record of major upheavals or depopulation... Prior to the Seljuk Empire most of this area was Greek- or Persian-speaking, and afterwards mostly Turkish-speaking, showing how complex are the interwoven strands of nomad migration, ethnic affiliation and regional economy' (1991: 153-54).

settlements, or the later Israelite monarchy.[24] The problems inherent in this assumption were referred to by Coote and Whitelam (1987: 179 n. 3). In the light of the above discussion, it needs to be made clearer that the identification of 'Israel' with the highland settlements is even more questionable on the basis of available evidence. The term 'Israel' in this context is misleading and diverts attention away from an important discussion about the sociopolitical conditions that accompany this marked settlement shift. This was not made clear enough in Coote and Whitelam (1987), despite the important proviso that was added to the earlier cited statement (1987: 179 n. 3):[25] 'The reference to "Israel" in the Merneptah stela may not refer to the settlement of the highland or to any social group directly ancestral to monarchic Israel'. Bimson objects to this on the ground that such a view is not justified by the evidence (1991: 17). He suspects that the suggestion derives from a realization that 'even with the traditional dating of the Iron I settlements, there may not have been time for Israel to emerge through the process which they envisage before Merneptah's fifth year' (1991: 17-18). However, this is not the reason for the qualification. The problem arises out of an understanding of the complex and variable nature of tribal organization. Far from ignoring the evidence of the Merneptah stela, its evidence is seen to be significant. If 'Israel' of the stela was organized tribally, as Bimson accepts, but which is not evident from the stela itself, then the very nature of tribal organization calls into question the precise relationship between this entity, the highland settlements, and any later Israelite monarchy. However, once again the major distraction for virtually all proponents in the recent debate has been the concentration upon Israel and the assumption that there is a close fit between 'Israel' and the spread of highland settlement in early Iron Age Palestine.

The Transformation and Realignment
of Late Bronze–Iron Age Palestine

The search for early Israel has proven to be a serious distraction which, in the absence of further unambiguous evidence, ought to be abandoned for the time being, while we concentrate on historical

---

24. Similarly, Thompson (1992b: 311) argues for a difference between 'Israel' of the stela and the referent of the same name in the Assyrian period.

25. However, see n. 6 above.

judgments, which need to be constantly revised and improved, regarding the probabilities of the history of Palestine in the thirteenth to eleventh centuries BCE. In particular, the historian needs to explain the processes at work in the settlement shift that took place during the Late Bronze–Iron Age transition. Hitherto the discussion of early Israel and its emergence has advanced primarily through the juxta-position of archaeological data and biblical texts. From now on the discussion of peoples, societies and cultures—including whatever may be designated 'Israel'—will need to advance largely without the bibli-cal text, for this period at least. The traditions of Israel's origins are more important as sources of information for the nature of later monarchic, exilic and Second Temple Israel. Those who have said that the history of early Israel cannot be written in any conventional sense of a text-based reconstruction are correct, at least until major bodies of historical texts from the period are discovered—and even then such texts would have to find their place within the constellation of other categories of evidence. Research strategies need to break free from the constraints of traditional text-based reconstructions by pursuing insights gained through the juxtaposition of archaeological data and historical parallels generated by such broad comparative disciplines as anthropology, historical geography, macrosociology and historical demography. Furthermore, Braudel's conception of *la longue durée* offers a perspective from which to view familiar problems and encourages the search for patterns in history that are often obscured or overlooked by intense concentration on limited periods of time or geographical area.

Any study of the history of Palestine has to take into account the complex arrangement of micro-environments which have ensured that the region as a whole has seldom been unified and which have con-ferred a large degree of autonomy on the different sub-regions and their inhabitants, thereby contributing to the diversity of Palestine. Thompson's (1992b) study rightly emphasizes the importance of Palestinian regional variation in trying to understand its history. However, it is also important that such an emphasis does not lose sight of world history. Palestine has been and remains a part of world history; its strategic location on the trade and military routes by land and sea at the hub of three continents has meant that its history is intricately linked to global history. The ways in which the micro-environments have been exploited has often been determined by outside factors such as imperial investment of finance, labour and technology. Once the history of this area and its populations are set in the context of 'world history' then it is possible to ask important comparative questions about the nature of cultural, social, political, economic and religious interrelationships and changes.

The settlement variation which occurred in Palestine during the Late Bronze–Iron Age transition cannot usefully be studied as though it arose in a temporal and spatial vacuum. The disruptions that occurred throughout the eastern Mediterranean towards the end of the Late Bronze Age appear familiar enough for us to talk in terms of a collapse or even dramatic collapse on an interregional scale. The use of such terminology, however, raises expectations and assumptions that such a collapse was immediate and gave rise to a radical break in material culture in different regions. It is important to be continually reminded of the imprecision of our terminology and chronology in which distinctions between centuries, for instance, for purposes of classification, are arbitrary and particularly dangerous when they lead to assumptions that something dramatic happened in 1200 BCE that distinguishes what had gone on immediately before from what followed. Such distinctions encourage the study of history as a series of discrete events in which sociopolitical changes are neatly categorized (Bloch 1954: 183-84). In what sense do the destructions of Late Bronze Age urban sites in Palestine represent a collapse? The dating of the destruction layers of Late Bronze Age urban centres in Palestine is controversial and constantly being revised (Fritz 1987: 86-89), but it is to be doubted that this was a 'sudden' occurrence. Present estimates at dating point to the fact that this was part of a protracted process that lasted at least half a century, if not more, and can only be understood as part of longer-term trends in the history of the region.

The historian needs to explain the restructuring of the social system expressed in the changes of settlement patterns which are so evident at the end of the Late Bronze and the beginning of the Iron Ages. It might be a better reflection of the situation if we adopted the terms transformation and realignment of Late Bronze–Iron Age Palestine rather than collapse. Sabloff (1986: 114) has recently argued for a similar reappraisal of the so-called Mayan collapse (800–1200 CE) in terms of a demographic, political and economic realignment. Such terms overcome expectations of a radical break at a particular point in time—a radical break that fits well with assumptions about external invasion, conquest or infiltration by different ethnic groups. It also challenges our perspective on basic data by encouraging appreciation of continuities rather than an undue emphasis on differences and discontinuities in material culture. The historian is dealing with complex and protracted processes that cannot easily be reduced to or analysed simply in terms of particular moments in time but must be understood in the widest geographical and temporal context. H. Weippert (1988: 26-27) has drawn attention to the problem of the different rates of development between different subregions of Palestine and to the fact that the dates for periods of transition can only be approximations.[26] Similarly, T. Dothan (1989: 1-14) in a recent reassessment of the initial appearance and settlement of the Philistines and other Sea Peoples in Palestine illustrates that cultural change during the transition period from Late Bronze–Iron I Age was not uniform or simultaneous throughout the country. It was characterized by a complex process in which indigenous, Egyptian and Philistine cultures overlapped for certain periods.

The realignment and transformation of Late Bronze–Iron I society was clearly a very complex process, as we would expect, and it is in the discussion of the processes at work that the greatest differences are likely to occur. Thompson (1992b: 180) doubts that the breakdown of international trade at the end of the Early Bronze and Late Bronze

26. Finkelstein pointed out in an oral response at the Boston symposium that it is extremely difficult to date early Iron I sites within a margin of error of fifty years. This is obviously a critical problem for the historian who needs such information in order to produce an understanding of the relative chronology of settlement shift but who is dependent upon the judgments of specialists. Finkelstein states the case well: 'It has been practically impossible to make fine chronological distinctions in the pottery from Settlement sites. The problem will naturally crop up at various points in this work, since it is crucial for understanding the processes of occupation and the development of material culture at early Israelite Settlement sites... In some instances, we will thus try to make the distinction between early and late pottery of the Iron I period, despite the risks inherent in this attempt; to refrain from doing so would obviously impede our attempts to advance the analysis of the process of Settlement.'

Dever (1991: 83) notes that Finkelstein's analysis of Iron I pottery is pivotal but only 'for the few specialists capable of judging Finkelstein's arguments. (They *are* few; so hereafter generalists, biblical scholars, and historians must defer to experts, rather than continuing to offer historical-cultural conclusions based on their own ceramic evaluations, which are invalid and misleading).'

Ages could have such an effect upon the Palestinian economy as to result in 'wholesale dislocations throughout the region, and especially in so many sub-regions (such as the hill country and the Northern Negev)', since such regions were only marginally affected by trade routes. He believes (1992b: 215) that the evidence points to major climatic change resulting in widespread drought and famine from c. 1200–1000 BCE.[27] Climate is obviously an important factor, given the marginal nature of the sub-regions of Palestine, where dramatic variations in rainfall over two or more years can have devastating effects. Famine, however, is not always a direct result of periods of drought but is frequently the result of sociopolitical factors, as the tragic events in parts of modern-day Africa all too vividly illustrate (cf. Thompson 1992b: 219-20). It is also the case that Palestine has witnessed important shifts in settlement during more modern periods when the climate in the region has remained stable. Thompson (1992b: 261) points out that the Phoenician cities survived the drought without widespread collapse, attributing their political and economic autonomy to their relative geographical isolation. This would suggest that it is sociopolitical factors that are of greater importance in understanding the settlement shifts rather than climatic change. Geographical isolation is no protection against catastrophic climatic change.

The complex of trade networks which in antiquity linked the Mediterranean, Red Sea, Persian Gulf and Indian Ocean means that Palestine has long been part of a 'world economy' in which the urban elite benefited from interregional trade. Palestine has occupied a strategic place in the world trade axis throughout history, and the urban and bedouin elite have often benefited from their participation in or control of transit trade through the area. But their position on the transit routes to and from core areas has meant that their roles and opportunities were particularly sensitive to any disruption or decline

---

27. Thompson (1992b: 204) goes so far as to claim that the change in climate was 'a primary cause of the changes in economy and settlement patterns in Palestine during the Middle Bronze period'. This is surprising in the light of the fact that he criticizes (1992b: 150) Coote and Whitelam for imposing a mono-causal explanation—the disruption of international trade—on settlement shift, when in fact they only refer to correlations between such settlement shifts and trade cycles, leaving open the question of causal priority (Coote and Whitelam 1987: 79). However, Thompson has reintroduced an important topic into the discussion which needs careful consideration.

in the core. The existence of such a closely integrated world economy, in particular in the eastern Mediterranean during the Late Bronze Age, also meant that any disruption to part of the trade network influenced other areas. Palestine invariably played a dependent role in trade, since it provided the land bridge, and a hub of the waterways, to the infrastructurally more important economies of the major continents. Palestinian urban centres were therefore sensitive and vulnerable to trade cycles and suffered severely from the disruption of the Mycenaean world, whatever the causes may have been.[28] Societies are not monolithic entities but overlapping networks of different power structures and groups (Mann 1986: 1). Since the eastern Mediterranean was a closely interlocking network of different power groups and spatial entities, any structural alterations on such a widespread scale were bound to influence Palestinian society. It is not possible then simply to concentrate our attention on settlement shifts in the highlands of Palestine at the beginning of the Iron I period without taking adequate account of the structural changes brought about by changes in the wider network. The decline of trade and economy along with the many circumstances that attended it were integral to the transformation of economic, political and social relations in Palestine.[29]

The most evident result of this realignment in Palestine is an increase in highland rural settlements as part of similar settlement shifts in other areas of the eastern Mediterranean. Desborough (1972: 19-20, 82, 88) notes that the decline of the Mycenaean palace centres

28. Liverani (1987) provides a good account of the interconnections throughout the eastern Mediterranean during this period.

29. There is no adequate account of the factors that contributed to the decline of interregional trade in the eastern Mediterranean. Renfrew's comparative study (1979) of general systems collapse offers an introduction to an important area of future research, but clearly much more needs to done in order to understand the transformation of the eastern Mediterranean in general. It should be noted that the disruption of trade and economy is not considered as some mono-causal explanation of settlement change. The significance of fluctuations in the Palestinian economy is the way in which they often correlate with major settlement change. Coote and Whitelam (1987: 49-50) stated that 'although it is appropriate for us to give thorough attention to interregional economic exchange, it is not our purpose to prove its causal priority. Its relative explanatory significance in any particular instance will and should always be a matter for assessment.' Trade here is understood in the widest possible terms as an indicator of regional and interregional economy.

was accompanied by a shift in settlement to highland or more remote areas. Interestingly he notes that Sub-Mycenaean pottery represents a clear cultural continuum, even though there was a sharp deterioration in material terms (Desborough 1972: 29, 41; Snodgrass 1971: 34, 40). This is in striking contrast to earlier assumptions that the destruction of the Mycenaean world was caused by external invasion and represented a radical cultural break (see also Lemche 1985). Such settlement shifts as a response to urban decline can be observed in many areas of the world. For example, Iron Age Zealand in Denmark experienced a similar urban decline and corresponding increase in autonomous settlements in remote, often virgin, areas (Kristiansen 1987). The mountains have long been a place of refuge for peasant communities from the periodic political instability of the exposed lowlands throughout the history of the Mediterranean (Braudel 1972: 34, 53). The settlement of the Palestinian highlands and steppes during the Iron I period is not a unique event, but part of the centuries-long cycle of growth, stagnation, decline and regeneration in the history of Palestine (Coote and Whitelam 1987: 27-28).

The importance of the various material features is not that they confirm or deny the ethnicity of populations at different sites, but that they provide evidence of important continuities in material culture from the Late Bronze Age to Iron I that need to be recognized and given sufficient weight. Regional variations need to be acknowledged and accounted for not on the basis of ethnicity, itself the subject of continuing anthropological research, but rather on the basis of the socioeconomic and sociopolitical environment. The continuities in material culture add to the case that we are dealing with the realignment of Palestinian society rather than the collapse and destruction of Late Bronze Age culture and its replacement by new ethnic groups emerging from the desert fringes, the far north, Egypt, or anywhere else. The identification of aspects of the material culture or of particular sites as 'Israelite' is not based upon positive evidence in the archaeological record but rather upon assumptions about the existence or location of Israelite sites in particular areas on the basis of traditions within the Hebrew Bible. The various aspects of the material culture of Iron I need to be understood as functions of socio-environmental and political conditions rather than distinctive ethnic innovations or markers for the national ethnic entities posited by the religious traditions of the Hebrew Bible.[30]

The evidence that Finkelstein puts forward, once the distraction of the label 'Israelite' is removed, adds further weight to this view. As he states (1988: 338), 'Human material culture is influenced first and foremost by the socioeconomic situation and by the environmental conditions'. The appearance and use of pillared buildings, silos, cisterns, terracing, and pottery forms such as collared-rim ware are explicable in terms of the topographical and environmental conditions facing the inhabitants of highland and marginal settlements in the context of the disruption of local and regional economies (see also Dever 1991: 83-84). The technological solutions and expertise displayed in the use of cisterns, terracing, or the construction of pillared buildings militate against the view that the population of these sites were nomads in the process of sedentarization (Coote and Whitelam 1987: 123-34). The evidence put forward by Finkelstein, when stripped of the distractions of putative ethnic labels, provides further support for the view that the settlement shift at the end of the Late Bronze Age and beginning of the Iron I period was a reaction to economic disruption which had an impact on all aspects and levels of Palestinian society rather than being the direct result of social conflict brought about by class struggle or external invasion or infiltration.

Historians must await the results of further archaeological research, particularly comprehensive surveys of the lowlands and coastal areas, along with comparative excavations of sites of differing sizes in these areas, in order to produce a more complete regional picture of the settlement patterns. The lack of comprehensive surveys of all regions of Palestine, and particularly of the lowlands, is a major obstacle in trying to understand the processes at work in the Late Bronze–Iron Age transition. London (1989: 42) makes the point that 'until now

30. It is not possible on the basis of the archaeological record to assume that the Iron I sites indicate common ethnic identity. Alternatively, the regional interactions or environmental conditions that contributed to material similarities among the rural groups may have led eventually to the recognition or imposition and acceptance of ethnic identity in these areas of Palestine. In a sense, the tendency has been to pose the question the wrong way round by identifying similarities and then asking what ethnic group was responsible. There may be little or no ethnic identity at first, but such identity may result from the common solution to problems of subsistence among interacting polities over a period of time. In this sense ethnic identity would be more relevant to a discussion of the processes involved in the formation of an Israelite state or later.

archaeologists have been comparing rural sites in the hill country with urban sites in the lowlands and then attributing the differences to Israelite versus Canaanite communities. The differences may be more indicative of rural versus urban lifestyles.'[31] The existence of villages on the exposed edge of the highlands, or other villages with or without outer defences, indicates that social conflict was only part of the processes that explain the shift in settlement. Progress in this field is now even more dependent upon the continued publication and judgments of archaeologists, so that historians can interpret the material in a comparative interdisciplinary context.

The power of the Hebrew Bible over historians, even those who profess to try to free themselves of its hold, is clearly demonstrated in recent discussions of the emergence of early Israel, as Miller (1991a) has shown. The Merneptah stela illustrates that some entity called 'Israel' was in existence, and possibly as a relatively significant political force, in the thirteenth century BCE. Even though many historians and archaeologists suspect that some entity called Israel was involved in the settlement of the Palestinian highlands in the Late Bronze–Iron Age transition, this cannot be stated with any degree of certainty on the basis of the evidence currently available. Furthermore, it is distracting and misleading to retain references to Israel, however much they may be qualified or however much we may try and encode our uncertainties with quotation marks ('Israel').[32] It is distracting because the use of the term Israel also brings with it the inevitable assumptions

31. Finkelstein (1991: 51), in replying to the criticisms of London that he had compared the rural site of 'Izbet Ṣarṭah with urban sites such as Aphek, Qasile and Gezer, responds by pointing out that Aphek and Qasile were apparently no larger than 'Izbet Ṣarṭah. However, Dever (1991: 78) similarly believes that the proliferation of collared-rim ware in Iron I hill country sites, compared with its absence at large sites such as Gezer, is evidence for differences in urban–rural distribution rather than an ethnic dichotomy.

It is interesting to note that Finkelstein has revised his original and restrictive view of the applicability of archaeological data from 'Canaanite' sites. He was previously of the opinion (1988: 22-23) that evidence from 'large Canaanite mounds' may contribute to our understanding of the Late Bronze Age but is of little value for understanding the processes at work in 'Israelite Settlement'. More recently, he has recognized (1991: 48-49) that comprehensive surveys in the lowlands to match the work already carried out in the hill country need to be completed along with the excavation of single period Iron I sites in different parts of Palestine.

32. This is also true of Dever's (1991: 88 n.7) reference to 'Proto-Israel'.

of tribal organization and ethnic or religious unity. Once we are able to relinquish our attachment to the label it allows us to concentrate on the critical issues of the processes involved in the transformation and realignment of Palestinian society. It means that historians are freed to ask crucial questions about the processes at work unencumbered by the theological baggage and agenda of the Hebrew Bible which has had such a profound hold on the study of the region and the presentation of its history.

BIBLIOGRAPHY

Ahlström, G.W.

1986   *Who Were the Israelites?* (Winona Lake, IN: Eisenbrauns).

1991   'The Origin of Israel in Palestine', *SJOT* 2: 19-34.

1993   *The History of Ancient Palestine from the Palaeolithic to Alexander's Conquest* (JSOTSup, 146; Sheffield: JSOT Press).

Ahlström, G.W., and D. Edelman

1985   'Merneptah's Israel', *JNES* 44: 59-61.

Bimson, J.

1989   'The Origins of Israel in Canaan: An Examination of Recent Theories', *Themelios* 15: 4-15.

1991   'Merenptah's Israel and Recent Theories of Israelite Origins', *JSOT* 49: 3-29.

Bloch, M.

1954   *The Historian's Craft* (Manchester: Manchester University Press).

Braudel, F.

1972   *The Mediterranean and the Mediterranean World in the Age of Philip II* (2 vols.; London: Collins).

Coote, R.B.

1990   *Early Israel: A New Horizon* (Minneapolis: Fortress Press).

1991   'Early Israel', *SJOT* 2: 35-46.

Coote, R.B., and M. Coote

1990   *Power, Politics, and the Making of the Bible* (Minneapolis: Fortress Press).

Coote, R.B., and D.R. Ord

1989   *The Bible's First History* (Philadelphia: Fortress Press).

Coote, R.B., and K.W. Whitelam

1987   *The Emergence of Early Israel in Historical Perspective* (Sheffield: Almond Press).

Cribb, R.

1991   *Nomads in Archaeology* (Cambridge: Cambridge University Press).

Davies, P.R.

1992   *In Search of 'Ancient Israel'* (JSOTSup, 148; Sheffield: JSOT Press).

Desborough, V.R.
1972   *The Greek Dark Ages* (London: Benn).
Dever, W.G.
1991   'Archaeological Data on the Israelite Settlement: A Review of Two
         Recent Works', *BASOR* 284: 77-90.
Dothan, T.
1989   'The Arrival of the Sea Peoples: Cultural Diversity in Early Iron Age
         Canaan', in S. Gitin and W.G. Dever (eds.), *Recent Excavations in
         Israel: Studies in Iron Age Archaeology* (Winona Lake, IN: ASOR/
         Eisenbrauns): 1-14.
Emerton, J.A.
1988   Review of G.W. Ahlström, *Who Were the Israelites?*, *VT* 38: 372-73.
Finkelstein, I.
1985   'Excavations at Shiloh 1981–1984: Preliminary Report', *Tel Aviv* 12:
         123-80.
1988   *The Archaeology of the Israelite Settlement* (Jerusalem: Israel
         Exploration Society).
1991   'The Emergence of Israel in Canaan: Consensus, Mainstream and
         Dispute', *SJOT* 2: 47-59.
Fritz, V.
1987   'Conquest or Settlement? The Early Iron Age in Palestine', *BA* 50:
         84-100.
Garbini, G.
1988   *History and Ideology in Ancient Israel* (London: SCM Press).
Giveon, R.
1971   *Les bédouins Shosou des documents égyptiens* (Leiden: Brill).
Gottwald, N.K.
1979   *The Tribes of Yahweh: A Sociology of Liberated Israel, 1250–1050
         BCE* (London: SCM Press).
Halpern, B.
1983   *The Emergence of Israel in Canaan* (Chico, CA: Scholars Press).
Jamieson-Duke, D.W.
1991   *Scribes and Schools in Monarchic Judah: A Socio-Archaeologial
         Approach* (Sheffield: Almond Press).
Kristiansen, K.
1987   'Center and Periphery in Bronze Age Scandinavia', in M. Rowlands,
         M. Larsen and K. Kristiansen (eds.), *Centre and Periphery in the
         Ancient World* (Cambridge: Cambridge University Press): 74-85.
Lemche, N.P.
1985   *Early Israel: Anthropological and Historical Studies in the Israelite
         Society before the Monarchy* (Leiden: Brill).
1991   *The Canaanites and their Land: The Tradition of the Canaanites*
         (JSOTSup, 110; Sheffield: JSOT Press).
Liverani, M.
1987   'The Collapse of the Near Eastern Regional System at the End of the
         Bronze Age: The Case of Syria', in M. Rowlands, M. Larsen and K.
         Kristiansen (eds.), *Centre and Periphery in the Ancient World*
         (Cambridge: Cambridge University Press): 66-73.

London, G.
   1989   'A Comparison of Two Contemporaneous Lifestyles of the Late Second Millennium BC', *BASOR* 273: 37-55.
Mann, M.
   1986   *The Sources of Social Power.* I. *A History of Power from the Beginning to AD 1760* (Cambridge: Cambridge University Press).
Martin, J.D.
   1989   'Israel as a Tribal Society', in R.E. Clements (ed.), *The World of Ancient Israel: Sociological, Anthropological and Political Perspectives* (Cambridge: Cambridge University Press): 95-117.
Mendenhall, G.E.
   1962   'The Hebrew Conquest of Palestine', *BA* 25: 66-87.
Millard, A.R.
   1991   'Texts and Archaeology: Weighing the Evidence. The Case for King Solomon', *PEQ* (Jan–Dec): 19-27.
Miller, J.M.
   1991a   'Is It Possible to Write a History of Israel without Relying on the Hebrew Bible?', in D. Edelman (ed.), *The Fabric of History: Text, Artifact and Israel's Past* (JSOTSup, 127; Sheffield: JSOT Press): 93-102.
   1991b   'Solomon: International Potentate or Local King?', *PEQ* (Jan–Dec): 28-31.
Redford, D.B.
   1986   'The Ashkelon Relief at Karnak and the Israel Stela', *IEJ* 36: 188-200.
   1992   *Egypt, Canaan, and Israel in Ancient Times* (Princeton: Princeton University Press).
Renfrew, C.
   1979   'Systems Collapse as Social Transformation: Catastrophe and Anastrophe in Early State Societies', in C. Renfrew and K.L. Cooke (eds.), *Transformations: Mathematical Changes to Culture Change* (New York: Academic Press): 481-506.
Rogerson, J.W.
   1986   'Was Early Israel a Segmentary Society?', *JSOT* 36: 17-26.
Sabloff, J.A.
   1986   'Interaction among Classic Maya Polities: A Preliminary Examination', in C. Renfrew and J.F. Cherry (eds.), *Peer Polity Interaction and Socio-Political Change* (Cambridge: Cambridge University Press): 109-16.
Snodgrass, A.
   1971   *The Dark Ages of Greece: An Archaeological Survey of the Eleventh to the Eighth Century BC* (Edinburgh: Edinburgh University Press).
Stager, L.E.
   1985   'Merneptah, Israel and the Sea Peoples: New Light on an Old Relief', *Eretz Israel* 18: 56*-64*.
Thompson, T.L.
   1992a   'Palestinian Pastoralism and Israel's Origins', *SJOT* 6: 1-13.

1992b *Early History of the Israelite People: From the Written and Archaeological Sources* (Leiden: Brill).

Weippert, H.
1988 *Palästina in vorhellenistischer Zeit* (Handbuch der Archäologie, 2.1; Munich: Beck).

Weippert, M.
1971 *The Settlement of the Israelite Tribes in Palestine: A Critical Survey of Recent Scholarly Debate* (London: SCM Press).

Weippert, M. and H. Weippert
1991 'Die Vorgeschichte Israels in neuem Licht', *TRu* 56: 341-90.

Whitelam, K.W.
1986 'Recreating the History of Israel', *JSOT* 35: 45-70.
1995 'New Deuteronomistic Heroes and Villains: A Response to T.L. Thompson', *SJOT* 9: 97-118.
1996 *The Invention of Ancient Israel: The Silencing of Palestinian History* (London: Routledge).

Wightman, G.J.
1990 'The Myth of Solomon', *BASOR* 228: 5-22.

Yurco, F.J.
1986 'Merenptah's Canaanite Campaign', *Journal of the American Research Center in Egypt* 23: 189–215.

THE REGULATION OF SOCIAL LIFE:
LAW, ETHICS AND DEVIANCE

JSOT 38 (1987), pp. 47-72

CUSTOMARY LAW AND CHIEFTAINSHIP:
JUDICIAL ASPECTS OF 2 SAMUEL 14.4-21*

Elizabeth Bellefontaine

The judicial activities of any society can only be understood within their social and political contexts. This paper proposes that in Israel (as in comparable societies elsewhere) the deeply entrenched customary law of an acephalous segmentary society undergoes modification when the society and its sub-groups are caught in the throes of social, economic and political transformation. The modifications, by way of adaptation in substance or procedure, suspension, or transfer of authority, may not only reflect the genesis of new forms of social structure and control but may even be means of mediating the transition.[1] The study focuses on the phenomenon of transfer of judicial authority from one socio-political level to another in a transitional period of Israelite history, that of the chieftainship of David. The proposal is exemplified by an analysis of the judicial elements discernible in 2 Sam. 14.4-21 and the sociopolitical contexts it reflects.

I

The case presented to David by the widow of Tekoa in 2 Sam. 14.4-20 is, according to its context (vv. 1-24), the ruse used by Joab in manipulating David to permit the return of Absalom from exile, where he had

* I wish to acknowledge the assistance of the Social Sciences and Humanities Research Council of Canada which provided me with a research grant during a sabbatical leave, 1985–86.
1. Some modifications, such as committing customary law to written form, might be attempts by traditionalists to resist rather than mediate such transition. Such a consideration, however, lies outside the scope of this article.

fled after killing his brother. According to the text, Joab's artifice was successful and David allowed Absalom to return to his home but not to Jerusalem and his father's court.

In form, 2 Sam. 14.4-20 has been designated by Simon a juridical parable (Simon 1967: 220-21, 224-25; cf. Hoftijzer 1970: 421-24) and by Gunn a judgment-eliciting parable (Gunn 1982: 40-43). Gunn correctly argues against Simon's interpretation of the legal nature of the story, contending that 'the legal element is merely an accident of these particular cases where the one to whom the parable is addressed happens to be a king with (implicit) judicial powers' (Gunn 1982: 41; cf. Coats 1981: 380-82).[2] Nevertheless, the contention does not prevent our peering through the screen of the story at the legal elements which may be there—even if by accident. It is the judicial structures impinging upon the characters in the story and providing the background for their interaction which are the object of this article. The account presents a story whose plot is plausible enough for the king to believe and which is realistic enough to allow us to glimpse through it the dynamics of a politically sensitive judicial situation.

An intriguing element in the drama is that David relented on Absalom's banishment even after he learned that he had been tricked by the woman's plea (v. 21). The point has generated a continuing debate about whether or not the Israelite leader was bound in parallel cases by a previous judicial decision such as the one David made at the woman's request (Simon 1967: 224; Hoftijzer 1970: 421-24; Ackroyd 1977: 129, 132; Whitelam 1979: 127-31; Coats 1981: 382; Gunn 1982: 41). However, there is no evidence that any legal necessity or precedent existed that would require David to make a parallel judgment in Absalom's case and end his exile. What, then, moved him to do so at this point? We learn in 2 Sam. 13.39 and 14.1 that David had already been yearning for his son's return. Yet he had done nothing to bring it about. What was there about his dialogue with the woman which suddenly triggered him into action? We are looking here not for emotional or psychological reasons, though these may have played a significant role (Camp 1981: 21-22). We are interested, rather, in a possible judicial factor in the sociopolitical context of the situation

---

2. Coats does not view 2 Sam. 14.4-20 as a parable but describes it as an 'anecdote' which has 'a parabolic function'. The function is not to elicit a judgment to serve as a legal precedent but to point out the 'absurdity that would result' from a strict application of the law (Coats 1981: 382).

which gave impetus to David's order to recall his son.

A second curious element of the story is the hesitancy of David to make a clear and immediate judgment on the widow's case (vv. 8-11). Only in his third response, and at the woman's determined prodding, did he fully commit himself by oath to protect her son. Whitelam assumes that the Israelite leader could legally postpone a decision in difficult cases. Yet he admits that David's attempt to defer judgment is 'apparently unique in Old Testament contexts' (1979: 132). There is, in fact, no proof of the existence of such a legal provision for deferral of judgment. This study suggests a different explanation. It proposes that the hesitancy of David to decide in the one case and then his surprisingly swift decision in favour of Absalom in the second case devolve— at least in part—upon the central issue of judicial authority as perceived by David at the time. The judicial dynamics of the episode only become clear when viewed from the perspectives of (1) the customary law which constituted the judicial sphere of Israel as an acephalous, politically non-centralized society in the pre-Saulide period and (2) David as paramount chief in the process of becoming king in Israel.

II

Organizationally, Israel in its earliest period (ca. 1200–1020 BCE) was a segmentary lineage society composed of 'separate, equal, and autonomous segments' (Frick, 1985: 65; but cf. Rogerson 1986) and politically decentralized (Malamat, 1973; Crüsemann 1978: 201-208; Gottwald, 1979a: 237-341; Frick, 1985: 51-69; cf. Fortes and Evans-Pritchard 1940: 1-23; Middleton and Tait 1958: 1-31; Sahlins 1967: 91-119; Lewis 1976: 323-33) which under Saul and early David was transformed into a chiefdom (Flanagan, 1981; Frick, 1985: 71-97) before achieving nationhood under a fully developed monarchy during the later reign of David and his successors.

In the judicial sphere, cross-disciplinary studies have stressed the socio-political contexts of rule-making and enforcing which have led to general agreements about the type of judicial authority which would have been exercised within the social organization of early Israel. Without suggesting the existence of a rigid social system, scholars generally accept that the social units constituting pre-Saulide Israel were the *bêt-'āb*, the *mišpāḥâ*, and the *šēbeṭ/maṭṭeh* (DeGeus 1976: 133-50; Gottwald, 1979a: 237-92; Boecker 1980: 27-40; Wilson,

1983a: 59-75; 1983b: 229-48; Stager 1985: 20-22).

The *bêt-'āb*, that is, the extended family or multiple family house-hold (Stager 1985: 18-23), was the basic social and economic unit of Israelite life.[3] Within it, absolute authority over all internal household affairs rested in the head male figure, the *paterfamilias* (Gen. 31; 38). This authority—including even the power to pronounce the death penalty (Gen. 38)—was strong during the early sedentary period with its mainly agrarian economy but appears to have weakened during the time of the monarchy with the establishment of more complex economic, social and religious structures (DeGeus 1976: 136; Belle-fontaine 1979: 23-24).

The family did not survive in isolation but existed within the next unit of social organization, the *mišpāḥâ* The *mišpāḥâ* was formed by the joining together of several *bêt-'ābôt* who lived in close proximity and expressed their relationship in kinship terms although questions are raised about whether the kinship was real or fictive. While *mišpāḥâ* is generally translated as 'clan', anthropological data indicate that this designation is not totally accurate when applied unqualified to Israelite *mišpāḥâ* which, contrary to usual clan practice, where endo-gamous (Gen. 24.15, 38, 67; 29.10-30; Lev. 18.6-18) rather than exo-gamous (Gottwald, 1979a: 257-67; 301-15; 1979b: 77-79; 1985: 285; Stager 1985: 20-21). Thus Gottwald simply describes the Israelite *mišpāḥâ* as a 'protective association of extended families' which 'had a vital regional or neighborhood character' (Gottwald, 1979a: 257-58, 316; cf. Stager 1985: 2). In most instances the *mišpāḥâ* was coexten-sive with the village or town (Mendenhall 1976: 144; DeGeus 1976: 138; Gottwald, 1979a: 316). The interdependence of family and 'clan'/village forged a kin-like solidarity among the members and provided identity to individual Israelites who knew themselves as belonging to *bêt-'āb* of a particular *mišpāḥâ* (Judg. 9.1; 2 Sam. 16.5).

---

3.   There is growing archaeological evidence, based on the Israelite two-to-four-room houses, for the existence of a single household (= nuclear family) units smaller than the extended family (Shiloh 1970: 180-90; Mazar 1981: 44-46; Stager 1985: 11-18; cf. Wilson, 1983a: 62-63). Frick (1979: 243) views such dwellings as housing 'egalitarian small extended families'. However, in a more recent extensive interpreta-tion of the archaeological data, Stager concludes that such dwellings could not accommodate 'a coresident domestic group larger than the nuclear family' (Stager 1985: 18; cf. 29 n. 9). He further describes how groups of two or three individual houses form clusters or compounds each of which would have housed an extended or multiple family household, the *bêt-'āb* (Stager 1985: 18-20, 22).

The *mišpāḥâ* was the larger body within which members of the constituted families intermarried, shared a common territory and culture (Mendenhall 1976: 144) and experienced mutual support and protection. As the fundamental sociopolitical units of Israel, the *mišpāḥôt* were essentially autonomous entities and in them inhered the real power of the people with the authority to regulate their own affairs. The *mišpāḥâ* then, would have exercised a significant judicial function in ancient Israel, judging according to its customary law all cases of disputes between families, including those involving homicide (DeGeus 1976: 141; Wilson, 1983b: 234-38; Whitelam 1979: 44; Köhler 1956: 145-75).

The *šēbeṭ/maṭṭeh,* the tribe, constituted both a loosely organized social entity and a territorial grouping providing secure access to resources and protection to the *mišpāḥôt* which formed it (Gottwald, 1979a: 245-56).[4] Though conceived of as an endogamous lineage system, kinship was fictitiously derived from an eponymous ancestor. At this level of organization, membership is greater but less stable than in the *mišpāḥâ*. In a segmentary lineage system such as early Israel, where the significant sociopolitical organizational units are the *mišpāḥôt* decision-making at the tribal level hardly occurs; common decisions would be difficult to achieve and enforce (Hoebel and Frost 1976: 306). There is no textual evidence of judicial authority being exercised by the Israelite tribes (Wilson, 1983a: 65).

Even less can be said with certainty about the existence of judicial activity on an Israel-wide scale before the monarchy. The absence of any centralizing figure or structure rendered attempts at judicial action mostly ineffective (Judges 19–20).[5] We may conclude, therefore, that the strongest bonds of Israelite life and law outside the family were rooted in the closely knit, autonomous 'clan'/village communities.

III

Comparative studies by ethnographers of law of social systems analogous to early Israel are helpful in understanding the general nature,

4. Gottwald's retribalization theory views Israel's tribal structure as a deliberately devised decentralized society formed in opposition to and in resistance against the centralized control system and hierarchically ranked society of the Canaanite city-states (Gottwald 1975; 1979a; 1985: 284-88).

5. Nor do the judges qualify as such centralizing political–juridical figures (DeGeus 1976, 204-206; Mayes 1985: 83-87).

procedure and locus of authority of customary law as it would have developed and operated in these local communities. The legal historians and social anthropologists have spilt much ink trying to formulate generally acceptable definitions of law and custom and to specify their interrelationship (Seagle 1941: x-xv, 3-35; Bohannan 1965: 33-42; Gluckman 1965: 178-215; Mair 1972: 139-59; Hoebel 1967: 18-28; Barkun 1968: 83-90; Pospišil 1967: 2-26; 1971: 11-37, 44-126; Moore 1978: 13-24).[6] No consensus has been reached but important distinctions have been drawn which will be helpful in our inquiry. Theoretically, the distinctions in themselves are not uniformly defined; nor can they in practice always be distinguished with secure clarity since their spheres of interest and authority often overlap. Nevertheless, distinctions are helpful and, indeed, necessary. Thus, customary law (= custom) is distinguished from: (1) simple customs— that is, habitual ways of behaving: non-sanctioned normal practices; (2) norms—seen as non-judicial, value-based directives of conduct;[7] and (3) law—either as rules or as judicial processes or both—as a means of social control by a centralized, permanent authority above the kinship level with a legitimate monopoly of force to ensure compliance or impose sanctions in a consistent manner; law thus defined resides in the state. Within early Israel's decentralized society, simple customs, norms and customary law would have operated and would have retained a degree of 'residual' power (Newman 1983: 37) even into monarchical times.

Certain basic features characterize customary law although they do not conform rigidly to every concrete situation. Customary law may be described as (1) local; (2) oral; (3) general but concrete; (4) sanctioned; (5) requiring a judge.

1. 'Nothing is more characteristic of customary law than its particularism and localization' (Hamnett 1975: 11). It originates in a small locality and is generally associated with the autonomy of peasant village communities (Lobingier 1950: 663; Fallers 1969: 3). Within such

6. The history of the discussion, and the resultant literature by both legal theorists and social scientists, are extensive. For summaries and further references, see the authors cited.

7. Like 'law', so the term 'norm' is defined and employed in a variety of ways by jurisprudents and anthropologists (cf. Stone 1936: 288; Allott 1980: 16-17; Christie 1982). It is clear that greater precision is needed in labelling the various biblical statements usually subsumed under the designation 'law'.

communities, it is the accepted means of social control above the family level. Diffusion of customary law to neighboring or affiliated clans or tribes may eventually result in common customary laws at tribal or inter/intra-tribal levels. The establishment of a centralized political system, such as a chiefdom or state, does not of itself cause local law to cease functioning. However, if a custom of a village or tribe becomes a general law of the state, the law loses its customary character even though it remains in force locally (Pospišil 1967: 24-25).

2. Customary law originates and 'flourishes' as oral law even when the art of writing is known (Lobingier 1950: 663; Fallers 1969: 3; Moore 1978: 249-50). When set down in writing, it tends to lose quickly its customary character since it is no longer open to adaptation in the manner possible in its oral and less specific form.[8]

3. A particular feature of customary law is that it is both general and concrete, permanent but flexible (Hamnett 1975: 16-17). The general custom is applied to a particular case where it is given one of several possible specific interpretations and judgments. After each concrete application, the law reverts to its general form, ready to be applied to the next concrete situation with perhaps a different judgment (Fallers 1969: 312; Hamnett 1975: 11; Gluckman 1955: 282). Some researchers hold that customary law is unchanging and permanent in reference to its general prescriptions but, in its concrete application, codicil-like provisions may emerge as concrete 'subordinate norms' which 'can and do change, in response to varying social conditions' without altering the principle of the provision (Hamnett 1975: 11; cf. Num. 27). Others, however, maintain that customary law, like all types of law, has the potentiality to change in any aspect: in substance, by the addition, subtraction or alteration of key elements; in procedure, by alteration of the judgment process or by the transfer of authority from one level to another; or even in its nature by codification or universalization (Allott 1980: 15-16; Bohannan 1965: 33-38). Flexibility may engender vagueness and indeterminacy, which is seen by some as the strength of

---

8.   Its character as local law is also weakened as diffusion of written records allows for its adoption in whole or in part by neighboring communities (Watson 1984: 36, 50; Hamnett 1975: 16-17). A number of explanations have been proposed for the need to commit customary law to writing. These involve social and political factors as well as judicial ones (Lobingier 1950: 663; Kaiser 1975: 57; Allott 1980: 162-64; cf. Oates 1977: 480).

customary law and by others as its weakness (Allott 1980: 54-59; Watson 1984: xv-xvi).[9]

4. It is principally, if not exclusively, the attachment of sanctions, together with an authority to impose them, that supplies the 'legality' aspect of custom. This has been one of the most debated points in the attempt to distinguish law from custom (Lobingier 1950: 662-63; Gluckman 1965: 201-202; Lasswell and Arens 1967; Pospišil 1971: 87-96; Hamnett 1975: 12; Allott 1980: 51). Service avoids speaking of customary law, preferring instead 'sanctioned customs', which he defines as 'forms of social control that are reinforced positively or negatively by the public or some part of it' (1975: 86). Positive reinforcement may include persuasion, praise and rewards, while negative sanctions may range from psychological constraints, exclusion and fines to the death penalty. Some researchers distinguish social sanctions, which include all types of social pressures, from strictly legal sanctions, that is, those supported by physical force (Moore 1978: 122-23). With the imposition of sanctions, an authority has been imputed to customary law which legitimates it and makes it socially functional (Hamnett 1975: 128).

5. The fifth feature is less clearly dealt with in the literature. Lobingier holds as 'a particular characteristic of customary law that the availability of a judge is more important than the availability of settled rules of law. The right of judgment has to be vested in some person or class of persons' (1950: 663; Allott 1980: 52-53). However, such persons are not professional jurists (Service 1975: 86). The legal authority may be vested in the entire community, in its representatives such as a council of elders or in a specially deputed individual who acts as mediator or adjudicator, never as originator of law. Even where self-help is the common mode of redress, it must operate within the customary rules and under the approval or direction of the community (Epstein 1968: 3). The local authority applies the general law to particular cases and oversees compliance with the verdict. The territorial range of the local authority determines the geographical limits of the customary law (Watson 1984: 43).

In light of this general description of customary law and of what

9. This characteristic is due partly to its oral form and is a prime reason for its eventual more precise formulation in written form. Perhaps it owes something, too, to its small community locus, where the need to restore severed social relations would require flexibility (Aubert 1983: 62-63; Fallers 1969: 11).

was said above about the significant judicial activity in Israel at the
'clan'/village level, we may accept that customary law was deeply
entrenched and directive of life in these local autonomous units of
Israelite social organization. And it is at this level that the widow of
Tekoa found justice too harsh. By applying the characteristics of customary law to her account, it becomes clear that her community
responded to the homicide in keeping with accepted customary law.

1. It was the woman's *mišpāḥâ*, her local community, which judged
the case and gave the verdict requiring blood vengeance for the death
of her son (v. 7). It is the law of the *mišpāḥâ* which is operative.

2. It is not unreasonable to accept that the custom was held orally by
the community and was not in written form. The widow relates a
story; she does not quote a statute or text. Some biblical commentators
hold that the pronounced death penalty for the fratricide derived from
known laws now found in the biblical text, specifically, the prohibition
of murder in Exod. 20.13 and the death sentences for murder in
Exod. 21.12 and Num. 35.31, 33 (Phillips 1970: 85; Fokkelman 1981:
132; Patrick 1985: 195). This is not clearly evident. In particular, it is
difficult to accept Phillips's assertion that the only law operating here
is the decalogue prohibition of murder and the covenant code obligation that 'the murderer had to be executed in order to propitiate
Yahweh' (Phillips 1970: 85). No reference is made in the account to
such laws; nor is there any clear indication that a covenant obligation
was thought to have been violated. Had covenant law been the issue, it
is unlikely that the mother would have considered an appeal against a
divinely ordained verdict or believed that David could exempt others
and himself from it. Nonetheless, the woman and the paramount are
clearly adherents of Yahwism (vv. 11, 13-14, 16-17). The key to
understanding the situation must lie in the fact that even when provisions for such crimes as homicide are incorporated into covenant law,
they frequently have their basis in pre-existing 'clan' or tribal law (cf.
McKeating 1975: 47, 50; Schulz 1969: 113-27; Phillips 1982: 230;
Gerstenberger 1965: 107-108, 143-44). McKeating maintains that
'religion is in effect a device for wresting from the kin group their
rights to self-help and to compensation' (1975: 50). Later, the sacral
offence may be secularized and made a crime subject to the courts
(McKeating 1975: 50; cf. Porter 1967: 8). In 2 Samuel 14 homicide
still appears to be normally handled by the local community.

3. It is not the general custom of blood vengeance that is questioned

by the widow but its strict application to her son. To the paramount she pleads on the side of the flexibility of the law on the basis of certain extenuating circumstances: there were no witnesses to the crime; it appeared to be unpremeditated; the mother's widowhood and dependence on the remaining son; and the role of the son as heir and preserver of the lineage (vv. 5-7). Another reason for questioning the strict judgment is hinted at, namely the 'conflict of interest' issue by which the vengeful kin would gain possession of the family property on the death of the heir (v. 16). All of these particulars would have been known to the local authorities, but evidently they were not seen as outweighing the law's demand for blood vengeance.

4. The sanction is clear: custom demands the death of the killer, a sanction which in the view of the *mišpāḥâ* is commensurate with the crime (v. 7). While the community pronounces judgment, the *gō'ēl haddām* is appointed to carry out the sentence (v. 16).

5. We know nothing of the judicial process leading to the decision. However, the competence and authority of the *mišpāḥâ* to have judged the case remains unquestioned. It is the verdict which is not accepted by the widow. And so she hides her son (v. 7) until she can appeal to the king against the customary law and against the legitimate authority of her *mišpāḥâ*.

IV

What was David's status and authority in this situation? We know that at a time later than David, under the fully established monarchy, a formal, hierarchically structured judicial system under royal control was in place throughout the realm. According to 2 Chron. 19.4-11, Jehoshaphat set up a clearly defined hierarchy of courts, with royally appointed judges in each fortified city and a higher-level court in Jerusalem which would oversee judicial functioning of the lower courts and decide difficult cases referred to it. While the passage raises textual and historical questions, recent scholars tend to accept Jehoshaphat's reform as basically historical (Albright 1950; Phillips 1970: 18-19; Macholz 1972b: 318-21; Gottwald 1979a: 370-71; Whitelam 1979: 186-208; Williamson 1982: 287-89). Taken together with Deut. 17.8-13, which reflects a later and more complex judicial system (cf. also Deut. 16.18-20), the Chronicles passage indicates that at some point under the monarchy the centralized power of the state succeeded in wresting a considerable degree of judicial power from the local authorities in the town and cities. Authority in the family and local communities was not totally eclipsed, but was progressively and considerably weakened, especially with regard to the law on homicide with which our text is concerned. McKeating has shown that, at first, vengeance was the prerogative of 'clan' law and authority; but with the shifts in social, religious and political organization occasioned by the monarchy and the influence of the priests, it became in time a crime, an offense, not against a particular family or kin group, but against the 'whole national community' (1975: 46-68).

It remains to ask about judicial activity during the time of the chieftainship, that period of transition which, although relatively brief, formed a sociopolitical bridge between the decentralized tribal society of early Israel and the socially ranked, centralized control structures of full monarchy. The time of the chiefs in Israel, that is, the period from the loss of the ark (1 Samuel 4) to Solomon's accession to the throne (1 Kings 1–2), is shown by Flanagan to have been a confused and tumultuous time of transformation involving shifts in the economic, political, social and religious spheres of Israelite life (Flanagan 1981; 1983). Recently, Frick has demonstrated the beneficial application of the systems theory of social anthropology to analyse Israel in this transition period (1985). The systems theory of societies stresses the interrelationship of all systems within a society so that changes in one area effect changes of some kind and degree in the others (Frick 1985: 15). Neither Flanagan nor Frick considers judicial activity in Israel during the transitional time of chiefdom. However, during a process of systemic transformation such as they describe, reglementary procedures (cf. Moore 1978: 18) would also have been affected although perhaps not as swiftly as some other areas of social life. It is necessary, therefore, to consider from a comparative stance the nature of judicial authority of chiefdoms before considering David's judicial role in 2 Samuel 14.

The most complete and helpful description of the legal dimensions of chiefdoms is given by Newman as part of her typology of legal institutions based upon an analysis of sixty pre-industrial societies (Newman 1983).[10] The typology is one step in her study of the

---

10. Among the twenty features of chiefdoms outlined by Renfrew (1974: 73) none appears to have direct reference to chiefly judicial functions, although they may be included in a few of the features mentioned. The last feature, stating that

relationship in simple societies between legal structures, substantive law (especially in relation to social stratification), and pre-industrial modes of production (1983: 204). We need not present or debate her entire thesis but shall concentrate on the typology and on her description of legal complexities in chieftainships.

Newman's typology of legal institutions rests on five variables (1983: 52):

> The existence of a third party or 'hearing body'.
> A social requirement to use the third party.
> The authoritativeness of third-party 'decisions'.
> The centralization of decision-making.
> Multiple levels of jurisdiction or appeal.

The range of legal complexities across the societies studied extends to eight types of legal systems (1983: 115):

1. Self- or kin-based redress
2. Advisor systems
3. Mediator systems
4. Elders' councils
5. Restricted councils
6. Chieftainships
7. Paramount chieftainships
8. State-level legal systems

Since David has been described as attaining the status of paramount chief (Flanagan 1981; Frick 1985), we restrict our remarks to Newman's description of chieftainships and paramount chieftainships (1983: 54, 86-91, 91-95, cf. 207-208).

In chieftainships, ultimate legal authority is centralized in the individual in whom all socio-political authority resides at the highest point of political power. The chief is formally recognized as the final judge or court of appeal in any dispute although he may not always be appealed to. His authoritative decision is binding. He has the power to impose sanctions, although he may need the help of others to enforce

chiefdoms have 'no true government to back up decisions by legalized force', can be taken to include legal along with other types of decisions. The centralization of judicial activity can be inferred from the existence in chiefdoms of 'centers which coordinate social and religious as well as economic activity' (number 9), and from the 'reduction of internal strife' (number 17) although both the strife and its reduction likely relate more to political and military causes than legal ones.

them (also Service 1975: 86-90). In particular, self-redress must now have the support of the chief rather than be the first resort of vengeance. In such cases, the family of the victim may not retaliate. Further, chiefs are usually noted for their oratory, their wisdom, and their knowledge of the people's customary ways. Their office tends to be hereditary, a factor indicating legal centralization (Newman 1983: 86-91).

Paramount chieftainships exhibit these same features but are hierarchically more complex, legally as well as politically, and extend over a much larger geographic and population base. The paramount is often the first and last judge within his own residential centre. Members of his family sometimes advise him and assist in administration. In highly structured chieftainships, a regional level of jurisdiction is established and functions above the village level; each level is ultimately subordinate to the paramount chief. More egalitarian structures and procedures are exhibited at the lower levels. Newman compares the paramount chieftainship to a 'royal kingdom', although the latter is more centralized in all its powers (cf. Service 1975: 90). Despite the centralization of authority in the chiefs, some degree of judicial autonomy is retained at the local, village level. 'In fact', Newman observes, 'the tension caused by the opposing organizational 'principles' of centralization and local control runs throughout the ethnography of paramount chieftainships' (1983: 91). She further contends that the degree of 'vertical integration of legal and political authority' marks the difference between chieftainships and states. 'The paramount's inability to completely subordinate the authority of regionally based (and opposition-orientated) power groups is often cited as an important feature distinguishing these systems from "true states"' (1983: 94). Where the social complexity gives rise to social stratification, issues which were previously resolved by kin and local community authorities come under the control of the central power. In particular, integration of the judicial authority at the centre leads to prohibitions against self-redress. The administration of justice becomes part of a general trend towards political consolidation (Newman 1983: 96-97, 207-208).

We may now return to the period of the chief in Israel. In discussing the 'monarchical judicial authority' of Saul, Whitelam (1979: 69-89) demonstrates that Saul's judicial authority was unspecified and ambiguous; that no strictly judicial decision of Saul has survived; that his authority depended solely upon his position as military leader; and that he was ineffectual in his efforts to have his followers (including his son) carry out his decision (1 Sam. 14.36-46; 22.7-8, 9-19). Such features are characteristic, not of monarchical, but of chiefly rule— and a not very secure or successful one at that. The Saulide period was only the beginning of a longer transition period from tribal to monarchical Israel. Saul's accession to leadership was based mainly on military status and achievement. He established no legal system for decision-making; there is not even any clear evidence that he ever heard an appeal.

David continued the transition from acephalous, non-centralized tribal Israel to monarchy, ultimately consolidating his various powers in the office of king. Establishing himself in Judah and successfully wresting Israel from Saul's family, he first established his status into one resembling a paramount chieftain. Most of the parallels demonstrating his paramountcy have been drawn by Flanagan (1981; 1983). Thus, the leader before whom the widow of Tekoa appears is already functioning at the center of power as military leader, distributor of goods, expander and solidifier of his territory, and performer of cultic rituals (Flanagan 1981: 65-67; 1983). His authority to function as judge and final court of appeal would be, as we have seen, not merely consonant with his status, but an essential element of it.

David appears to have operated throughout his reign as sole judge in Israel above the local courts (2 Sam. 8.15). He did not institute a complex legal structure or even, as in most chieftainships, a mid-level regional judicial system (2 Sam. 15.3; cf. Gottwald 1979a; 369). Perhaps his paramountcy was not secure enough to bear the risk of delegating a power which was such a functional and symbolic element of chiefly authority. At any rate, it is on this point that Absalom so cunningly criticizes his father, accusing him of negligence of his office in not establishing a judiciary system for the speedy and just resolution of cases (2 Sam. 15.2-6). Absalom's motives, however, are highly suspect, as is the picture he paints of David as judge. Absalom's purpose is clearly to undermine the people's confidence in David as a just judge and to win them over to himself who, if he were in his father's position, would certainly appoint such judges! It is significant that he waylays the petitioners *before* they reach the court to present their cases. If his accusation were true, it would be more to his advantage to meet them *after* they had unsuccessfully sought the chief's judgment and been turned away, to commiserate with them, to articulate the chief's failures, and then to stress how more fortunate they would be if Absalom were their leader. His approaching the people prior to their reaching the court seems propagandistic, intended (1) to turn them away in their quest convinced that their suit would not be heard; (2) to raise doubts about David's competence to rule; and (3) to sow the seeds of yearning for Absalom to be chief judge—that is, paramount—in Israel. Hence, 2 Sam. 15.2-6 is not a trustworthy statement of David's fulfillment of his role as judge. It does, however, demonstrate that Absalom's desire to be 'judge' in Israel was due, not to a concern about justice, but to his ambition to replace his father as chief in the land.

Aside from this text, there is no textual basis for questioning David's faithful fulfillment of his judicial role. The fact that petitioners came from outlying areas to Jerusalem, the residential capital of the paramount, for his judgment in concrete cases (cf. Macholz 1972a: 168-70) is evidence that his position as 'warrior–intensifier–redistributor' (Harris 1979: 94, Flanagan 1981: 66) embodied also a judicial status and function. By his subjects he was regarded as the highest judicial authority in the hierarchical sociopolitical system. Chiefly leadership does not distinguish judicial authority from political, military and economic control. Chieftainship consists in consolidating in one person a 'plurality of tasks', not a separation of powers and roles performed by the same person. Every activity of the paramount was directed towards consolidating control in himself as leader at the highest level of power. The one role of the chief is to be a chief (Hamnett 1975: 90). So the appearance before him of the suppliant widow of Tekoa would have been no surprise to a chief such as David. Nor is it surprising that the chiefly characteristics of sagacity and knowledge of judicial affairs are attributed to David by the woman who praises his wisdom, his knowledge and his justice (2 Sam. 14.17, 20; McCarter 1984: 340; cf. Newman 1983: 86; Mettinger 1976: 242; Hoftijzer 1970: 441; Whitelam 1979: 134-35). It is likewise in keeping with his status as paramount chief that David had as his principal advisor a member of his own family, Joab, his nephew (1 Chron. 2.9-17; Flanagan 1981: 62-65).

V

Keeping in mind the sociopolitical contexts of its setting, we return to the dialogue between David and the widow which, despite its controlled formality, betrays a deep-set tension. The dynamics of the interchange demonstrate that the critical issue is one of authority or, more precisely, of authority in tension.

From a judicial perspective, the case being considered consists of an appeal of a member of a 'clan'/village community to a third party above the group with both the authority to override customary law and local authority and the means to enforce compliance. The appeal is made directly to the higher authority from the local level with no indication that an intermediary authority is involved or, indeed, exists. Such an appeal is, we have seen, characteristic of the chieftainship or of the nation state in process of being established (Aubert 1983: 58; Newman 1983: 86). What is noteworthy is the widow's willingness, even her desperate determination, to go beyond the sphere of the local authority and to recognize the authority of the chief to make a binding decision in a case which ordinarily would have been finally settled by the *mišpāḥâ* internally. She almost seems to force that authority upon a reluctant paramount or, at least, to prod him to act upon the power inherent in his office. For the woman's legal appeal (Mettinger 1976: 146, 241-42; cf. Hoftijzer 1970: 425-27) places David in a difficult position and introduces tension into the dialogue. As paramount, David is confronted with a request to suspend the normal operation of deeply rooted customary law in a particular *mišpāḥâ* of his realm (contra McKeating 1975: 50-51) and to interfere in local judicial activity by overturning a legitimately reached judgment of the *mišpāḥâ*. David's hesitancy in responding to the woman's request to act against the decision of her *mišpāḥâ* derives from his chiefly position which dictates caution in countermanding the authority of strong local power bases (Newman 1983: 94). He is caught up in the tension created by the chiefdom's pull towards the centralization of power and the opposite pull towards autonomy of the regional 'clan'/village units. Risk of alienating a group which forms part of his own power base deters him from making a clear and forceful decision. So he attempts to dismiss the woman with a vague promise to issue some 'orders' (v. 8).

But the mother will not be put off. She is not content until she maneuvers the paramount into committing himself to save her son and confirming his judgment by invoking Yahweh (v. 11). The chief is now totally involved and committed to use his chiefly powers to enforce his decision. The usurpation of the power of the local community over this particular case is total and final. The chief, the ultimate judicial authority, decides that a man who by local law should die, shall live, and that the kinsman who, despite the chief's judgment, would kill him in accord with local custom, would die (vv. 10-11). By order of the chief, the self-help procedure of 'clan'/village life has been eclipsed in this particular instance. The risk has been taken; despite his initial reluctance, the paramount has exercised his judicial authority in opposition to local authority (contra Macholz 1972a: 171-75). The chief must ultimately have judged that his weakening of the power of both customary law and the local community would not greatly endanger the equilibrium of power between the centre and the margins of the sociopolitical system. The balancing element in this case rests in the fact that the general customary law related to homicide and blood-guilt remains and will be invoked again by the local group when the need arises. Neither the widow nor the paramount questions the customary law itself. Self-redress has not yet been abolished in Israel nor local authority totally annulled. Yet the custom does not remain unchanged. By interfering in its normal application to the widow's son, the chief suspends the customary law on homicide in this instance. In effect, it has begun to be subsumed into the power of the realm and its first characteristic of localization has been diminished. Moreover, a transfer of authority from the local sphere to the centre has been initiated, a directional flow which will continue until homicide in Israel becomes a crime against the whole community (2 Chron. 19.10; cf. Deut. 17.8; McKeating 1975: 64-68). But a sacral element has entered into the present situation. In addition to the political risk, David is aware that he also risks possible repercussions from the supernatural sphere by failing to avenge the dead brother's blood. This may have been another cause of his initial reluctance to act on the woman's request. However, the woman relieves him of that danger by taking upon herself any consequences of a positive decision (v. 9).

Having finally exercised his judicial wisdom (vv. 17, 20) in making one judgment, David now does not hesitate to make a second decision. He orders Joab to bring back Absalom from exile (v. 21). He acts even after learning that he has been cleverly manipulated to make this decision. One perceives a shift in David's exercise of his authority between the two judgments. This change permits us to infer a similar underlying shift in David's perception of the judicial authority of his status. It has been noted that there is no clear evidence that the paramount is legally bound in parallel cases by the verdict he pronounces in a previous case. A different determinant is at work here. Except for the fratricides, scholars usually find no obvious parallels between the woman's story and Absalom's situation. It is interesting to note, however, that Absalom had fled to Geshur, to his mother's family (2 Sam. 3.3; 14.37-38) who were protecting him just as the Tekoite woman claimed to be protecting her son (v. 7) and further, that some of the arguments put forward in the widow's plea for her son's life could also have been pleaded by Maacah for her son Absalom (vv. 6-7).[11] The final and explicitly stated parallel involves the consequences to others if David does not act (vv. 7, 13, 16). For Joab's purpose, these consequences provide the strongest and most serious argument for changing 'the course of affairs' (v. 20). The account suggests that the judicial authority of the chief included the power to annul, for adequate reasons, the ordinary operation of the law. The chief can suspend customary law and overrule a legitimately reached 'clan'/village judgment. As chief, he can also suspend the punishment accruing to Absalom's crime and overrule his own banishment edict (v. 13).[12] The first appeal asks that a fratricide go unpunished and that the offender be restored to his family and to his status as son and heir (v. 7). The second appeal (by Joab through the woman) requests that another fratricide go unpunished and the

---

11. We may question, then, the general labelling of the woman's story as 'fictitious'. The text says only that Joab put her up to it and directed her to speak wisely (vv. 2-3). Deception was necessary to avoid exposing the ploy too soon, but there seem to have been more parallels between the story and Absalom's situation than the act of fratricide.

12. It is not clear that a banishment edict was ever formally issued by David. We are told three times that, after his crime, Absalom fled on his own initiative into exile (2 Sam. 13.34, 37, 38). Yet, the Tekoite woman (and Joab) holds David responsible for his son's ongoing absence. Absalom must have known that his life would be in danger if he fell into David's hands so he fled out of royal territory. The text does not indicate whether the threat to his life derived from an existing (local) law on homicide similar to the one reflected in the woman's story, or from the possibility of David's exercising familial justice. In any event, when no edict of return was issued after three years, exile becomes, in effect, banishment by the paramount. So David would have to act against a (tacit) royal edict to bring Absalom home free from the fear of sanction.

offender be restored to 'the people of God' (v. 13) and, by implication, to his status as son and heir. In neither case is the murderer
declared innocent, granted pardon or excused for his deed. But their
actions with their consequences are weighed in the balance of a
broader context, namely, the suffering and disaster which would
befall others if due sanctions were imposed (contra Coats 1981: 382).
In one case this involves the widow and her dead husband; in the
other, 'the people of God' (v. 13).

So for Joab the ruse was not a question of eliciting from David a
precedent-setting legal judgment. Rather, it was a matter of convincing
him of the power and wisdom of chiefly judicial authority by which
for sufficient reasons exceptions could be made to previously pronounced legal decisions. The making of an exception with regard to
Absalom would not be perceived as weakness. Rather, it would demonstrate that David, the wise judge, was in control. He could banish and
he could recall. He could bring Absalom back but keep him at a distance. His judgment would send a message throughout the land that
power and authority rested ultimately in the paramount in Jerusalem.
Again, the role of a chief is to be chief and to be seen to be chief.

In both cases, the alternative was for David to do nothing, in which
case the law would have followed its normal course. But then David
would not have proven himself a wise chief. Once this chiefly judicial
authority has been exercised and the risk taken, it is easier to make a
second decision. The tension and indecisiveness which marked David's
first judgment quickly dissipate and the judgment rendered in favor of
Absalom is authoritative, decisive and free of tension. Only later will
David learn the risk he has taken with this decision (2 Sam. 15.1-37).

VI

The episode of David and the Tekoite woman viewed within a comparative setting allows us to draw certain conclusions.

1. The realistic nature of the woman's story and of David's response
permits us to accept 2 Sam. 14.4-20 as an example of the process by
which the judicial authority of the chief was expanded and strengthened while that of the autonomous local groups was gradually
weakened. It offers an illustration from just one perspective—the
judicial—of the process by which local community and regional functions would have been assumed by the coordinating power at the
sociopolitical centre. Since judicial authority was linked to other

modes of power and control, the transfer of final legal authority from the smaller social units to the chief (and later to the king) must be seen as an element in the systemic transformation of Israel from segmentary lineage society to monarchy.

2. That the episode occurs in a transitional period in Israel is betrayed by the tension in the unit. David has achieved paramountcy and is well on his way to monarchy. But the residual power of the local communities and the lack of any intermediate court or regional judges shows that full integration of judicial authority to the centre of power has not yet been achieved.

3. Caught up in the dynamics of sociopolitical change, even the deeply rooted customary law of autonomous social groups undergoes transformation and some elements of it eventually lose their customary character altogether. We have seen from one example how customary law can be suspended or annulled and how there takes place a transfer of its controlling authority from its original sphere to a higher level outside the local community.

4. A distinct shift in social ordering is initiated in Israel during the critical transition period of chieftainship, a shift which eventually will be institutionalized in the state. The modification of customary law not only reflects that transformation of society of which it is a part, but it also serves both to mediate and to promote the transition to a new form of social organization.[13] This is achieved by the transposition of legal authority from the margins to the centre of sociopolitical control. The legal modification functions as a part of a wider process of 'displacement' of disparate power groups and corresponding

13. Other features in the story about David have been seen as serving mediating functions related to the sociopolitical transformation of Israel to chiefdom and monarchy. Flanagan (1983: 361) describes the ritual aspects of David's transferring of the ark to Jerusalem (2 Sam. 6.1-20) as 'a rite of passage which mediated and legitimated the temporal, spatial, and social transformations occurring at the time'. Analyzing the literary context of the account of the transfer (2 Sam. 5.13–8.18), Flanagan demonstrates the use of ritual in the process by which power shifted from the house of Saul to the house of David. In a related vein, Brueggemann analyzes the same passage, noting along with the sociological shift from 'tribe' to 'state', a parallel 'intellectual' shift embedded in the literature and serving to 'legitimate and authorize' the transfer of political and economic power (1985: 68-69). Supporting Flanagan's discussion, he concludes that 'not only ritual structure but also literary structure mediates social transition to new forms of social power' (1985: 124 n.6). We propose the same mediating and legitimating function for judicial structures.

'ascendancy dominance' of centralized governance under David (cf. Flanagan 1983: esp. 362).

5. Along with a new *form* of sociopolitical organization, chieftain-ship (and monarchy) provided a new *concept* of social ordering. Social anthropologists observe that a society's lineage system may operate not only as a mode of social organization, an observable pat-tern of relationships, but may function concomitantly as an 'ideology', a 'set of notions' which constitutes for that society a world-view, or a 'myth' (Holy and Stuchlik 1983: 5-15).[14] Such an ideology operates not only as a group's organizational model, but also as their 'funda-mental guide to conduct and belief in all areas of their social life' (Fortes 1969: 290-91). While such a proposal as it relates to ancient Israel cannot be fully pursued here, it is reasonable to conclude that the process of shifting social, political, religious, economic and judicial control from the lineage groups to the powerful figure at the centre not only created a new mode of social organization which weakened (and eventually destroyed) the existing one, but that it weakened at the same time the lineage principle itself, substituting for it a different conception of reality, one based not on lineage principles but on a hierarchical model of reality expressed politically in chiefdom and monarchy, socially and economically, in a ranked society, and religiously, in the priesthood. Judicial ordering, always closely tied with sociopolitical organization, could not escape the practical and conceptual changes nor avoid becoming both object and agent of the new ordering.

BIBLIOGRAPHY

Ackroyd, P.R.
       1977   *The Second Book of Samuel*, The Cambridge Bible Commentary on
                    the New English Bible (Cambridge: Cambridge University Press).
Albright, W.F.
       1950   'The Judicial Reform of Jehoshophat', in S. Lieberman (ed.), *Alexander
                    Marx Jubilee Volume* (New York: Jewish Theological Seminary of
                    America): 61-82.

14. Holy and Stuchlik note that the two are not always in tandem (1983: 11-14). They explain that the domain of ideas, that is, the notions of ideology confessed by the people, is often not matched in the domain of social reality, that is, by what people do. Their distinction has important implications for anthropological methods of research and reporting and for scholars of other disciplines who draw upon such work.

Allott, A.
1980   *The Limits of Law* (London: Butterworth).
Aubert, W.
1983   *In Search of Law. Sociological Approaches to Law* (Law in Society Series; Oxford: Martin Robertson).
Barkun, M.
1968   *Law Without Sanctions. Order in Primitive Societies and the World Community* (New Haven: Yale University Press).
Bellefontaine, E.
1979   'Deuteronomy 21.18-21: Reviewing the Case of the Rebellious Son', *JSOT* 13: 13-31.
Boecker, H.J.
1980   *Law and the Administration of Justice in the Old Testament and Ancient East* (Minneapolis: Augsburg).
Bohannan, P.
1965   'The Differing Realms of Law', in L. Nader (ed.): 33-42.
1969   'Ethnography and Comparison in Legal Anthropology', in L. Nader (ed.) 1965: 401-18.
Brueggemann, W.
1985   *David's Truth in Israel's Imagination and Memory* (Philadelphia: Fortress Press).
Camp, C.
1981   'The Wise Women of 2 Samuel: A Role Model for Women in Early Israel?', *CBQ* 43: 14-29.
Christie, G.C.
1982   *Laws, Norms and Authority* (London: Duckworth).
Coats, G.W.
1981   'Parable, Fable, and Anecdote: Storytelling in the Succession Narrative', *Int* 35: 368-82.
Cohen, R., and R. Elman Service (eds.)
1978   *Origins of the State: The Anthropology of Political Evolution* (Philadelphia: Institute for the Study of Human Issues).
Crüsemann, F.
1978   *Der Widerstand gegen das Königtum: Die antiköniglichen Texte des Alten Testaments und der Kampf um den frühen israelitischen Staat* (WMANT, 49; Neukirchener Verlag: Neukirchen–Vluyn).
DeGeus, C.H.T.
1976   *The Tribes of Israel* (Assen: Van Gorcum).
Epstein, A.L.
1968   'Sanctions', *International Encyclopedia of the Social Sciences* 14: 1-5.
Fallers, L.A.
1969   *Law Without Precedent: Legal Ideas in Action in the Courts of Colonial Busoga* (Chicago: University of Chicago Press).
Flanagan, J.W.
1981   'Chiefs in Israel', *JSOT* 20: 47-73.
1983   'Social Transformation and Ritual in 2 Samuel 6', in C.L. Meyers and M. O'Connor (eds.), *The Word of the Lord Shall Go Forth*: *Essays in*

Honor of David Noel Freedman in Celebration of his Sixtieth Birthday (Winona Lake, IN: Eisenbrauns): 361-72.

Fokkelman, J.P.
1981   *Narrative Art and Poetry in the Books of Samuel 1* (Studia Semitica Neerlandica, 20; Assen: Van Gorcum).

Fortes, M.
1969   *Kinship and the Social Order* (Chicago: Aldine).

Fortes, M., and E.E. Evans-Pritchard
1940   *African Political Systems* (Oxford: Oxford University Press).

Frick, F.S.
1979   'Religion and Sociopolitical Structure in Early Israel: An Ethno-Archaeological Approach', in P.J. Achtemeier (ed.), *Society of Biblical Literature 1979 Seminar Papers* (Missoula, MT: Scholars Press): 233-53.
1985   *The Formation of the State in Ancient Israel* (The Social World of Biblical Antiquity Series, 4; Sheffield: Almond).

Gerstenberger, E.
1965   *Wesen und Herkunft des 'Apodiktischen Rechts'* (WMANT, 20; Neukirchener Verlag: Neukirchen–Vluyn).

Gluckman, M.
1955   *The Judicial Process Among the Barotse of Northern Rhodesia* (Manchester: Manchester University Press).
1965   *Politics, Law and Ritual in Tribal Society* (Oxford: Blackwell).

Gottwald, N.K.
1975   'Domain Assumptions and Societal Models in the Study of Pre-Monarchic Israel', VTSup 28: 89-100.
1979a   *The Tribes of Yahweh: A Sociology of the Religion of Liberated Israel, 1250–1050 BCE* (Maryknoll, NY: Orbis Books).
1979b   'Sociological Method in the Study of Ancient Israel', in M.J. Buss (ed.), *Encounter with the Text* (Philadelphia: Fortress Press; Missoula, MT: Scholars Press): 69-81.
1985   *The Hebrew Bible—A Socio-Literary Introduction* (Philadelphia: Fortress Press).

Gunn, D.M.
1982   *The Story of King David: Genre and Interpretation* (JSOTSup 6; Sheffield: JSOT Press).

Hamnett, I.
1975   *Chieftainship and Legitimacy: An Anthropological Study of Executive Law in Lesotho* (London and Boston: Routledge & Kegan Paul).

Harris, M.
1979   *Cultural Materialism: The Struggle for a Science of Culture* (New York: Random House).

Hoebel, E. Adamson
1967 (1954)   *The Law of Primitive Man: A Study in Comparative Legal Dynamics* (Cambridge, MA: Harvard University Press).

Hoebel, E. Adamson, and L. Frost Everett
1976   *Cultural and Social Anthropology* (New York: McGraw–Hill).

Hoftijzer, J.
1970 'David and the Tekoite Woman', *VT* 20: 419-44.

Holy, L., and M. Stuchlik
1983 *Actions, Norms and Representations: Foundations of Anthropological Inquiry* (London: Cambridge University Press).

Kaiser, O.
1975 *Introduction to the Old Testament: A Presentation of its Results and Problems* (Oxford: Basil Blackwell).

Köhler, L.
1956 *Hebrew Man* (London: SCM Press).

Lasswell, H.D., and R. Arens
1967 'The Role of Sanction in Conflict Resolution', *The Journal of Conflict Resolution* 11: 27-39.

Lewis, I.M.
1976 *Social Anthropology in Perspective* (Harmondsworth: Penguin Books).

Lobingier, C.S.
1950 'Customary Law', *Encyclopedia of Social Sciences* 4: 662-67.

Macholz, G.C.
1972a 'Die Stelung des Königs in der israelitischen Gerichtsverfassung', *ZAW* 84: 157-82.
1972b 'Zur Geschichte der Justizorganisation in Juda', *ZAW* 84: 321-40.

Mair, L.P.
1972 *An Introduction to Social Anthropology* (2nd edn rev.; Oxford: Clarendon).

Malamat, A.
1973 'Tribal Societies: Biblical Genealogies and African Lineage Systems', *Archives Européennes de Sociologie* 14: 126-36.

Mayes, A.D.H.
1985 *Judges* (OTG; Sheffield: JSOT Press).

Mazar, A.
1981 'Giloh: An Early Israelite Settlement Site near Jerusalem', *IEJ* 31: 1-36.

McCarter, P.K., Jr
1984 *II Samuel* (AB, 9; Garden City, NY: Doubleday).

McKeating, H.
1975 'The Development of the Law on Homicide in Ancient Israel', *VT* 25: 46-67.

Mendenhall, G.E.
1976 'Social Organization in Early Israel', in F.M. Cross, W.F. Lemke and P.D. Miller, Jr (eds.), *Magnalia Dei: The Mighty Acts of God. Essays on the Bible and Archaeology in Memory of G. Ernest Wright* (Garden City, NY: Doubleday): 132-51.

Mettinger, T.N.D.
1976 *King and Messiah: The Civil and Sacral Legitimation of the Israelite Kings* (ConBOT 8; Lund: Gleerup).

Middleton, J., and D. Tair (eds.)
    1958   *Tribes Without Rulers: Studies in African Segmentary Systems*
            (London: Routledge & Kegan Paul).
Moore, S. Falk
    1969   'Comparative Studies: An Introduction', in L. Nader (ed.), *Law in
            Culture and Society* (Chicago: Aldine): 337-48.
    1978   *Law as Process: An Anthropological Approach* (London: Routledge
            & Kegan Paul).
Nader, L. (ed.)
    1965   *The Ethnography of Law* (American Anthropologist Special Publica-
            tion), LXVII, 6.2.
Newman, K.S.
    1983   *Law and Economic Organization: A Comparative Study of Preindus-
            trial Societies* (Cambridge: Cambridge University Press).
Oates, J.
    1977   'Mesopotamian Social Organization: Archaeological and Philological
            Evidence', in J. Freidman and M.J. Rowland (eds.), *The Evolution of
            Social Systems* (London: Duckworth): 457-85.
Patrick, D.
    1985   *Old Testament Law* (Atlanta: John Knox).
Phillips, A.
    1970   *Ancient Israel's Criminal Law: A New Approach to the Decalogue*
            (New York: Schocken).
    1973   'Some Aspects of Family Law in Pre-Exilic Israel', *VT* 23: 349-61.
    1982   'Prophecy and Law, in R. Coggins, A. Phillips and M. Knibb (eds.),
            Israel's Prophetic Heritage. Essays in Honour of Peter R. Ackroyd
            (Cambridge: Cambridge University Press): 217-32.
Porter, J.R.
    1967   *The Extended Family in the Old Testament* (Occasional Papers in
            Social and Economic Administration, 6; London: Edutext).
Pospišil, L.
    1967   'Legal Levels and Multiplicity of Legal Systems in Human Societies',
            The Journal of Conflict Resolution 11: 2-26.
    1971   *Anthropology of Law: A Comparative Theory* (New York: Harper &
            Row).
Renfrew, C.
    1974   'Beyond a Subsistence Economy: The Evolution of Social Organiza-
            tion in Prehistoric Europe', in C.B. Moore (ed.), *Reconstructing
            Complex Societies* (Cambridge, MA: American Schools of Oriental
            Research): 69-95.
Rogerson, J.W.
    1986   'Was Early Israel a Segmentary Society?', *JSOT* 36: 17-26.
Sahlins, M.D.
    1967   'The Segmentary Lineage: An Organization of Predatory Expansion',
            in R. Cohen and J. Middleton (eds.), *Comparative Political Systems*
            (American Museum Sourcebooks in Anthropology; Garden City, NY:
            The Natural History Press): 91-119.

Schulz, H.
  1969   *Das Todesrecht im Alten Testament: Studien zur Rechtsform der Mot-Jumat Sätze* (BZAW, 114; Berlin: Töpelmann).
Seagle, W.
  1941   *The History of Law* (New York: Alfred A. Knopf).
Service, E.R.
  1975   *Origins of the State and Civilization: The Process of Cultural Evolution* (New York and Toronto: W.W. Norton).
  1978   'Classical and Modern Theories of the Origins of Government', in R. Cohen and E.R. Service (eds.), *Origins of the State* (Philadelphia: Institute for the Study of Human Issues): 21-34.
Shiloh, Y.
  1970   'The Four-Room House—Its Situation and Function in the Israelite City', *IEJ* 20: 180-90.
Simon, U.
  1967   'The Poor Man's Ewe Lamb: An Example of a Juridical Parable', *Biblica* 48: 207-42.
Stager, L.E.
  1985   'The Archaeology of the Family in Ancient Israel', *BASOR* 260: 1-35.
Stone, R.L.
  1976   'Norm and Normative', in D.E. Hunter and P. Whitten (eds.), *Encyclopedia of Anthropology* (New York: Harper & Row): 288.
Watson, A.
  1984   *Sources of Law, Legal Change, and Ambiguity* (Philadelphia: University of Philadelphia Press).
Whitelam, K.W.
  1979   *The Just King: Monarchical Judicial Authority in Ancient Israel* (JSOTSup, 12; Sheffield: JSOT Press).
Williamson, H.G.M.
  1982   *1 and 2 Chronicles* (NCB; Grand Rapids: Eerdmans; London: Marshall, Morgan & Scott).
Wilson, R.R.
  1983a   'Enforcing the Covenant: The Mechanisms of Judicial Authority in Early Israel', in H.B. Huffmon (ed.), *The Quest for the Kingdom of God: Studies in Honor of George E. Mendenhall* (Winona Lake, IN: Eisenbrauns): 59-75.
  1983b   'Israel's Judicial System in the Preexilic Period', *JQR* 74: 299-348.

JSOT 49 (1991), pp. 47-76

SHAME AS A SANCTION OF SOCIAL CONTROL IN BIBLICAL ISRAEL:
JUDICIAL, POLITICAL, AND SOCIAL SHAMING

Lyn M. Bechtel

Shame, like guilt, can be used by a society as a sanction of behavior which may or may not elicit a response of the emotion of shame. In the Old Testament there are many instances of shaming and a great abundance of shame vocabulary; yet in looking for research on the Old Testament sanction of shaming, there is relatively little available.[1] In much of the existing research there are two problems. First, some scholars assume that shame and guilt are the same emotional response and the same sanction, so shame is treated as if it were guilt. Modern psychoanalytic theory and social anthropological theory find that shame is a separate emotional response and sanction from guilt, stemming from different psychological forces, reflecting different patterns of behavior, and functioning in different social constructions, although shame and guilt could often be interrelated (see below for differences between shame and guilt). Secondly, in the analysis of shame, particularly in the commentaries, shaming instances are recognized and perceived as isolated experiences. There is a lack of understanding of how shame functions as a major sanction of behavior within the society, and of the social dynamics that are necessary for the society to use shame as a sanction of behavior.

1. M.A. Klopfenstein, *Scham und Schande nach dem Alten Testament* (Zürich: Theologischer Verlag, 1972); H. Seebass, '*Bosh; Bushah; Bosheth; Mebhushim*', *TDOT*, II, pp. 50-60; F. Stolz, 'Bosh zuschanden werden', *Theologisches Handwörterbuch zum Alten Testament*, pp. 269-72; J. Pedersen, 'Honour and Shame', *Israel: Its Life and Culture* (London: Oxford University Press, 1962), II, pp. 213-44; D. Daube, 'The Culture of Deuteronomy', *Orita* 3 (1969), pp. 27-52. Cf. E.R. Dodds, *The Greeks and the Irrational* (Berkeley: University of California Press, 1951), but this work deals more with Greek society than the Old Testament.

In comparing the use of shame and guilt in biblical society, I have concluded that both were determinants of behavior and checks on unacceptable behavior; and because of the great prevalence of public shaming, it is my contention that shame was equally important, if not slightly more important, than guilt as a means of social control. The purpose of this study is to show that shame is a different emotional response and sanction from guilt, to present a broad picture of the use and function of shaming as a sanction of behavior, and to point out the social dynamics necessary for it to function effectively in the society. To give the broad picture of the place of shame in biblical society, the study will investigate a few of the many instances of shaming, using the observations of David Daube on shame in the book of Deuteronomy as a foundation. It will focus on the function of shame within the judicial, political, and social systems. To help analyse the sanction of shame in the Old Testament, modern psychoanalytic and social anthropological theory will be utilized to inform the working definition of shame and guilt.

Working Definition of Shame and Guilt

In examining shame in the biblical texts an important consideration is the basic description and general understanding of shame and guilt that forms the foundation and colors the presumptions of the research. The following definition of shame and guilt is based on modern psychoanalytic, social-anthropological, and social-scientific theory.

Shame
There is a distinction between the emotional response of feeling shame or being ashamed and the social sanction of shaming or putting to shame (the action that causes the emotion of shame and that controls behavior). According to Gerhart Piers (whose theory is a standard one within the field of psychology), the main difference between shame and guilt lies in the kind of internalized norm that is violated and the expected consequences. The emotional response of shame relates to the anxiety aroused by 'inadequacy' or 'failure' to live up to *internalized, societal and parental goals and ideals.*[2] These goals and ideals contain four important elements:

---

2.   G. Piers and M. Singer, *Shame and Guilt* (New York: W. Norton, 1953).

1. the core of narcissistic omnipotence—necessary to establish healthy integrative functioning;
2. the sum of the identifications and images of the self presented by parents;
3. a layer of social identifications and roles inculcated by the society; and
4. an awareness of the potential of the self and the goals of self-realization.

These goals and ideals dictate expectations of what a person 'should' be able to do, be, know, or feel as well as a picture of what the society should be like. Shame relates to failure or inadequacy to reach or live up to a socio-parental goal or ideal, and it impacts on 'who a person is'. Helen Merrill Lynd, in her lengthy study of shame, points out that shame often arises in situations of incongruity, a reversal of expectations, or inappropriateness because these situations put 'who a person is' in jeopardy.[3]

Karen Horney notes that an individual's healthy sense of pride is based on sustaining these goals and ideals.[4] For instance, there may be pride in achievement, in feats of moral or physical courage, in a job well done, or in feelings of dignity or belonging or acceptance. Failure or inadequacy violates pride, and the response to a violation of pride is shame. Franz Alexander suggests that the feelings of failure and violation of pride associated with shame are inhibiting and repressive and shake people's confidence in themselves, their abilities, and their worth.[5] The fear that shame stimulates is that of contempt which leads to the *fear of psychological or physical rejection, abandonment, expulsion* (separation anxiety), *or loss of social position.*

One of the most prevalent impulses for people who have been shamed is the need to take revenge for their humiliation—that is 'face-saving'. Because of the involvement of pride in the experience of shame, 'getting back' at the offender seems to restore the shamed person's wounded

3. H. Lynd, *Shame and the Search for Identity* (New York: Harcourt, Brace, 1958).

4. K. Horney, *Neurosis and Human Growth* (New York: W. Norton, 1950); A. Isenberg, 'Natural Pride and Natural Shame', *Philosophy and Phenomenology* 45 (1950), pp. 329-49.

5. F. Alexander, *Fundamentals of Psychoanalysis* (New York: W. Norton, 1948); *idem*, 'Remarks about the Relation of Inferiority Feelings to Guilt Feelings', *International Journal of Psycho-Analysis* 19 (1938), pp. 129-36.

pride. And because the shamers have had the power to hurt the pride of the shamed, that puts them above or superior to the shamed. By taking revenge and shaming the shamer, the situation is reversed. The shamed person, then, feels triumphant and has defeated the shamer.[6] Unfortunately, because of the inhibiting aspect of shame, face-saving is rarely possible.

Another tendency for people who have been shamed is to look for pity through further self-abasement. As a means of preventing further shaming by others they bring it about themselves and thus take control of the shaming process. People often exaggerate their shame and lowliness by making themselves look even more lowly. The humbling techniques will depend on the society, but degrading body positions (such as hanging the head or lying prostrate on the ground) are common.

At the present time, the major contribution of social anthropologists and sociologists to the understanding of shame lies in the area of its function as a sanction of social behavior. In older comparative studies of 'shame cultures' and 'guilt cultures', shame cultures were considered those that relied on the external sanction of shame. They were assumed to be primitive, industrially backward, lacking in moral standards and a sense of sin, and lacking in concern for the individual. Guilt cultures were considered to be those that relied on the internal sanction of guilt and the conscience. They were assumed to be the highly developed, industrialized and individualized western cultures that possessed moral standards and were concerned for the welfare and dignity of the individual.[7]

More recently the idea of primitive, amoral shame cultures versus progressive, moral guilt cultures has been questioned and re-examined. It is now realized that both types of cultures have moral standards, which can be predominantly enforced by pressure from public opinion and shame or which can be predominantly enforced by pressure from the conscience and by guilt.[8]

In older comparative studies shame was considered solely an external

6.   Horney, *Neurosis and Human Growth*, p. 103; Hu Hsien-Chin, 'The Chinese Concept of Face', in *Personal Character and Cultural Milieu* (Syracuse: Syracuse University Press, 1956), pp. 447-67.

7.   R. Benedict, *The Chrysanthemum and the Sword* (Boston: Houghton Mifflin, 1946), pp. 222-24; cf. D. Ausubel, 'Relationship between Shame and Guilt in the Socializing Process', *Psychological Review* 62 (1955), pp. 378-90.

8.   Piers and Singer, *Shame and Guilt*, pp. 59-62.

sanction, and guilt solely an internal sanction. Nowadays, most social scientists feel that both shame and guilt arise from external pressure and internal pressure.[9] Shame relies predominantly on external or group pressure and is reinforced by the internal pressure of fear of being shamed. Guilt relies predominantly on internal pressure from the conscience and is reinforced by the external pressure from the society.

The work of Mary Douglas on 'group' and 'grid' is helpful in understanding the kind of social structure that permits the use of the sanction of shame or guilt.[10] In group-orientation, people's main source of identity comes from belonging to the strongly bonded group; consequently, the group is capable of exerting great pressure on people, in order to control their behavior. In grid-orientation (I call it 'individual-orientation') people's main source of identity comes from within the self. There is great value in individuality, and in order to control behavior the internalized grid of society (in the form of the conscience) is capable of exerting great pressure on people. No society is purely group-oriented or purely grid-oriented; they are all comprised of a mix in varying proportions of group and grid. Since shame relies heavily on external pressure from the group, it works most efficiently on a predominantly group-oriented society. In that type of society public opinion and outward appearances will influence the behavior of the individual because group rejection means being cut off from the major source of identity (the threat that shame presents is that of psychological or physical rejection, abandonment, and so on). Consequently, the importance of shame in a society will correspond to the amount of group-orientation present. In contrast, guilt works most efficiently in a predominantly grid-oriented (or individual-oriented) society, since guilt relies heavily on a stress on individuality and internal pressure from the conscience.

In Western society the lack of understanding of the sanction of shaming relates to the predominant guilt-orientation and individual-orientation of the society. Most psychologists and social scientists agree that the majority of people in Western society function with a highly individualistic focus and a more pronounced guilt sensitivity

---

9. M. Mead, *Cooperation and Competition Among Primitive Peoples* (New York: McGraw–Hill, 1937); Piers and Singer, *Shame and Guilt*, pp. 63-70; K. Riezler, 'Comments on the Social Psychology of Shame', *American Journal of Sociology* 48 (1943), pp. 457-65.

10. M. Douglas, *Natural Symbols* (New York: Vintage Books, 1973).

than shame sensitivity, which makes it more difficult to be aware of shame and shaming sanctions.[11]

Because of the importance of belonging to the group in a group-oriented shame culture, people's standing in the community or status is important, making people status-conscious. These societies are usually layered by an 'honor' hierarchy which designates the amount of authority held: ruler over subject, parents over children, husband over wife, elder over younger. Only friends are equals. Of great importance is the honor and respect the younger generation must show for the elderly and the honor shown to parents. Honor increases status, while shame decreases honor and lowers status.

Again because of the group-orientation, the family group and a group of close friends are important. Most people have life-long friends from whom they expect complete loyalty in the same way they expect loyalty from their family.

The functions of the sanction of shame are primarily:

1. as a means of social control which attempts to repress aggressive or undesirable behavior;
2. as a pressure that preserves social cohesion in the community through rejection and the creation of social distance between deviant members and the group;[12]
3. as an important means of dominating others and manipulating social status.

---

11. Lynd, *Shame and the Search for Identity*; Piers and Singer, *Shame and Guilt;* Horney, *Neurosis and Human Growth*; A. Kardiner and R. Linton, *The Individual and his Society* (New York: Columbia University Press, 1939); Alexander, *Fundamentals of Psychoanalysis*; *idem*, 'Remarks about the Relation of Inferiority Feelings to Guilt Feelings'; H. Lowenfeld, 'Notes on Shamelessness', *Psychoanalytic Quarterly* 45 (1976), pp. 62-72; S. Levin, 'Some Metapsychological Considerations on the Difference between Shame and Guilt', *International Journal of Psychoanalysis* 52 (1967), pp. 355-62.

12. Lowenfeld, ' Notes on Shamelessness', pp. 62-72; Piers and Singer, *Shame and Guilt*; R. Lowie, *Primitive Society* (New York: Liveright, 1947); D. Leighton and C. Kluckhohn, *Children of the People* (Cambridge, MA: Harvard University Press, 1947); Kardiner and Linton, *The Individual and his Society*; Lynd, *Shame and the Search for Identity*; Alexander, *Fundamentals of Psychoanalysis*; F. English, 'Shame and Social Control', *Transactional Analysis Journal* 5 (1975), pp. 24-28.

Guilt

According to Piers guilt relates to the *internalized, societal and parental prohibitions or boundaries* that cannot be transgressed (as opposed
to the internalized goals and ideals). These imperatives, once internalized, form an internal authority which the individual attempts to obey
(the conscience). Guilt, then, is the tension which arises when a prohibition or boundary has been 'transgressed'. It is the act of transgression that is wrong (not the essence of the person or who a person
is). The transgression of a boundary creates a feeling of wrongdoing
which causes guilt. Guilt is accompanied by the *fear of punishment*.[13]

The difference between shame and guilt is subtle, but important.
Yet despite the subtle differences shame and guilt are often interrelated—they can overlap, one can lead to the other, one can conceal the
other, and both can be a reaction to the same stimulus.[14]

Shame as Sanction of Behavior in Biblical Israel:
Linguistic Evidence

The linguistic evidence on Hebrew shame vocabulary will convey the
prevalence of the emotion and sanction of shame as well as the breadth
of meaning of the vocabulary. The emotion and sanction of shame
were expressed in Hebrew by (1) the verb *bwš*, 'to shame' (and the
nouns *bûšâ*, 'shame', *bōšet* 'shame', *bošnâ*, 'shame'); (2) the verb *klm*,
'to humiliate/ shame' (and the nouns *kᵉlimmâ*, 'humiliation/shame',
kᵉlimmût, 'humiliation/shame'); (3) the verb *qlh* (niphal; perhaps by a
by-form of *qll* 'to be light'), 'to be lightly esteemed or dishonored/
shamed' (and the noun *qālôn*, 'dishonor/ shame'); (4) the verb *šrp*, 'to
reproach/verbally shame' (and the noun *ḥerpâ*, 'reproach/verbal
shame'); (5) the verb *ḥpr*, 'to be ashamed, blush'; (6) the verb *špl*, 'to
be low, abased, be humiliated' (and the noun *šiplâ*, 'lowliness, humiliation'); (7) the verb *mkk*, 'to be low, humiliated'; (8) and the nouns
nablût, 'shamelessness', and *nᵉbālâ*, 'disgrace'. The differences in
meaning among the words are slight but discernible. Shame words are
often accompanied by phrases that express shame on the face (blush-
ing) or shame expressed in the body position (i.e. hanging the head in
shame) or that show that a person has been shamefully reduced to a

13. Piers and Singer, *Shame and Guilt.*
14. Piers and Singer, *Shame and Guilt*, p. 44.

lower social position in his or her own eyes and in the eyes of others (e.g. Jer. 48.39, *bwš;* 2 Sam. 10.5, *klm*; Isa. 16.14, *qlh*; Jer. 50.12, *ḥpr*). *Ḥrp*, the verb *qls*, 'to mock/shame' (and noun, *qeles*, 'derision/ shame'), the verb *l'g*, 'to mock/shame' (and the nouns, *la'ag*, 'derision/ shame', *lā'ēg*, 'derision/shame'), the verb *lyṣ*, 'to scorn/shame' (and the noun, *lāṣôn*, 'scorning/shaming') denoted verbal shaming, taunting, mocking, or scorning with insulting words. The main oppositional term to shame was the root *kbd* (signifying honor or heaviness). Honor increased status or heavy esteem, while shame decreased status, causing light esteem (see *qlh* above). The evidence suggests that there was no inherent sense of 'guilt' in the shame vocabulary.

Strikingly, the vocabulary for guilt was far less extensive than that of shame. The emotion and sanction of guilt were expressed in Hebrew by (1) the verb *'šm*, 'to offend/be guilty/ commit iniquity' (and the nouns *'āšām*, 'offense/guilt/iniquity', *'ašmâ*, 'wrongdoing/ guiltiness', and the adjective *'āšām*, 'guilty'); (2) the verb *rš'*, 'to be wicked/condemn as guilty' (and the adjective, *rāšā'* 'wicked/guilty'); and (3) the noun *'āwōn*, 'iniquity/guilt/punishment'. *Rš'*, *'šm*, and *'āwōn* alternated between meaning 'guilt' and meaning 'iniquity' or 'wrongdoing'. As a result, it is often difficult to decipher which meaning was intended.

Linguistically, there was no connection between shame and guilt. Consequently, there is a prima facie case for investigating shame as a separate, distinctive emotional experience and as a separate means of social control, though at times shame may have been associated with guilt.

The Formal Sanction of Judicial and Political Shaming

Shame functioned effectively in the Israelite community because the society was predominantly group-oriented with a less prominent grid-orientation. It was close-knit, and people's major (but certainly not only) source of identity stemmed from the group. People relied on and were strongly pressured by the opinion of others. What influenced those opinions was the external appearance of things. This social structure made people particularly susceptible to shaming. Shaming was effective because people were socially conditioned by the society during the process of socialization to find their identity in group belonging, to be concerned about the opinion of others, and to 'pride' themselves in the social and religious ideals of the community. Most people developed a sensitivity to shaming which far exceeded that common to most of modern Western society. And in contrast to the use of the sanction of shame is the concern for the honor of the group and the honor of the individual.

Shaming sanctions can be found in a variety of contexts: formal judicial shaming; formal political shaming within warfare and diplomacy; and public, informal social shaming. Scholars have recognized most of the instances as shameful, but they have not analyzed them as sanctions of behavior that fit within a social construction that allowed them to function coercively. In other words, scholars have not been aware of the broad pattern of shaming within Israelite society.

The Formal Sanction of Judicial Shaming
The importance of the sanction of shaming was evident in the area of law and the judicial system as reflected in the book of Deuteronomy. Although the primary concern and sanction of the judicial system was guilt, shame was a significant concern and sanction that interfaced guilt. There were official shaming sanctions as well as a concern for the abuse of shaming sanctions.

Here I turn to the work of David Daube for the foundation of my investigation. Daube has recognized that 'the Book of Deuteronomy contains a strong shame-cultural element...',[15] although he attributes it to an affiliation with Wisdom. He points out that there is an emphasis, not so much on the fearfulness of a crime, but on the fearfulness of the resulting appearances in the eyes of the beholders. The problem was more the inadequacy that was revealed, rather than the crime itself.[16] Daube gives numerous examples, such as 22.1-4, regarding the temptation of avoiding a shameful sight; 22.13ff., regarding bringing a shameful reputation on a bride and her family; 23.12ff., regarding the spot outside the camp in which the army was to relieve itself; 25.11-12, regarding the shame of a woman grabbing a man's genitals in a fight; 27.16, regarding people who were publicly cursed for shaming their father or mother; and so on. He also points out two important forms employed by Deuteronomy, *lō' tûkal* or *lō' yûkal* ('you/he should not', 12.17; 16.5; 17.15; 21.16; 22.3; 22.19; 24.4) and

15. Daube, 'The Culture of Deuteronomy', p. 27.
16. D. Daube, 'To Be Found Doing Wrong', *Studi in onore di Volterra* (Rome, 1969), II, p. 7; cf. 'The Culture of Deuteronomy', p. 47.

kî yimmāṣē' ('if there be found', 17.2; 21.1; 22.22; 24.7). The phrase *lō' tûkal/lō' yûkal* ('you/he should not') related to the religious and social ideals of the community—things that people 'should' or 'should not' do[17]—in contrast to the 'you shall' or 'shall not', which related to the societal and parental prohibitions and boundaries. *Kî yimmāṣē'* ('if there be found') related to the concern for appearance,[18] characteristic of a close-knit, group-oriented society.

For Daube's analysis of most of this material, I will refer the reader to his works cited above. I will deal with two examples from the book of Deuteronomy, 25.5-10 and 25.1-3.

Public Humiliation as a Sanction of Behavior
An excellent example of a shaming sanction within the judicial system is found in Deut. 25.5-10, a provision concerning Levirate marriage.[19] This sanction showed the importance of public humiliation and public opinion as a means of social control. The provision stated:

> If brothers dwell together and one of them dies and has no son, the wife of the dead brother shall not be married outside the family to a stranger; her husband's brother shall go in to her and take her as his wife to perform the duty of a husband's brother to her. And the first son whom she shall bear shall succeed to the name of his brother who is dead, that his name may not be blotted out of Israel. And if the man does not wish to take his brother's wife, then his brother's wife shall go up to the gate to the elders and say, 'My husband's brother refuses to perpetuate his brother's name in Israel; he will not perform the duty of a husband's brother to me'. Then the elders of his city shall call him and speak to him; and if he persists, saying, 'I do not wish to take her', then his brother's wife shall go up to him in the presence of the elders and pull his sandal off his foot and spit in his face, and she shall answer and say, 'So shall it be done to the man who does not build up his brother's house'. And the name of his house shall be called in Israel, the house of him that had his sandal pulled off (25.5-10).

17. Daube, 'The Culture of Deuteronomy', pp. 41-43.
18. Daube, 'The Culture of Deuteronomy', pp. 43-50.
19. An old practice found in Hittite and Middle Assyrian law. See R. de Vaux, *Ancient Israel*, pp. 37-38; N.H. Snaith, 'Daughters of Zelophehad', *VT* 16 (1966), pp. 124-27; P.C. Craigie, *The Book of Deuteronomy* (Grand Rapids, MI: Eerdmans, 1976), p. 313; S.R. Driver, *A Critical and Exegetical Commentary on Deuteronomy* (Edinburgh: T. & T. Clark, 1896), pp. 281-83.

There is disagreement among scholars as to the central concern in this provision. Was the function of Levirate marriage to beget an heir for the dead brother and his wife so that the brother's name was not blotted out?[20] Or was it to prevent the division of ancestral property?[21] In response to the question of the central concern, Daube points out that

> by begetting an heir to his dead brother, the survivor obviously deprives himself of half the property. If the deceased is definitely gone without an heir, everything will unreservedly belong to the survivor. The temptation to leave the widow alone and thus remain in sole possession must be considerable, and the indications are that many succumbed.[22]

So 'name' and 'property' were closely tied. But, the widow complained to the elders at the city gate that her husband's brother refused to raise up a 'name' for his brother; she did not complain that he was trying to retain all the 'property' for himself. Property was a secondary concern. I would stress the enormous importance of 'name' in biblical culture. In a group-oriented society, it was not individual survival (as in individual-orientation) that guaranteed what we would call 'eternal life', but family-group survival which was accomplished by begetting children, that is the perpetuation of 'name'. The heir would be a central concern in this society.

The widow lodged her complaint, and the man was summoned. If he publicly refused to carry out his obligation, a shaming sanction was used in which the widow publicly (in front of the elders and all who were witnessing at the city gate) shamed the brother-in-law by pulling off his sandal and spitting in his face, thus bringing a shameful reputation on him and his family. The public nature of the shaming sanction was essential.

There has been a great deal of speculation on why the sanction was shameful. Spitting in a person's face was a common informal, social shaming sanction which defiled and degraded people and rendered them unclean and socially unacceptable. In Num. 12.14, in connection with Miriam's leprosy, it is said: 'if her father spit in her face, she would hide in shame for seven days. Let her be shut up outside the

---

20. E.g. A.D.H. Mayes, *Deuteronomy* (London: Oliphants, 1979), p. 328; G. von Rad, *Deuteronomy* (London: SCM, 1966), p. 154; Driver, *A Critical and Exegetical Commentary on Deuteronomy*, p. 281; Craigie, *The Book of Deuteronomy*, p. 314; Daube, 'The Culture of Deuteronomy', p. 35; cf. Gen. 38.1-10.

21. Mayes, *Deuteronomy*, p. 328.

22. Daube, 'The Culture of Deuteronomy', p. 35.

camp for seven days, then bring her in again' (cf. Lev. 13, 15; 15.8). Spitting was not only shameful, but because it rendered the person unclean and unacceptable, it threatened the person with being cut off from the community. In Leviticus 15 all bodily fluids, once discharged (including saliva), were considered extremely defiling. Mary Douglas points out that, symbolically, the body is a bounded system that is a symbol of the community.[23] Any substance produced by the body is acceptable while in the body, but becomes unacceptable or unclean when it is expelled from the body. In spitting, the saliva is expelled from the body and is then unclean, similar to unclean things that are cast out of the community. Another clue regarding why spitting was a shaming gesture is found in Lev. 15.8. Here the text suggests that if an unclean person spat on a clean person, the latter had to wash the clothes, bathe, and be unclean until the evening. This would explain why it was unpleasant or even dangerous to be spat upon by an unclean person, but not why spitting itself was unpleasant.

In addition, spitting may have symbolized the incident in the other example of Levirate marriage in Gen. 38.1-11, where Onan had intercourse with Tamar, his brother's widow. He spilled his semen on the ground so Tamar would not conceive, which was considered an insulting, shameful act (vv. 8-10). Carmichael proposes that the patriarchal tradition formed the basis for the Deuteronomic law;[24] and so in Deuteronomy 25 spitting may have symbolized the man's spilling his semen on the ground and refusing to cause the woman to conceive.

Sandal removal is more difficult to explain. The ceremony of sandal removal was presumably not shameful in itself, since there are several such instances in the OT. In Gen. 13.17 ownership of land was legally effected by walking over it, and in Ruth 4.7-8 taking off the shoe symbolized the transfer of or giving up the right of redemption of property.[25] In Deut. 25.9 sandal removal was put in a different

23. M. Douglas, *Purity and Danger* (London: Routledge and Kegan Paul, 1966), pp. 118-23.

24. C. Carmichael, 'A Ceremonial Crux: Removing a Man's Sandal as a Female Gesture of Contempt', *JBL* 96 (1977), pp. 321-36.

25. E.F. Campbell, *Ruth* (AB; Garden City, NY: Doubleday, 1975), pp. 149-50. Attempts to unravel the custom have not dispelled the problems; see E. Lacheman, 'Notes on Ruth 4.7-8', *JBL* 56 (1937), pp. 53-56; E. Speiser, 'Of Shoes and Shekels (1 Sam. 12.3; 13.21)', *BASOR* 77 (1940), pp. 15-20, where surrender of the sandal is assumed to be similar to surrender of an item of clothing in a situation

context, and it was the context that added the element of shame to the ceremony. In this context sandal removal was accomplished by a woman and was combined with shameful spitting. I conclude with Carmichael[26] that in the sandal-removal ceremony here the sandal probably represented the woman's vagina and the foot represented the man's penis. In Ruth 3.4, 7 Ruth was instructed to go, uncover Boaz's feet, and lie down. The sexual meaning of 'feet' as a euphemism for the penis is widely attested (cf. also Judg. 3.24; 1 Sam. 24.3; 2 Kgs 18.27 = Isa. 36.12; Isa. 7.20; Ezek. 16.25; and in all probability, Exod. 4.25; Deut. 28.57; Isa. 6.2). When the widow removed the brother-in-law's sandal from his foot, she symbolized the removal of his Levirate privilege of having sexual intercourse and producing an heir. And this was combined with spitting, which symbolized the shameful refusal to cause the woman to conceive. Additionally, the sandal removal could have symbolized the loss of the property to the brother-in-law if the widow then married outside the family and produced an heir.

A further shaming was introduced into the sanction by the fact that it was inappropriate for a 'dominant' male to be dealt with aggressively and shamefully by a 'submissive' female. For the man this made the ceremony even more shameful.

The sanction did not end with the pulling off of the sandal and spitting. The brother-in-law and his family were then labeled publicly by the community as 'The House of Him That Had His Sandal Pulled Off'. It was a label that would remain with the family in the form of a perpetually shameful reputation. Because of the fear of this shameful reputation, the family, no doubt, was to have placed pressure on the man to carry out his duty.

This was no casual sanction; it negatively affected the status of the man and his family in the community, which, then, threatened their

---

where land was surrendered to another (Nuzi texts of the fifteenth century); J. Sasson, *Ruth* (Baltimore: The Johns Hopkins University Press, 1979), pp. 142-46; G. Tucker, 'Witnesses and "Dates" in Israelite Contracts', *CBQ* 28 (1966), pp. 42-45; T. and D. Thompson, 'Some Legal Problems in the Book of Ruth', *VT* 18 (1968), pp. 79-99; cf. Craigie, *The Book of Deuteronomy*, p. 315; Mayes, *Deuteronomy*, p. 329.

26. C. Carmichael, *Women, Law and the Genesis Traditions* (Edinburgh: Edinburgh University Press, 1979), pp. 65-73; *idem*, 'A Ceremonial Crux', pp. 321-36; cf. Campbell, *Ruth*, p. 150.

very survival. Von Rad wonders if the policy had legal consequences as well;[27] but a sanction that threatened the status and thus the very survival of a family in the community was severe enough punishment! And the fact that guilt and legal punishment for having violated a policy of the community was not involved indicated that shaming was often the more powerful sanction because of the group-orientation of the community.

The Concern for Excessive Shaming

There was a delicate balance between appropriate shaming and inappropriate, excessive shaming. The legal system attempted to maintain that balance. For example, in Deut. 25.1-3 the policy stated:

> If there is a case between men, they shall come to the court, they shall judge them, and they shall make right (*ṣdq*, hiphil) the right person and make guilty (*rš'*, hiphil) the guilty person. Then if the guilty person deserves to be beaten, the judge shall make him lie down and be beaten publicly as many times as fits his guilt. He shall give no more than forty (lashes);[28] if one should go on to beat him with more stripes than these, it will dishonor (*qlh*, hiphil) your brother in your eyes (25.1-3).

The policy began with an explanation of the legal process, a process involving guilt and innocence. If the person was found guilty, he or she was punished. What is important to recognize is that the provision dealt with the public revelation of both legal guilt (not internal feelings of guilt) and shame, and that the real concern was excessive shaming so that the guilty person was not inappropriately shamed in the eyes of the community. There was no concern for excessive feelings of guilt.

We have seen above that shaming was necessary when it was used as an official means of social control, but it had to be controlled and not carried out in excess of what the crime dictated. The text does not deal with the degree of shame the guilty person suffered by having his guilt revealed publicly at the gate and by being made to lie down

---

27. Von Rad, *Deuteronomy*, p. 154.

28. Forty lashes were the prescribed punishment in Middle Assyrian law (*ANET*, I and II [ed. J.B. Pritchard; Princeton: Princeton University Press, 1950], A 18, p. 981; G.R. Driver and J.K. Miles, *The Assyrian Laws*, p. 343) and later, in order to avoid accidental excess, the number was fixed in Israel at thirty-nine. The practice is also mentioned in Josephus, *Ant.* 4.238, 248; 2 Cor. 11.24; cf. H.E. Golin, *Hebrew Criminal Laws* (1952), pp. 49-53, 258-81.

prostrate and be beaten in front of the judge and anyone passing. The position was inappropriate for an honored person. Such a position fostered feelings of helplessness and degradation, which led to feelings of shame. Even without the shame of excessive punishment, the ordeal was inherently shameful; and the shame functioned as an important deterrent and means of control. This was acceptable shame under the circumstances.

But excessive beating beyond what was appropriate for the crime stripped people of their dignity and self-esteem and left them thoroughly shamed and degraded in the eyes of others. In a group-oriented society, preserving the basic dignity of an individual was essential for the basic dignity and status of the group. Having a policy against excessive shaming pointed to the importance that was attached to controlling a prevalent means of social control and to protecting the dignity of the individual.

The Formal Sanction of Political Shaming

Shaming Sanction Used in Warfare

One of the important contexts within which much shaming occurred was warfare, and in particular the experience of capture at the hands of an enemy. One of the characteristics of warfare in the ancient Near East (and especially in Assyria) was the use of psychological warfare. It was within this area of psychological warfare that shaming was employed. Saggs, in his study of Assyrian warfare,[29] observes that inhumane treatment and punishment of defeated warriors and leaders were not carried out for sadistic purposes alone. Such tactics were important because of their psychological impact. A captured vassal was not just vindictively tortured; he was made a *public* example for all to see, so that he served as warning by demonstration of what happened to delinquents. It was publicity, not necessarily pain, that was the primary motive for shameful and inhumane treatment of captives. The Assyrians openly boasted of their shaming and violence because a reputation for shame and violence was the main means of softening up and incapacitating an enemy population in advance.

One of the common ways of treating a captive in war (warriors or kings, both of whom symbolized their nation) in a shameful and

29. H.W. Saggs, 'Assyrian Warfare in the Sargonic Period', *Iraq* 25 (1963), pp. 149-51.

dehumanizing manner was to strip them and lead them off into captivity naked and bound, a practice which can be seen visually in the war reliefs of Assyria and Babylon.[30] Nakedness exposed the prisoners to the heat and cold, but most shamefully their private sexual parts were publicly exposed to the mocking eyes of those who gazed and jeered at them. The captured men were stripped of their ability to defend themselves and their nation. They were literally without protection. Their nakedness was symbolic of the defenselessness of their nation and demonstrative of its failure to attain victory.

In the context of warfare the function of this shaming sanction was primarily to attempt to control the undesirable, aggressive behavior of the enemy. Shaming made it possible to dominate and control defeated warriors because shame was restrictive and psychologically repressive. The victors would not have to worry about a counter-offensive if the enemy warriors were psychologically demoralized and rendered physically ineffective and defenseless.

Healthy pride was based on sustaining community ideals, such as dignity, strength, adequacy, honor, significance, or relatedness—things on which the group prided itself. The shaming action of stripping warriors was designed to withhold some of these assets and thus to violate their pride. This violation left warriors feeling exposed, inadequate, insignificant, unacceptable, isolated, abandoned, or stripped of their human dignity. Most importantly, this reflected on the nation.

A second function was status manipulation. In group-oriented societies status was largely (but not entirely) dependent on the evaluation and opinions of others. The more recognition, respect, or honor nations or people had in the eyes of others, the more influence, superiority, dominance, and status they had. These qualities were not conferred 'once for all time'; they were tenuous, shifting entities which

30. For illustrations, see Y. Yadin, *Art of Warfare in Biblical Lands* (New York: McGraw–Hill, 1963), I, pp. 151, 243 (the Megiddo piece); II, p. 39; G. Loud, *Megiddo Ivories* (Chicago: University of Chicago Press, 1939), plate 4.2a-b; J.B. Pritchard (ed.), *The Ancient Near East in Pictures Relating to the Old Testament* (Princeton: Princeton University Press, 1954), fig. 385, p. 124. For defeated (mostly dead) enemies shown naked, see R. Barnett and M. Falkner, *The Sculpture of Assur-nasir-apli II (883–859 BC), Tiglath-Pileser III (745–727 BC), Esarhaddon (681–669 BC) from the Central and Southwest Palaces at Nimrod* (London: British Museum, 1962), pls. xxxvii-xl, xliv; *Assyrian Sculpture in the British Museum* (Toronto: McClelland & Stewart, 1975), pls. 78, 81, 152; O. Kaiser, *Isaiah 13–39* (Philadelphia: Westminster, 1974), p. 114.

shaming threatened. One way of maintaining or raising an individual's or group's status was by lowering the status of other people or groups. Humiliating captive warriors lowered them and their nation to an inferior position and raised up the victors in status. Consequently, captive warriors or kings were made to walk naked, to grovel in the dust abjectly, or to feel helpless and defenseless in order to 'put them down' into a humiliating position and to lower their status. Conversely, putting others down had the effect of strengthening the confidence and sense of superiority of the victors. There was, then, less chance that neighbors would side with and assist the shamed defeated warriors and more chance that they would side with the confident winners.

To achieve all of this, a sanction involving guilt was out of place and would simply not have been effective. Within a group-oriented culture, a shame sanction was the best option.

One example of the shaming sanction of leading prisoners into captivity naked is reflected in Isa. 20.1-5. Around 715 Sargon II of Assyria became preoccupied with events in and around his own empire. Egypt, under the rule of the Twenty-fifth (Ethiopian) Dynasty, was once again in a position of relative strength, though it remained an Assyrian vassal. As a result, a spirit of rebellion pervaded Egypt, and other weaker rebellious Assyrian vassals began to look to Egypt for support. In 714 the Philistine cities under the leadership of Ashdod attempted to get out from under Assyrian domination by refusing to pay tribute to Assyria. Their action was supported by Egypt. Hezekiah, too, wanted liberation from Assyrian domination, and he considered having Judah join the revolt, hoping, of course, for Egyptian support. Isaiah was strongly opposed.

Part of the Isaiah tradition (possibly not completely historical) claimed that Isaiah walked the streets of Jerusalem for three years 'naked and barefoot' to express his opposition to dependence on Egypt for protection. This symbolic action on the part of Isaiah symbolized the shameful experience of warriors being led into captivity naked. It suggested that Egypt and Ethiopia themselves might experience this cruel treatment, and it served as a warning to Israel that they would experience shame if they relied on Egypt for help in defying the Assyrians. Most importantly, the action was designed to stimulate fear of the warfare shaming sanction in the people of Jerusalem and to discourage them from joining the revolt. It was not until 711, after the defeat of Ashdod by the Assyrians, that Isaiah announced the meaning of the warning:

> As my servant, Isaiah, has walked naked and barefoot for three years as a sign and portent against Egypt and Ethiopia, so the king of Assyria will lead the captive Egyptians and exiled Ethiopians, young and old, naked and barefoot, with buttocks uncovered, to the nakedness/shame (*'erwat*) of Egypt.[31] Then they shall be dismayed and shamed (*bwš*) because of Ethiopia their hope and Egypt their boast (20.3-5).[32]

There are two relevant issues with which scholars have been concerned. First, there is disagreement whether Isaiah walked stark naked or wore a loincloth. Some scholars assume that since nakedness was a 'scandal' in Israel (e.g. Gen. 3.7, 10; 4.22), Isaiah would not, in all common decency, have walked completely naked, but rather in a loincloth.[33] However, captive warriors were not led into captivity in loincloths, but rather completely naked. There would have been considerably less shame and less of an impact if warriors had worn a loincloth. Isaiah was simulating what the nation would experience; and thus, he would, no doubt, have portrayed the actual practice of publicly walking captives naked with genitals exposed. In doing so, he was attempting to stimulate Israel's fear of a well-known shaming sanction associated with defeat.

Walking naked entailed double shame: the shame Isaiah experienced from being naked in the presence of his community, and the shame the people of Jerusalem would have experienced when they saw the shameful sight. People's reaction to public nakedness was, at the least, to turn their heads away. Part of the socialization process in Israel involved an awareness that public nakedness was inappropriate and unacceptable behavior (see Gen. 2–3) and that people should react to being naked in public by feeling ashamed and react to public nakedness of others by averting their eyes.[34] It was unpleasant to see because the public shame of one member of the community reflected shame on the entire community.

---

31. *'Erwat miṣrāyim* is regarded as a gloss.

32. Other examples of the shame of nakedness are found in Isa. 47.2-3; 2 Sam. 10.5; Nah. 3.5-7; 2 Chron. 28.15; Mic. 1.8.

33. Cf. G.B. Gray, *A Critical and Exegetical Commentary on the Book of Isaiah 1–27* (Edinburgh: T. & T. Clark, 1921), p. 346; R.E. Clements, *Isaiah 1–39* (Grand Rapids, MI: Eerdmans, 1980), p. 174.

34. Although it was allowed at times in the cult (2 Sam. 6.20-22).

The meaning of the word *'erwâ* shows the connection between nakedness and shame. *'Erwâ* had a primary meaning of 'nakedness', but under certain circumstances it meant 'shameful exposure' or 'the genitals' (suggesting that public nakedness was considered shameful because of the exposure of the genitals) or 'the exposed undefended parts of a person or country' (suggesting vulnerability or defenselessness which caused defeat and shame). People's clothing formed a covering which protected their vital parts from the physical environment (rain, heat, cold, wind) and, most of all, psychologically from having the private areas of the body exposed to the gaze of others. Public nakedness made people feel self-conscious and psychologically vulnerable or defenseless, as if this had exposed a person's 'inner self'.

Feelings of being dominated, controlled, inferior in status, physically ineffective and defenseless, exposed, unacceptable, isolated, abandoned, and degraded were the emotions and experiences associated with this shaming sanction that Isaiah was trying to make Hezekiah and the people of Jerusalem fear.

Secondly, there is some scholarly discussion as to whether either Isaiah or the people of Jerusalem understood the significance of Isaiah's action before God announced its meaning three years on.[35] It seems clear, however, that, in light of the atmosphere of potential war, the people of Jerusalem would have known instantly what was being symbolized, since the sanction of walking captives naked was widely practiced. The later announcement in 711 simply pointed out that what Isaiah had announced and had symbolized for three years was now being accomplished.

Shaming Sanction Used in Diplomacy
A shaming sanction used in the world of international diplomacy can be found in 2 Sam. 10.1-5. Due to the death of the Ammonite king, Nahash, there had been a change of rulers, and Hanun, his son, ruled in his place. According to the text David pledged to deal as loyally with the new administration as he had with the previous one. So he sent ambassadors[36] as his personal representatives to Hanun to console

---

35. See Kaiser, *Isaiah 13–39*, p. 115; J. Hayes and S. Irvine, *Isaiah* (Nashville: Abingdon, 1987), pp. 267-71; H. Wildberger, *Jesaja 13–27* (Neukirchen–Vluyn: Neukirchener Verlag, 1978), pp. 749-60.

36. The word *'ebed*, 'servant', is translated 'ambassador' to give greater impact

him concerning his father's death. But the advisors to the new Ammonite king questioned David's action—probably with good reason:

> Do you think because David has sent comforters to you, that he is honoring (*kbd*) your father? Has David not sent his ambassadors to you to search the city and spy it[37] out, and overthrow it? (v. 3).

Although David's publicly announced intentions were to honor, he was a shrewd politician, and the advisors of Hanun dealt with him cautiously. As a result of their assumption of David's aggressive motives,

> Hanun took David's ambassadors and shaved off half[38] their beards and cut off half their garments, at their hips, and sent them away. When it was told to David, he went to meet them, for the men were greatly humiliated (*klm*). And the king said, 'Remain at Jericho until your beards have grown and then return' (vv. 4-5).

From Hanun's point of view the behavior of the ambassadors of David needed to be controlled. The ambassadors were not yet guilty of spying, so a guilt sanction would have been inappropriate. Instead, a shaming sanction was resorted to: shaving off half the beard[39] (cf. 1 Sam. 11.1-4) and cutting off half the garments to expose the genitals.

Again, the public nature and the group focus of the sanction has to be stressed. We have seen previously that public nakedness was shameful because it was inappropriate and unacceptable to have the genitals exposed publicly. It was particularly inappropriate for the dignified representatives of the king and nation to be naked from the waist down, walking through the city streets before the people of Ammon. The ambassadors 'should' have been clad in flowing garments of respect, but now unexpectedly they had their sexual parts publicly

---

to the shaming actions which were performed against David's servants who actually functioned as ambassadors.

37. An alternative text has 'land', *hā'āreṣ*.

38. MT has 'half', *ḥᵃṣî*, perhaps in anticipation of cutting off half (*ḥᵃṣî*) their garments. LXX has merely 'their beards'.

39. W. McKane (*I & II Samuel* [London: SCM Press, 1963], p. 226) observes that the Hebrew words for 'beard' (*zāqān*) and 'elder' (*zāqēn*) had the same consonants, and so concludes that the beard was also a symbol of seniority and rank in the community.

exposed. And they looked foolish—they were elegantly dressed from the hips up and naked from the hips down, with one side of their beards shaven off. It was inappropriate to treat men of honor and status in such a shameful manner. And the shaming reflected on Israel!

In ancient Israel a man's beard was a symbol of his dignity and vitality, particularly his sexual vitality.[40] Because of this veneration of the beard, one way of degrading a man and making him look foolish was to cut off or pull at his beard (cf. Isa. 50.6).[41]

One of the characteristics of shame (pointed out by Lynd) was that it arose in situations of violation of expectations. The declared intention of David and his ambassadors was to console and honor, and their expectation was to be honored and respected in return. Instead, the response of Hanun was to shame David's representatives, and this reversal of expectations made the shame more intense. Yet from the point of view of the Ammonites the action was justified—an uncovering of the undercover agents who were assumed to be spying for their nation.

Like all shaming actions, these sanctions had an inhibiting effect. To prevent spying and aggressiveness, Hanun made the ambassadors ineffective by shaming them. And by shaming and belittling David through his representatives, Hanun and the Ammonites were the ones who took control of the situation.

In addition, the shaming was a means of status manipulation. One way that Hanun and the Ammonites could raise their own status was by lowering the status of Israel through David and his ambassadors by shaming them and 'putting them down' into a humiliating position.

A further complication of the shaming action was the men's necessary exclusion from the Israelite community. The ambassadors would have displayed their shaming if they walked the streets of Jerusalem in their shamed condition, and they would have suffered additional shame if they had returned to their own community looking foolish with only half a beard. David protected himself, his representatives, and the nation by having them remain in seclusion in Jericho until their beards had grown back. Their seclusion minimized the shaming

40. Shaving the beard was also associated with expressions of mourning (cf. Isa. 15.2; Jer. 41.5; 48.37) or judgment (cf. Isa. 7.20).

41. Cf. P.R. Ackroyd, *The Second Book of Samuel* (Cambridge: Cambridge University Press, 1977), p. 97, and H. Hertzberg, *First and Second Samuel* (Philadelphia: Westminster, 1964), p. 304.

of David and the nation, and thereby reduced the pressure for immediate retaliation.

Viewed as shaming sanctions intended to prevent spying and aggressive behavior and to manipulate status, the incident was surely a challenge to David. Hanun must have assumed that David was too weak to save face and take revenge. David did indeed respond and save face for himself subsequently by putting the Ammonites and their allies, the Syrians, through a humiliating defeat (2 Sam. 10.6-19).

The Informal Shaming Sanction in Social Use

Shaming sanctions were not confined to the official shaming techniques used in the legal process, warfare and diplomacy. Unlike other means of control, such as the use of force and punishment which were restricted in their use to authorized persons, anyone in the society had access to shaming sanctions. Consequently, it was employed publicly and informally by ordinary folk in the midst of everyday life.

In the book of Psalms, particularly in the complaint psalms, there were constantly repeated concerns about being shamed by members of the community or by enemies, who may or may not have been part of the community:[42]

> To you, O Lord, I lift up my soul. O my God, in you I have trust, let me
> not be shamed (*bwš*); let my enemies not exult over me; let none that wait
> for you be shamed (*bwš*); let them be shamed (*bwš*) who are wantonly
> treacherous (Ps. 25.1-3; cf. Pss. 4, 22, 31, 34, 35, 37, 39, 40, 42, 44,
> 55, 57, 69, 70, 71, 74, 79, 80, 89, 102, 109, 119, 123).

Although scholars have recognized the shaming, they have not understood the inter-group shaming some of these psalms manifest. Aside from external enemies of the nation, there seemed to be a group of less pious (or possibly impious) people in the community who shamed the orthodox because of their trusting relationship with YHWH. From the point of view of the orthodox psalmists, the shaming sanctions used against them were inappropriate and evil. As a result of this shaming the wicked shamers often strutted confidently and arrogantly, displaying their superiority (Pss. 9.3; 10.2-5; 31.19; 140.5), while the shamed people felt afflicted, inferior, and bowed down (e.g. Pss. 10.12;

---

42. See H. Birkeland's study of the 'enemies' in the Psalms (*The Evildoers in the Book of Psalms* [Oslo: Jacob Dybwad, 1955]).

22.6, 14-15; 31.9-10; 42.11; 69.20-21, 30; 102.3-11; 109.22-24). For the less pious, the extreme righteousness of the pious was an annoyance that could not have been dealt with by a guilt sanction. The pious were guilty of nothing. A shaming sanction was the only option.

Feeling shamed and afflicted caused the psalmists to need pity and comfort from their community or at least from their friends. Receiving none, they turned to God: 'I look for pity, but there is none; and for comforters, but I find none' (Ps. 69.21). When they did not receive the pity and comfort they expected, they would often humble themselves further by fasting or wearing sackcloth to elicit it (e.g. Ps. 69.10-12).

For the pious, revenge or face-saving through counter-shaming was inappropriate behavior which violated the ideals of their religion (see below). Thus, they called on God to take revenge for them by shaming the shamers:

> Let them be shamed (*bwš*) and humiliated (*klm*) who seek after my life.
> Let them be turned back and be disgraced (*ḥpr*) who devise evil against
> me... Let them be put to shame (*bōšet*) and disgrace (*ḥeprâ*) together who
> rejoice at my calamity. Let them be clothed with shame (*bōšet*) and humil-
> iation (*kᵉlimmâ*) who magnify themselves against me (Ps. 35.4, 26; cf.
> 6.10; 31.18; 35.4; 40.14-15; 53.5; 59.13; 70.2; 71.13; 83.16-17; 86.17;
> 97.7; 109.28-29, 78; 129.5).

The Common Shaming Sanctions

It is important to be aware of the common shaming techniques used: making a person a laughing-stock, slandering, taunting, scorning, or mocking (e.g. 2 Chron. 30.10; Job 12.4; Pss. 22.6-8; 30.9; 35.15-16; 39.8; 42.11; 44.14; Isa. 57.4; Jer. 20.7; Lam. 3.14; Ezek. 23.32); wagging or shaking the head mockingly (e.g. 2 Kgs 19.21; Job 16.4; Pss. 22.7[8]; 109.25; Isa. 37.22; Jer. 18.16; Lam. 2.15; Zeph. 2.15; and in the NT Mt. 27.39; Mk 15.29); gaping with open mouth (e.g. Pss. 22.7, 13; 35.21; Job 16.10) and sticking out the tongue (Isa. 57.4); gnashing the teeth (e.g. Pss. 35.15-16; 37.12; 112.10; Lam. 2.1); spitting (Num. 12.14; Deut. 25.9; Job 17.6; 30.9-10; Isa. 50.6; also Mt. 26.67; 27.30; Mk 10.34; 14.65; 15.19); hissing (e.g. Job 27.23; Jer. 18.16; 19.8; 25.9, 18; 29.18; Lam. 2.15-16; Zeph. 2.15); striking the cheek shamefully (e.g. Job 16.9-10; Lam. 3.30); winking (e.g. Ps. 35.19; Prov. 6.13; 10.10; 16.30); and defiling the beard (2 Sam. 10.4-5; Isa. 50.6).

Probably most common was the practice of taunting (scorning, mocking, slandering, or making a person a laughing-stock). Examples of taunts are: (to those of Jerusalem after the 587 destruction) 'Is this the city which was called the perfection of beauty, the joy of all the earth?' (Lam. 2.15), or (to an orthodox worshipper who trusts solely in God and not in earthly powers) 'He committed his cause to the Lord, let the Lord deliver him, let him rescue him, for he delights in him' (Ps. 22.8).

The Shaming of Job

One of the many examples of informal social shaming sanctions used by the community to control behavior is found in the shaming of Job.

Job was once a man with a reputation in the community for piety, honor, and prosperity. Then he was suddenly overwhelmed by conditions of misfortune and disease, imposed by God to test the genuineness of his piety. Job's pious friends assumed that Job's misfortune was a sign of God's disfavor. They accused him of being guilty (e.g. 15.6; 32.3), while Job claimed he was innocent (e.g. 9.15-35; 10.2-7). When their attempts to impose guilt upon him failed, they turned from honoring him to shaming him:

> I am a laughing-stock (*śᵉḥōq*) to my [lit. his] friends; I, who called upon God and he answered me, a just and blameless man, am a laughing-stock (*śᵉḥōq*; 12.4)...Bear with me, and I will speak, and after I have spoken, mock (21.3) (*l'g*) on.[43]... How long will you torment me, crush me with words? Ten times you have humiliated (*klm*) me, are you not ashamed (*bwš*) that you have insulted[44] me? (19.2-3, 5).

He was bewildered by the fact that his friends were not the least bit ashamed of treating him in this way, although it was inappropriate for pious folk to shame others (see below).

Job was also emotionally rejected and abandoned by his own family and household, which caused him to be emotionally debilitated in his time of need (19.13-19; cf. Ps. 55.14-15). His family and friends were the ones who 'should' have remained loyal and supportive of him (2.11; 6.10, 14; 16.2-5) and have given him pity (19.21). He was

---

43. The verb is in the singular, and scholars agree that the statement is directed to Zophar; see N. Tur-Sinai, *The Book of Job* (Jerusalem: Kiryath Sepher, 1967), p. 295.

44. The meaning of *hkr* is dubious. I follow N. Habel (*The Book of Job* [Philadelphia: Westminster, 1985], p. 272) who sees *hkr* as parallel to *klm*, meaning 'insult, abuse, disgrace'.

confident in their loyalty, but they disappointed him (6.14-21). This violation of his expectations caused additional shame for Job.

Primarily their actions were used as a means of social control which tried to maintain the purity of the pious community. Secondarily, they seemed to be interested in taking advantage of his situation to raise their own status and esteem by 'putting Job down' and treating him as an inferior, that is by indulging in status manipulation (12.3b; 13.2): And even if it be true that I have erred, my error remains with me. You have made yourself superior to me, so you are able to verbally shame me (*ḥrp*) (19.4-5).

People in his community also took advantage of his unfortunate state to humiliate him. They stared at him, gaped with their mouths, slapped him on the face shamefully (*ḥrp*, 16.10), and spat at him (17.6).[45] Often Job was shamed by members of the community who were the lowest in status—young people, slaves and ruffians:

> But now they laugh (*śḥq*) at me, those who are younger than I, whose fathers I disdain so much that I would not even set them with my dogs of my flock... They are driven from society; they are shouted at like a thief... Scoundrels and nonentities, outcasts of the land! And now I have become their joke, I am a byword among them. They abhor me, they keep aloof from me; they do not hesitate to spit in my face... They break up my path, they promote my calamity; no one restrains them (30.1, 5, 8-10, 13; cf. 19.16).

Once again these people used shaming for status manipulation. What made their shaming more humiliating for Job was the fact that it was done by inferiors, people of lower social status who should have honored him simply because of his higher status.

Much of Job's humiliation came in the incongruity between his previous situation of being honored (29.2-25) and his present situation of being shamed, even by the lowest of society (19.1-20; 30.1-19). In 29.8-10 Job remembers how he was once treated with respect and honor. Young people respected and honored people of higher status (elders, leaders, nobles, and Job); and people of high status respected and honored Job, the epitome of the honored person. It was inappropriate for a once honored man to be treated shamefully by anyone, let alone by socially inferior people. The inappropriateness of his shaming added to his humiliation.

---

45. Cf. Tur-Sinai, *The Book of Job*, ad loc.

Control of Excessive Social Shaming

Just as excessive official shaming sanctions had to be controlled, so excessive social shaming had to be curtailed also. There were attempts to control unofficial social shaming within the policies of the cult.

Most exegetes regard Psalm 15 as a cultic liturgy which stated the moral behavior required for admission to the temple (cf. Ps. 24.3-5; Isa. 33.14-16; Mic. 6.6-8). But without a broad understanding of the extensive use of social shaming and its function, the full impact of the shaming aspect of the Psalm can be misunderstood. The Psalm stated that a person had to have integrity and speak truth from the heart (v. 2), had to be loyal in fulfilling oaths (v. 4c), was not to loan money at interest or bribe the innocent (v. 5a, b), had to be one on whose tongue there is no slander,[46] could do not evil to a friend, and 'could not take up a taunt (*ḥerpâ*) against his neighbor' (v. 3; see Exod. 23.1; Lev. 19.16). For the pious person, ideal behavior excluded the use of the informal sanction of taunting or shaming one's neighbor (cf. Prov. 3.34-35; 6.12-15; 9.7-8; 10.10, 18; 11.2; 13.5; 18.3; 22.10). In a society that used shaming as a major means of social control, the very presence of the prohibition indicated that excessive informal shaming was prevalent and problematic, even within the pious community. The Psalm must have been influential, since the pious folk complained to God about being shamed and often suggested the kind of counter-shaming they would like God to carry out, but we have no evidence of the psalmists actually saving face for themselves by shaming the shamers.

Conclusion

I have presented selected examples of the variety of uses of shaming to show that it was a prevalent and important sanction of behavior. Its coercive power was available officially to state or local authorities as a formal sanction of behavior (judicial and political shaming) and unofficially to the community or general public as an informal social sanction of behavior (social shaming). Both the formal and informal sanctions were used to control undesirable or aggressive behavior, to manipulate status, and to dominate others. Shaming was used so

---

46. *Rāgal 'al-lᵉšōnô* is problematic, but there is a parallel in Ps. 39.2 ('stumble over my tongue') and in Ps. 73.9.

extensively that it became necessary to attempt to limit its use in the judicial system and among the general public. Excessive shaming stripped people of their dignity and self-esteem and left them thoroughly degraded in the eyes of others. In a shame/honor society, preserving the basic dignity of an individual was essential because the individual reflected the dignity and status of the group.

Shaming was predominantly a public experience; its power stemmed from its ability to reveal publicly inadequacy or failure to meet societal or religious ideals. It was effective because the social structure of Israelite society was heavily group-oriented, and shame relied predominantly on external group pressure, while being reinforced by the internal pressure of fear of shaming. In the group-oriented social structure, the main source of people's identity came from belonging to the group, and shame threatened people with being abandoned and cut off by the group. Part of the socialization process of the Israelite society involved developing a sensitivity to shaming. The reaction people had to being shamed was to take revenge or save face. This need for revenge suggested that their pride had been violated by their shaming. Revenge would restore pride by reversing the positions of those involved.

The history of Judeo-Christian biblical interpretation reflects a strong emphasis on guilt; yet, in the biblical community the sanction of shaming also played a significant role in the structure of the society. Part of the difficulty scholars have had in distinguishing shame and guilt arises out of situations where shame and guilt were interrelated.

STRATIFICATION, POWER AND SOCIAL JUSTICE

JSOT 33 (1985), pp. 3-25

THEODICY IN A SOCIAL DIMENSION

Walter Brueggemann

The issue of *theodicy* in current theological discussion is articulated in three distinct but not unrelated conversations:

1. The most obvious and popular is the pastoral question: 'Why did this happen to me?' That is, the question is focused on a negative experience of a person who seems not to deserve such treatment. This question is effectively posed in the popular book by Rabbi Lawrence Kushner, *When Bad Things Happen to Good People*.[1] The pervasiveness of the issue is evident in the popularity of the book, even though its argument seems romantic and scarcely adequate.[2]

2. In Old Testament studies, theodicy is conventionally related to the crisis of 587 BCE, and the emergence of the relatively miserable situation of exilic and post-exilic communities.[3] It is a situation in which the older historic traditions of confession are found wanting. On the one hand, it is conventionally thought that the question is posed in an early form of Habakkuk,[4] in Jeremiah and Job. More recently it is proposed

---

1.   Lawrence Kushner, *When Bad Things Happen to Good People* (New York: Schocken, 1981).

2.   A more solid, reflective discussion is offered by Sibley Towner, *How God Deals with Evil* (Philadelphia: Westminster Press, 1976). However, this book has not captured popular imagination as has Kushner.

3.   On the literature related to these issues in that context, see Peter Ackroyd, *Exile and Restoration* (Philadelphia: Westminster Press, 1968) and Ralph W. Klein, *Israel in Exile* (Philadelphia: Fortress Press, 1979).

4.   See the pastoral discussion of Donald E. Gowan, *The Triumph of Faith in Habakkuk* (Atlanta: John Knox, 1976).

that *wisdom, apocalyptic* and *creation* faith are responses to the issue, when the historical traditions are inadequate. In particular, James Crenshaw has contributed to this conversation in most helpful ways.[5]

3. The reality of the holocaust has focused the question of God's justice in inescapable ways and has muted old answers.[6] In some ways, the holocaust is an echo of the dilemma of Job. But Rubenstein[7] and others have shown that the holocaust is of such unutterable magnitude and irrationality that it violates any parallel with the old tradition. Indeed it is such a unique happening among us that it must be bracketed out provisionally from most discussions. Such a bracketing is not to dismiss the issue but to avoid trivializing it with frivolous comparisons.

I

These three ways of putting the question are all important and none can be taken lightly. The following discussion, however, attempts to press the issue in a different direction. The notion of *theodicy*, of course, combines the issues of God (*theos*) and justice (*dikē*). However, the theodic questions are largely treated as speculative questions about the character and person of God, so that the justice issue is too much shaped in religious categories.[8] In fact justice is a social question about social power and social access, about agreed-upon systems and practices of social production, distribution, possession and consumption. Scholarship has taken a largely idealistic view of the issue, which

5. James L. Crenshaw, *A Whirlpool of Torment* (Philadelphia: Fortress Press, 1984); *Theodicy in the Old Testament* (Philadelphia: Fortress Press, 1983); 'Popular Questioning of God in Ancient Israel', *ZAW* 82 (1970), pp. 380-95; 'The Problem of Theodicy in Sirach', *JBL* 94 (1975), pp. 47-64.

6. Emil Fackenheim, *To Mend the World* (New York: Schocken, 1982), has provided an excellent statement on the implications of the holocaust for both Jewish and Christian faith. Of course the various writings of Elie Wiesel have provided the most helpful and most disturbing commentary. On his work, see the introduction by Robert McAfee Brown, *Elie Wiesel: Messenger to All Humanity* (Notre Dame: University of Notre Dame Press, 1983).

7. Richard Rubenstein, *After Auschwitz* (Indianapolis: Bobbs Merrill, 1966).

8. On the question handled in more speculative, philosophical fashion, see John Hick, *Evil and the Love of God* (New York: Harper & Row, 1966).

likely reflects the social location of those in the conversation.[9]

Here I shall argue instead that the subject of *God-justice* (i.e. theodicy) requires a 'materialist' reading of text and experience,[10] for Yahweh functions and is discerned either through a *practice* of social consensus, or a *challenge* to a social consensus still held, but under assault. The justice of God cannot be separated from the actual experience of justice in the social process, because Yahweh's presence in Israel is known through and against the social process.

It is odd that our scholarly characterization of justice, and therefore theodicy, in the Old Testament is bifurcated. In the eighth-century prophets, for example, justice surely has to do with social practice in which Yahweh is understood to have a crucial concern.[11] We have enough critical data to know that in the strictures of the prophets, the advocacy of justice concerns both social systems and the God confessed through the practice of the social system.[12] That is hardly in doubt both in the text and in our usual interpretations. The justice questions in the

9.   I am using 'idealistic' here in the sense critiqued by Norman K. Gottwald, *The Tribes of Yahweh* (Maryknoll, NY: Orbis Books, 1979), pp. 592-607.

10.   It should be clear that 'materialist' here does not require Marxist categories, but requires taking into account the material basis and the historical context of real social life. The use of the word 'material' is not remote from conventional use of 'history' in Old Testament scholarship, as in the phrase, 'God acts in history' as long as 'history' is understood as the actual social processes of communal interaction which includes process of organization and technology as much as ideology and mythology. On a materialist reading, see Kuno Füssel, 'The Materialist Reading of the Bible', in N.K. Gottwald (ed.), *The Bible and Liberation* (Maryknoll, NY: Orbis Books, 1983), pp. 134-46, Walter J. Hollenweger, 'The Other Exegesis', *Horizons in Biblical Theology* 3 (1981), pp. 155-79, and *God of the Lowly* (ed. W. Schottroff and W. Stegemann; Maryknoll, NY: Orbis Books, 1984).

11.   See the fine article by James L. Mays, 'Justice', *Interpretation* 37 (1983), pp. 5-17. For justice in relation to social processes, see Bernhard Lang, 'The Social Organization of Poverty in Biblical Israel', *JSOT* 24 (1982), pp. 47-63, and Robert Coote, *Amos Among the Prophets* (Philadelphia: Fortress Press, 1981), pp. 24-45.

12.   Norman K. Gottwald, *The Tribes of Yahweh*, is most helpful in showing how Yahwism holds together the agency of Yahweh and the social practice of the community. The two are inseparable, even though many of us are more inclined than Gottwald to maximize the theological rather than the sociological counterpart. On the interface of Yahwism and social practice, see also Robert Wilson, *Prophecy and Society in Ancient Israel* (Philadelphia: Fortress Press, 1980), and Paul D. Hanson, *The Dawn of Apocalyptic* (Philadelphia: Fortress Press, 1975).

eighth-century prophets clearly concern social goods, social power, social access, and the way those are configured in society.

In contrast to the eighth-century prophets, however, our conventional handling of Job (and similar materials) tends to disregard those understandings of justice and remove the justice question from the arena of social processes to the reified air of theological speculation. Such an interpretive move tends to make theodicy an odd or peculiar question of exilic and post-exilic periods, whereas in fact theodicy is a regularly functioning presupposition that permeates every text either as consensus or as challenge. That is, theodicy may be peculiarly in crisis in the Joban literature, but it is not a new social phenomenon. The entire literature of the Old Testament, since the Exodus narrative, concerns the interface of God and social justice.

This change of our perception of justice from a *prophetic-social issue* (in the eighth century) to a *speculative theological issue* (in the sixth century) results in a separation of the God question from issues of social reality, from the ways of production and distribution of social goods and social power. Such a separation is hinted at in Crenshaw's conventional inventory of theodic categories in which he lists the dimensions of theodicy as 'moral evil, natural evil and religious evil'.[13] In this paper I want to urge that *social evil* is a crucial, if not central matter for theodicy in the Old Testament. Social evil concerns those arrangements of social power and social process that enable goods and access to be systematically legitimated by religious ideology though nonetheless unjust. It is an important fact of the sociology of our scholarship that the enormous concern of Israel for social power and social goods is characteristically bracketed out when we come to the question of theodicy.

It may be argued that a focus on social evil is not ontologically serious. But such an argument only presses us to a more basic conversation about God and God's enmeshment in the social processes. I

---

13. James L. Crenshaw (ed.), *Theodicy in the Old Testament* (Philadelphia: Fortress Press, 1983), p. 2. Rainer Albertz, 'Der sozialgeschichtliche Hintergrund des Hiobbuches und der "Babylonischen Theodizee"', in *Die Botschaft und die Boten* (ed. Jorg Jeremias and Lothar Perlitt; Neukirchen–Vluyn: Neukirchener Verlag, 1981), pp. 349-72, has made a formidable argument that the question of theodicy in the poem of Job represents a social crisis in the Persian period which endangers the conventional class structure. The parallels he draws to Neh. 5 may be too specific, but his point is congruent with this paper. See esp. p. 238 for his thesis.

propose then that social evil (by which I mean unjust power arrangements in society for which God is claimed as the legitimator and guarantor) is at the center of Israel's reflective thought. This way of
understanding theodicy is an overriding concern for marginal people
whose daily task of survival does not permit the luxury of more
speculative questions. From the 'edge',[14] the justice or injustice of
God is encountered in the way social process enhances or denies life,
and the justice or injustice of God is not otherwise experienced. Thus
the issue of theodicy for Israel is not an interesting speculative question, but is a practice of social criticism of social systems which do or
do not work humanely, and of the gods who sponsor and guarantee
systems that are or are not just. A god is known by the system it sanctions. Theodicy becomes in fact an irrelevant speculative issue if the
God question is not linked to systems of social access and goods.

II

I propose that we begin a fresh discernment of theodicy by noticing
how the concept is used in social analysis, particularly by those who
are not interested in the God question as such. Here I cite the contributions of three scholars whose views are representative in the field.

1. Peter Berger offers a typology of theodicies that runs a continuum of rationality–irrationality.[15] His articulation of the theodic problem includes a reference to a religious dimension, but he makes it
clear that theodicy of any type is nonetheless a social agreement about
how to handle the 'anomic experience' of communal life, i.e. how to
justify, order and understand meaningfully the experiences of actual
disorder. To some extent theodicy, then, exists to rationalize and make
things palatable. Berger suggests that a theodicy may be a 'collusion,
on the level of meaning, between oppressors and victims'.[16] Such an
agreement (characteristically not explicit) may be a theodicy of
suffering for one group and a theodicy of happiness for the other.[17]

---

14. See Mary Douglas and Aaron Wildavsky, *Risk and Culture* (Berkeley: University of California Press, 1982), chs. 5–8, on 'center' and 'border'. Their use of
'border' may include social marginality.

15. Peter L. Berger, *The Sacred Canopy* (Garden City, NY: Doubleday, 1967),
pp. 53-80.

16. Berger, *Canopy*, p. 59.

17. Berger, *Canopy*.

Following Durkheim, Berger regards the transcendent dimension of theodicy as central. That is, a concern for justice requires relation to divine symbolization. But it is clear that the transcendent serves to legitimate social power, goods and access in a certain configuration. The function of God is to establish a kind of givenness about a particular arrangement and to invest it with a quality of acceptability and legitimacy, if not justice. Examples might be the tacit agreement of society that Blacks have custodial jobs, that women receive less income than men for comparable work. These are deeply legitimated practices in our society, not much challenged until recently. Such socially accepted inequities presume the *operation* of a theodicy long before the *crisis* of oppression and the yearning for equity becomes a public act.

2. Robert Merton takes up the same question in less direct and more technical language without a primary religious reference.[18] He offers a sociological analysis of *nomos*,[19] i.e. the norms by which a society maintains itself and sets criteria for what is right and wrong, good and evil, what is to be rewarded and punished. *Nomos* thus functions as a set of criteria to govern social benefits and settlements.[20] The positive benefits are for those who meet the norms. Those benefits are made available in certain parameters: 'The range of alternative behaviors permitted by culture is severely limited.'[21] Obviously behavior that is deviant from those norms, which violates the reward system, is not rewarded and may be punished.[22] There is no doubt that the system of benefits is in part informed by and grows out of the ontological realities of life. Merton, along with Berger, concedes the legitimating function of ritual in this regard. But Merton's sociological realism is more critical than that of Berger in arguing that the *nomos* is not a gift of heaven, but is a contrivance of earth, which requires that the theodic consensus be read critically, as a decision about who will have

18. Robert K. Merton, *Social Theory and Social Structure* (Glenco, Ill: The Free Press, 1957).

19. Merton, *Social Theory*, pp. 121-94. Cf. James L. Crenshaw, *Theodicy in the Old Testament*, pp. 133-34.

20. Merton, *Social Theory*, pp. 137-38.

21. Merton, *Social Theory*, p. 134.

22. For a particular scriptural example, see Brueggemann, 'A Neglected Sapiential Word Pair', *ZAW* 89 (1977), pp. 234-58.

access to social goods and social power. The extent to which *nomos* is a social contrivance is that extent to which theodicy is an enquiry about social reality, social benefits, social decisions about reward and punishment. Violation of *nomos* may be regarded as disobedience to God. It also threatens social stability and will not be tolerated extensively.

The argument of this paper, on the ground of Merton's analysis, is that every theodic settlement (including its religious articulation) is in some sense the special pleading of a vested interest. Indeed, it cannot be otherwise, because there are no statements about God's justice that are not filtered through a social reality and social voices which have a stake in such social reality. The point to be stressed is that more theoretical and speculative treatments of theodicy have acted as though the discussion can be conducted without reference to those life realities. There is no theodicy that appeals to divine legitimacy that is not also an earthly arrangement to some extent contrived to serve special interests. This paper insists on this point, and urges, derivatively, that scholarly consideration of theodicy must recognize the ways in which *nomos* is mediated through such social reality and social interest.

3. Most helpful for our purposes is the analysis of Jon Gunnemann.[23] Influenced by Weber, Berger and Kuhn, Gunnemann understands social revolution as a shift of paradigms for theodicy, a different perception of evil. Theodicy is a settlement made in a society concerning how much evil and suffering is necessary, legitimate and bearable. It concerns the relative assignment of suffering to different members and groups in the community. Theodicy is an agreement on the amount of suffering to be borne in situations of unequal power and privilege in which some are happy while others suffer. Theodicy as a crisis occurs when some—usually the sufferers—no longer accept that reading of evil, that assignment of suffering, and insist that evil be perceived differently and suffering be distributed differently. When evil is perceived in new ways, then the distribution of social power must be done differently to redress the unacceptable arrangements. The odd reality is that a settlement may be long-standing and only late rejected, but the crisis is nonetheless acute when the question is raised. Revolution, then, according to Gunnemann, is not simply a seizure of

23. Jon P. Gunnemann, *The Moral Meaning of Revolution* (New Haven: Yale University Press, 1979), pp. 9-50.

power, but is a change in the rules through which power and access are apportioned.

What is clear in the analyses of Berger, Merton and Gunnemann is that theodicy concerns real power in real social communities. Any discussion of theodicy which fails to consider this dimension is likely to be ideology in the worst sense of the word, i.e. a cover-up of social reality. A catalogue of dimensions of theodicy which includes only the *moral, natural* and *religious*, and excludes the *social*, fails to address the ways in which evil is not a cosmic given but a social contrivance. Interpretations of scripture which are idealistic, i.e. which read theology only in natural, moral and religious categories without reference to social, institutional reality, have missed the crucial point. They offer a theological exercise that is irrelevant to real human life, even if it is a great comfort to the benefactors of present disproportions. In the Old Testament, the theodicy issue surfaces as early as the Exodus event which rejects the theodic settlement in the Egyptian empire and makes possible an alternative social arrangement. Israel, in its normative tradition since the Exodus, continues to reflect precisely on the social dimension of evil and suffering.[24] Moreover, Israel continues to believe that every theodic settlement is a contrivance that is open to change.[25]

24. At the heart of Israel's credo tradition is not speculation but a *cry* against unjust social power (cf. Exod. 2.23-25). It is that cry which is at the center of Israel's discontent which Herbert Schneidau, *Sacred Discontent* (Berkeley: University of California Press, 1976), properly calls 'sacred'. On the social power of 'cry' see the poignant lines of Ernst Bloch, *Atheism in Christianity* (New York: Herder and Herder, 1972), pp. 16-18. Bloch of course is concerned with a cry that is not heard, a conclusion which Israel's credo does not accept.

25. For ancient Israel, all such injustice is open to change and must be addressed to God who is the guarantor of social order, but also the transformer of social order. That is why the credo models out of such a change (the Exodus) were wrought through a cry to God. And that is why the credo as a paradigm of social possibility must be taught to each new generation. Cf. Michael Fishbane, *Text and Texture* (New York: Schocken Books, 1979), pp. 79-83. The 'core narrative' is a paradigm that must be in each case related to historical specifics, but the paradigm itself insists that social arrangements can be changed. On that central claim, see Walter Harrelson, 'Life, Faith and the Emergence of Tradition', in D. A. Knight (ed.), *Tradition and Theology in the Old Testament* (Philadelphia: Fortress Press, 1977), pp. 11-30.

III

The insights of social theory are not unknown in our own field of Old Testament study. I note three studies which are well-informed by attention to social reality.

1. Klaus Koch[26] has offered an important statement on theodicy in his argument of a deed-consequence system. That system operates as a sphere of destiny without active intervention of an agent. Unfortunately Koch's analysis does not pursue the sociological implications of his own insights. It is the case that the deed-consequence construct as a system of social rewards and punishments is not ordained in the cosmic ordering of things, but is a social construction to maintain certain disproportions, a fact which Koch does not take into account. It is when the system of advantage and disadvantage is no longer regarded as legitimate that a crisis in theodicy occurs. Koch makes these statements:

> It is when skepticism gained the upper hand that there was a *radical reassessment of the concept that there was a powerful sphere of influence in which the built-in consequences of an action took effect.*[27] ... In the later documents of the Old Testament, Qoheleth and Job show us that *the concept of actions with built-in consequences was shaken to the foundation.*[28]

Koch's statements can easily be related to the categories of social analysis offered by Berger, Merton and Gunnemann. The first quote concerning skepticism means that the entire system of benefits is in question. The second means that the benefit system is no longer regarded as a cosmic given, but is seen as a construction, or we may say, as a social contrivance. Once seen as a contrivance, its positivistic legitimacy is ended and it is subject to criticism and revision.

2. Patrick Miller[29] has examined the ways in which benefits, i.e. rewards and punishments, function in prophetic literature. First, his primary argument concerns the correspondence of sin and judgment.

---

26. Klaus Koch, 'Is There a Doctrine of Retribution in the Old Testament?', in J.L. Crenshaw (ed.), *Theodicy in the Old Testament*, pp. 57-87.

27. Koch, 'Is There a Doctrine of Retribution', p. 79. The italics are in the text.

28. Koch, 'Is There a Doctrine of Retribution', p. 82. The italics are in the text.

29. Patrick D. Miller, *Sin and Judgment in the Prophets* (Chico, CA: Scholars Press, 1982).

Second, his work carries on an important dialogue with Koch in which he identifies cases in which Koch has used the texts to serve his hypothesis, but in ways that are not the most compelling reading. But it is Miller's concluding statement that concerns us. He concludes:

> The correlation of sin and punishment while effected by Yahweh is not manifest in a capricious and irrational way unconnected to the nexus of events, as if it were an 'act of God' in the sense that insurance companies use such a term, a bolt of lightning from the sky that suddenly destroys. There is no such trivialization of the notion of judgment in the passages studied. On the contrary, they reveal a kind of synergism in which divine and human action are forged into a single whole or the divine intention of judgment is wrought out through human agency.[30]

For our purposes the telling phrases are 'the nexus of events' and 'wrought out through human agency'. That is, *benefits occur through social processes*, through control of access, goods and power. Any critique of God's justice must be a critique of the social agency through which that justice is made concrete. Theodicy is not an esoteric speculation about God, not a supernaturalism, but concerns the handling of power through human agency which claims religious legitimacy. What had been taken as divinely ordered is at least in part seen to be historically contrived. *Theos* is the legitimator of *dikē*, but the issues surface always about justice as experienced in the historical process.

3. D.N. Freedman, in his summary on the exilic period, concludes with 'The Final Response: Second Isaiah'.[31] He states:

> The simplest explanation of Second Isaiah's theology is to say that what everyone else thought was the question (Why do the innocent suffer?) was in fact the answer to a larger question, How does history work?[32]

That shift of the question proposed by Freedman is precisely correct, but I believe Freedman has not carried the shift far enough. To ask *how history works* is not a theoretical question about God, but an immediate political question about social power. Thus, for example, in Isaiah 46 the gods of Babylon are critiqued, but this is joined immediately in ch. 47 by a critique of arrogant political power. The two

---

30. Miller, *Sin and Judgment*, p. 138.
31. David Noel Freedman, 'Son of Man, Can these Bones Live?', *Intepretation* 29 (1975), pp. 185-86.
32. Freedman. 'Son of Man', p. 186.

cannot be separated.[33] The key interpretive point for our purposes is the decisive linkage of *divine authority* and *social power*. While scholarly attention has been on the matter of divine authority, the overriding question in the text itself, I propose, is the issue of social power. The ways of administrating social power are now deeply criticized and there is no going back. There is no appeal to divine legitimacy that can now nullify the critique. The conversation that Gottwald has boldly mounted concerns precisely this connection between divine legitimacy and social power which cannot be dismissed as Marxist. Israel's critical theological tradition since the Exodus is precisely a protest about and enquiry into the benefit systems of society in which God is affirmed to be present as dispenser, legitimator and guarantor. My concern here is to identify precisely what is at issue in the matter of theodicy. As soon as the fact of social evil is acknowledged, it becomes clear that theodicy is an enquiry into such arrangements that give excessive life to some at the expense of others. It takes no great imagination to see that that is how the theodicy question is posed in our time. I submit it is the way Israel characteristically posed the question.

IV

To test this proposal we take up the two texts commonly cited as most explicitly posing the question of theodicy (Jer. 12.1; Job 21.7).

  1. In Jer. 12.1, the theodic question is articulated as follows:

> Why does the way of the wicked prosper?
> why do all who are treacherous thrive?

The two pairs of terms yield a deed-consequence understanding: wicked (*rāšā'*)—prosper (*ṣālaḥ*), be treacherous (*bāgad*)—thrive (*šālâ*). Three observations are in order. First, the linkage of wicked–prosper is indeed a structure of act–consequence. The issue is raised by the poet because the consequence should not follow from the deed. The deed and the consequence contradict each other, which shows that the system of benefits has collapsed. The case is brought before Yahweh because he is the guarantor that certain deeds yield certain consequences, and certain consequences do or do not follow from

---

33. On the powerful connection between the two, see the essays in P. Richard (ed.), *The Idols of Death and The God of Life* (Maryknoll, NY: Orbis Books, 1983).

certain deeds. The question to Yahweh grows out of concrete experiences of social practice. It is not speculative.

Secondly, the decisive term 'prosper' (*ṣālaḥ*) is of special interest to us.[34] On the one hand the term is tightly tied to obedience in a clear scheme of deed and consequence. This is true in the sanctions of the Torah (Deut. 28.29; Num. 14.41; Josh. 1.8). It is used with reference to the reforming kings by the Chronicler (2 Chron. 14.6; 26.5; 31.21; 32.30). On the other hand, the term also refers to physical, material, social well-being, with an unmistakably eudaemonistic connotation (cf. Gen. 24.21, 40, 42; 39.3, 23; Isa. 48.15; 53.10; 54.17). Those who *ṣālaḥ* are those who benefit from the best rewards of the social system. It is not thought that the blessings and well-being are given like a bolt from the blue, but are given the way such matters are always administered, through the responsible and reliable function of the social system. The term has no special religious connotation, but refers to prosperity according to society's capacity and criteria.

Thirdly, in the text itself (Jer. 12.1) *ṣālaḥ* is exposited by the terms of v. 2, 'they take root, they grow, they bear fruit'. There are visible measures so that one can see for whom the social system functions. Elsewhere in Jeremiah this material–social dimension is evident: in 2.37 it means (negatively) well-being; in 5.28, it is linked with justice and welfare of orphans and in 22.30, it refers to longevity of the dynasty.

2. The second text commonly cited with reference to theodicy is in Job 21.7:

> Why do the wicked live,
> reach old age and grow mighty in power?

This surely is a challenge to God, as conventional discussions of theodicy have recognized. Verse 4 observes that this protest is not against *'ādām*, but against God who presides over the social system from which *'ādām* benefits. The conclusion of this unit in v. 16 speaks of prosperity (*ṭôb*) and observes that the wicked possess prosperity. The issue is the same as Jer. 12.1. But what is interesting here is that the issue does not revolve around a theological referent. Indeed God is not directly addressed any more than *'ādām* is. God is addressed by implication, but I submit it is not a theological statement, but a

---

34. On the term *ṣlḥ*, see Robert Davidson, *The Courage to Doubt* (London: SCM Press, 1983), pp. 21-26.

272

Social-Scientific Old Testament Criticism

critique of a social system of benefits for whom God is at best the invisible, unnamed guarantor. The accent is completely on the social, economic rewards that ought not to be but are because the system is skewed. The problem thus is not some speculative theological argument, or an existential anguish about an intimate relation, but the problem is the distribution of social goods.

A variety of texts explicate Job's concern for the social process as an instrument of God's injustice.

> Their children are established in their presence,
>   and their offspring before their eyes.
> Their houses are safe from fear,
>   and no rod of God is upon them.
> Their bull breeds without fail;
>   their cow calves, and does not cast her calf.
> They send forth their little ones like a flock,
>   and their children dance...
> They spend their days in prosperity (*ṭôb*)
>   and in peace they go down to Sheol (vv. 8-13).

The restatement in vv. 23-24 observes that the wicked go to their graves comfortable, untroubled, confident, rewarded:

> One dies in full prosperity (*'eṣem*)
>   being wholly at ease and secure,
> his body full of fat.
>   and the marrow of his bones moist.

They never see recompense (*šillēm*) nor destruction (cf. vv. 19-20).

How one reads this text depends upon one's interpretive posture. The conventional existentialist tendency of interpretation[35] can take this simply and directly as a critique of God alone. But if the sociological analysis of theodicy we have outlined has merit, then it is clear that the well-being of the children, houses, bulls and cows of the wicked is not caused directly by God as though by edict, but that the well-being takes place through the nexus of social processes.[36] Such

---

35. An existentialist interpretation has been made most attractive through the study of Samuel Terrien. Cf. his *Job: Poet of Existence* (Indianapolis: Bobbs–Merrill, 1957). It is noteworthy how this sort of interpretation tends to shy away from the materialist issues of social justice.

36. See the negation of these same social elements in Ps. 109, also through social processes. See my study of Ps. 109 as a statement about social processes, 'Psalm 109; Three Times "Steadfast Love"', in *Word and World* 5 (1985), pp. 144-54.

houses are safe from fear not because some spirit hovers over the house, but because the agents of finance, security and protection are favorably inclined. One's bull breeds without fail, not simply because of God's kindness, but because one has the best bulls and has the money to secure the most probable successes.[37]

My point then is not an exegetical, but a hermeneutical one. Our reading of Job (or any of the theodic literature) reads differently depending on our perspective, i.e. our social location. It is odd that an *existentialist* reading goes hand in glove with a kind of *supernaturalism* which simply overlooks all the functions of social process. But if the text is read with social realism and we ask how it is that the wicked are well-off, it is because the networks of social process which govern access and power are inclined and arranged that way. The theodic question addressed to God becomes at the same time skepticism about a social process that is less and less regarded as legitimate. The God of Israel (who is in some ways still linked to the revolutionary memories of the Exodus) is never a God apart from social processes, but is one who is mediated, experienced and practiced in those processes.[38] My judgment is that the entire question of theodicy has been misunderstood in our guild, because in the name of objectivity we have devised ways of reading and thinking about the question that screen out the problems that are most difficult for the 'haves' of society.

I do not want to claim too much or overstate the case, but I suggest that these two questions from Jer. 12.1 and Job 21.7 read differently if read in the presence of those who resent the wicked because the wicked have come to have a monopoly on social goods and social access, on bulls that breed without fail, on houses that are safe and on children that sing and dance and rejoice, on land that is too large while others are displaced.

---

37. James A. Michener, *Iberia* (New York: Random House, 1968), in commenting on the sociology of bullfighting concludes that if the Republicans had won the civil war in Spain, bullfighting would have come to an end. Bullfighting requires the luxury of enormous tracts of land, dependent on social monopoly. The point is not without parallel to Job's observation.

38. Proverbial sayings which lie behind the tradition of Job make connections between God and social process in the direction argued here. Cf. for example. Prov. 14.31; 17.5; 18.17.

V

One other evidence for relating theodicy to social evil needs to be considered. I have noticed how many times in Job the question of land is present. This is noteworthy because our existentialist readings of theodicy do not much concern land. I propose that where land is under debate, questions of God's justice concern not only God but the processes through which land is governed, distributed, taxed, mort-gaged and repossessed. In such contexts, God is the giver and author-ity of land.[39] At least to some extent the poem of Job asks about land and so shapes theodicy around issues of *social* evil.

1. The book of Job in its present form is bound by two statements concerning property:

> Thou hast blessed the work of his hands, and his possessions (*miqneh*) have increased in the land (1.10).
>
> And in all the land there were no women so fair as Job's daughters; and their father gave them inheritance (*naḥ⁽ᵃ⁾lâ*) among their brothers (42.15).

The structure of the book as loss and restoration (which has often been noted) is here articulated precisely around the land question, of land loss and land restoration. This movement is reflected as well in the formula *šûb š⁽ᵉ⁾bît* (42.10) which is also a formula of land restoration.[40]

2. The poem between these prose units is, among other things, an enquiry about land and the processes by which it is lost and held. We may begin with two statements which seem to be conclusions reflect-ing a consensus. In ch. 20, Zophar presents a massive assertion on the fate of the wicked. The wicked, says Zophar, are excluded from the reward system of society, and will receive no blessings. The con-clusion in v. 29 is:

---

39. Ps. 37 is a remarkable example of wisdom teaching preoccupied with how to secure and hold land. Cf. esp. vv. 9, 11, 22, 29, 34, with the word-play on 'cut off' (*kārat*) and 'possess' (*yāraš*). Such a perspective in wisdom supports the claim that wisdom teaching does indeed reflect a class interest, on which see Gordis, Kovacs, Kendenhall and Bryce.

40. On the meaning of this formula as it relates particularly to land, see John M. Bracke, 'The Coherence and Theology of Jeremiah 30–31' (unpublished disserta-tion, Union Theological Seminary, Richmond, 1983), pp. 148-55.

> This is the wicked man's portion from God,
>> the heritage decreed from him by God.[41]

The portion does not refer to communion with God (as in some Psalms) but to land. Zophar's verdict concerns social, economic, political nullification, so that the possessions of the wicked are taken from him (v. 28).[42] The form-critical analysis of Westermann suggests that one loses possessions, not by violence but through the agency of law, court and finance.[43] It is striking that at the end of the cycle of exchange with the friends, in 27.13 Job quotes Zophar's verdict and agrees with him:

> This is the portion of a wicked man with God,
>> and the heritage which oppressors receive from the Almighty.

The detailed exposition of Job in 27.14-23 speaks, among other things, of loss of children, silver, house, riches. Indeed the inversion of materials is such that:

> he may pile it up, but the just will wear it,
>> and the innocent will divide the silver.

3. We may consider what the three friends say about land. First, Eliphaz, speaking of the man who is reproved by God:

> You shall know also that your descendants shall be many,
>> and your offspring as the grass of the land (5.25).

In a parenthetical comment, he says,

> what the wise men have told
>> and their fathers have not hidden,
> to whom alone the land was given (15.18-19).

---

41. Brevard Childs, *Isaiah and the Assyrian Crisis* (SBT 3/2; Naperville, IL: Alec R. Allenson, 1967), pp. 128-36, has identified this formula as a 'summary appraisal'. Rhetorically then, the statement functions to assert a consensus which sociologically means a theodic settlement.

42. On 'portion', see von Rad, '"Righteousness" and "Life" in the Cultic Language of the Psalms', *The Problem of the Hexateuch and Other Essays*, pp. 260-66, and Walter Zimmerli, *Old Testament Theology in Outline* (Atlanta: John Knox, 1978), pp. 98-99.

43. Claus Westermann, *The Structure of the Book of Job* (Philadelphia: Fortress Press, 1981). The extensive use of the law-suit form draws the argument very close to such public processes, even if the usage is only an imitation. The form itself carries those nuances into the discussion.

Verse 20 offers a contrast by speaking of the wicked who has pain, and who must wander abroad for bread (v. 23), precisely because he has no land from which to receive bread. In v. 29, Eliphaz speaks of the wicked:

> He will not be rich, and his wealth will not endure,
>> nor will he strike root in the land.

In 22.8 Eliphaz catalogues Job's sins and says,

> The one with power possessed the land
>> and the favored man dwelt in it,
> You sent widows away empty, therefore...

That is, Job is seen as one who deserves to lose the land because he did not conduct his land possession according to the norms of his society.[44]

Bildad asserts that the land is not excessively troubled by the anger of Job (18.4), and then he comments on the wicked:

> His memory perishes from the land
>> and he has no name in the street (18.17).

This verdict apparently means he has no descendants to inherit the land. Concerning Zophar, we have already commented on 20.39 and his verdict.

Clearly all three friends have a theory about land possession: life is organized so that *socially responsible people possess land*. Clearly God governs so. Clearly as well, the social apparatus is organized to assure this. The destiny of the righteous and the wicked is not simply a heavenly verdict, but a social practice. *The verdict of God* and *the practice of the community* hold together, and the debate is about both, never about one without the other. The friends are the voice of a particular theodic ideology who keep in close connection social practice and religious legitimacy.

4. Job's response to this mode of social interpretation is clear. We have already seen in 27.13 that Job has the same judgment to make as his friends about the distribution and possession of land. Job's speech concerns social loss. He can remember when the system worked. The socially undesirable:

> are driven out from among men;
>> they shout after them as after a thief.

---

44. Job of course counters this in his statement of innocence in 31.16-17.

> In the gullies of the torrents they must dwell,
>> in the holes of the earth and of the rocks.
> Among the bushes they bray;
>> under the nettles they huddle together.
> A senseless, a disreputable brood,
>> they have been whipped out of the land (30.5-8).

That is as it should be. The systems of society work so that the socially undesirable should not have a place, and they do not.

But, of course, that is retrospect. The problem is that Job's present experience does not correspond to the theodic ideology of his friends. Most of the land references in the mouth of Job concern the *failure* of the deed-consequence system to function:

> The land is given into the hand of the wicked;
>> he covers the faces of its judges—
>> if it is not he, who then is it? (9.24).

> He takes away understanding from the chiefs of the people of the
>>> land,
>> and makes them wander in a pathless waste (12.24).

The reference in 9.24 is important, because it mentions judges, thus acknowledging human agency in the wrong distribution. The human agency of judges, closely allied with the inequitable God, is the subject in 24.2ff.:

> Men remove landmarks;
>> they seize flocks and pasture them.
> They drive away the ass of the fatherless;
>> they take the widow's ox for a pledge.
> They thrust the poor off the road,
>> the poor of the land all hide themselves (vv. 2-4).

In this text God does not directly exercise a time of judgment. Rather the established network of social practices favors the powerful rich against the helpless poor. The arena of conflict is land, displacement and the erosion of old boundaries. God is enmeshed in these practices which destroy society, but God's action is intimately linked to the judicial processes (cf. v. 12). God is assaulted not for direct actions, but because of the unfair, unreliable social practices and agents which God sanctions.

We have already examined the initial question concerning theodicy in Job 21.7. In the same unit, Job asks,

> How often is it that the lamp of the wicked is put out?
>   That their calamity comes upon them?
>   That God distributes pains in his anger (21.17)?

The verse is of interest because the term 'distribute' is *ḥālaq*, 'to apportion'. It is precisely the question of distribution that concerns Job. His question expects a negative answer. Never is the lamp of the wicked put out. Never is their calamity upon them. Never does God distribute pain in anger. Job wishes for God to distribute calamity. But Job does not believe that God will ever do it. Job no longer trusts the social system of rewards and punishment.

Job accepts the fundamental theodic premise of the friends, but he observes that the system has collapsed. Yet at the same time, Job continues to expect something from that system. In the great climactic statement of innocence in ch. 31,[45] we may observe at the beginning and at the end references to land as the measure of the function of the moral system of benefits. Land, as a blessing from God, is surely given through the social systems of law and finance. Job 31.2, reinforced by vv. 3-4, is a statement of innocence and of trust in the conventional processes of reward and punishment. Job in this passage counters the shrill question of 21.7 and affirms the conventional system of reward and ownership:

> What would be my portion (*ḥēleq*) from God above,
>   and my inheritance (*naḥ⁽a⁾lâ*) from the Almighty on high?

The use of *ḥēleq* and *naḥ⁽a⁾lâ* is worth noting. Though the reward is given by God, it is clearly a *material reward* that is given through *social processes*. Thus this assumption and its counter in 21.7 reflect the two theodicies of which Berger speaks. In 31.2-4 we hear the voice of those for whom the system *produces happiness*. In 21.7 we hear the voice of those for whom the system does not work and *produces misery*.

At the end of ch. 31 (vv. 38-40), the last conditional self-imprecation concerns land, care for the land, ability to have land, and the risk of what may come upon the land. Job's statement of innocence is, of course, a theological statement concerning blessing from God, but it is also a sociological statement about a system of sanctions. It is not simply a supernatural act of God that some have good land and others

---

45. On the chapter, see Georg Fohrer, 'The Righteous Man in Job 31', in J.L. Crenshaw and J.T. Willis (eds.), *Essays in Old Testament Ethics* (New York: Ktav, 1974), pp. 1-22.

have poor land, that some have thorns and briers and others have
myrtle and cypress (Isa. 55.13). This statement (31.38-40) is clearly
rooted in a conventional curse formula. The curse, however, does not
take place in a social vacuum, but through social process. The entire
chapter, bounded as it is in vv. 2, 38-40 by reference to land, assumes
a just social system. What is under discussion is not only *the good
intention of God, but the reliability of the system of benefits*. It is for
that reason that the language of the court is used (vv. 35-37), because
this is a statement about the workings of the system. Indeed, the inclination of Yahweh is not under review in this chapter, but only the
court system which adjudicates claims.

VI

As the poem of Job ends, Job has his material blessings restored and
increased (42.10-13), with credit for the rehabilitation given to
Yahweh. If the question of theodicy is posed around the issue of *theos*,
then the conclusion of this literature asserts that the faithful God of
Job answers and intervenes to work justice. But if the question of
theodicy is posed around the issue of *dikē*, then one may say that justice is done in the realm of social process. Because Job has spoken
what is right (vv. 7-8), he is given twice as much (v. 10).

The way in which Job is given twice as much is important for our
theme. To be sure, Yahweh guides the process of rehabilitation. But it
is of crucial importance for our argument that the mode of restoration
is through visible social channels:

> Then came to him all of his brothers and sisters and all who had known
> him before, and ate bread with him in the house; and they showed him
> sympathy and comforted him for all the evil that the Lord had brought
> upon him; and each of them gave him a piece of money and a ring of gold
> (v. 11).[46]

Job is given his reward as a just man through the social process.
Indeed this human, communal action is stated as a response to God's
evil. God may do evil, but redress is done through social process.

To be sure, this human action is matched by and corresponds to the
divine blessing (v. 12). But the divine blessing cannot substitute for
social process. It is the work of the human community which makes

---

46. 'All who had known him' perhaps refers not only to the three friends, but to
that whole company in ch. 30 who treat him with disdain.

Job's experience of God's justice possible. Indeed, one may believe it is freshly functioning social processes which permit this rehabilitation. Such processes do not displace divine justice but are the means through which it is practiced and experienced. *The fidelity and generosity of God and the equity of the social system* both operate. Indeed they function together. Job's vindication is unmistakably through the social system. Our supernaturalist and existentialist readings of Job have not sufficiently recognized that it is the *rehabilitation of the social process* that is evidenced along with and as the form of God's equity. Indeed our presuppositions have caused us not even to notice that the rehabilitation happens *through his fellows*.

In Jeremiah, to which we have also given attention with respect to theodicy, the same formula of *šûb šᵉbût* (cf. Job 42.10) is used for land restoration and for resumption of a place in the social functioning of the community. There is no doubt that this poetry of rehabilitation bears witness to the fidelity and generosity of God (chs. 30–31, 33).

For our purposes what is compelling is the function of regularized social process through which Jeremiah receives the just treatment for which he yearns. The narrative is at pains to stress that the hope of land is implemented through predictable and trustworthy social practice and social institution:

> I signed the deed, sealed it, got witnesses, and weighed the money on the scales. Then I took the sealed deed of purchase, containing the terms and conditions, and the open copy; and I gave the deed of purchase to Baruch the son of Neriah, son of Mahseiah, in the presence of Hanamel my cousin, in the presence of the witnesses who signed the deed of purchase and in the presence of all the Jews who were sitting in the court of the guard (vv. 10-12).

The detailed prose narrative is striking and unexpected after the rhapsodic poetry of chs. 30–31. In those chapters of consolation, the specific hope is homecoming to the land. But that glorious promise from God is in this narrative account made concrete in its specific description of the careful, detailed social practice which accompanies the reception of land. As is well known, Jer. 32.1-15 is a prose account of a legal transaction whereby Jeremiah, the righteous complainer who seeks justice and vengeance, receives the land to which he is entitled. There is no doubt that this quite personal episode is presented as a theological affirmation about the restoration of Israel in the land by God. The mode of the assertion, however, is that this rehabilitation in the land is done precisely through social, contractual processes, through payment, signed deed, secured witness and careful measure.[47] God's hope for justice is enacted through social processes. The derivative promise of vv. 42-44 presents precisely *social good* as the way Israel will know *God's justice*.

The grand promise of v. 15 and the specific historical details of vv. 10-12 are not in any tension. Their juxtaposition only indicates that in this tradition of theodicy, the righting of injustice is done through the structures and processes of society which make justice possible. To hope in God's future justice requires engagement with such historical concreteness. It takes deeds and witnesses and records to implement the promises of God in historical processes. The tradition acknowledges that in the end, the land promises are not fulfilled through supernatural intrusion, but through the transformations of historical process.[48]

In both Job and Jeremiah (the two places where the theodicy question is most explicitly posed) the resolution of the theodic crisis is restoration through social processes which are again known as functioning and reliable:

> Job 21.7 moves to 42.10-13 and restoration by the community
> *giving*.
> Jer. 12.1 moves to 32.1-15 and rehabilitation *by legal procedures*.

The attack on God's justice is resolved through rectified social process, the only rectification in which Israel has an interest.

Three methodological conclusions are hinted at in this argument:

1. Our conventional readings of theodicy through speculative, supernatural or existentialist lenses may be a misreading. It may be that theodic literature is finally more interested in *dikē* than in *theos*.

---

47. On the historical basis for the narrative of 32.1-15, Carroll, *From Chaos to Covenant: Prophecy in the Book of Jeremiah* (New York: Crossroad, 1981), p. 134, refuses to make a judgment. There seems no reason, in my opinion, to deny this narrative account to the historical experience of Jeremiah, thus permitting it to be a resolution of the issue raised in 12.1. On the specificity of the legal process, see G.M. Tucker, 'Witnesses and "Dates" in Israelite Contracts', *CBQ* 28 (1966), pp. 42-45.

48. Mic. 2.1-5, of course, shows how the gift of land from God takes place through disciplined and formal social processes. See especially Albrecht Alt, 'Micha 2.1-5, Gēes Anadasmos in Juda', *Klene Schriften zur Geschichte des Volkes Israel*, III (Munich, 1959), pp. 373-81.

2. To the extent that we have settled for a misreading through wrong categories, our habitual approach may be reflective of our social location as scholars, for we tend to be well-placed within the social system and therefore not inclined to let our theological reflection spill over into social criticism. It may be our social location that causes us to agree that theodicy concerns *moral, natural and religious* evil, to the disregard of *social* evil. I propose that putting the question differently invites a different reading of the text.

3. This argument may suggest (as I think is hinted by Koch, Miller and Freedman) that a materialist reading is required. The reality of God's governance is through social processes and not without them. This may make us more open to current exegesis which connects religious matters to issues concerning social power, social access and social goods. That is, read in relation to the crises of social process, the biblical literature has a different, more radical claim to make.

Freedman has tracked the change of the question of theodicy. The question 'Why do the innocent suffer?' is transformed into 'How does history work?' The answer that Israel knew very well is that history works through social processes (in Job's case through brothers and sisters and all who knew him and in Jeremiah's case through witnesses and court officials). Those social processes are either legitimated or judged by God. They operate either equitably or unjustly, either for the well-being of the community or for its destruction. That is how history works. Yahweh is discerned in Israel, sometimes as the *impetus of the social process*, sometimes as the *norm*, and sometimes as the *agent for the transformation* of the process.

JSOT 37 (1987), pp. 61-78

POVERTY IN THE SOCIAL WORLD OF THE WISE

J. David Pleins

Significant progress has been made in clarifying the social milieu of
the biblical wisdom literature. Although scholars are certainly not in
complete agreement on this issue, nevertheless many have convincingly argued for an urban elite educational background as the well-
spring of wisdom thought. This paper explores this thesis through a
consideration of wisdom teaching on poverty. The study begins with a
brief sketch of the royal tendencies and influences present in the book
of Proverbs. The view defended here is that the values and interests of
the wisdom writers are the same as those of the urban elite whom they
serve. There follows a detailed consideration of the distinctive use of
the Hebrew terms for poor in the book of Proverbs. An examination
of this vocabulary sets in sharp relief the view of poverty held by the
wise. In the course of this essay it will be seen that, in their understanding of the causes and theological dimensions of poverty, the wise
differed significantly from other strains of the biblical tradition, in
particular the Hebrew prophets. The evidence of the wisdom vocabulary on poverty confirms the view that the wise are the purveyors of
urban values.

1. *Social Background of the Wisdom Literature*

Many argue that the materials in Proverbs have their origins in the
life and needs of the royal court. Several scholars see evidence for this
view in the fact that the Egyptian and Mesopotamian wisdom writings
were produced by the court schools (cf. Gordis 1971: 163; Malchow
1982: 121; Mettinger 1971: 143-44; Olivier 1975). The Egyptian
wisdom instructions, in particular, are often connected with kings or
state officials and thus have their place in the scribal schools of the

royal court.[1] Israel, likewise, would have needed centers of learning to educate its officials (Lemaire 1984: 277; Crenshaw 1985: 607; cf. Mettinger 1971: 143-44; Hermisson 1968: 97-136; Olivier 1975: 56-59); and it is quite plausible that material such as that found in Proverbs served as instructional texts for aspiring court officials or their children (Heaton 1974: 103-14; cf. Mettinger 1971: 140-43).[2] The possibility of direct influence of Egyptian wisdom on the Israelite tradition and the importance of the instructional literary form to the Israelite scribal tradition (Prov. 1–9; 31.1-9; Mettinger 1971: 145) strengthen this consideration.[3]

The royal associations of Israelite wisdom literature are clear. Kings, such as Solomon and Hezekiah, are expressly connected with the text (Prov. 1.1; 25.1). The royal background of the wisdom literature helps to explain why the office of the king plays an important role in Proverbs.[4] The text's concern for the king and for attitudes toward the king are emphases quite proper to an education in royal society.

Some have argued that the biblical text of Proverbs is a document

1.   Examples include: crown prince Harjedef to his son (Lichtheim 1973: 58-59); an unknown vizier to his son, Kagemni, who was eventually elevated to a governing post (Lichtheim 1973: 59-60); Ptahhotep, a crown prince and governing official (Lichtheim 1973: 61-80); the *Instruction to Merikare*, an elder king to his son, the heir apparent (Lichtheim 1973: 97-109); *The Instruction of King Amenemhet I for his Son Sesostris I* (Lichtheim 1973: 135-45); the text of Any, the writing of a scribe to his son (Lichtheim 1976: 135-46); and the instruction of Amenemope, an agricultural overseer and scribe (Lichtheim 1976: 146-63).

2.   The Egyptian wisdom texts seldom refer to an educational setting in the course of the material (cf. Satire of the Trades [Lichtheim 1973: 185]; Any [Lichtheim 1976: 140]). A similar silence in Proverbs does not, therefore, allow one to conclude that the biblical wisdom material originates outside royal society.

3.   For a review of the arguments concerning the Egyptian influence on Israel's wisdom tradition, cf. Bryce 1979: 15-56; Emerton 1979: 214-15; Heaton 1974: 121-22; Ruffle 1975.

4.   The king is important to the maintenance of order and justice in society (cf. Prov. 16.12; 20.8, 26; 22.11; 29.4, 14; 30.22; cf. Bryce 1979: 189-210). In particular, he is the protector of the weak (Prov. 29.14; cf. Fensham 1962: 138). The king has special access to the divine, and therefore has extraordinary knowledge and powers of judgment (Prov. 16.10; 21.1; 25.2-3; Bryce 1979: 201; cf. 1 Kgs 3.4-14). Bryce indicates that the king 'is to be feared as God' (1979: 201; Prov. 14.35; 16.10, 14; 19.12; 20.2, 8; 24.21). The text repeatedly urges loyalty and respect for the king (Prov. 16.12, 15; 20.28; 24.21-22; 25.2-6; 30.31; cf. Bryce 1979: 141-62).

which reflects the traditions and attitudes of popular culture, namely the non-royal village society of the premonarchic period (cf. e.g. Murphy 1978: 37; 1983: 17-19; Nel 1982: 14-15; Clements 1975: 73-74, 81). We concur with Lemaire, however, that written collections such as the book of Proverbs would not have had their setting in popular culture: 'The *written* transmission of *collections* of proverbs presupposes a cultural milieu different from that of the oral transmission of isolated proverbs used occasionally in everyday life or in traditional palavers' (Lemaire 1984: 272).[5] While it is possible that some of the proverbial material comes from the popular culture, its transferral into writing indicates its urban educational function. On this basis it can be argued that the Proverbs collection would have served the needs of those who knew how to read and write and who were employed for scribal purposes.[6]

One of the implications of the royal background of wisdom writing in Israel is that this literature is a product of the ruling elite, a sector of the society that 'had little in common with the poorer peasants clinging desperately to their holdings, or with the petty tradesmen and the artisans in the cities, who suffered their own discontents and were evolving new values in their religious tradition' (Gordis 1971: 162). It is to be expected, then, that the values and practices advocated in the wisdom tradition are in accord with the political and economic leanings of the ruling classes (cf. Gordis 1971: 169). If this view is

5. I believe Nel (1982) does not take into account the full significance of his own view in this regard. He argues that while the court is associated with wisdom literature in Israel, one cannot ascirbe all the material to a single ethos. He offers a variety of settings for the material: family, school, court, priestly, prophetic, and individual (1982: 79-81). He contends that the city encompasses all these categories. It seems, however, that he is simply substituting the city for the court. There is no reason why the various materials would not be appropriate subject matter in a well-rounded elite education.

6. Those who convey these traditions—the wise—are to be regarded as professionals in the monarchic establishment (against Clements 1975: 81). The prophetic writings provide evidence that the wise were a distinct group of no small importance to the administrative bureaucracy. The prophets group the wise among the other members of the ruling elite, namely the priests, diviners, prophets, governing officials, and warriors (Isa. 19.11-12; 44.25; Jer. 8.8-9; 9.22 [Eng. 9.23]; 10.7; 18.8; 50.35; 51.57; Ezek. 27.8; Obad. 1.8; cf. Bryce 1979: 150-51). On the basis of this evidence Bryce terms the wise a 'professional class' (1979: 151). Similar views are propounded by McKane who contends that the wise were high political advisors in the employ of the state (1965: 17-18, 38-47; cf. Bryce 1979: 196).

correct then the wisdom teaching on poverty should bear the marks of values and attitudes adhered to by the educated elite.

2. *The Terms for Poor: Distribution Patterns*

The vocabulary used for 'poor' in Proverbs reveals patterns markedly different from those found in other blocks of biblical literature. The prophetic literature, for example, uses four terms when speaking of the poor: *'ebyôn* ('poor'; 17 times), *dal* ('weak, haggard, poor'; 12 times), *'ānî* ('poor, oppressed'; 25 times), and *'ānāw* ('humble'; 7 times). Similarly the Psalms prefer *'ebyôn* (23 times) and *'ānî* (31 times) when discussing poverty, but also make us of *dal* (5 times) and *'ānāw* (13 times). A glance at the statistics for Proverbs reveals a startling contrast. In the book of Proverbs the terms *'ebyôn* (4 times) and *'ānî* (8 times) occur rarely and in restricted contexts (see below). Of the terms for 'poor' used by the prophets and the Psalms, the adjective *dal* is the one used and preferred by the wisdom writers (15 times). Furthermore, when speaking about poverty, the writers of Proverbs add the adjective/participle *rāš* ('poor, indigent'; 15 times) and the noun *mahsôr* ('need, lack, poverty'; 8 times), terms which rarely appear in the Psalms (*rāš* in Ps. 82.3; *mahsôr* in Ps. 34.10 [Eng. 34.9]), and which are not found at all in the prophetic materials. This divergence in word choice between the prophets and the wise should be considered the sign that a different jargon is present, in this case the specialized language of the wisdom teachers.[7]

The use of *dal*, *rāš*, and *mahsôr* characterizes the value system adhered to by the wise, one which differed substantially from that of the prophets.[8]

---

7.   Clements says there is no technical vocabulary in Proverbs (1975: 78, 82), and Donald claims that in comparison to Proverbs the difference in emphasis of the terms for poor which is attested in Psalms is simply the result of 'sociological sympathies and obsessions of the Psalmists rather than as an extension of the meaning area of the words' (1964: 29). However, I would suggest that both writers miss the significance of the distribution patterns of the terms for poor. The special wisdom associations of *rāš* and *mahsôr* are indicated by their relative infrequency in the rest of the Hebrew Bible. The term *rāš* occurs outside of Proverbs only in 1 Sam. 18.23 (a royal context); 2 Sam. 12.1, 3, 4 (a wisdom tale); Ps. 82.3; Qoh. 4.14; 5.8 [Eng. 5.7]. Likewise, *mahsôr* appears only in Deut. 15.8; Judg. 18.10; 19.19-20; Ps. 34.10 [Eng. 34.9].

8.   Kuschke argued that the terms for poor could be separated into two groups.

3. *The Terms* 'ebyôn *and* 'ānî/'ānāw

The traditional paralleling of *'ebyôn* and *'ānî* found in the Psalms and
the prophets also occurs in Proverbs, but in restricted contexts. Curiously this pairing appears only in chs. 30–31, sections of the book of
Proverbs assigned to the sage Agur, the son of Yakeh (Prov. 30.1),
and to Lemuel's mother (Prov. 31.1), although the exact authorship of
the entire material remains uncertain (cf. McKane 1970: 643). The
peculiarity of these texts is further heightened by the fact that *'ebyôn*
and *'ānî* are used only rarely outside of chs. 30–31 (*'ebyôn*; 14.31'
'ānî, 3.34; 14.21; 15.15; 16.19; see discussion below). Moreover, the
terms *dal*, *rāš*, and *maḥsôr*, common to Proverbs 10–29, are not
found at all in chs. 30–31. This state of affairs suggests a differing
editorial history and authorship for chs. 30–31, and perhaps even a
differing social background for this material.

In Prov. 30.14 the *'ebyôn* and *'ānî* are placed in the context of
exploitation. The writer observes that 'There are those whose teeth
are swords, whose teeth are knives, to devour the poor [*'ānî*] from off
the earth, the needy [*'ebyôn*] from among men' (Prov. 30.14). Here
the wisdom writer approximates the social criticism of the prophets
using traditional phrasing shared with the prophets. If the prophets
offer any clue to the interpretation of this material, the agents of the
devouring of the *'ānî* and *'ebyôn* are the ruling elite (cf. e.g. Amos
4.1; 5.11; 6.1-6; Isa. 3.13-14; Jer. 5.4-5, 27-28). Next, the pair *'ebyôn*
and *'ānî* is found in ch. 31, where King Lemuel passes on the words
of his mother. He was exhorted to 'Open your mouth, judge righ-
teously, maintain the rights of the poor [*'ānî*] and needy [*'ebyôn*]'

On the one side he placed *'ebyôn*, *dal*, and *'ānî*, and on the other he grouped together
rûš (and its derivatives), *ḥsr*, and *miskēn* (1939: 53; cf. Donald 1964: 30). He
claimed that the two groupings reflected differing mentalities concerning poverty—
possibly the mentalities of two opposing social classes (Kuschke 1939: 53). He suggests that *rûš*, *ḥsr*, and *miskēn* are used in the wisdom literature when poverty is
subjected to scorn, but that *'ebyôn*, *dal*, and *'ānî* are used 'when an inner sympathy
(on religious grounds) with the fate of the poor is to be expressed and a call is made
for just and brotherly deeds on their behalf' (1939: 45). Kuschke is correct to assert
that differing mentalities concerning poverty are present in the biblical literature.
However, I believe his division is over-simplified and misses the fact that the
prophets and the wise infused radically differing estimations of poverty into terms
that they shared, such as *dal*.

(Prov. 31.9). A concern for justice surrounds these terms for poor, and it is a concern connected with the king who is treated as the protector of the poor. To this one might compare Jeremiah's exhortations to king Jehoiakim, who was reminded that Jehoiakim's father, King Josiah, 'judged the cause of the poor ['*ānî*] and needy ['*ebyôn*]; then it was well' (Jer. 22.16). Finally, in the acrostic poem concerning the wise and capable wife, this woman's just character is demonstrated by the fact that 'She opens her hand to the poor ['*ānî*], and reaches out her hands to the needy ['*ebyôn*]' (Prov. 31.20).

The term '*ānî*/'*ānāw* also occurs apart from '*ebyôn* and *dal* in Proverbs.[9] The term '*ānî* is found once in the instructions in wisdom collected in Proverbs 1–9. This in itself is unusual since neither '*ebyôn* nor *dal* appears at all in Proverbs 1–9; only *maḥsôr* is also found in the section in question (see below). The passage (Prov. 3.34) relates the response of Yahweh toward the wicked and the upright. In a series of antithetic pairs, vv. 32-34 reveal the divergent response Yahweh makes to these two groups: the devious man is loathed, the wicked man's house is cursed, and the scoffer receives scorn. By contrast the upright are taken into Yahweh's confidence, and the righteous man's house is blessed. The '*ānî*/'*ānāw* are grouped among the upright and righteous as people who are favored by God. The link between '*ānāw* and piety has been argued by some in relation to the Psalms (cf. e.g. Rahlfs 1892; Baudissin 1912; van der Ploeg 1950; van der Berghe 1962) and may find a counterpart in this text. Here the writer uses the link to good effect, contrasting Yahweh's attitude toward the upright/righteous/humble and the devious/wicked/scoffer. Altering the parallelism the writer concludes in Prov. 3.35, 'The wise will inherit honor, but fools get disgrace'. It is difficult to know if the writer intends this statement to be treated simply as another example of Yahweh's just ways or if through parallelism the writer seeks to identify the holders of wisdom with the humble and just, that is, those who are in Yahweh's confidence, and thus blessed and favored. In so doing the wise would be numbered among the ranks of the '*ānî*/'*ānāw*; however, this is not a typical posture for the wise according to the rest of the book of Proverbs.

9.   Some uncertainty in this regard is introduced by *kĕtîb-qĕrê* variations in these verses. In three cases in which '*ānî* is preserved as the reading in the MT text, the *qĕrê* is given as '*ānāw* (Prov. 3.34; 14.21; 16.19). In this study no distinction is made between '*ānî* and '*ānāw* in Proverbs.

The term *'ānî* occurs three times in the sentence literature of Proverbs 10–22. In the first instance, Prov. 14.21, those who show kindness to the *'ānî/'ānāw* are considered 'happy', while those who despise friends are treated as 'sinners'. Kindness to the poor is, as will be seen, a common exhortation in the wisdom literature, with charity being a mark of the truly wise. Next, the lot of the *'ānî* is presented as a continual struggle in Prov. 15.15. Their plight is the opposite of a 'continual feast', although the exact circumstances are not specified. McKane suggests that the 'good morale' which produces this feast is 'an inner resilience which is invulnerable to the whims of fortune' (1970: 481). He adds that 'whoever has it will not allow himself to be broken by the assaults of poverty. He will withstand them with unconquerable courage, with dignity and composure, and will not permit poverty to contaminate him. He will endure poverty without suffering degradation' (1970: 481). Finally, in 16.19 the text of Proverbs states: 'It is better to be of a lowly spirit with the poor [*'ānî/'ānāw*] than to divide the spoil with the proud [better: ruthless/arrogant]'. In the wisdom literature wealth is seen as something good; however, the wise often temper and limit the conditions under which it is to be enjoyed.[10] Here the sage seeks to distance the student from associations with the proud, arguing that a place among the *'ānî* would be preferable (see further below).[11] The understanding of poverty which attends *'ānî* in Proverbs (outside of chs. 30–31) closely resembles the view which the wise develop elsewhere in Proverbs using other terms for poor (see further below). Unlike the prophetic materials, Proverbs 1–22 does not link the term *'ānî* to the socioeconomic oppression of the poor by the ruling elite.[12]

10. Cf. Prov. 1.19; 10.2; 11.28; 16.8; 17.1; 20.17, 21; 23.20; 28.20. The Egyptian wisdom literature counsels that one show restraint in one's use of wealth (Ankhsheshonq 6.10; 7.7; 9.11, 24-25; 12.3; 25.6; P. Insinger 6.17, 24; 15.7; 26.16). Gluttony is to be avoided (Kagemni [Lichtheim 1973: 60]; Satire of the Trades [Lichtheim 1973: 191]; Ankhsheshonq 15.20; 24.12; P. Insinger 5.12). Greed brings strife and want, and is often condemned (Ptahhotep §19; Merikare [Lichtheim 1973: 100]; Amenemope 6.14-15; 10.10; Ankhsheshonq 9.22; 12.18; 14.7, 20; 15.7; 21.15; P. Insinger 4.7, 8; 15.7).

11. A further use of *'ānî* (Prov. 22.22) is made in connection with the *dal* in the 'Sayings of the Wise' (Prov. 22.17–24.34) discussed below.

12. For references to the prophetic social critique of the urban establishment's oppression of the poor see the following: Isa. 3.13-14; 5.8; Jer. 2.34; 5.28; 22.13-14; Ezek. 18.12, 17; 22.29; Amos 2.6; 5.11; 8.4.

4. *The Vocabulary of the Wise:* dal, rāš, *and* maḥsôr

These few references to *'ebyôn* and *'ānî* are overshadowed by the frequent use of *dal*, *rāš*, and *maḥsôr* in the text of Proverbs.[13] As noted above, it is these terms which constitute a special vocabulary of the wise for discussing poverty. Thus, even though the term *dal* is shared with the prophets and Psalms it is clear from the distribution patterns that *dal* is a term preferred by the wise, whereas neither the prophets nor the Psalms show a preference for this term. A study of the wisdom usage reveals that this divergence in distribution is accompanied by a divergence in value concerns between the prophets and the wise.

The wisdom literature is concerned with schooling the student in how to respond to life's many circumstances and demands. These sentences offer practical guidelines for meeting the challenges of the world, and reveal what principles were thought by the wise to govern the world order. The wisdom material in this section cultivates the virtues of wealth by warning of the hard realities of poverty. Many of the verses present the stark contrast between wealth and poverty in an effort to steer the student away from a lifestyle which would lead to indigence. The terms *dal*, *rāš*, and *maḥsôr* occur several times in the sentence literature of Proverbs 10–22, and it is with this material that we begin a survey of these words.

Poverty by its very nature consigns the poor to a miserable fate, one not to be sought or cherished. In Prov. 18.23 the *rāš* is presented as one who begs. The response the poor person receives from the rich, however, is harshness. Such an observation does not condone this attitude of the rich toward the poor. In fact, there are many exhortations from the wise that the poor are not to be mocked (see below). What this passage does indicate, however, is that poverty is an ugly situation, leaving one at the mercy of the often unsympathetic whims of the rich. The wise also know that the rich rule the *rāš* and that the borrower is a slave to the lender (Prov. 22.7). This too serves as a solemn warning to the student to avoid falling into poverty. Wealth and poverty are contrasted in Proverbs 10.15. 'A rich man's wealth is

---

13. For discussions of *rāš* and *maḥsôr* see: Fabry 1986; George 1966: 388; 1971: 17; 1977: 6; Kuschke 1939: 45; *THAT* II: 347-48; van der Ploeg 1950: 254-58; van Leeuwen 1955: 17.

his strong city; the poverty of the poor is their ruin.' McKane comments that 'Wealth is an insurance against the chanciness of existence, and whoever has it is not naked and defenceless before its vicissitudes' (1970: 417). There is no virtue or refuge in poverty from the perspective of the wise.

The terrible condition of poverty is stressed by reference to its friendless character. Prov. 14.20 states: 'The poor [*rāš*] is disliked even by his neighbor, but the rich has many friends'. The friendless character of poverty is highlighted in Prov. 19.7: 'All a poor man's [*rāš*] brothers hate him; how much more do his friends go far from him!'. Friendship is also the concern of Prov. 19.4. There it is observed that 'Wealth brings many new friends, but a poor man [*dal*] is deserted by his friend'. The friendless character of poverty is stressed even more forcibly in a sentence which suggests that the very worst situation to be found among the poor is when one poor person [*rāš*] oppresses another [*dal*] (Prov. 28.3).[14] Gordis comments,

> But what an irony to see a poor man making life miserable for his fellows and gaining nothing thereby! The observation comes with especial aptness from a perspicacious son of the upper classes, who was tired perhaps of the perpetual accusations levelled against wealthy malefactors by prophets, lawgivers and sages (Gordis 1971: 172).

There is no community among the poor according to the wise. It is a condition which lacks the camaraderie known by the wealthy, that is in 'civilized' society.

As aware as the wise appear to be of the brutal condition of the poor, it is clear that the writers of Proverbs do not look beyond the hard realities of this life in anticipation of a new order in which the poor will be vindicated—a transformation such as that proclaimed by the prophets (cf. e.g. Isa. 14.30; 26.6; 29.19; 32.7; Zeph. 3.12). Nor

---

14. Van Leeuwen notes that some emend *rāš* in Prov. 28.3 to read *raša'*, *rôš*, or even *'ašîr*. The only one of these suggestions that has any possible textual support at all is *raša'* but this requires a contorted derivation from the LXX's *en asebeiais*, 'with impieties', an analysis disputed by McKane (1970: 629). McKane contends that the MT reading be accepted, but that the translation be rendered by 'powerful' or the like on the basis of cognate evidence. However, this rendering seems forced especially in light of the frequent use of *rāš* in Proverbs. None of the proposed emendations improves upon the Hebrew text as it stands, and the meaning 'poor' figures sensibly in the text.

does the wisdom writer seem to see any terrible injustice in the exist-ing world order (cf. Gordis 1971: 177-78). For the wise, poverty is a reality to be avoided, but not protested against. Unlike the prophetic social critique, the wisdom writer draws no connection between the poverty of the poor and the wealth of the rich. The sole exception to this may be Prov. 28.15, which states: 'Like a roaring lion or a charg-ing bear is a wicked ruler over a poor [*dal*] people.' However, in gen-eral the writers of Proverbs betray no awareness that the poor as a group are poor because they have been wronged by the ruling elite, as the prophets consistently proclaimed. Instead the wise merely observe that taking from the *dal* is as pointless as giving to the rich. In the end one ends up with nothing (Prov. 22.16). How different the prophetic view which contends that much gain is made by those who take from the poor! For the wise, poverty, like wealth, was accepted as one of the givens of existence with which the student must learn to cope. One presumes that the student, who comes from an elite background, would be able to avoid a lapse into poverty if only the advice of the wise were followed.

The terms *rāš* and *maḥsôr* are often connected with laziness in Proverbs. The wisdom teachers show a great concern for diligence and offer strong warnings against laziness. In the poems on wisdom in Prov. 1–9 *maḥsôr* results from too much sleep and not enough atten-tiveness to one's labors (Prov. 6.11). The wise hold up the ant as the model of success:

> Go to the ant, O sluggard: consider her ways, and be wise. Without having any chief, officer or ruler, she prepares her food in summer, and gathers her sustenance in harvest. How long will you lie there, O sluggard? When will you arise from your sleep? A little sleep, a little slumber, a little fold-ing of the hands to rest, and poverty [*rē'š*] will come upon you like a vagabond, and want [*maḥsôr*] like an armed man (Prov. 6.6-11).

Diligence and laziness are also the concern of 10.4: 'A slack hand causes poverty [*rāš*], but the hand of the diligent makes rich'. The wise cultivate a work ethic. It is work (*'eṣeb*) that brings profit (*môtār*), but mere talk that breeds want (*maḥsôr*; Prov. 14.23). Simi-lar sentiments are expressed elsewhere (for *maḥsôr* see Prov. 21.5, 24.34; cf. Prov. 19.15, 24).[15]

The attempt to locate the roots of poverty in laziness is entirely absent from the prophetic literature. As van Leeuwen observes, the

15. Drunkenness is associated with *rîš*, 'poverty', in Prov. 31.7.

perspective in Proverbs is that of one who has not known poverty. Van Leeuwen writes: 'Poverty can thus only be judged by someone who has never become its victim personally, and who consequently has never experienced it as a pressing problem' (van Leeuwen 1955: 153). For the wise poverty was 'a chastisement that one brings upon oneself' (1955: 153). It is the deserved result of drunkenness and lack of industry (Prov. 10.4; 12.11; 19.15; 20.4; 20.13; 21.17; 23.20; cf. Davies 1981: 106). Such an understanding of the cause of poverty might have been congenial to the well-to-do, but the prophets argued that it was the socioeconomic structures of the society that produced poverty. Herein lies a major point of contention between the prophets and the wise—theirs is a disagreement over the causes of poverty (van Leeuwen 1955: 153). On the prophetic analysis the plight of the poor was not something for which the poor were themselves responsible. Indeed the poor were 'victims of poor social conditions, dupes of oppression and of the possessiveness of the great' (van Leeuwen 1955: 153).

Even though the poor are considered a despised and lazy lot in the proverbial literature, the mistreatment of the poor is discouraged as behavior inappropriate to the truly wise person. The student must learn what the proper posture toward the poor should be. In the first place the text states that one should not despise or mock the *rāš*, for this is an insult to the Creator (Prov. 17.5). Likewise, in Prov. 14.31 the oppression (*'šq*) of the *dal* is condemned as an affront to God, but kindness to the *'ebyôn* is lauded. The basis for this posture toward the poor rests on the belief that the Lord makes both the rich and the poor; both poverty and wealth are thought of as given by God or fate (cf. Prov. 22.2; 29.13; Donald 1964: 29).[16]

Opposition to the mistreatment of the poor is expressed rather more strongly in the 'Sayings of the Wise' (Prov. 22.17–24.34), a text which has clear connections to the Egyptian instruction of Amenemope (Bryce 1979: chs. 1–3; see references in n. 3).[17] The writer states, 'Do not rob the poor [*dal*], because he is poor [*dal*], or crush the afflicted [*'ānî*] at the gate' (Prov. 22.22). The close paralleling of *dal* and *'ānî*

16. Poverty can come by fate and the hand of god according to the Egyptian wisdom literature (Ptahhotep §10; Amenemope 7.1-6; 21.15-16; Ankhsheshonq 12.3; 22.25; 26.8, 14; P. Insinger 7.18; 17.2; 28.4; 30.15).

17. This text differs from the other wisdom literature in not using *rāš*; nor is *'ebyôn* found. The term *maḥsôr* appears in Prov. 24.34.

is unusual in the text of Proverbs. The subject of the gate is also striking since this is the only instance in Proverbs of a concern for justice at the gate (cf. Prov. 24.7). The motivation against oppression is likewise unparalleled in Proverbs: one must not rob the poor because 'the LORD will plead their cause and despoil of life those who despoil them' (Prov. 22.22; cf. Exod. 22.20-22 [Eng. 22.21-23]). McKane (1970: 377) draws attention to the parallel in Amenemope ch. 2: 'Beware of robbing a wretch, of attacking a cripple' (Lichtheim 1976: 150). This text reveals how ancient the teaching against robbing the poor was in wisdom circles.[18] McKane points out that the Egyptian text of Amenemope differs from the Hebrew injunction in that the Egyptian text lacks a religious motivation to encourage the support of the poor. In the Hebrew text Yahweh is presented as a God who defends the poor, and for that reason one should not mistreat the poor. Yet it must be observed that this passage is not typical for the wisdom of Proverbs. If this text could be dated more securely one might have evidence for an important development in the biblical wisdom tradition. The writers of Proverbs are generally unconcerned with the notion of Yahweh as the bringer of justice. It was the prophets who felt compelled to elevate the ancient values ignored by the wise, or to which the urban elite's educators only paid lip service.

Assisting the poor through giving—charity—was an important concern to the wise. The student is warned against neglecting the poor (*dal*, Prov. 21.13). It may be that one day the student might be in distress and the neglect of others would rebound to leave the student naked before disaster, with no one to assist. The wise person shares food with the poor (*dal*, Prov. 22.9). The defining feature of just rulers is their treatment of the poor (*dal*) in legal contexts (Prov. 29.14). Similarly in chs. 28–29 of Proverbs—a section which is concerned with contrasting the wicked and the righteous, and subsets of these two groups—the character of righteousness is defined in Prov. 29.7 as showing concern for justice to the poor (*dal*).[19] It is not the

---

18. The wisdom writings often counsel against mistreating the weak (Ptahhotep §4; Merikare [Lichtheim 1973: 100]; Amenemope 4.4-7; 14.5-8; 15.6-7; 26.9; P. Insinger 33.16). People are to aid the poor (Amenemhet [Lichtheim 1973: 136]; Any [Lichtheim 1976: 141-42] Amenemope 16.5-10; 26.13-14; 27.4-5; Ankhsheshonq 15.6; P. Insinger 15.22; 16.12, 13, 14; 25.6).

19. Bryce thinks chs. 28 and 29 are more favorable to the poor than to the rich,

case, as McKane claims, that this verse is 'another...of the few examples of a wisdom sentence which is an instrument of prophetic teaching' (1970: 641). Such an attitude is not foreign to wisdom thought, but the type of social justice envisioned here differs from that found in the prophetic literature (see discussion below). Nevertheless, to the wise the just treatment of the poor is a mark of righteousness.

Malchow attempts to show that the wisdom literature's approach to the poor extends beyond charity. He believes the writings advocate an active posture toward the poor—a posture which deserves the label of 'social justice' (1982: 122). Against this I would argue, first, that Malchow has failed to separate the attitudes found in the book of Proverbs from those in Job. The understanding of poverty and the usage of the terms for poor in Job differ markedly from Proverbs. Job overlaps much more with the prophetic materials than it does with Proverbs both in its selection of terms for poor (Job uses *'ebyôn, dal*, and *'ānî*, but never *rāš* or *maḥsôr*) and in its understanding of poverty as a condition which results from injustice (cf. e.g. Job 24.4, 9, 14; 29.12; 30.25; 31.16; 34.28; 36.6, 15). Thus the understanding of poverty found in Job might be termed social justice. However, the book of Proverbs never moves beyond charity. The concern found in Proverbs over false weights and measures (Prov. 11.1; 16.11; 20.10; 20.23), and its call for the respect for property lines (Prov. 23.10-11) is ancient in the wisdom tradition, but this hardly qualifies as a comprehensive concern for social justice such as that found in the prophetic literature.[20] Next, the text of Proverbs exhibits no consciousness that the wealth of the cities was obtained at the expense of the peasant population, as the prophets so tellingly indicate was the case. There is no awareness on the part of the wise that there are institutional evils which need to be addressed. Such an awareness constitutes the prerequisite for labeling a perspective one of 'social justice' rather than one of simple charity. By contrast, the wise focus on the charitable care of individuals, and seem oblivious to the plight of the

and takes this an indication of late date (Bryce 1978: 118). The contrast between rich and poor is frequent in ch. 28 (vv. 6, 8, 11, 19, 20, 22, 25, 27; cf. McKane 1970: 621).

20. The Egyptian wisdom material exhibits a concern, though rare, over measures and property lines. For weights and measures see Amenemope 17.18-19; 18.4; 18.15–19.7. For property lines see Merikare (Lichtheim 1973: 100); Amenemope 7.11–8.4; 8.11-12.

poor as a group. In general the wise treated poverty as one of life's inevitable, unpredictable misfortunes brought about by the mysterious ways of Yahweh.[21] All that the wise person could do was work diligently in the hope of avoiding such a fate. One showed concern for the poor only to avoid mistreatment should one also happen to fall into poverty.

The motivation for charity is perhaps not for the noblest reasons. Negatively it is said that: 'He who oppresses the poor [*dal*] to increase his own wealth, or gives to the rich, will only come to want [*maḥsôr*]' (Prov. 22.16), and elsewhere: 'He who closes his ear to the cry of the poor [*dal*] will himself cry out and not be heard' (Prov. 21.13). The practice of usury is condemned for similar reasons. The student is warned that wealth gained in such a manner will pass on to one who is generous to the poor (*dal*, Prov. 28.8; cf. Lev. 25.36; Exod. 22.23 [Eng. 22.24]; Deut. 23.21 [Eng. 23.20]; McKane 1970: 626). Thus the wise warn that both the failure to help the poor and the attempt to make gains at their expense can bring poverty on the evildoer.

The inducement offered by the wise for assisting the poor is that blessings and rewards from God are promised in return for charitable giving. Prov. 11.24 states: 'One man gives freely, yet grows all the richer; another withholds what he should give, and only suffers want [*maḥsôr*]'. In Prov. 19.17 kindness to the *dal* is treated as lending to Yahweh (cf. Prov. 14.21). Note that one is not exhorted to aid the poor in order to right injustice, following the prophetic call; rather, one aids the *dal* with material reward in mind. When one lends to Yahweh, 'he [i.e. Yahweh] will repay him [i.e. the lender] for his deed' (Prov. 19.17). Similarly Prov. 28.27 states: 'He who gives to the poor [*rāš*] will not want [*maḥsôr*], but he who hides his eyes will get many a curse'. The way one overcomes society's inequities according to the wise is through a reliance on the generosity of the rich who will in turn benefit from their own giving.

The wisdom teachers use the notion of poverty to remind their audience that there are worse things in the world than poverty.[22] One would be better off poor (*rāš*) than a liar (Prov. 19.1, 22). Similarly,

---

21. See n.16 above for the Egyptian references to God making people poor.

22. It is doubtful that this material was used to console the poor in their poverty as van Leeuwen maintains (1955: 161, 164). Awareness of wealth's unstable nature is meant to refine the attitude of the student toward fate and the use of wealth. One is warned not to waste wealth (cf. Prov. 22.22).

one would be better off poor (*rāš*) than 'perverse' in one's deeds (Prov. 28.6).[23] Wealth too has its dangers according to the wise. Wealth is transitory (cf. e.g. Prov. 11.28; 20.17, 21; 23.4-5, 23-27; 28.22, 29.3).[24] Since wealth can cloud one's self-esteem, the wise state that it is better to have the perspective of the poor person: 'A rich man is wise in his own eyes, but a poor man who has understanding will find him out' (28.11). The wise warn that excessive concern for wealth can lead to poverty (*maḥsôr*, Prov. 21.17). Finally, the sages maintain that wealth can enslave (Prov. 13.8). McKane suggests that the intent of this verse is to warn that the wealthy can be the subject of threats and blackmail (1970: 458). The poor, by contrast, have little or no property that can be extorted.

5. *Conclusion*

The patterning of terms in Proverbs appears to reflect the divergent understanding of poverty cultivated by the wise—an understanding which forms a contrast to the position developed by the prophets. The teachings of the wise support their concerns for social status, class distinction, and the proper use of wealth—concerns which are rooted in the values cultivated by the ruling elite from which the wisdom literature arises. To the wise the poor are insignificant elements in the social order from whom nothing can be taken. In its instructional use of poverty, however, Proverbs seems to display an ambivalence in its attitude toward the poor, at times elevating the poor and at times disdaining them. But in this, the wisdom teacher is only concerned to make the student aware of the need to limit one's enjoyment of wealth, and for this purpose, reference to poverty was a useful teaching device. Nevertheless, this does not mean that the wise took vows of poverty! Poverty is called upon for its heuristic value, enabling the student to grasp the proper attitude toward wealth and wisdom. There is no attempt to elevate the condition of the poor or to treat poverty as a desirable existence. Nor is there any awareness that, in fact, the urban

23. The Egyptian wisdom writings indicate that there are things worse than poverty, stressing the importance of a life of happiness and integrity (Amenemope 8.19-20; 9.5-6, 7-8; Ankhsheshonq 21.22; 23.8, 9; P. Insinger 27.9).

24. The Egyptian wisdom writings show an acute awareness of the transitory nature of wealth (Ptahhotep §6; §30; Any [Lichtheim 1976: 142]; Amenemope 9.10–10.5; 18.12-13; 19.11-15; 24.15-17; Ankhsheshonq 9.11; 18.17; P. Insinger 18.5).

population was making great gains from its exploitation of the poor—
a fact which was foremost in the denunciations of the prophets.[25]

BIBLIOGRAPHY

Albright, W.F.
    1942   'A Teacher to a Man of Shechem about 1400 BC', *BASOR* 86: 28-31.
Baudissin, W.W.G.
    1912   'Die alttestamentliche Religion und die Armen', *Preussische Jahrbücher* 149: 193-231.
Berghe, P. van den
    1962   "*ānî* et *'ānāw* dans les Psaumes', *Le Psautier, Orientalia et Biblica Lovaniensia,* 4 (ed. R. de Langhe; Louvain: Publications Universitaires): 273-95.
Bright, J.
    1976   'The Organization and Administration of the Israelite Empire', in F.M. Cross, W.E. Lemke, and P.D. Miller, Jr (eds.), *Magnalia Dei: The Mighty Acts of God* (Garden City, NY; Doubleday): 193-208.
Bryce, G.E.
    1979   *A Legacy of Wisdom: The Egyptian Contribution to the Wisdom of Israel* (Lewisburg: Bucknell University Press).
Clements, R.E.
    1975   *Prophecy and Tradition* (Oxford: Basil Blackwell).
Crenshaw, J.L.
    1985   'Education in Wisdom', *JBL* 104: 601-15.
Davies, E.W.
    1981   *Prophecy and Ethics: Isaiah and the Ethical Traditions of Israel* (JSOTSup 16; Sheffield: JSOT Press).
Donald, T.
    1964   'The Semantic Field of Rich and Poor in the Wisdom Literature of Hebrew and Accadian', *OrAnt* 2: 27-41.
Emerton, J.W.
    1979   'Wisdom', in G.W. Anderson (ed.), *Tradition and Interpretation* (Oxford: Clarendon Press); 214-37.
Fabry, H.J.
    1978   '*dal*', *TDOT* 3: 208-30.
    1986   '*ḥāsēr*', *TDOT* 4: 80-90.
Fensham, F.C.
    1962   'Widow, Orphan and the Poor in the Ancient Near Eastern Legal and Wisdom Literature', *JNES* 21: 129-39.
George, A.
    1966   'Pauvre', *DBSup* 7 (Paris: Letouzey et Ané), cols. 387-406.

---

25. Unfortunately the useful lexical analysis of Wittenberg (1986) arrived too late to be included in this study.

1971   'La pauvreté dans l'Ancien Testament', in Constantin Koser (ed.), *La Pauvreté Evangélique* (Paris: Cerf): 13-35.

1977   'Poverty in the Old Testament', in M.D. Guinan (ed.), *Gospel Poverty: Essays in Biblical Theology* (Chicago: Franciscan Herald Press): 3-21.

Gordis, R.

1971   *Poets, Prophets, and Sages: Essays in Biblical Interpretation* (Bloomington, IN: Indiana University Press).

Heaton, E.W.

1974   *Solomon's New Men: The Emergence of Ancient Israel as a National State* (New York: Pica Press).

Hermisson, H.-J.

1968   *Studien zur israelitischen Spruchweisheit* (WMANT, 28; Neukirchen–Vluyn: Neukirchener Verlag).

Kennedy, J.

1898   *Studies in Hebrew Synonyms* (London: Williams and Norgate).

Kovacs, B.W.

1974   'Is There a Class-Ethics in Proverbs?' in J.L. Crenshaw and J.T. Willis (eds.), *Essays in Old Testament Ethics* (New York: Ktav): 171-87.

Kuschke, A.

1939   'Arm und Reich im Alten Testament mit besonderer Berücksichtigung der nachexilischen Zeit', *ZAW* 57: 31-57.

Leeuwen, C. van

1955   *Le développement du sens social en Israël avant l'ère chrétienne* (Studia Semitica Neerlandica, 1; Assen: Van Gorcum).

Lemaire, A.

1984   'Sagesse et Ecoles', *VT* 34: 270-81.

Lichtheim, M.

1973   *Ancient Egyptian Literature. 1. The Old and Middle Kingdoms* (Berkeley: University of California Press).

1976   *Ancient Egyptian Literature. II. The New Kingdom* (Berkeley: University of California Press).

1980   *Ancient Egyptian Literature. III. The Late Period* (Berkeley: University of California Press).

1983   *Late Egyptian Wisdom Literature in the International Context: Study of Demotic Instructions* (Orbis Biblicus et Orientalis, 52; Göttingen: Vandenhoeck & Ruprecht).

Malchow, B.V.

1982   'Social Justice in the Wisdom Literature', *BTB* 12: 120-24.

McKane, W.

1965   *Prophets and Wise Men* (Naperville, IL: Alec R. Allenson).

1970   *Proverbs: A New Approach* (Philadelphia: Westminster Press).

Mettinger, T.N.D.

1971   *Solomonic State Officials: A Study of the Civil Government Officials of the Israelite Monarchy* (Lund: Gleerup).

Murphy, R.E.

1978   'Wisdom—Theses and Hypotheses', in J.G. Gammie, W.A. Brueggemann, W.L. Humphreys and J.W. Ward (eds.), *Israelite Wisdom:*

Theological and Literary Essays in Honor of Samuel Terrien
(Missoula, MT: Scholars Press): 35-42.

1983　*Wisdom Literature and Psalms* (Nashville: Abingdon Press).

Nel, P.J.

1982　*The Structure and Ethos of the Wisdom Admonitions in Proverbs*
(BZAW, 158; Berlin: de Gruyter).

Olivier, J.P.J.

1975　'Schools and Wisdom Literature', *JNSL* 4: 49-60.

Ploeg, J. van der

1950　'Les pauvres d'Israël et leur piété', *OTS* 7: 236-70.

Rahlfs, A.

1892　*'ānî und 'ānāw in den Psalmen* (Göttingen: Dieterichsche Verlags-
buchhandlung).

Ruffle, J.

1977　'The Teaching of Amenemope and its Connection with the Book of
Proverbs', *TynBul* 28: 29-68.

Wittenberg, G.H.

1986　'The Lexical Context of the Terminology for "Poor" in the Book of
Proverbs', *Scriptura: Tydskrif vir bybelkunde* (Stellenbosch) 2: 40-85.

JSOT 40 (1988), pp. 49-60

LATIFUNDIALIZATION AND ISAIAH 5.8-10

D.N. Premnath

8 Woe to those who accumulate house to house,
 And add field to field
 Until there is no small landholding;
 And you have become possessors of land
 All by yourselves in the midst of the land.

9 In my hearing... Yahweh of Hosts:
 Indeed the large estates shall become desolate,
 Large and beautiful, no one to sit in possession.

10 For ten acres of vineyard shall yield but one bath,
 And a homer of seed shall yield but one ephah.

These verses reflect the growth of large estates, or 'latifundialization'. Latifundialization in social-scientific literature is generally defined as the process of land accumulation (large estates, hence latifundia) in the hands of a few wealthy landowners to the deprivation of the peasantry. While this process is the central phenomenon, there are various aspects related to it. Rather than address a single factor or phenomenon, a more useful way of dealing with the subject will be to get a fuller picture of its various dimensions. Such is the aim of this article.

The best context for interpreting the process of latifundialization would be the transition from a subsistence to a market economy. However, in this development it is important to discern the nature of changes in various sectors. The transition brings about significant changes in the systems of production and distribution; these systems are in turn to be broken down further into their component parts. The categories relating to the system of production are (a) factors of production, i.e. land, labor and capital and (b) nature of production (method of tillage). Under distribution, the pertinent categories are (a) consumption, (b) systems of exchange and (c) distributive systems.

1. *Production*

a. *Factors of Production*

Land. The process of latifundialization creates a steady worsening of the plight of the peasantry which is directly related to the loss of easy and secure access to arable land. The peasants' access to cultivable land, particularly with reference to the cost involved, terms under which such access is available, and the security of such a privilege, are dictated and/or controlled by the system(s) of land tenure. To express the change in terms of land tenure relations, there is a shift from the peasant-held small plot type of domain to a combination of patrimonial, prebendal and mercantile domains (Wolf 1966: 50-57). Patrimonial domain refers to inheritance on the basis of lineage (Wolf 1966: 50); prebendal domain is not inheritable, but granted to officials in return for their services through a particular office (Wolf 1966: 51); under mercantile domain, land is viewed as private property, becoming an entity to be bought and sold (Wolf 1966: 53). These three forms can exist side by side in the same social order. A shift towards a combination of the above-mentioned domains involves a change in the direction of large landholdings, in which the growth of large estates is inversely proportional to the size of the landowning class. In this process, peasants are at the losing end with maximum risk and minimum security of tenure.

Labor. A shift takes place from free-holding peasant proprietors to landless day laborers. Under a subsistence economy, labor is considered as a social duty. The bonds of kinship which govern social life within the community also govern economic activities (Nash 1967: 5). Under a subsistence economy the productive units tend to be multi-purposed. There is a complete change in the membership and structure of the productive units. With the rise of a market economy, there is an increasing division of labor, giving rise to specialized structures of productive units which are geared to markets.

Capital. In a subsistence economy, capital is not considered as a commodity for sale. But with the change in the system of land tenure in a market economy, the factors of production become saleable entities. Rent capitalism becomes an important component of the new domain, that is, the process of splitting up the means of production into several units to which money value is attached. Payment of rent is required not only for the use of land but also for various other means of production such as water, seed, work animals and others. In order to produce, the peasant will have to pay rent for these. Needless to say, the high cost of production with these segmented means of production forces the peasant into debt. Unable to pay for these means, the peasant resorts to borrowing, probably at a high rate of interest. Loans are usually raised on the value and security of the next harvest. If the crops fail in a bad season, the peasant goes deeper into debt. Besides interest on loans, there are other ways the landlords and money-lenders can squeeze the peasants of their income. The peasants can be forced to sell their crops at harvest time when prices are the lowest (Feder 1971: 147). The peasants are also short-changed through false weights and measures when the crop is divided. The outcome of all this is heavy indebtedness on the part of the peasant which finally leads to foreclosures, which in turn afford a further means of land accumulation in the process of latifundialization. In all this, the courts, instead of safeguarding the interests of the peasants, endorse and facilitate the whole process.

b. *Nature of Production*
In this area the basic shift is from a mixed subsistence to a single cash crop type of farming. The introduction of cash crops 'marks a differentiation between the contexts of production and consumption' (Smelser 1967: 34). Under a subsistence economy the productive as well as consumptive units are the same. But in the market economy production is geared to the market for an unknown consumer whether local or distant. Commercial crops require extensive plantations and thus have to occupy large expanses of land in response to market pressures. Growing cash crops for export and local consumption adversely affects the production of staple crops. Here again the peasants are the hardest hit. The need to buy their own staple foods forces them into an unfamiliar market system where they can be cheated by false measures and rigged scales.

2. *Distribution*

a. *Consumption*
Under a market economy the agricultural surplus is no longer distributed within the community. It is transferred to the ruling class

which has control over the economic activity. In the distribution of goods, the major portion goes for the conspicuous consumption of the ruling elite who not only do not produce, but plainly disdain physical labor. Consumption becomes a sign of wealth.

b. *Systems of Exchange*
The shift here is from local exchange arrangements to a wider market network. Under a subsistence economy, there is very little exchange outside the family or kinship or village circle. But the market system puts an end to group monopolies at the local level. Goods and services are more and more pulled into an ever-expanding market, leading to ever-expanding trade. Such a development in the systems of exchange has implications for the composition of society. There is the growth of a class of merchants and traders as well as money-lenders. We have already noted the role played by money-lending and usury in the impoverishment of the peasantry.

c. *Distributive Systems*
In 'simpler' societies the available goods and services are distributed mainly on the basis of need. But in 'more advanced' societies distribution is determined by power (Lenski 1966: 27). In a subsistence economy, political power is not related to economic control in the same way as in a more developed economy, where there is a close relationship between economic and political power. Where market conditions play a vital role, the peasant is subject to a wide variety of economic controls. Particularly, the three dimensions of production which serve as potential sources of economic power are: (a) control of land use, (b) control of markets, and (c) control of credits (Parsons 1963: 9). By a skillful and/or devious manipulation of these factors, the ruling class is able to extend its power over the majority.

Specific aspects of the process of latifundialization have thus to be seen not in isolation but as part of an interrelated and complex process. The changes that take place in conjunction with the rise of market economy are in the direction of growth and development. But the beneficiaries of this growth and prosperity are a small percentage of the total population—the upper class. They live off of the labor and surplus of the majority—the peasants. The extracted surplus goes to underwrite the wealthy life style of the privileged class and to ensure the security of a state which protects the interests of the ruling class.

In this sense, 'growth' and 'development' contribute very little to the improvement of the condition of the common peasantry. The opulence of the rich is achieved at the expense of the poor. The consequence of all the aspects of latifundialization is the steady deprivation and impoverishment of the peasantry.

The beginnings of latifundialization in Israel can be seen already during the emergence of monarchy. With the rise of David to power, Israelite control gradually extended to the Canaanite plains. The vast territorial expansion under David necessitated major changes in the governmental system. The administration and supervision of such an expanded realm resulted in the creation of a bureaucracy, a process which had far-reaching consequences for the systems of land tenure. Payment for different categories of office was made through a system of land grants in patrimonial and prebendal domains. It is conceivable that David gave the Canaanite plains as grants rather than the Judean hill country; these areas already consisted of a combination of the patrimonial and prebendal domains, and thus merely acquired new overlords, that is Israelite bureaucrats (Chaney 1986: 67-68). The new Israelite landed aristocracy thus created imbibed the values of the typical agrarian elites. The extraction of surplus from the primary producers to afford a life of luxury and leisure became their main objective.

Hence the land tenure system that came into practice with the institution of the monarchy in Israel was a complete change from the one which existed previously. In premonarchic Israel, family members had access to a plot of land which was probably used for the purposes of cultivation as well as residence. It has also been suggested that some of these fields were held by the village as a whole and all the plots periodically redistributed (Alt 1959: 348-72; Chaney 1983: 64-65). Such periodic redistribution would prevent any one particular family having monopoly over a particular strip of land. Under these circumstances, however, permanent improvement is hardly to be expected. It is implied that this type of land tenure would only promote the cultivation of subsistence crops such as cereals and vegetables. The premonarchic dwellers in the Judean hill country thus had a mixed subsistence type of economy producing cereals and vegetables for their own consumption. (For a detailed discussion, see Gottwald 1979: 657-60 and Chaney 1983: 64-65; 1986: 63-64.) With the shift in domain under the monarchy, lands once freely held by peasants began to fall into the hands of the rich landowners, even in the highlands, and peasants became landless laborers. Newly formed large estates were now being used for commercial crops like vines and olives (in the highlands) for the market. Wine and oil were much in demand by the elite and, moreover, were worth more than grain per unit of volume and weight in terms of exchange value. Because of this, they were key items in trade exchange for strategic military items and other luxury goods.

It seems likely that these changes were taking place even during the time of David. But it is not until the reign of Solomon that we see a full-fledged agrarian nation state. The success of Solomon's rule lay in his exploitation of the economic possibilities of his empire (1 Kings 4). The commercial activities of Solomon brought wealth into the state (1 Kgs 5.10; 9.26-28; 10.15-28). But the expenditure of the state far outweighed the income. The building of the temple, maintenance of a huge army (1 Kgs 4.26), other mammoth building projects (1 Kgs 9.15-20), maintenance of a large harem (1 Kgs 11.1-3) and the ever-increasing royal court establishments took their toll on the agrarian economy.

These dynamics were operative again during the rule of the Omrides in the north and Jehoshaphat in the south in the ninth century BCE, and during the reigns of Uzziah in the south and Jeroboam II in the north during the eighth century BCE. The worst form of latifundialization is witnessed in this latter period. It is very significant that precisely in these periods we get prophetic oracles which speak against economic injustice in society either generally or specifically. (A detailed discussion of the social reality of eighth-century Israel and Judah is found in Coote [1981] and Lang [1983] and in a more elaborate discussion by this author elsewhere [1984].)

Isaiah 5.8-10
In this passage the word *bayit* (v. 8) needs some explanation. The meaning cannot be restricted to 'house', even though in the translation given at the beginning it has been rendered thus. W. Moran has studied extensively the use of the Accadian *bītu* in Ugaritic documents from the second millennium dealing with the transfer of immovable property. On the basis of his analysis, he concludes that property in these texts was referred to as house (*bītu*) or as field (*eqlu*) or as house and field (1967: 549-52). The term *bītu* was used in a variety of

ways to refer to house, house and land or just land. Building on Moran's treatment, Marvin Chaney in his discussion of the Tenth Commandment has argued that the *bayit*:

> ... of one's neighbor originally referred to a plot of arable land held in redistributional domain by an Israelite extended family which, as a unit of both production and consumption as well as of residence, farmed the plot in mixed, subsistence agriculture (1982: 6).

It is significant that the Ugaritic formula linking houses and fields occurs in this condemnation of land accumulation as well as in Mic. 2.2. Consequently it seems quite likely that Isaiah is using *bāttîm rabbîm* to mean large landholdings. The same phrase occurs in Amos 3.15 also, where H.W. Wolff says that it conjures up 'the amassing of real estate and landholdings in the hands of the small upper class, a phenomenon which thus dissolved the ancient Israelite system of property loans' (1977: 202).

In v. 8 *māqôm* has been translated as 'small landholding', following W. Johnstone's study of technical expressions regarding property holdings in the Old Testament in the light of the Ugaritic texts. According to Johnstone, *māqôm* refers to estate or property, in addition to its general meaning of locality, place or spot (1969: 314). This follows G.R. Driver's translation of *mqmh* (1956: 30) as a 'share of his estate' and Johnstone further cites: Gen. 23.20; Judg. 9.55; 19.28; 1 Sam. 2.20; 27.5; 29.4; 2 Sam. 19.40 (1969: 314) in support. However, he does not cite Isa. 5.8, where *māqôm* is also used in a technical sense to refer to the small landholding of the peasant.

Crucial to the rendering of the last part of v. 8 is *hûšabtem*. The semantic field of *yšb* includes the ownership of land. A. Alt recognized the upper-class political nuance of the term *yôšᵉbê* in his discussion of Judg. 5.23, where *yôšᵉbê* designates the proprietors or lords of the aristocratic Canaanite political structure ('die Besitzer und Herren des aristokratisch verfassten Kanaanäischen Gemeinwesens' [1953: 276]). More recently, Gottwald has concluded that *yôšēb/yôšᵉbê*:

> ... are leaders in the imperial feudal statist system of social organization, with primary reference to every king but embracing other functionaries in the statist system. As Israel developed statist socio-political organization of its own, the term was increasingly applied to Israelite functionaries in the state apparatus and, on occasion, referred to persons of power in the upper socio-economic strata irrespective of their holding political office (1979: 532).

It is these members of the ruling class who owned large estates, and in Isa. 5.8, 9 the verbal and nominal forms of *yšb* should be seen in the context of the process of land accumulation.

The accusation in v. 8 is followed by judgment in vv. 9 and 10. This calls for a total reversal of the present situation: a total desolation of the large estates of the upper class. The use of *gᵉdōlîm* and *bāttîm rabbîm* underlines the magnitude of their landed possessions. It is significant that the judgment in v. 9 ends with a reference to *yôšēb*. The prophet predicts that there will be no one to possess land, that is there will be no landlords: the rich landowners will be bereft of their large landholdings. Their crime of accumulating large estates by joining the small plots of land which were the inheritance of the peasants was a violation of the sacred ordinance, the principle of distribution of land under Yahweh's ultimate ownership.

Further, to the avaricious motives of the landed elite to gain maximum economic advantage through the cultivation of cash crops, Yahweh will respond with a total failure of the harvest. It is noteworthy that v. 10 lists two of the major items of export from Palestine: wine and grain. These items were exported in exchange for luxury and military items. The primary producers were in no way benefited by the fruits of their own labor. The judgment speaks of depriving the rich of the very things of which they had deprived the peasants.

The present treatment differs from previous treatments of the passage in question on three counts. First, in its systematic use of the comparative evidence. The process of latifundialization reflected in Isa. 5.8-10 is analyzed with the help of categories drawn from the studies of agrarian economies past and present. Comparative perspective can lead to asking useful and sometimes new questions. At an important level, comparisons can serve as an effective check on accepted explanations and conclusions (Lenski 1976: 559-60). Finally, the comparative perspective can lead to new generalizations (Moore 1966: xiii-xiv).

Secondly, the present treatment has sought to propose a context for the passage as a whole while at the same time making sure that the various details in the passage fit together cogently in relation to the overall context. Thus the interpretation of *bayit*, *māqôm*, *hûšabtem* and *yôšēb* all belong in the context of the growth of large estates and the deprivation of the peasantry.

Thirdly, the present treatment has tried to understand the context of the passage in its *systemic* interrelatedness. The growth of large estates is a multi-faceted phenomenon. Hence, the force of v. 10 cannot be understood if one does not see the place of cash crops in the consumption of the elite and their export/exchange operations. That is why the judgment is seen precisely in terms of failure of these crops.

No single treatment, to the best of this author's knowledge, has tried to incorporate all the three above-mentioned aspects. Otto Kaiser's treatment focuses on the change in the ownership pattern reflected in this passage as a violation of the sacred ordinance concerning land (Lev. 25.23b). He does identify the main reason for this crisis as the rise of monetary economy but does not develop the thesis, giving little attention to the details of the text (1972: 65-67).

The means by which the large cultivated estates were formed, according to R.E. Clements, 'can only be guessed at, but analogies would suggest that it was achieved by the taking over of common land and by the buying up of neighboring properties' (1980: 62). I am uncertain whether Clements is thinking of comparative evidence from the field of social sciences or passages such as Mic. 2.2 and 1 Kgs 23.3. I suspect it is the latter. In relation to the accumulation of land, Clements also recognizes the role of the legal process in legitimating corrupt practices. He does not, however, elaborate on this aspect, and again, very little is said about the individual details of the text. Some of Alt's general comments on Mic. 2.1-5 are of significance for understanding Isa. 5.8-10 also, because both these passages attest the same situation. A discussion of Alt's comments is beyond the scope of this paper. But what is of particular relevance is his observation that the growth of large estates was a violation of the original redistributional land-tenure system where the peasants had access to small plots of land. Hence the judgment (in Mic. 2.4, 5) speaks of a total reversal in that the large estates would be redistributed and there would be none to cast the measuring line by lot for the guilty (1955: 13-23).

Among earlier scholars, Duhm has some perceptive comments on the Isaianic passage, pointing out that access to land was important for the Hebrews and to be without land was to be without any kinship affinity. He also recognized the landowning nuance of the term *yšb* (1922: 56-57). Bardtke's exposition of this passage, however, misses the mark both in trying to provide a general background for this passage and also in some details (1971: 135-54). His argument that Isa. 5.8-10 reflects the condition of the second half of the eighth century

BCE, particularly during the time of Hezekiah, is not convincing. Also, his explanation that the indebtedness and impoverishment of the common populace is to be seen in the context of protracted payment of tribute to the Assyrians has limited relevance. It is true that the common people bore the brunt of taxation for raising the tribute money. But this does not explain why the condition of the peasantry deteriorated even at a time of unprecedented political supremacy and economic growth as seen in the Israelite and Judahite kingdoms in the first part of the eighth century. This is precisely what the eighth-century oracles of Amos, Hosea, Isaiah and Micah attest. The reference to 'joining house to house' is understood by him as referring to the acquisition of buildings in cities (1971: 238). Also, his argument that 'the poor and the unpropertied' were not affected by this buying of houses in the cities is baffling. Comments such as these only go to show the need to take comparative evidence on agrarian societies more seriously. Insights from the field of social sciences concerning agrarian societies are crucial in bringing to light aspects of the text which have been overlooked, misunderstood, or not covered by previous exegesis.

BIBLIOGRAPHY

Alt, A.
    1953   'Meros', in *Kleine Schriften zur Geschichte des Volkes Israel* (Munich: Beck), I: 274-77.
    1955   'Micha 2, 1-5, *GĒS ANADASMOS* in Juda', in *Interpretationes ad Vetus Testamentum pertinentes Sigmundo Mowinckel septuagenario missae* (Oslo: Forlaget Land og Kirke) 13-23 = pp. 373-81 in *Kleine Schriften zur Geschichte des Volkes Israel*, vol. 3 (Munich: Beck, 1959).
    1959   'Der Anteil des Königtums an der sozialen Entwicklung in den Reichen Israel und Juda', in *Kleine Schriften zur Geschichte des Volkes Israel*, vol. 3: 348-72.
Bardtke, H.
    1971   'Die Latifundien in Juda während der zweiten Hälfte des achten Jahrhunderts v. Chr. (Zum Verständnis von Jes. 5, 8-10)', *Hommages A. André Dupont-Sommer* (Paris: Adrien–Maisonneuve): 235-54.
Chaney, M.L.
    1982   'You Shall Not Covet Your Neighbor's House, *Pacific Theological Review* 15: 3-13.
    1983   'Ancient Palestinian Peasant Movements and the Formation of Premonarchic Israel', in D.N. Freedman and D.F. Graf (eds.), *Palestine in*

Transition: The Emergence of Ancient Israel (The Social World of Biblical Antiquity Series, 2; Sheffield: Almond Press): 39-90.

1986   'Systemic Study of the Israelite Monarchy', in N.K. Gottwald (ed.), *Social Scientific Criticism of the Bible: The Monarchy* (Semeia, 37; Missoula, MT: Scholars Press): 53-76.

Clements, R.E.
1980   *Isaiah 1–39* (NCB; Grand Rapids: Eerdmans).

Coote, R.B.
1981   *Among among the Prophets: Composition and Theology* (Philadelphia: Fortress Press).

Driver, G.R.
1956   *Canaanite Myths and Legends* (Edinburgh: T. & T. Clark).

Duhm, B.
1922   *Das Buch Jesaja* (Göttingen: Vandenhoeck & Ruprecht).

Feder, E.
1971   *The Rape of the Peasantry* (AB; Garden City, NY: Doubleday).

Fohrer, G.
1962   'The Origin, Composition and Tradition of Isaiah I–XXXIX', *Annual of the Leeds University Oriental Society* 3: 3-38.

Gottwald, N.K.
1979   *The Tribes of Yahweh: A Sociology of the Religion of the Liberated Israel 1250–1050 BCE* (Maryknoll, NY: Orbis Books).

Gray, G.B.
1912   *A Critical and Exegetical Commentary on Isaiah I–XXVIII* (ICC; Edinburgh: T. & T. Clark).

Johnstone, W.
1969   'Old Testament Expressions in Property Holding', *Ugaritica* 6: 308-17.

Kaiser, O.
1972   *Isaiah 1–12* (OTL, 1; Philadelphia: Fortress Press).

Lang, B.
1983   'The Social Organization of Peasant Poverty in Biblical Israel', in *Monotheism and the Prophetic Minority* (The Social World of Biblical Antiquity Series, 1; Sheffield: Almond Press): 114-27.

Lenski, G.E.
1966   *Power and Privilege: A Theory of Social Stratification* (New York: McGraw–Hill).
1976   'History and Social Change', *American Journal of Sociology* 82: 548-64.

Lenski, G.E., and J. Lenski
1982   *Human Societies: An Introduction to Macrosociology* (4th edn; New York: McGraw–Hill).

Moore, B.
1966   *Social Origins of Dictatorship and Democracy: Lord and Peasant in the Making of the Modern World* (Boston: Beacon).

Moran, W.
1967   'The Conclusion of the Decalogue (Ex. 20.17 = Dt. 5.21)', *CBQ* 29: 543-54.

Nash, M.
    1967   'The Organization of Economic Life', in G. Dalton (ed.), *Tribal and Peasant Economies* (New York: The Natural History Press): 3-11.
Parsons, K.H.
    1963   'Land Reform and Agricultural Development', in K.H. Parsons, R.J. Penn and P.M. Raupp (eds.), *Land Tenure: Proceedings of the International Conference on Land Tenure and Related Problems* (Madison: University of Wisconsin Press): 3-22.
Premnath, D.N.
    1984   'The Process of Latifundialization Mirrored in the Oracles Pertaining to 8th century BCE, in the Books of Amos, Hosea, Isaiah and Micah', (ThD dissertation, The Graduate Theological Union; Berkeley, CA).
Skinner, J.
    1915   *The Book of the Prophet Isaiah I–XXXIX* (rev edn; London: Cambridge University Press).
Smelser, N.J.
    1967   'Toward a Theory of Modernization', in G. Dalton (ed.), *Tribal and Peasant Economies* (New York: The Natural History Press): 29-48.
Smith, G.A.
    1908   *The Book of Isaiah* (2 vols.; New York: Armstrong).
Wildberger, H.
    1972   *Jesaja 1–12* (BKAT; Neukirchen–Vluyn: Neukirchener Verlag).
Willis, J.T.
    1980   *Isaiah* (The Living Word Commentary on the Old Testament; Austin, TX: Sweet Publishing Company).
Wolf, E.
    1966   *Peasants* (Foundations of Modern Anthropology Series; Englewood Cliffs, NJ: Prentice–Hall).
Wolff, H.W.
    1977   *Joel and Amos* (Hermeneia; Philadelphia: Fortress Press).

SOCIAL GROUPINGS AND SOCIAL ROLES

JSOT 23 (1982), pp. 3-31

SEEING IS BELIEVING:
THE SOCIAL SETTING OF PROPHETIC ACTS OF POWER*

Thomas W. Overholt

We generally think of the Old Testament prophets as speakers rather than actors, and as a consequence much more scholarly attention has been directed to the forms of their speech than to the patterns of their actions. And yet we realize that the prophets are sometimes pictured as acting in ways significant to the exercise of their office. I.M. Lewis has recently suggested that some observable trauma must attend a prophet's call, so that the audience may be aware at first hand of the non-verbal aspects of his or her power,[1] and R.R. Wilson puts the matter somewhat more broadly by focusing on the social aspects of both the selection of an intermediary and the intermediary's characteristic behaviour.[2]

The purpose of this paper is to survey a specific category of prophetic actions, which I will refer to as 'acts of power', and to examine one subgroup of this category in more detail, asking in particular what these actions might suggest to us about the relationship between a prophet and his or her society.

* Much of the work on this paper was done during the summer of 1981, while I was participating in a seminar on 'Religion and Society in Ancient Israel' sponsored by the National Endowment for the Humanities. I would like to acknowledge the support of the Endowment, the stimulation provided by Professor Robert R. Wilson, the leader of the seminar, and the hospitality of Yale University.

1. I.M. Lewis, 'Prophets and their Publics', *Semeia* 21 (1981).

2. R.R. Wilson, *Prophecy and Society in Ancient Israel* (Philadelphia: Fortress Press, 1980), pp. 48-51, 62-68.

Prophetic Acts of Power in the Old Testament

'Acts of power', as I shall be using the term, is not intended to be a formal literary category. It refers, rather, to reported actions of prophetic figures which in their narrative context appear somehow unusual, extraordinary, or miraculous. There are more than 60 instances of such actions reported in Kings and the prophetic corpus.

In terms of the relationship in which they stand to 'ordinary' human activities these reports can be divided into two broad categories.[3] First, there are acts which in themselves are fully within the capabilities of any person to perform. The naming of children (Isa. 7; Hos. 1) and the intentional breaking of a pot (Jeremiah 19), or even a yoke (Jer. 27–28), are not in themselves especially startling or indicative of power. It is their context which calls attention to them and makes them so. Similarly, anyone can walk the streets naked (Isa. 20; Mic. 1.8), though not many choose to. Such an act calls attention to itself, but again it is the particular context which gives it its significance. Other actions may border even more closely on the exotic or bizarre—Ezekiel's eating a scroll (3.1-3) and temporary dumbness (3.22-27, 24.25-27), or Hosea's marriage to a prostitute (1.2-3)—but are still within the range of possible human activities.[4]

A second and smaller group of passages report what we might refer to as actions which abrogate the 'laws of nature', by which I simply mean those which fall outside of normal expectations about what it is generally possible for humans to accomplish. I do not want to raise the question of whether anyone believed such things could happen

---

3. There are, of course, other ways of analyzing the stories. A. Rofé has divided them into three types: simple legenda, legenda which have undergone literary elaboration, and vita. His intention is to describe the stories as literary creations, and he has little to say about the effects the prophets' actions had on their society beyond the suggestion that the beneficiaries of the 'simple miracles' (2 Kgs 2.19-22, etc.) were 'expected to respond with respect and veneration' ('The Classification of the Prophetical Stories', *JBL* 89 [1970]), p. 432. My classification of the stories, also based on their content, can lump them into a single class because it is the actions themselves and not the nature of the accounts about them which is my main concern.

4. The passages assigned to this category are: Isa. 7.3, 10-17; 8.1-4, 18; 20.3; Jer. 16.1-9; 19; 27-28; 32; 35; 43.8-13; 51.63-64; Ezek. 3.1-3; 3.22-27/24.25-27; 4-5; 6.11-14; 12.1-16, 17-20; 21.6-7, 14-23; 24.1-2, 15-24; 37.15-28; Hos. 1.2-9; 3.1-5; Mic. 1.8; Hab. 2.2; Zech. 6.9-14; 11.4-6; 1 Kgs 11.29-30; 19.19; 20.37; 22.11.

(presumably, some did so believe), but only suggest that such acts would certainly be perceived as more 'special' than 'normal'. Isaiah's causing the shadow of the sun on the dial to move backwards (38.7-8 = 2 Kgs 20.9-10) is an example of such an action, but the bulk of them are to be found in the Elijah and Elisha narratives.[5]

Occasionally the report of a prophetic act of power will give an indication of the actual or intended response of the audience. From these we can see that some such acts seem to have encouraged those who witnessed them toward a certain course of action (1 Kgs 22.11; Isa. 7.3-5; Hab. 2.2), while others provoked a puzzlement which became the occasion for a verbal exposition of the prophet's message (Jer. 16.10-13; Ezek. 12.8-16, 21.7 [Hb. = 12], 24.19-24; 37.18-28). Several times the actions evoked a hostile response (1 Kgs 13.4; Jer. 28.1-4, 10-11, 12-16). Sometimes they led to the recognition that Yahweh is God (1 Kgs 18.39; Ezek. 24.24, 27), but more often to the recognition that the prophet who performed them is an authentic prophet (1 Kgs 17.24; 19.20; 2 Kgs 1.13-14; 2.15; 4.37; 5.15 and 17-18; 8.4-6). The latter is the predominant response in the Elijah and Elisha stories, and it is possible that the contest between prophets recorded in Jeremiah 27–28 should also be seen in this light. Here we should also take note of the Deuteronomist's assertion that, while the prophets may perform acts of power, they are still subject to a theological test to determine their authenticity (Deut. 13.1-5). That is, acts of power are not to be considered the final proof of a prophet's authority. The fact that the Deuteronomist felt the need to make such a stipulation seems to indicate that there were those for whom 'signs and wonders' were enough to establish the authority of a prophet. But the Deuteronomist could not allow such a practice to go unassailed, since in his theologically-conditioned view the true prophet was *the* mediator to whom Yahweh spoke directly and through whom Yahweh's true words were delivered to the people.[6] But though he had no use for

---

5.   The passages assigned to this category are: Isa. 38.7-8 (= 2 Kgs 20.9-11); 1 Kgs 17.13-16, 19-22; 18.36-38; 2 Kgs 1.10-12; 2.8, 14, 21, 24; 4.1-7, 25-37, 41, 43; 5.26-27; 6.6, 15-20. Cf. also Isa. 38.21-22. As the years passed, some of these reports, like Elijah's and Elisha's raising of the dead boys, may have contributed to the development of widely-held beliefs. Cf. P. Lapide, *Auferstehung: Ein Jüdisches Glaubenserlebnis* (Stuttgart: Calwer Verlag, 1977), pp. 19-32.

6.   Cf. Wilson, *Prophecy and Society*, pp. 157-66.

such prophetic actions, it appears that others did.[7]

The only full-length study of prophetic actions, G. Fohrer's *Die symbolischen Handlungen der Propheten*, differs from the present essay in two ways: the scope of the activities accepted for examination and the context within which they are interpreted. With respect to the former Fohrer includes fewer specific episodes in his classification 'symbolic actions' than I have in my initial broad categorization. This is most noticeable in Kings, where he finds only four such acts (1 Kgs 11.29-31, 19.19-21, 22.11; 2 Kgs 13.14-19). This narrowing of the field of inquiry is the result of Fohrer's distinction between magical and symbolic acts. The former are numerous in the Old Testament, and can even be considered the broader phenomenological context out of which the latter arose. But it is Fohrer's contention that while in some of the prophetic actions the magical *element* is stronger than in others, none can be viewed as a magical *action*. The prophets overcame magic.[8]

This leads us to the second difference. At the very outset Fohrer informs us that the symbolic actions need to be seen in the broad phenomenological context of acts of magic and sorcery,[9] and his entire second chapter is devoted to examining parallels to the prophetic symbolic actions. The upshot of this effort is to show that the prophetic acts are not entirely idiosyncratic in external form. They have analogues in other cultures, and an examination of these may shed some light on the underlying significance of the act. So, for example, when discussing 2 Kgs 13.14-19 he points out the magical character of the act and refers to the 'shooting' of arrows, bones, and the like to harm enemies, citing specific examples from the Australian Aborigines, the African Bushmen, African stone-age art, the Elephantine papyri, Jewish magic, Sweden, and Mexico.[10] His search for analogies is

---

7. It may be noted that very few of these acts of power, and none in the second group, are designated *'ôt* or *môpēt*, the terms used in Deut. 13.1-5. Since the Elijah and Elisha narratives to which I will be turning my attention show very little influence from the Deuteronomist, this is perhaps not surprising. And since the Deuteronomist does use these terms to designate both objects which serve as reminders (Deut. 6.8; 11.18) and manifestations of unusual power (Deut. 6.22; 7.19; 11.3; 26.8; 28.46; 29.2), it seems reasonable to assume that the reference in 13.1-5 is to acts like those under discussion.

8. G. Fohrer, *Die symbolischen Handlungen der Propheten* (Zurich: Zwingli Verlag, 2nd edn, 1968), chs. 1 and 4.

9. Fohrer, *Die symbolischen Handlungen*, pp. 9-10.

10. Fohrer, *Die symbolischen Handlungen*, pp. 23-25.

wide-ranging in both space and time, and this chapter is the longest in the entire book.

This grounding of prophetic symbolic actions in magic is, however, only Fohrer's first assertion about them, not his last. As the final three chapters make abundantly clear, he considers the primary context for their interpretation to be theological. His basic assertion is that the prophetic symbolic actions and their magical parallels are neither identical nor externally the same, the parallels between them being in 'details', not in the 'core'. It is not simply that the magical elements are abolished, leaving only the symbolic, as he holds to be the case with profane symbolic actions. Rather, there is an 'inner and funda-mental overcoming of the magical elements'.[11] The characteristics of this prophetic 'alteration' of the magical foundation may be stated as follows: the prophetic actions are undertaken at the command of Yahweh, and not as the result of a human wish;[12] they are usually accompanied by an interpretation; and there is a promise by Yahweh that the symbolized occurrence will take place. This latter gives a certainty which is absent in magical acts and shows the prophets' dependence upon Yahweh. While profane symbolic actions symbolize and teach, but do not establish a result, prophetic action is the bearer of divine revelation and is, therefore, certain of result. But by the same token the magical is fundamentally overcome, since the prophet is not working his own will but is expecting a special act of God, which by divine command he symbolizes. Nor is the prophetic action to be considered a 'third possibility' alongside profane and magical actions, for the symbol is not chosen by the prophet himself, but commanded by God.[13] Thus Fohrer can speak of a broken or dialecti-cal relationship of the prophetic symbolic action to magic.[14]

This means that the apparently more 'magical' acts (e.g. 1 Kgs 17.14-16, 21) can be viewed rather as survivals of an earlier, nomadic stage of Israel's social and religious development.[15] Since it is not my

---

11. Fohrer, *Die symbolischen Handlungen*, pp. 94-95.

12. For Fohrer a magical act is one which is believed to carry its efficacy within itself, an act in which one seeks to grasp some secret, numinous power in the inter-ests of wish-fulfillment. Cf. 'Prophetie und Magie', *ZAW* 78 (1966), pp. 27-28, and *Die Symbolischen Handlungen*, pp. 10-11.

13. Fohrer, *Die symbolischen Handlungen*, pp. 94-98, 104-107.

14. Cf. 'Prophetie und Magie', pp. 46-47.

15. 'Prophetie und Magie', pp. 30, 46,

intention to offer a detailed critique of Fohrer's position, I will content myself with the observation that modern anthropology has cast doubts on the utility of the notion of survivals in general and of the category 'nomadism' for the understanding of Israelite cultural background.[16] Instead, I will move directly to a consideration from a somewhat different perspective than Fohrer's of a group of 'magical' episodes in the Elijah and Elisha narratives, to see if something of their social functions can be discerned.

The actions to be considered from this cycle are those belonging to the category of acts which seem to abrogate 'laws of nature'. About them we can make three observations. The first is that for the most part they occur in pairs: both Elijah and Elisha miraculously provide for the sustenance of a widow (1 Kgs 17.8-16; 2 Kgs 4.1-7, cf. 4.42-44), bring a dead boy back to life (1 Kgs 17.17-24; 2 Kgs 4.18-37), and cause the waters of the Jordan River to part by striking them with a mantle (2 Kgs 2.8, 14). Twice Elijah calls down fire from heaven (1 Kgs 18.36-38; 2 Kgs 1.9-16), and twice Elisha acts to eliminate poison from water or food (2 Kgs 2.19-22, 4.38-41). Only four episodes, all of them attributed to Elisha, stand without parallel (2 Kgs 2.23-25; 5; 6.1-7, 15-20). Whatever these reports may mean, it is clear that Elijah and Elisha are being depicted in a similar light.

We can in the second place observe that in some of these episodes there is embedded an indication of someone's response to the prophet's action. After the raising of her son, the widow said to Elijah: 'Now I know that you are a man of God and that the word of Yahweh in your mouth is truth' (1 Kgs 17.24). When they saw the fire, the Israelites assembled on Carmel exclaimed: 'Yahweh, he is God; Yahweh, he is God!' (1 Kgs 18.39), and faced with a similar catastrophe the army captain recognized Elijah's power and prayed to be spared (2 Kgs 1.13-14). The sons of the prophets, having witnessed Elisha splitting the waters of the Jordan, are said to have exclaimed: 'The spirit of Elijah rests on Elisha' (2 Kgs 2.15), and the woman whose son Elisha had raised from the dead 'came and fell at his feet, bowing to the ground' (2 Kgs 4.37). Likewise Naaman, cured of his leprosy, acknowledged Yahweh's power and, implicitly, that of his prophet (2 Kgs 5.15-19). Two additional responses connected to other episodes are worth noting. Elisha responded to Elijah's casting his

16. Cf. J.W. Rogerson, *Anthropology and the Old Testament* (Atlanta: John Knox, 1978), pp. 22-45.

mantle on him by abandoning his home and following him (1 Kgs 19.20). Even more suggestive is the episode in 2 Kgs 8.4-6 where, at the king's request, Elisha's servant, Gehazi, tells of 'all the great things that Elijah has done'. During this telling, which included 'how Elisha had restored the dead to life', the woman and her resurrected son appeared on the scene, and the king treated her more favorably than she even requested (cf. vv. 3, 6). We notice, then, the tendency to connect responses to accounts of prophetic acts of power.

The third observation has to do with the apparent social situations mirrored in the accounts of prophetic acts of power. Here it will be useful to consider the patterns of social relationships exhibited in the cycle as a whole. These can be roughly diagrammed as follows (episodes containing prophetic acts of power are italicized: episodes containing responses are marked *; + indicates ambiguity in the relationship depicted):

1. the prophet interacts with a king
     adversarial relationship: 1 Kgs 17.1; 18.17-20; 19.1-3
          (queen); 21.17-29; 2 Kgs *1.1-16**; 6.24–7.20
     cooperative relationship: 1 Kgs 18.41-46; 2 Kgs 3.9-20;
          8.1-6*; 9.1-13; 13.14-19
2. the prophet interacts with individuals and small groups
          (Israelite and other)
     adversarial: 1 Kgs *17.17-24**+; 2 Kgs *1.1-16**+; *2.23-25*
     cooperative: 1 Kgs *17.8-16*; 18.7-16; 2 Kgs *4.1-7*, 8-17,
          *18-37**
3. the prophet interacts with Israelite people (in sizeable groups)
     adversarial: none
     cooperative: 1 Kgs *18.21-40**+; 2 Kgs *2.19-22*
4. the prophet interacts with 'foreign' functionaries
     adversarial: 1 Kgs *18.21-40**; 2 Kgs *6.8-23*; *8.7-15*
     cooperative: 2 Kgs *5.1-19a**
5. the prophet interacts with his 'servant' or with the 'sons of the prophets'
     adversarial: 2 Kgs *5.19b-27*
     cooperative: 1 Kgs 18.41-46; 19.19-21*; 2 Kgs *2.1-18**;
          4.38-41, 42-44; *6.1-7*

As indicated, there are several passages in which the relationship depicted is difficult to categorize as either adversarial or cooperative. For example, 1 Kgs 17.17-24 begins with the widow accusing Elijah of causing her misfortune ('What have you against me, O man of God? You have come to bring my sin to remembrance, and to cause the death of my son!'), though the episode ends on a more positive note ('Now I know that you are a man of God, and that the word of Yahweh in your mouth is truth'). Similarly, in 2 Kgs 1.1-16 Elijah is set against both the king and his troops, though the captain of the third group recognizes his power and prays for mercy. At the beginning of the Carmel episode (1 Kgs 18.21-40) the people are not overtly hostile, but neither are they actively supporting Elijah.

Now several things of interest emerge from this schematization of social relationships. With respect to 1. it is striking that while the tendency is to portray Elijah's relationships to the king as adversarial in nature, the opposite is true for Elisha.[17] R. Wilson has suggested that Elijah was throughout his life a 'peripheral prophet' attempting to reform the central cult, while Elisha, though he began his career similarly, moved in the period after Jehu's rise to power in the direction of becoming a 'central prophet' exercising social maintenance functions.[18] We also note that in reality there are no acts of power in which the prophet interacts directly with the king, and only one response attributed to a king (while the king is important behind the scenes in 2 Kgs 1.1-16, it is his messengers and soldiers who actually confront the prophet).[19] This is surprising, given the intensity of the relationships between king and prophet mirrored in the narratives as they have come down to us.

We notice about 3. that only positive relationships are described

17. G. Hentschel believes that during the first part of his career the relationship between Elijah and Ahab was marked by cooperation rather than conflict. For his view of the developing relations between the prophet and the royal house, cf. *Die Elija-erzählungen* (Leipzig: St Benno–Verlag, 1977), pp. 275-333. On Elisha as a supporter of the monarchy, cf. M. Sekine, 'Literatursoziologische Beobachtungen zu den Elisaerzählungen', *Annual of the Japanese Biblical Institute* 1 (1975), pp. 39-62.

18. Wilson, *Prophecy and Society*, pp. 201, 206.

19. Hentschel believes that vv. 10-14 constitute a pre-Deuteronomistic expansion of an earlier narrative pointing out that (a) they seem to convey a different picture of the prophet than the context (e.g. in v. 15 Elijah is no longer fearsome, but afraid), (b) the title 'man of God' and harsh treatment of opponents is reminiscent of the Elisha stories, and (c) v. 15 forms a good conclusion to v. 9 (*Elija-erzählungen*, pp. 11-12; on the redaction history of the passage, cf. pp. 202-208). In his view it was the changing social situation that brought about the change in the tradition. Thus, while the oldest tradition of the Ahaziah narrative was passed on among a North Israelite population faithful to Yahweh, the story later came to be transmitted in prophetic circles. The people were more interested in the sober facts of Elijah's encounter with the king, while the prophetic circles incorporated material about the prophet's experiences, turning the narrative into a miracle story (cf. pp. 353-55).

between the prophets and groups. Interaction with large groups of people is clearly not the focus of attention in the narratives of this cycle.[20] 2. and 5. combined contain roughly two-thirds of the acts of power and half the responses, suggesting that such actions were more at home in individual and small group situations. With respect to 1 Kgs 17.8-16, 17-24 Hentschel argues that these episodes were not originally part of the drought narrative, but derive from a prophetic circle like that of Elisha. More interesting is his suggestion that an earlier form of the story of the prophet's raising the dead boy (identifiable in the dialogue-free core of the passage, vv. 19b, 21a^a, b^b, 22b, 23a) plays up the prophet's independent power, while later additions served to increase his dependence upon God.[21] If this should be correct, and if the original story was indeed connected with Elijah, our impression of the prophet as a powerful worker of wonders would certainly be strengthened.

As the table shows us, acts of power and responses to such acts may occur in both adversarial and cooperative situations, though their appearance is slightly more frequent in the latter. They may thus be performed for the benefit of two kinds of individuals or groups, sometimes simultaneously (cf. 1 Kgs 18.21-40): those inclined to be ill-disposed and those inclined to be well-disposed toward the prophet. But the nature of the response is essentially the same in each case, viz. to acknowledge the prophet's power and, therefore, his authority. The responses in 3. and 4. are not really an exception to this. There the explicit acknowledgement is of the power of the prophet's God, but since this comes as a result of a successful act of mediation by the prophet, it also has the effect of acknowledging the latter's authority as well. Finally, both acts of power and responses appear to be scattered throughout the prophets' careers, insofar as they can be known to us.

It might be added that there are differences of opinion over whether or not some of these episodes really refer originally to Elijah and Elisha. For example, H.-C. Schmitt argues that 2 Kgs 4.8-37 and 6.8-23 were originally about an anonymous 'man of god', whom the collector

---

20. In Hentschel's opinion 1 Kgs 18.21-40 was not originally part of the drought narrative. The oldest layer of tradition to be found in this passage is vv. 21, 30 and 40, with vv. 38-39 representing the next stage of development (*Elija-erzählungen*, pp. 134-39, 156-78).

21. *Elija-erzählungen*, pp. 93-98, 188-95, 271-73.

of the stories identified with Elisha.[22] I am not fully convinced that this is the case, but even if it were, it would not alter the hypothesis being presented here. It might even strengthen it, since it would widen the scope of this type of prophecy beyond the figures of Elijah and Elisha. Among somewhat different lines L. Bronner sees the whole series of miracle stories as the product of a 'well informed author' whose intention was to mount a polemic against Canaanite mythology in general and 'Baal worship' in particular. One notices, however, that the settings depicted in many of the stories themselves (e.g., actions within a group of supporters) do not reflect such a polemic. Thus, even if her suggestion contains some truth, this polemic does not appear to constitute the original function of the stories.[23] A similar point might be made about A. Rofé's classification of 2 Kings 5 among the 'didactic legenda', in which the miracle itself is down-played in order to stress something of deeper significance which transcends the immediate circumstances, viz. 'to prove to foreigners' both that 'there is a prophet in Israel' (v. 8) and that 'there is no God in all the earth, but in Israel' (v. 15).[24] Rofé assumes the transformation of 'popular, venerative' stories, and considers the present version of Naaman's cure to be late, reflecting the dispersion of Israelites in Assyria after 721 BCE. It seems to me one could grant such an interpretation and still maintain that the story had an earlier function which the later author consciously moved into the background.

How is one to assess this evidence? The following proposition seems attractive: If these prophets demonstrated their power for both opponents and allies to see, if they did this at several stages of their careers, and if these demonstrations of power elicited similar responses, then it seems reasonable to conclude that the social function of such acts of power was the legitimation of the prophets in the exercise of their office.[25] The Old Testament narratives themselves do

22. H.-C. Schmitt, *Elisa: Traditionsgeschichtliche Untersuchungen zur vorklassichen nordisraelitischen Prophetie* (Gütersloh: Mohn, 1972), pp. 89-91, 153-54.

23. L. Bronner, *The Stories of Elijah and Elisha as Polemics Against Baal Worship* (Leiden: Brill, 1968). Bronner's argument is sometimes forced; cf., for example, her attempts to free Elijah and Elisha from any association with 'magic' (especially pp. 105, 133).

24. A. Rofé, 'Classes in the Prophetical Stories: Didactic Legenda and Parable', *Studies in Prophecy* (VTSup, 26; Leiden: Brill, 1974), pp. 145-48, 152-53.

25. Cf. B.O. Long, 'Prophetic Authority as Social Reality', in G.W. Coats and

not give us a very clear picture of this social process, however, and so examples from other cultures will be useful in illustrating the logic of this suggestion.[26]

Acts of Power Outside Israel

It is a truism that we do not know as much as we would like about the social setting of the Old Testament. In that respect, as in others, the concerns of the authors did not match our own. Recently there has been some interest in utilizing the materials and methods of sociology and anthropology to help bridge the gaps in our knowledge of the social context of certain biblical phenomena.[27] I believe such an attempt will also be fruitful in the present case, and with this as a motivation now turn to two examples of shamanic acts of power.

For our first example we will centre on a single shaman, Wovoka, a Paiute Indian of western Nevada who from the late 1880s functioned

B.O. Long (eds.), *Canon and Authority* (Philadelphia: Fortress Press, 1977), pp. 10-11; Wilson, *Prophecy and Society*, pp. 42-68. R. Kilian refers to Elijah's raising of the dead boy as a 'proof-legend' (*Erweislegende*), but since his interest lies elsewhere, viz. in establishing that the Elijah narrative originated earlier than the version connected with Elisha, he does not pursue this observation; 'Die Totenerweckungen Elijas und Elisas—eine Motivwanderung?', *BZ* 10 (1966), pp. 44-56.

26. We ought to note H.-C. Schmitt's reference to non-biblical materials to interpret the function of the prophet Elisha as he appears in a group of miracle stories which Schmitt contends were connected with Gilgal (2 Kgs 4.1-7, 38-41; 6.1-7). There the prophet appears not as a preacher but as a miracle worker concerned with the special welfare of his group of followers. Ecstasy is a central characteristic of these prophets, and Schmitt compares them to modern Islamic dervishes, whose numerous 'paranormal capabilities' function as 'signs of holiness'; *Elisa*, pp. 162-69. Schmitt does not explain the social implications of this 'special welfare' or the 'signs of holiness', however.

27. Cf., for example, Wilson, *Prophecy and Society*, especially pp. 1-19, and N. Gottwald, *The Tribes of Yahweh* (Maryknoll: Orbis Books, 1979). With respect to the comparative approach to cultural phenomena I am fond of the following statement by E.E. Evans-Pritchard: 'In comparative studies what one compares are not things in themselves but certain particular characteristics of them. If one wishes to make a sociological comparison of ancestor cults in a number of different societies, what one compares are sets of structural relations between persons. One necessarily starts, therefore, by abstracting these relations in each society from their particular modes of cultural expression.' 'Social Anthropology', in *Social Anthropology and Other Essays* (New York: Free Press, 1964), p. 18.

for a time as the leader of a new religious movement known as the Ghost Dance of 1890. This movement, which was founded on a hope that the whites would soon be eliminated through some supernatural agency and that dead Indians would be resurrected and with their still-living relatives restored to the old way of life, spread widely throughout the Rocky Mountains and Great Plains. It attracted a great deal of attention among whites, and has been extensively studied, beginning with the classic work of James Mooney, an ethnologist who began his research into the dance in late 1890 while it was still expanding and who was able to interview Wovoka himself.[28]

Wovoka had a reputation for acts of power. Mooney tells us that after his revelation he began to preach, 'convincing the people by exercising the wonderful powers that had been given him'. He goes on to say that Wovoka '...occasionally resorts to cheap trickery to keep up the impression as to his miraculous powers. From some of the reports he is evidently an expert sleight-of-hand performer.'[29] Many of the Indians, however, did not speak of Wovoka's powers in such negative terms.

Let us review his reputation. Wovoka is said to have performed many wonders. He could reportedly control the weather, making it 'rain or snow or be dry at will'.[30] One document which came into Mooney's possession, an account of Wovoka's teachings to a delegation of Cheyenne and Arapaho Indians in August 1891, written down by one of them on the spot, has him saying:

> I, Jack Wilson, love you all, and my heart is full of gladness for the gifts you have brought me. When you get home I shall give you a good cloud... which will make you feel good... There will be a good deal of snow this year and some rain. In the fall there will be such a rain as I have never given you before.[31]

28. J. Mooney, *The Ghost-Dance Religion and the Sioux Outbreak of 1890* (*Annual Report of the Bureau of American Ethnology*, vol. 14; Washington, DC: Government Printing Office, 1896). For more on the Ghost Dance and the problems connected with evaluating the sources of our information about it, cf. T.W. Overholt, 'The Ghost Dance of 1890 and the Nature of the Prophetic Process', *Ethnohistory* 21 (1974), pp. 37-63.

29. Mooney, *Ghost-Dance Religion*, pp. 772-73.

30. Mooney, *Ghost-Dance Religion*, p. 772.

31. Mooney, *Ghost-Dance Religion*, p. 781. Because of his long-time association with a family of white settlers named 'Wilson', Wovoka was sometimes called 'Jack Wilson'.

The agent of Wovoka's reservation, C.C. Warner, reported in a similar vein:

> The originator of this craze[32] is one of my Pah-Ute Indians. His name is Jack Wilson, and like all such cranks he is a fraud, but a pretty smart fellow. He obtained his notoriety by telling the Indians that he would invoke the Great Spirit and bring rain (after there had been two years of drought), and it so happened that his promised invocation was in the commencement of our severe winter of 1889 and 1890, during which time it stormed almost incessantly from October to April. His success was rapidly spread abroad, and from that time on he has had many followers.[33]

He could precipitate unusual events, making the 'whole world' appear in his hat, or appearing before the eyes of assembled delegates in a cloud.[34] Porcupine, a Cheyenne Indian, found him to be clairvoyant (he could immediately discern any inattention among those to whom he was speaking) and capable of communicating his desires at a distance (Indians came to visit him from distant reservations as a result of having been 'sent for' by him[35]). Though buffalo were by this time virtually extinct, Wovoka could provide them for his followers. He told a delegation of Sioux that, if they should meet and kill a buffalo on their journey home, they should cut off the head, tail, and feet and leave them behind so that the animal could resuscitate. They later reported that this happened,[36] and a 'favorite' ghost song used among the Kiowa refers to such an event:

> I shall cut off his feet (repeat)
> I shall cut off his head (repeat)
> He gets up again (repeat)[37]

32. The Ghost Dance came to be widely referred to among whites as the 'Messiah craze'.

33. Warner in *Sixtieth Annual Report of the Commissioner of Indian Affairs* (Washington, DC, 1891), I, p. 301. G.B. Grinnell reports a story which circulated among the Cheyenne to the effect that General Miles and his troops went to arrest Wovoka, but the latter made it rain for seven days and nights, so that all but Miles himself were drowned ('Account of the Northern Cheyenne Concerning the Messiah Superstition', *Journal of American Folklore* 4 [1891]), p. 67.

34. Mooney, *Ghost-Dance Religion*, pp. 775-76, 797.

35. Mooney, *Ghost-Dance Religion*, p. 795.

36. Mooney, *Ghost-Dance Religion*, p. 797.

37. Mooney, *Ghost-Dance Religion*, p. 1088.

In the ceremony of the Ghost Dance large groups of Indians danced slowly in a circle, singing specially-composed ghost songs. During these lengthy performances it was common for individual dancers to fall to the ground in a trance and visit the spirit world. Mooney reports that:

> During the first year or two of the excitement, it several times occurred at Ghost dances in the north and south... that meat was exhibited and tasted as genuine buffalo beef or pemmican brought back from the spirit world by one of the dancers. It is not necessary to explain how this deception was accomplished or made successful. It is sufficient to know that it was done, and that the dancers were then in a condition to believe.[38]

And this belief had important consequences. One Sioux follower of Wovoka explained that the meat and other items brought back from the spirit world by the dancers were proof that their trances were authentic, and the trances were proof of Wovoka's power and authenticity.[39]

One group of Sioux delegates reported that Wovoka promised that if they became tired on their long trip home and called upon him for help, he would shorten their journey. They did this one night, and in the morning awoke to find themselves 'at a great distance from where we stopped'.[40] G.B. Grinnell found that in the autumn of 1890 enthusiasm for the Ghost Dance was revived among the Cheyenne by a report of some Shoshone and Arapaho who said that 'while travelling along on the prairie they had met with a party of Indians who had been dead thirty or forty years, and who had been resurrected by the Messiah'.[41] Wovoka's public trances themselves were signs of his power, and the same was true for those of certain of his followers who became leaders of the dance among their own tribes.[42]

The trances of the dancers were a way in which this power was brought vividly into the lives of many individuals. There is evidence that many of the trance experiences were induced by leaders skilled in

38. Mooney, *Ghost-Dance Religion*, p. 991; cf. Grinnell, 'Account', p. 66. For an eyewitness account of one such performance, cf. Mooney, *Ghost-Dance Religion*, pp. 916-17.

39. Mooney, *Ghost-Dance Religion*, p. 799; cf. E.W. Foster (agent at the Yankton Sioux Agency in South Dakota) in *Sixtieth Annual Report of the Commissioner of Indian Affairs*, p. 427.

40. Mooney, *Ghost-Dance Religion*, p. 797.

41. Grinnell, 'Account', p. 61. Wovoka was frequently referred to as the 'Messiah'.

42. Mooney, *Ghost-Dance Religion*, pp. 795, 894, 904.

hypnotic techniques,[43] but they were real enough to those who had them. Upon reviving, individuals commonly told of visiting the place where the dead were encamped. There they had met relatives and acquaintances living again the old Indian life and had seen herds of buffalo and other game.[44] What was seen in the trances affected the physical features of subsequent dance performances, new songs, paraphernalia, and symbols being added in imitation of the visions.[45] These trances became a routine, institutionalized part of the dance performances, and sometimes came so easily that Mooney notes hypnotic techniques were no longer needed.[46] It is worth noting that the trancers were said to have 'died', and that this mirrors what was reported of Wovoka's own revelatory experience: '...he fell down dead, and God came and took him to heaven'.[47]

Comparatively speaking, not many of the adherents of the Ghost Dance met Wovoka face-to-face, but they knew of his acts of power. They knew through reports of those who had witnessed them, and they knew from their own trance experiences, which in their minds confirmed the prophet's power and his promise of a new world soon to come. But whether or not one had personally experienced a trance, the ghost songs based on trance visions and sung at every performance were testimonials to Wovoka's power. The dead relatives and friends, the artifacts of the old life, the game animals were all waiting, poised to return:

> The whole world is coming,
> A nation is coming, a nation is coming,
> The Eagle has brought the message to the tribe.
> The father says so, the father says so.
> Over the whole earth they are coming.
> The buffalo are coming, the buffalo are coming,
> The Crow has brought the message to the tribe,
> The father says so, the father says so.[48]

43. Mooney, *Ghost-Dance Religion*, pp. 775-76, 798, 899, 922-96.
44. Mooney, *Ghost-Dance Religion*, pp. 797, 904.
45. Mooney, *Ghost-Dance Religion*, pp. 898-99, 916, 921, 923, 1075.
46. Mooney, *Ghost-Dance Religion*, p. 924.
47. Mooney, *Ghost-Dance Religion*, p. 772; cf. pp. 795, 798, 922. Fr. J. Jutz says that this is the way the dancers themselves described the experience ('Der "Ghost Dance" der Sioux Indianer', *Central Blatt and Social Justice* [St Louis, May, 1918]), pp. 49-50.
48. Mooney, *Ghost-Dance Religion*, p. 1072. 'Father' refers to Wovoka.

These songs were in effect personal confirmations of and testimonials to Wovoka's power and authenticity.

> My children, my children,
> Look! the earth is about to move, (repeat)
> My father tells me so. (repeat)[49]

Wovoka's acts of power were widely reported in his own day, though we have seen that Indian and white attitudes toward them tended to differ considerably.[50] A recent 'biography' of Wovoka by P. Bailey makes the claim that he consciously sought to become a 'mighty magician' like Jesus (about whom he had learned through his contact with the Wilson family) and John Slocum, founder of the Indian Shaker religion. To this end he consciously sought to build an image by holding 'seances' at which he performed sleight-of-hand tricks and at the crucial moment staged a decisive 'miracle'. The latter took place in the heat of midsummer, and involved a prediction by Wovoka that at noon on the following day ice would come floating down the river. The event in fact occurred and became famous in the region, and local tradition persists that Wovoka was aided in his feat by the Wilson brothers, who were stationed upstream with a wagon-load of ice which at the proper moment they dumped into the river.[51] Bailey also refers to other tricks performed by Wovoka—he made a block of ice fall from the 'sky', created a lode of gold by loading a shotgun with gold dust and shooting a rock face, contrived to prove his 'invulnerability' by being shot with a gun loaded only with powder and dropping pellets from his hand onto the blanket on which he stood—each time emphasizing a naturalistic explanation and suggesting that the prophet wilfully deceived his own people in order to enhance his own personal standing.[52]

---

49. Mooney, *Ghost-Dance Religion*, p. 973; pp. 953-1103 contain an extensive collection of ghost songs and commentaries on them. Cf. also L.W. Colby, 'The Ghost Songs of the Dakota', Nebraska State Historical Society, *Proceedings and Collections*, Series 2.1 (1895), pp. 131-50.

50. It should not be assumed that all Indians believed in Wovoka and participated in the dance. Cf. Mooney, *Ghost-Dance Religion*, pp. 913-14, 926-27; T.W. Overholt, 'Short Bull, Black Elk, Sword, and the "Meaning" of the Ghost Dance', *Religion* 8 (1978), pp. 171-95.

51. P. Bailey, *Wovoka the Indian Messiah* (Los Angeles: Westernlore Press, 1957), pp. 62-66, 211 n.7; cf. G.M. Dangberg, 'Wovoka', *Nevada Historical Society Quarterly* 11 (1968), p. 14 n.11.

52. Bailey, *Wovoka*, pp. 67-91, 121-28. Bailey has a second book, *Ghost Dance*

By contrast G. Dangberg's biographical sketch of Wovoka is much more balanced. She cites her sources faithfully, and provides several lengthy quotations from an unpublished manuscript, 'Wizardry—The Jack Wilson Story', written by E.A. Dyer, a white contemporary of Wovoka who was the latter's long-time friend and confidant. According to Dyer, 'Jack Wilson's trances were, at least to Indians, very impressive productions... He wasn't shamming. His body was as rigid as a board. His mouth could not be prised open and he showed no reaction to pain inducing experiments.'[53] Dangberg, whose ties with the Walker Lake area where Wovoka lived are long-standing, reports that 'it was generally conceded by residents of Mason Valley that Wovoka correctly prophesied the "hard winter" of 1889–90', and that some said he accurately forecast all storms during the period 1886–91/92.[54] She reports two other episodes of interest. 'Sometime during the 1880s the body of an Indian girl who had died was burned near Hawthorne. It is reported that 200 Indians saw Jack, as he had promised, raise the girl from the flames to "God's house".' Finally, there is the anecdote that Jack attributed having escaped injury in a haying accident to his being 'bullet proof'.[55]

There is much in these reports that will seem to us bizarre, and we cannot rest content with simply narrating them. One of the good features of Dangberg's sketch is that she makes some attempt to relate Wovoka's actions to the larger context of Paiute shamanism, and we must do likewise if we want to see these acts of power in their proper perspective. Fortunately, we have at our disposal for this task W.Z. Park's study of Indian shamanism in Western North America.[56]

Messiah (Los Angeles: Westernlore Press, 1970) which, though the fact is nowhere explicitly acknowledged, is an extensive revision of his earlier *Wovoka*. In the earlier edition Bailey acknowledged his dependence upon written sources and informants, and cited them in 60 footnotes. Despite that, the book has a certain novelistic quality, containing a great deal of dialogue which one must assume has been invented. The second edition is longer, cuts out all references to sources, and greatly expands the dialogue sections. In my opinion it would be perilous to depend upon either to be an accurate biography of the prophet.

53. Quoted in Dangberg, 'Wovoka', p. 12.

54. Dangberg, 'Wovoka'.

55. Dangberg, 'Wovoka', pp. 27, 30.

56. W.Z. Park, *Shamanism in Western North America: A Study in Cultural Relationships* (Evanston: Northwestern University Press, 1938). One half of this book is devoted to Paviotso (i.e. Northern Paiute) shamanism, the other to the relationship

Among the Paiutes a shaman is 'one who acquires supernatural powers through direct personal experience'.[57] The Paiutes believed that many among them possessed supernatural power through which they became more successful hunters, or gamblers, or the like, but the shaman possessed it in greater quantity, often demonstrating it in curing illness and in certain other characteristic performances. Such persons were thought to be able to control the weather,[58] to be bullet proof,[59] and/or to swallow heated arrow points.[60] Some had power over the antelope, and served as leaders of the communal antelope hunts which were an occasional feature of Paiute life.[61] It is evident that Wovoka was not unique among Paiutes either in performing acts of power or in the general nature of the acts he performed.

The shamans' strong power enables them to cure illnesses, and this is their 'chief function' among the Paiutes.[62] In some cases they are believed even to have brought the dead back to life by journeying into the other world, finding the departed soul of the person who had died, and inducing it to return to the body.[63] The performances at which these healings took place differed from each other because of differences in the experiences of the individual shamans. But they were invariably social occurrences in which everyone participated in some way (e.g. by singing) and in which the shaman's tricks played an important part:

of that phenomenon to the shamanism prevalent in surrounding cultures. Cf. also Park's 'Paviotso Shamanism', *American Anthropologist*, 36 (1934), pp. 98-113. Wovoka was a Northern Paiute.

57. Park, *Shamanism*, p. 10.

58. O.C. Stewart, *Culture Element Distributions: XIV, Northern Paiute* (Berkeley: University of California Press, 1941), p. 444; F.A. Riddell, 'Honey Lake Paiute Ethnography', Nevada State Museum, *Anthropological Papers*, 4 (1960), p. 70.

59. R.H. Lowie, *Notes on Shoshonean Ethnography* (New York: American Museum Press, 1924), pp. 292-93; J.H. Steward, *Ethnography of the Owens Valley Paiute* (Berkeley: University of California Press, 1933), p. 310; B.B. Whiting, *Paiute Sorcery* (New York: Viking Fund, 1950), pp. 28-30.

60. I.T. Kelly, *Ethnography of the Surprise Valley Paiute* (Berkeley: University of California Press, 1932), p. 192.

61. S.W. Hopkins, *Life Among the Paiutes, Their Wrongs and Claims* (Boston: Cupples, Upham and Co., 1883), pp. 55-57; Stewart, *Culture Element Distributions*, p. 423; Riddell, 'Honey Lake Paiute', p. 40.

62. Park, *Shamanism*, p. 45.

63. Park, *Shamanism*, pp. 40-41.

When Paviotso shamanism was in full swing, these performances, held in a small closely packed house, must have been exciting and impressive. The singing and the shaman's tricks appear to have excited the spectators to a high emotional pitch which was followed by a relaxation of tension attended often by a general feeling of satisfaction when control of the sickness was demonstrated by the return of the soul or the extraction of the disease-object.[64]

Park goes on to say that 'legerdemain is not generally characteristic of the shamanistic performance. Apparently the shamans of today perform no tricks when curing, but several informants recall that in the past some practiced sleight-of-hand'.[65] Among the tricks mentioned are making pine nuts mysteriously appear in a basket (a sign that the patient would recover), putting hot coals or a heated knife blade in the mouth, and licking the end of a bundle of burning reeds.

Some acts of power, especially control of the weather, seem to have served mainly a demonstrative function, proving 'the shaman's *rapport* with powerful spirits, which give him power to cure the sick and heal the wounded'.[66] Occasionally, however, such power was used for the benefit of the community, for example, by causing the ice to melt in a river so that a run of badly-needed fish could begin.[67] Though the practice is not specifically reported among the Paiute, Park notes that among neighboring tribes it is common to find midwinter performances of novice shamans, one of the purposes of which is the exhibition of power.[68] Among the Klamath, the novice shaman, after receiving power, waits until winter to 'prove' it; only then does he perform his first cure. Interestingly enough, the repertoire of 'tricks' attested for Klamath shamans has many parallels with those of Paiute shamans.[69]

As to the social position of Paiute shamans, Park reports that not every powerful shaman was a chief, but they were typically consulted in secular matters. Specifically of Wovoka he says:

> ... [he] was a powerful and influential figure among the Paviotso. He was held in high esteem by members of all the bands, and five years after his death (in 1932), he was spoken of by nearly all Paviotso with admiration

64. Park, *Shamanism*, p. 47.
65. Park, *Shamanism*, p. 57.
66. Park, *Shamanism*, p. 15.
67. Park, *Shamanism*, pp. 60-61.
68. Park, *Shamanism*, pp. 122-23.
69. L. Spier, *Klamath Ethnography* (Berkeley: University of California Press, 1930), pp. 259ff.

and respect. Perhaps some of the influence he enjoyed in later years
among his own people can be traced to the demand by other Indians for
his advice on religious matters.[70]

Yet in another place he says, 'prestige and status are expressions of
individual accomplishment, the result of personality and ability'.
Therefore, no generalization can be made about the 'social importance' of Paviotso shamans. 'One shaman may be respected by the
entire group and consulted on a variety of problems involving personal affairs or matters of importance to the group, another may be
merely a practitioner who is more or less successful in treating the
illnesses of members of the tribe.'[71]

It is thus the case that among a certain class of Paiute religious
practitioners acts of power were expected, and that one of the functions of such acts was to engender belief in the power and authority of
the practitioner. In this respect Wovoka, though he advocated a doctrine which had appeal far beyond the bounds of his tribe, is clearly
recognizable as a Paiute shaman.

From Western North America let us turn somewhat more briefly to
the various Tungus peoples of Siberia, whose culture and beliefs have
been so exhaustively described by S.M. Shirokogoroff. 'Shaman' (and
its variants) is itself a term from the Tungus languages in which it
'refers to persons of both sexes who have mastered spirits, who at
their will can introduce these spirits into themselves and use their
power over the spirits in their own interests, particularly helping
other people, who suffer from the spirits'.[72] Like their counterparts
elsewhere, these shamans are reported to have performed acts of
power, including self-infliction of 'wounds', various manipulations
with fire, and ventriloquism (as Western observers were wont to
explain the voices heard during the performances).[73] Shirokogoroff

70. Park, *Shamanism*, p. 70.

71. Park, *Shamanism*, p. 103.

72. S.M. Shirokogoroff, *Psychomental Complex of the Tungus* (London: Kegan
Paul, Trench, Trubner, 1935), p. 269; cf. p. 271. On mastery as it relates to the
shaman's trance and for a discussion of the communal context of the trance and an
extensive bibliography, cf. L.G. Peters and D. Price-Williams, 'Towards an Experi-
ential Analysis of Shamanism', *American Ethnologist* 7 (1980), pp. 397-418.

73. Cf. M.A. Czaplicka, *Aboriginal Siberia* (Oxford: Clarendon, 1914), pp. 228-
33. A.F. Anisimov gives a vivid account of a shamanic performance among a related
group of Siberians in which the manifestations of power included various sounds
(screams, snorting of beasts, bird calls, whirring of wings) and walking on hot coals

remarks that such actions are frequently and erroneously portrayed 'as imposture and tricking of the audience'. But if we are to be fair, they should be seen from another perspective:

> As shown, the shamans, especially among the Manchus (under the Chinese influence, I suppose), use a great number of tricks for proving the presence of spirits. Such are e.g. all operations with fire. As a matter of fact, an inexperienced ordinary man cannot take into his mouth burning incense or step on a heap of burning charcoal, etc. without hurting himself. The shamans do it, sustaining sometimes only slight injuries which do not prevent them from going ahead with the performance. These facts are interpreted as due to the power of mastered spirits, and not to the shaman personally. If he succeeds in these tricks, the audience and himself believe that the spirit is actually present.[74]

In the same context he gives the example of a performance at which two members of the audience doubted the shaman's power. 'The shaman took a coin from one of them and continued his performance. After a while he asked one of the skeptical men to open his hand and the man, to his great surprise, discovered the coin in his hand. Naturally, he, as well as the audience, were convinced of the great power of the shaman.'[75]

('The Shaman's Tent of the Evenks and the Origin of the Shamanistic Rite', in H.N. Michael (ed.), *Studies in Siberian Shamanism* [Toronto: Arctic Institute of North America, 1963]), pp. 101, 104-105. N.K. Chadwick quotes liberally from eye-witness accounts of shamanic performances, in the process calling attention to such phenomena as 'ventriloquism'. But her overall concern to highlight the 'intellectual' aspect of shamanic activity and the shaman's 'solemn religious function' caused her to subordinate the more dramatic aspects of the performances and not inquire into their social functions ('Shamanism Among the Tartars of Central Asia', *Journal of the Royal Anthropological Institute* 66 [1936]), esp. pp. 93-102.

74. Shirokogoroff, *Psychomental Complex*, p. 331. I.M. Casanowicz describes various shamanic 'miracles' and comments: '...the shamans could hardly, for any length of time, keep up the belief in their superiority without convincing the people by "miracles"—that is, by executing feats which exceed the power of the laity to perform or understand—of their supernatural endowments' ('Shamanism of the Natives of Siberia', *Annual Report of the Smithsonian Institution, 1924* [Washington, DC: Government Printing Office, 1925]), p. 432.

75. Shirokogoroff, *Psychomental Complex*, pp. 331-32. Barbara Myerhoff writes of an occasion on which she witnessed the Huichol shaman (*mara'akame*), Ramon, perform a death-defying series of leaps high up in a mountain canyon. Of the performance she says: 'I could not be sure whether Ramon was rehearsing his equilibrium or giving it public, ceremonial expression that day in the barrancas. In

This can be put in a slightly different way. In order for a shamanic performance to be effective, it is necessary for the audience to be appreciative and sympathetic. When such is not the case, the shaman may have to utilize various tricks to win over the audience. Over time some of these may become conventionalized and may be incorporated as a regular part of the ritual.[76] Some, like walking on coals or diving into the water and emerging out of a series of holes chopped in the ice, may become trials to test the power of new candidates. It may be noted in passing, since both the Old Testament and the Paiute materials contain examples of it, that Tungus shamans were thought to have the power to revive the dead.[77]

We ought to pay particular attention to the social support which formed the basis of a Tungus shaman's authority. When, for example, Shirokogoroff describes the formal characteristics of shamanism,[78] one is struck by the predominant place which society plays in them. The shaman is a 'master of spirits', indeed, he must have several spirits at his disposal, but these are for the most part spirits already known to the clan and the larger group. His knowledge is to an important extent limited by what the society already knows, and if it does

societies without writing, official statements about a person's status and skill are often made in dramatic, public, ceremonial form. Whether seen as a practice session or as ritual, the events of the afternoon provided a demonstrative assertion that Ramon was a true *mara'akame* and, like all authentic shamans, a man of immense courage, poise, and balance' ('Shamanic Equilibrium: Balance and Mediation in Known and Unknown Worlds', in W.D. Hand (ed.), *American Folk Medicine: A Symposium* [Berkeley: University of California Press, 1976]), p. 101. To give one further example, T.O. Beidelman has pointed out that 'unlike priests, Nuer prophets must manifest anomalous, extraordinary attributes to demonstrate the validity of their claims to a new and unusual authority... Confirmation of a prophet's calling is mainly through the public evaluation of the kinds of acts the nascent prophet claims to have performed after his strange behaviour begins...' ('Nuer Priests and Prophets', in T.O. Beidelman (ed.), *The Translation of Culture* [London: Tavistock, 1971]), p. 390. For a description of the miracles attributed to two well-known Nuer prophets earlier in this century, Ngundeng and his son, Gwek, cf. C.A. Willis, 'The Cult of Deng', *Sudan Notes and Records* 11 (1928), pp. 195-208; P. Coriat, 'Gwek, the Witch-Doctor and the Pyramid of Dengkur', *Sudan Notes and Records* 22 (1939), pp. 221-38; A.H. Alban, 'Gwek's Pipe and Pyramid', *Sudan Notes and Records* 23 (1940), pp. 200-201.

76. Shirokogoroff, *Psychomental Complex*, pp. 333-34, 339-40.

77. Shirokogoroff, *Psychomental Complex*, pp. 353, 320.

78. Shirokogoroff, *Psychomental Complex*, pp. 271-74.

not conform sufficiently to this standard, he may not be recognized as an authentic shaman. Furthermore, the methods by which the shaman deals with the spirits and the paraphernalia he or she employs are for the most part traditional, as is the 'general theory of spirits, their particular characters, and the practical possibilities of dealing with spirits' which form the 'theoretical basis' of shamanic activity. Finally, most shamans are connected with the clan organization. Of all the persons who want to be or 'pretend' to be shamans, only those acknowledged by the clan (or some specific group) are considered to be authentic.[79] All of this is illustrated quite nicely by a lengthy example of the election of a shaman among the Manchus in which public opinion is seen to play a decisive role, first in favoring the creating of a new shaman, and then in a continuous evaluation of the performances of two candidates in terms of a rather well-defined set of communal expectations. As it turned out, neither of the candidates was perfectly acceptable, but one was confirmed:

> Although the new shaman did not know all of the spirits and could name only a part of them, he seemed to have reached extasy on the last day of the performance and fell down unconscious, 'as white as paper, so that it was distressing to look at him', and the public opinion turned in his favour; he had 'power' and for a long time there had not been such a good shaman.[80]

The successful shaman forms close bonds with his clients, and as the number of his clients increases, he becomes more and more influential. But if a shaman is perceived to have a 'bad heart', the group will often turn against him.[81] For the audience has a stake in the shaman and his performance, and enters emotionally into the latter. One does not remain aloof. Clan relationships generate sorrow and a desire to help the person for whom the performance is being staged. The

79. On this latter point, cf. Shirokogoroff, *Psychomental Complex*, pp. 348-50. Of persons who try to perform outside of a proper social context he says, 'These are not shamans, because they cannot produce a real extasy, especially without an audience, and they have no social functions, usually no paraphernalia, but they are either dishonest impostors or psychomentally affected people. By this I do not intend to say that they cannot become shamans, but I want only to indicate that they do not function as shamans, have no milieu and probably cannot assume the functions of shamans, because they are not recognized; this may be dependent, at least sometimes, on personal considerations' (p. 350).

80. Shirokogoroff, *Psychomental Complex*, p. 358; cf. pp. 353-58.

81. Shirokogoroff, *Psychomental Complex*, pp. 177-78.

performance itself is exciting, and since the spirits which the shaman controls and embodies are considered to be real, 'emotive reactions are quite easy and natural'. Further, 'the rhythmic music and singing and later the "dancing" of the shaman gradually involve every participant more and more in a collective action. When the audience begins to repeat refrains together with the assistants, only those who are defective fail to join the chorus'.[82] But if the audience contains too many individuals who are skeptical or not susceptible to ecstasy, 'it may react too slowly to the shaman's suggestions, and the performance may therefore fail'.[83] In a real sense, then, the community is in control, is itself, as Shirokogoroff puts it, 'the acting agent':

> The issue of a performance depends on the personal ability of the shaman, in so far as his performing corresponds to the expectations of the community, and in so far as it is accepted and thus becomes effective. His individuality in the performance is thus greatly limited by the existing ethnographical and ethnical complexes. The performance must therefore have a form which would correspond to the ideas of the community about the performance and be in accordance with its susceptibility to the influence of suggestion, to hypnosis, and to ecstasy.[84]

We appear, therefore, to be confronted with a movement that is circular in nature. Tungus society has a certain knowledge of the spirits and certain expectations of those who would claim to control them and manifest their power. The acts of power of a good shaman conform in a broad way to these expectations, with the result that the society accepts the authenticity of his or her calling. Tradition defines the actions, the performance of which proves the presence of authentic power.

Conclusion

The results of the three case studies may now be summarized. With respect to the Elijah–Elisha cycle we have seen that the two prophets are depicted in a similar light, viz. as perpetrators of acts of power. There is a tendency for accounts of these acts to be accompanied by

---

82. Shirokogoroff, *Psychomental Complex*, p. 331. Anisimov's account shows remarkably well the extent of the audience's active participation and the intensity of the ecstasy of both shaman and audience; 'Shaman's Tent', pp. 100-105.

83. Shirokogoroff, *Psychomental Complex*, p. 333.

84. Shirokogoroff, *Psychomental Complex*, p. 335; cf. pp. 326, 328, 331, 343.

responses from those who witnessed them, and such responses are always of essentially the same nature: they acknowledge the prophets' power and authority. Finally, these acts of power are directed at both those who were ill-disposed and those who were well-disposed toward the prophets. The observations on Wovoka and Paiute shamanism showed that among such individuals acts of power were to be expected, and that one of their functions was to engender belief in the power and authority of the shaman. In the case of the Tungus it was evident that acts of power were expected. Such acts conformed in general to society's expectations for them, and were taken as proof of the shaman's power and authority. Without such socially-sanctioned proofs the shaman would either never be confirmed initially, or, having been confirmed, would stand in danger of rejection. It is worth noticing that the Tungus shaman faced the task of proving him- or herself to all members of the group, whether friendly, indifferent, or hostile.

On the basis of the apparent congruence of these three cases it seems reasonable to conclude that the accounts of Elijah's and Elisha's acts of power, whatever else they may 'mean' in the tradition and in the present form of the text, give us a glimpse of the process by which these early Israelite prophets were authorized. However, such a conclusion ought to be accompanied by certain provisos. In the first place it is the process of authorization, and not the specific contents, which I am suggesting is fundamentally the same in the three cases.[85] Elijah and Elisha are early Israelite prophets, and not simply shamans in the Paiute or Tungus sense. The three display important differences, as well as similarities, though I would hold that the former lie primarily in the specific content of their beliefs, while the latter are found predominantly in the structure of their relationships with the other members of their society. Secondly, it is not particularly important to me to come to a judgment about whether the specific acts of power attributed to any of these figures 'really happened'. What is clear is that acts of power (or 'tricks', or 'miracles'), whether witnessed or heard of, had a particular effect upon the relationship which existed between these religious functionaries and their societies. It is an interesting question why there are so few miraculous acts of power in the Old Testament outside the Elijah and Elisha cycle. Is this a localized

85. Cf. T.W. Overholt, 'Prophecy: The Problem of Cross-Cultural Comparison', *Semeia* 21 (1981), pp. 55-78.

or even individualized phenomenon? Was there a certain segment of
Israelite society which did not tolerate such actions, or (perhaps more
likely) a series of tradents who did not recognize or were not interested in the original function of such accounts, and therefore altered
or ignored them? A study of the other broad category of prophetic
acts of power (cf. n.4) from the point of view of the conclusions
arrived at here might throw some light on this problem.

Finally, some additional words about the social setting of such
actions and the stories about them are also in order. In my opinion
B.O. Long has correctly emphasized that such stories are not to be
understood as deriving primarily from circles of pious followers
which sought to glorify the prophets. Citing parallels from other cultures, he observes that miracle stories are often encountered in societies where shamanism is in a state of decline, where one of their
'important functions' is to reinforce belief in the institution of
shamanism by recounting the feats of powerful shamans of the past,
while at the same time allowing skepticism about specific individual
shamans of the present to exist.[86] Now the fact that shamans and
prophets find themselves the center of controversy and have their
authority disputed does not necessarily indicate that their particular
religious function is in a state of decline, as Shirokogoroff's observations on the 'present state and future of shamanism' make clear.[87] Be
that as it may, such a setting would appear to me to fit a later use to
which some such stories were put. One should notice that in the case
of Wovoka it was his own power that was recounted and not that of
some more powerful predecessor, and the same is true of the Siberian
shamans. Like Long and many others, I think of the Elijah–Elisha
cycle as a complex literature in the episodes of which several levels of
functioning may be evident. In their original setting it seems to me the
prophetic acts of power served primarily to legitimate the authority of
the prophet, while subsequent tellings of the story could serve to bolster that authority, whether in a given situation the influence of the
prophets was waxing or waning. And, of course, at later stages of the
tradition the stories could be taken over altogether into the service
of larger points of view.[88] In this respect I find myself in closer

86. B.O. Long, 'The Social Setting for Prophetic Miracle Stories', *Semeia* 3
(1975), pp. 46-59.

87. Shirokogoroff, *Psychomental Complex*, pp. 391-94, 399.

88. R.P. Carroll, for example, suggests that 'the compilers of the books of

agreement with Long's more recent remarks on prophetic signs, in which he suggests that certain actions by Elijah and Elisha served to demonstrate their legitimacy and reinforce their claims of authority.[89]

All this having been said, the basic conclusion remains: seeing *is* believing (or *should be*), at least as far as the relationship of the shaman or prophet to his society is concerned.[90]

Kings' were influenced in their selection of stories about Elijah and Elisha by a desire 'to draw attention to the resemblance' between these prophets and Moses: 'The Elijah–Elisha Sagas: Some Remarks on Prophetic Success in Ancient Israel', *VT* 19 (1969), pp. 412-13.

89. B.O. Long, 'Prophetic Authority as Social Reality', pp. 11, 15. Cf. also his '2 Kings III and Genres of Prophetic Narrative' (*VT* 23 [1973], pp. 337-48), where the present shape of some of the stories is shown to be 'defined by' a specific literary schema in the service of 'demonstrative theology', though this represents a reworking and not their original function; and along somewhat broader lines, 'Social Dimensions of Prophetic Conflict' (*Semeia* 21 [1981], pp. 31-53).

90. That a certain way of looking at the world is presupposed in such a relationship is nicely suggested by B. Toelken's turning of a familiar phrase: 'If I hadn't believed it I never would have seen it' ('Seeing with a Native Eye: How Many Sheep Will It Hold?', in W.H. Capps (ed.) *Seeing with a Native Eye* [New York: Harper, 1976], p. 23). But that is another topic.

JSOT 52 (1991), pp. 77-94

THE SOCIAL LOCATION OF THE DEUTERONOMISTS:
A SOCIOLOGICAL STUDY OF FACTIONAL POLITICS
IN LATE PRE-EXILIC JUDAH

Patricia Dutcher-Walls

The provenance of the Deuteronomistic History is a topic which has received varied treatments and answers over the last fifty years of biblical scholarship. The basic approach of scholars has been to use an exploration of the language, content, themes and interests evident in the books of Deuteronomy through 2 Kings to suggest possibilities for the origin, provenance, stream of tradition, authors and/or location of the text. This type of methodology has been able to illuminate several important facets of the text and its origins. But because of the seemingly wide-ranging interests that the Deuteronomists display, this approach has not led to a consensus about where and from whom the Deuteronomistic History emerged.

While building on, and indebted to, the work of previous scholarship, this article takes as its starting point a sociological methodology for increasing our understanding. The insights of a social-scientific analysis of Israelite society bring a new and needed perspective to the question of the provenance of a text, particularly one as significant as the Deuteronomistic History. Indeed, such an approach rephrases the question to become one of social location: can we locate within ancient Israelite society the place where the compilers of the Deuteronomistic History stood? To answer this I will utilize the social and political analysis of agrarian and aristocratic societies done by two prominent social scientists, in order to build a model useful for understanding ancient Israel in the time of the late monarchy.

A number of important assumptions on which this paper is based should be clarified. Since the time of Noth's groundbreaking work, the Deuteronomistic History has been widely understood as a 'unified and self-contained whole' (Noth 1981: 6). With many scholars, I assume that we are dealing in the Deuteronomistic History with a text heavily edited and shaped by editors. They used sources in either oral or written form to tell a continuous historical narrative betraying their own interests and theological concerns. Further, I understand Cross's proposal (1973) about two editions, as updated by Nelson (1981), to be a useful and probable solution to the production of the work.

It is the time period between the two editions of the History that this essay will focus on, examining six narratives from the closing years of Judah's existence, one from 2 Kings (chs. 22–23) and five from Jeremiah (chs. 26, 29, 36, 37, 38). In doing this, my assumption is that the Deuteronomists were involved in the life and events of this time and kept their own viewpoint and Deuteronomistic tradition alive.

I am aware of the many significant critical problems surrounding the narratives examined here, for example, the myriad issues about 2 Kings 22–23 (see Lohfink 1985), and those about the prose traditions in Jeremiah (see, for example, Holladay 1989). However, this type of study does not require specific decisions about these critical issues, because the model used allows us to read sociological data from a text in a manner not directly dependent on historical or literary analysis. A broader question of social relationships is being addressed, one which overarches historical events and survives redactional activity. A text, as theologically shaped as it is, contains material that was not the primary focus nor carrier for an editor's interests. Thus, following an approach used by Long, I will be 'focusing on elements in the tradition not directly expressive of the editor's apologetic and homiletic interests' (Long 1982: 42). It is these elements that contain the sociological and political data necessary to the study of Judah's social structure and the probable location of the Deuteronomists within it.

I should indicate several further assumptions. In all cases, I assume the narratives used are historically based, even if they are not in detail 'factual' or in editorial stance 'objective'. The chapters from 2 Kings (22–23) I of course take as a Deuteronomistic composition, perhaps the capstone of the ideological interests of the Deuteronomistic History in the edition under Josiah. However, the question of editorial viewpoint is not so clear-cut for the Jeremiah chapters. Generally, I take an approach to the Jeremiah material close to that of Nicholson (1970), who holds that the traditionists, the Deuteronomists, who shaped the prose and narrative materials in Jeremiah during the exile to portray their own theology and meet the needs of their own time, did so using Jeremiah's own words and incidents from his life that have historical validity. This is thus a position intermediate between that of Holladay (1989), who gives more credence to the historical witness of the Jeremiah tradition, and that of Carroll (1981), who places more emphasis on the creative work of the traditionists to the virtual exclusion of historicity.

That the carriers of the Deuteronomistic tradition can be located within the social and religious life of Judah is one assumption common to previous studies about the tradition. However, a review of four scholars will illustrate the wide variety of proposals for the tradition's provenance and development.

Von Rad (1966: 25) proposes the theory that the Deuteronomic tradition had roots in northern Israelite religion and was brought to Judah and cultivated there by rural Levitical priests who 'set themselves the task...of awakening the spirit of the old religion of Yahweh'. This priestly circle produced Deuteronomy around the time of Josiah to keep alive the old, northern tradition in which they stood, and to make this tradition applicable to their own historical situation.

While Clements accepts both the origins of the Deuteronomic tradition in the northern kingdom and its Levitical ties, his analysis indicates that Deuteronomy was 'composed as an attempt at reforming and reinterpreting the cult tradition of Jerusalem', and that this best accounts for 'a number of significant features of the Deuteronomic theology' (1965: 301). By seeing the group behind Deuteronomy as descendants of the priesthoods of the northern shrines who were familiar with but critical of the Jerusalem cult tradition, Clements is able to identify Deuteronomy's conditional covenant tradition as a deliberate counterbalance to Jerusalem's eternal and unconditional covenant tradition.

Nicholson proffers a significant contrast to von Rad's thesis; he states that the best location for the preservation of northern sacral and cultic traditions is in the prophetic, not the priestly, circles of Judah, because of the 'vital contacts between Deuteronomy and the teaching of the prophetic party in northern Israel' (1967: 69). His proposal is that the northern ideas were carried by members of a prophetic circle who fled south after 721 BCE, and formulated those ideas into a 'programme of reform and revival which they intended to be carried out by the Judaean authorities' (1967: 94).

Weinfeld, in his 1985 study, emphasizes and explores the flow of tradition from the northern circles in a way similar to Nicholson's. However, highlighting the didactic purpose of the Deuteronomic style ('to demonstrate that the divine word acted in all stages of Israel's history' [Weinfeld 1972: 16]), he stresses that those responsible for the Deuteronomic program and literature were scribes of the Jerusalem court who worked during the period from Hezekiah to Josiah (Weinfeld 1972: 161). He notes:

> ...only scribes who deal with literary and written documents and who have access to the court could have assembled so variegated a collection of documents as are encountered in Deuteronomy and the whole deuteronomic composition (1967: 254).

Rural Levites? Reforming priests? A prophetic circle? A scribal school? Each of these proposals holds that the Deuteronomistic History was the product of a single professional interest group. And all of these make some sense, given the manifest interests of Deuteronomy and the History, but do they make sense sociologically? This review shows the distinct lack of agreement among scholars on the location of the Deuteronomists, and indicates the limitations of a methodology that examines biblical texts without a sociological understanding. My proposal is that a model of the social stratification and political culture of monarchic Israel will allow a better understanding of where in that social structure the Deuteronomists might have been located.

The model I will use is based on the extensive cross-cultural work of two social scientists in analyzing and describing the social and political systems of pre-industrial societies. Gerhard Lenski, as a part of his larger study on social stratification (1966), has reviewed the social structure of agrarian societies, a type of society marked by relatively advanced agricultural technology but no industrialization. His thoroughly researched study highlights the typical pattern of societal interactions, roles and power relationships in these agrarian cultures, the societal type that fits ancient Israel. T.F. Carney (1975) explores the uses and possibilities of models for understanding societies in antiquity. Building largely on data from ancient Rome but including other ancient cultures as well, his results provide a good model for the politics, city life, economics and militarization of ancient aristocratic societies in general; this again is the typology that fits Judah under the late monarchy.

The broad outlines of the model are based on Lenski's analysis showing the social structure typically found in agrarian societies. Lenski notes several general aspects of such agrarian societies, particularly that they contain marked social inequality. Lenski (1966: 210) further notes that 'the unequal distribution of power, privilege, and honor in [agrarian societies] arises largely from the functioning of their political systems'. He goes on to explain that this is not an unexpected finding:

> Given the nature of man and society... we should logically anticipate an increase in social inequality as the economic surplus expands, as military technology advances to the point where the average man can no longer equip himself as well as certain others, and as the powers of the state increase. Furthermore, we should expect that the actions of men of power, who act in the name of the state, would be the primary source of this increase in social inequality (p. 210).

The highest and most powerful class in such a society is made up of the ruler (in a sense a class unto him- or herself) and the various state officers, advisors to the king, civil and military officials and the landed elites who own large tracts of land either by inheritance or royal grant (p. 220). This class makes up a tiny minority of the population, yet owns or controls most of the resources, power and wealth. One modification which Lenski's general pattern needs in order to fit ancient Israel is that in a society where religion is a state affair, and the temple the king's sanctuary, the high priests must be ranked in power and prestige in the uppermost class (see pp. 208-209 and especially p. 257).

The next most powerful class is made up of various people. Foremost among these are members of the retainer group dependent on the political elite (p. 243)—people such as servants, soldiers and lower-level civil officials. By and large, their tasks are the maintenance of the distributive economic system whereby goods and wealth are redistributed from the lower classes to the higher—in particular to the crown—through taxes, rents and fees (p. 246). Also included here would be the temple staff (in a state religion) and the small estate owners, whose land-owning status is more tenuous or less extensive than that of the elites. Finally, Lenski notes that the merchant class,

despite its humble origins, has a source of accruing wealth and therefore some political power through its trade. It stands in a market
relationship with the government, not an authority relationship, and so
can maximize these market forces and minimize the effects of royal
authority and elite control (pp. 250-54).

In the vast underclass, making up the large majority of the population, stand the peasants. On their labor falls the burden of supporting
the whole state apparatus and the privileged class (p. 266). This they
do through the payment of land taxes and rents, and by supplying
labor services, all of which often constitute a large portion of their
production. Lenski notes the bare subsistence level and condition of
their life: 'To compound the misery created by their economic situation, the peasants were often subjected to cruel and inhumane treatment by their superiors' (p. 271). Joining the peasants in misery is the
artisan class, who are often the semi-skilled and unskilled workers for
the merchants. They are recruited from the peasant class, but often
are lower in income and stability than the more stable peasants
(p. 278). Finally, the dregs of the social order are the expendables—
those whose employment and existence are not needed by the society
at large. These beggars, outlaws, itinerant workers and others form a
sub-class in any society 'where methods of limiting population growth
fail to prevent more births than are required to satisfy the demand for
labor' (p. 281).

A look at the dynamics of the highest class will reveal some of the
political interactions which affect state policy and power relationships.
Lenski describes the internal struggles which characterize agrarian
states. These are 'struggles between opposing factions of the privileged
class, each seeking its own special advantage' (p. 211). In particular,
the goal is the 'capture of the machinery of government... that brought
fabulous wealth and immense power to the victor' (p. 212). Thus the
elite class and the ruler struggle for power among themselves, seeking
to retain or gain advantages which increase wealth, status, stability in
office, and/or effective control of resources. The ruler is pitted against
those elites who seek control over the crown's resources and policies;
there are variations in states along an autocracy–oligarchy continuum
depending on whether the ruler or elites hold more power (pp. 235-
37). But there are also divisions within the governing class creating
factions and affecting their possible influence on the ruler (p. 239).
And all of these struggles, however they affect the governing class and

the policies of the state, take place only within the elite stratum:

> ... the outcome of all the countless struggles between rulers and their governing classes had almost no effect on the living conditions of the common people, except as these struggles sometimes led to violence and destroyed their very livelihood (p. 241).

Carney's analysis of bureaucratic politics dovetails with Lenski's more systemic study by focusing on the political machinations of the upper class. The ruler in an aristocratic state basically has to maintain power over against the ministers and bureaucrats who seek to limit the ruler's power to their own advantage. Thus the ruler operates 'in a structured situation, in a pre-set field of very powerful forces' (Carney 1975: 54). The ministers' aims are 'to secure a docile emperor and to maximize the scope of their own powers', while the autocrat's prime concern is to control his or her ministers (p. 55). The moves which rulers can make to dominate the bureaucracy include creating a counter-bureaucracy, limiting the number of 'indispensable' office holders, limiting tenure in office, making appointments only at their own discretion so that there are no automatic promotions or accumulated seniority, and controlling communications in the state (pp. 56-57). Further, wise autocratic politics dictate that strategic positions in the inner court and in the inner circles of the bureaucracy should be protected from powerful subjects of aristocratic pedigree or bureaucratic expertise. They should be filled by those 'who had the least power to oust or replace' the ruler, often freed slaves, eunuchs and provincials, those without social status, heirs or connections (p. 59).

In contrast, the elites in the government, the ministers, advisors and officials of the ruler, have their own aims and political survival tactics. Carney notes explicitly that these officials are in the same social class as the landed elites and thus represent their interests—they have 'the same reference group in common, that of the landed gentry' (p. 60), and 'they came from and intended to return to the land-owning gentry' (p. 61). There are serious consequences from this connection because the elites seek lower taxes on their own estates, which limits the income to the state and king and concurrently limits the king's power. The three large sectors which the ruler confronts are the military, with its power of organized force, the administrators, who have the power to block actions, and the ecclesiastical structures, which have the power to confer legitimacy (p. 62). By wielding these powers successfully, these sectors can limit, control and even depose the ruler. 'Hence, an

emperor's plans were variously limited by his bureaucracy's pre-
paredness to execute them—or him' (p. 62).

However, Carney points out that the politics of an aristocratic state
dictate that officials can get nowhere by themselves against the king.
To accrue power, they cannot act alone in such a complex situation.
Rather, two things are necessary—the formation of coalitions and the
loyalty of subordinates (p. 63). Power blocks can develop within a
bureaucratic department, and those that successfully wield influence
have a related clientele among the landed gentry and a coalition group
in the inner court (p. 64).

I should make explicit several modifications that I am making to factors mentioned by Lenski and Carney. These changes are needed to
account for particular aspects of Judah's situation in the late monarchic
period. The first is to include directly the status and influence of the
state religion and temple in Jerusalem. Secondly, I have put less stress
on the politics of middle-level bureaucrats and on the intricacy of the
bureaucracy than Carney does using data from the Roman empire.
That empire was much larger and more far-flung than Judah, so we
must not expect the same geographically and politically extensive
bureaucratic politics. Finally, I include an awareness of the international situation in which Judah found itself: it was a tiny state caught
between large empires, namely Egypt, Assyria and Babylon. Carney
mentions the influence that such external factors can have (pp. 352-
53), but we must make that influence a central part of our awareness.

In turning to a detailed study of several biblical texts, the discussed
model will be kept in mind throughout because it will provide the new
perspective we need to examine sociological data in the passages. I
begin with the narrative in 2 Kings 22–23 about King Josiah and the
reform based on the law book found in the temple. This story provides a useful starting point, because it is here that the people most
closely associated with the Deuteronomistic movement in a sense sur-
faced in Judah's history.

We notice first that the 'people of the land', who are otherwise
unspecified, are the ones who make Josiah king (2 Kgs 21.24) after
killing the servants who had assassinated his predecessor, Amon. Moti-
vations are not noted, but the demise of the Assyrian empire at this
time, the switch from Manasseh's and Amon's pro-Assyrian policy to
Josiah's independence policy, and the likely impact of international
affairs on internal Judean factions, make political speculations enticing.

Those who support Josiah in his role as reformer come from varied social positions. Hilkiah, the high priest, and Shaphan, the scribe, are associated with the finding of the law book and its reading to the king (2 Kgs 22.8-10). The delegation sent by the king to inquire about the book includes the high priest, the scribe, the scribe's son, Ahikam, one person whose role is not identified, and another who is the king's servant (2 Kgs 22.12). This delegation seeks and gets a prophecy from a prophetess, Huldah; her husband, Shallum, is mentioned as a court official, the keeper of the wardrobe (2 Kgs 22.14). Finally, specific social stations are mentioned in the references to the highest priests of the temple staff, the high priest, the second priests, and the door-keepers, who are appointed to carry out the reform in the temple (2 Kgs 23.4).

Using our model to reflect upon this narrative and the social roles mentioned in it, it is clear that the reform is carried out in and by the highest and most powerful class. The king and some of his closest advisors are involved. But it is also evident that the reform supporters are spread across various social stations—priests, a prophetess, the king's servants, scribes and nobles are all a part of the action. Although the apologetic nature of the narrative can only display unanimity among the top officials, our model helps us be aware that what is portrayed here is most likely a faction at work supporting its king and its policies. That there were other opposing factions is likely, although the nationalistic fervor of the time may have made them quieter than usual.

I follow this analysis along similar lines in the book of Jeremiah. Here I have selected five passages from the narrative sections of the book, all of which deal with conflicts between the prophet Jeremiah and various opponents just before the fall of Judah. While the passages appear on one level as biographical incidents from Jeremiah's life and on another as characteristic Deuteronomistic conflict stories, the narratives also reveal social data not directly related to the homiletic interests of the editors.

Jeremiah 26 gives a picture of conflict involving large societal groups in Jerusalem. Our model alerts us to the import of its data. Here is a conflict which seems to involve the highest classes as well as some of the general population. At least the very public nature of the event is portrayed so that all the people can see and take sides. More significantly, 'priests' and 'prophets', albeit general terms, do refer to groups with more social standing and power; they are powerful enough to put Jeremiah's life in danger. What is implied is that they have enough standing in the court to hand Jeremiah over to the king for the death sentence. However, they are opposed by another group whose equal or greater connections are shown by their coming up from the palace of the king. We have here our first direct indication of factions among the elites of Judah, for in the very court and palace of the king who would put Jeremiah to death stand those who support him and save his life. Further, given the fact that the two specific prophets mentioned as prophesying Jerusalem's destruction (Jeremiah and Uriah) stand opposed by those prophets who demand Jeremiah's death, it is clear that there was a split in this group, too. And the presence of the elders of the land who support Jeremiah alerts us that here too there must have been varying viewpoints.

The two specific names mentioned are also interesting. Elnathan, who seems to be on the king's side—at least if being an agent of the king's will implies support—is identified as the son of Achbor, quite possibly the Achbor who was a part of Josiah's reform. (For an excellent study of conflict between prophetic groups and of the familial connections in these narratives, see Long 1982.) Finally, Ahikam, the son of Shaphan who saves Jeremiah's life is the son of Josiah's scribe and also has served at Josiah's court. In the figure of Ahikam, we see a direct indication that the social faction supporting Jeremiah had connections with Josiah's Deuteronomistic reform party.

Our second passage in Jeremiah is ch. 36, where the prophet is again in conflict, this time more directly with King Jehoiakim. We certainly have in this chapter a paradigmatic episode of conflict between king and prophet, where the issue is the hearing and heeding of the Lord's word. But, in addition to the paradigm, we have valuable social and political data. Here the controversy engulfs the inner circles of the court, with Jeremiah being caught in the middle. We see immediately that those involved are from the highest class closest to the seat of power—the officials and attendants of the king. One group is represented by the officials gathered in the secretary's room. They listen to the scroll in fear, and they support Jeremiah and Baruch with the warning to hide. Three among them in particular urge the king not to burn the scroll, implying a respect for, and fear of, the message and messenger. Quite the opposite is shown by the king and his attendants; especially evident is the king's scorn for and rejection of the import of the scroll. Again we have an indication of factional divisions in the highest circles of Judah's government.

Some of the names mentioned also give interesting bits of information. The scroll is first read from a room in the temple belonging to Gemariah, son of Shaphan. His son, Micaiah, is the messenger to the officials. At a later point, Gemariah is one of the three who urge the king not to destroy the scroll. We see here the son and grandson of Josiah's scribe involved in the group which hears Jeremiah's word and supports the prophet. This is a further indication of the links between the deuteronomistically-minded associates of Josiah and Jeremiah's support group. The figure of Elnathan, seen above to be the son of another Josianic reformer, remains ambiguous, however. Here he seems to be one of Jeremiah's adherents—although in the last passage we studied he functioned as the king's agent against a prophet whose message was similar to Jeremiah's. Long (1982: 46) takes him to be one of Jeremiah's symphathizers, or at least as not openly hostile to his message, and this may be as close as we come to seeing one of the ways that the generation after Josiah dealt with the prophet who brought the word of the Lord to Judah *in extremis*. (For an alternative reconstruction of the text, see Holladay 1989: 252.)

Jeremiah 29 highlights a conflict between prophets during Zedekiah's reign, at some point after the first group from Judah had been taken into exile. The prophets in the exile who foretold a short exile clearly continue to resist the fact of Babylonian victory and its meaning. Jeremiah, in contrast, advises a policy of accommodation to the situation. In both cases, the understanding of Yahweh's will has direct consequences in both the political and everyday spheres of life—continued resistance and restlessness as against accommodation and prospering in the new situation. Long (1982: 49) phrases it that both prophets here, and in particular Jeremiah, 'were part of a larger struggle between factions for "autonomist" or "coexistence" political action'; this type of analysis is in line completely with our model. Further, the prophet Shemaiah tries to line up a priest's help in restraining Jeremiah with his 'wild' prophecies in the temple (vv. 24-28). Zephaniah as priest is supposed to control the temple precincts, but he does not do Shemaiah's bidding. He emerges thus as one who is friendly to Jeremiah's side of the conflict, and this helps us see that there were divisions among the priests, too, especially in light of the priests of ch. 26 who stood against Jeremiah. The detail of Shemaiah

seeking Zephaniah's help is understandable in terms of our model as
an attempt at building a coalition: factions gain power against the king
or other factions by lining up support for their position among various groups and parts of the governmental and ruling-class structures.

The figure of Zephaniah presents still another possible link between
Jeremiah's supporters and what we might call the Deuteronomistic
party under Josiah (see Long 1982: 46 for further exploration of this
connection). He is the son of Maaseiah, a priestly official himself, who
is the son of Shallum. This is the same Shallum who is Jeremiah's
uncle (Jer. 32.7), and he may be the husband of Huldah, Josiah's
prophetess (2 Kgs 22.14). If the tradition is accurate at this point, then
Jeremiah's support group is again linked to Josiah's circle. At any
rate, Zephaniah is Jeremiah's second cousin as well as being a sympathetic official in the right spot to help at the right time.

Conflict between Jeremiah and the court's inner circles is again
portrayed in ch. 37. As the drama in the story increases and the day of
doom for Jerusalem draws near, the political divisions and social
conflict in the inner court intensify, with Jeremiah again being caught
in the middle. Identified first are two general social groups, the king's
attendants and the people of the land (Oded 1977: 457); this latter is a
possible reference to landed elites, who do not listen to Yahweh's
word. This reference underlines the fact that the highest classes did
take sides in the political/religious turmoil of the time. However, in
this chapter, there is little hint of a support group or faction on
Jeremiah's side, and we see the power of his opponents at court displayed in a more open and aggressive fashion. To Jeremiah's prophecy
that resistance to the Babylonians is foolhardy and that Jerusalem will
indeed fall, his opponents react with anger and an attempt to silence
the spokesman of such a position. The accusation that Jeremiah is
attempting to defect and desert the city points up the tense and volatile
nature of the situation in which these elites see themselves. While the
faction supporting resistance to the Babylonians emerges in stark
relief, the king is seen as a more ambiguous and ambivalent character.
He does not listen to Jeremiah (we are told), yet he sends a delegation
to him to seek his help in prayer. Later, he calls Jeremiah to himself
privately and seeks the word of Yahweh through the prophet. His disposition towards Jeremiah, in spite of the enmity of his officials, is
seen in his granting Jeremiah's request not to be returned to the
prison.

The proper names also reveal some sociologically interesting data. We notice that the tradition indicates that two who may be brothers are part of the circle against Jeremiah—Jehucal and Irijah, each listed as a son of Shelemiah. Given the close-knit associations possible in a monarchic court, this possibility is not surprising, although we can say no more than that with this evidence. Also worth noting is that the priest Zephaniah shows up in a role that leaves open the question of his attitude toward Jeremiah. In the passage studied above, he appears in a role friendly to the prophet, and his status here as the ambivalent king's messenger does not contradict that role.

Our final passage, ch. 38, tells a story following closely the one just examined. Indeed, the chapters may well narrate different versions of the same series of events: a threat to Jeremiah's life from some court officials, a timely rescue, and an audience with the king. Be that as it may, this passage is rich in data that correspond to and are explained by our model. The presence of factionalism in the inner circles around the king is undeniably clear. One group of officials, angered at Jeremiah's public calls for accommodation and even surrender to the Babylonians, attempts to silence him and his political position. The other side, which supports Jeremiah and respects the word he brings from Yahweh, is represented by Ebed-melech. Our model has alerted us to the suggestion that, as a foreigner and eunuch, he is 'safe' and can be trusted by the king more than those who may push a family connection to put a son in power. In these two factions we again get an indication of the political import and power of religious claims; the presentation, maintenance and function of the state religion is an integral part of a faction's control of power. The impact of foreign domination on internal factionalized politics is similarly quite evident. We also see that the factionalism has had repercussions outside the court's inner groups, in that some have already gone over to the Babylonians.

Proper names again reveal insights. Jehucal is mentioned here as one of Jeremiah's enemies, whereas in ch. 37 his status as king's messenger leaves open the question of his political leanings. Gedaliah, likewise listed among the prophet's adversaries, is probably the son of Pashur, the priest named in ch. 20, who was also an opponent of Jeremiah. We see thus the kind of connections possible among such factions.

The figure of the king emerges again in its ambivalence. The picture is of a ruler who does not have power over against some of his

officials, for Zedekiah admits that he cannot stop Jeremiah's opposition from seizing him. Yet he commands Ebed-melech to take a small
group from the king's house and carry out a rescue. Our model helps
us understand this situation perfectly in terms of the politics of elites
in a monarchic situation, each group trying to gain power over the
ruler. The level of suspicion and intrigue present in the court in the
last days of Judah is indicated by the king's secrecy in talking to
Jeremiah. Especially revealing is the comment that the conversation
between the king and the prophet had *not* been overheard—the norm
must be for the walls to have ears!

Through the series of textual studies carried out in the above section, we have seen the usefulness of our model in understanding the
political and social situation in Judah in the late monarchy. The studies
allow us to see the inner workings of the court and members of the
upper class in the situation in which Judah finds itself just before its
demise. We see the existence of conflicting factions among the elites of
the nation, and we see the vying for power and influence that took
place among them. Each tries to have an impact on the policies of the
king and nation; their battles are played out in the very court of the
king while having ramifications throughout the elite class and beyond.
Yet, as in our model, the lowest classes are little affected or involved
in the intrigues of the court, until those political struggles bring violence down on their heads in the form of the Babylonian invasions.
Even then, they are left on the land to maintain agricultural
productivity.

We have gained some idea of the political ideology of these factions
in the pre-exilic years. Judah, a small vassal state caught between the
clashes of world empires, contains within its elites factions urging
particular responses to the international scene. Each faction claims
religious legitimation for its political program.

Further, we have seen that the membership of each faction cuts
across the various social groupings and roles that make up the highest
class of society of the day. There is not one faction of priests versus
prophets, or gentry versus king's officials. Rather, each faction seems
to include the full range of elite social roles—prophets, officials,
priests and gentry—in its circle of influence and power. Family connections are often evident and important, for fathers and sons often
follow the same world-views. Coalitions are formed to increase influence and power. The divisions thus lie between political ideologies,

not between roles, status levels or occupations among the elites.

The secrecy, intrigue and deadly seriousness of the conflicts between the factions are also clear. People's lives are at stake as well as the nation's direction and future. This is a 'game' played for keeps, in which it is hard, if not impossible, to be neutral or unconcerned.

It is clear that the theology and world-view that has usually been associated with Deuteronomistic circles in the many critical studies of their work is, in the above analysis, aligned with, and carried by, one of the factions active in these years right before the exile. This Deuteronomistic faction has its roots in the time of Josiah, if not before. Our texts identified the group of reformers associated with Josiah's renewal program as the focal point for the open and active political life of the faction, although a study of earlier time periods might reveal its predecessors. The faction is associated with Josiah's enthronement and carries out his reform.

The faction continues to pursue its interests in the closing years of the state, under kings less open to its influence. Instead of being the dominant ideology, or at least the most persuasive one, as under Josiah, the group must push its view against at least one other ideology among the elites and in the courts of both Jehoiakim and Zedekiah.

The faction's ideology includes a view of Yahweh's sovereignty over Judah's affairs, and a sense of the nation's sinfulness and of the possibility of deserved punishment if no repentance becomes evident. It also urges a political accommodation to Babylonian hegemony which entails less than an arrogant and stubborn claim on Yahweh's unconditional graciousness toward the nation and its Davidic dynasty.

The faction's opponents also lay claim to a Yahwistic ideology, but one which emphasizes God's unconditional covenant with David's heirs and permanent presence in Jerusalem. A narrow and stubborn nationalism is concurrently maintained. Against this view no dissent is tolerated—at least when these opponents have the political power to silence their detractors.

In these later years, the faction contains the sons, nephews and grandsons of Josiah's reformers and is closely associated with one particular family grouping, that of Shaphan the scribe. The descendants of Shaphan figure prominently in the circle, although the influence of the Deuteronomistic world-view extends well beyond that family, cutting across and including various social roles among the elites it draws on.

The faction finds a kindred spirit in Jeremiah, and it supports his prophetic stance against those who would silence him and his word. Jeremiah is the prophet of Yahweh *par excellence* for this circle's world-view. I deliberately leave vague the connections between the Deuteronomists and Jeremiah; the available data will allow only a description of the social and political roles played by the faction and the prophet, not a reconstruction of their historical or literary relationship.

The faction is unsuccessful in promoting its political program, since the kings Jehoiakim and Zedekiah neither listen to nor follow its advice of repentance and accommodation. Both kings are swayed by the nationalistic faction into rebellion against Babylon and thus they bring Babylon's destructive wrath down on Judah.

It is now clear that using a systemic sociological model of elite political factions to 'read' Biblical texts has given us a new perspective on the social location of the Deuteronomistic circle in the final years of Judah's national existence. Our study shows who at the time was open to, and who promoted, what is usually called the Deuteronomistic theology. It shows what types of people they were, their social roles and political interactions, and their status in society. Thus it gives us a sociologically sensitive analysis which points to the Deuteronomists' location at the heart of the political power structure with its struggles in Judah's closing years.

Most importantly, this analysis highlights the Deuteronomists as a coalition of elite professional groups, joined in a political alliance so necessary for power in the factionalized politics of aristocratic states. Thus, this analysis provides a more comprehensive view than von Rad's, Clements's, Nicholson's or Weinfeld's various proposals of priestly, prophetic or scribal provenance for Deuteronomy and the Deuteronomistic tradition. One should not choose between these social groups; rather, the interests which the text betrays in things cultic, prophetic and scholarly reflect the social location of its adherents as a mixed elite grouping of priests, prophets, scribes, court officials and gentry. To choose only one group is to overlook the social reality of political structures and factional struggles in agrarian societies in antiquity. To put it another way, such a mixed elite faction better accounts for the wide variety of interests in Deuteronomistic texts, because it reflects the variety of concerns of the social location from which it came.

BIBLIOGRAPHY

Bright, J.
1965   *Jeremiah* (AB; Garden City, NY: Doubleday).

Carney, T.F.
1975   *The Shape of the Past: Models and Antiquity* (Lawrence, KS: Coronado Press).

Carroll, R.P.
1981   *From Chaos to Covenant* (New York: Crossroad).

Clements, R.E.
1965   'Deuteronomy and the Jerusalem Cult Tradition', *VT* 15: 300-12.

Cross, F.M.
1973   'The Themes of the Book of Kings and the Structure of the Deuteronomistic History', in *Canaanite Myth and Hebrew Epic* (Cambridge, MA: Harvard University Press): 274-89.

Holladay, W.L.
1989   *Jeremiah*. II (Minneapolis: Fortress Press).

Lenski, G.
1966   *Power and Privilege: A Theory of Social Stratification* (Chapel Hill: University of North Carolina Press).

Lohfink, N.
1985   'Das neueren Diskussion über II Kön 22–23', in *Das Deuteronomium: Entstehung, Gestalt, und Botschaft*, (Leuven: Leuven University Press): 24-48.

Long, B.O.
1982   'Social Dimensions of Prophetic Conflict', *Semeia* 21: 31-53.

Nelson, R.D.
1981   *The Double Redaction of the Deuteronomistic History* (JSOTSup, 18; Sheffield: JSOT Press).

Nicholson, E.W.
1967   *Deuteronomy and Tradition* (Philadelphia: Fortress Press).
1970   *Preaching to the Exiles* (New York: Schocken Books).

Noth, M.
1981   *The Deuteronomistic History* (JSOTSup, 15; Sheffield: JSOT Press).

Oded, B.
1977   'Judah and the Exile', in *Israelite and Judaean History*, J.H. Hayes and J.M. Miller (eds.), (Philadelphia: Westminster Press): 435-88.

Rad, G. von
1966   *Deuteronomy* (Philadelphia: Westminster Press).

Weinfeld, M.
1967   'Deuteronomy—The Present State of Inquiry', *JBL* 86: 249-62.
1972   *Deuteronomy and the Deuteronomic School* (Oxford: Clarendon Press).
1985   'The Emergence of the Deuteronomic Movement: Its Historical Antecedents', in *Das Deuteronomium* (Leuven: Leuven University Press): 76-98.

JSOT 57 (1993), pp. 23-37

ROLE DEDIFFERENTIATION IN THE BOOK OF RUTH

Jon L. Berquist

The simple story of Ruth often proves a difficult ground for precise exegesis. In recent years, many studies have utilized literary methods to understand the narrative structure of the book and its plot and characterization.[1] It is common to view the book of Ruth as an artistic short story, a literary fiction with no precise historical setting, although there is a consensus that Ruth is post-exilic. In these studies, sociological analysis has been conspicuously absent.

The potential of sociological methods for the interpretation of the book of Ruth is great. In order to be understandable to their readers, stories must possess a degree of conformity with familiar elements of the readers' social world. Specifically, the interaction between characters within a narrative must correlate to observable social processes, and these processes create possible foci for sociological investigation. This does not imply that the story's characterization depicts historical persons; rather, with appropriate suspension of belief, the reader must imagine these literary characters to be persons who behave in recognizable ways.

---

1. E.F. Campbell, *Ruth* (AB, 7; Garden City, NY: Doubleday, 1975); P. Trible, *God and the Rhetoric of Sexuality* (OBT; Philadelphia: Fortress Press, 1978), pp. 166-99; J.M. Sasson, *Ruth: A New Translation with a Philological Commentary and a Formalist-Folklorist Interpretation* (Sheffield: JSOT Press, 1979); R.E. Murphy, *Wisdom Literature: Job, Proverbs, Ruth, Canticles, Ecclesiastes, and Esther* (FOTL; Grand Rapids: Eerdmans, 1981), pp. 83-96; A. Berlin, 'Ruth', in J.L. Mays (ed.), *Harper's Bible Commentary* (San Francisco: Harper & Row, 1988), pp. 262-67; and D.N. Fewell and D.M. Gunn, *Compromising Redemption: Relating Characters in the Book of Ruth* (Literary Currents in Biblical Interpretation; Louisville, KY: Westminster Press/John Knox, 1990).

Sociological approaches, therefore, can be helpful in the study of the book of Ruth through a nuanced understanding of human social behavior. Of course, the interpreter must be careful not to assume that the literary depictions are historically 'accurate', that is, that the depictions can be used as sociological evidence. This use of sociological methodology does not deny the literary nature of texts, but instead finds ways in which literary and sociological approaches can cooperate in exegesis.[2]

In the book of Ruth, the social roles of the main characters (Naomi, Ruth and Boaz) undergo observable changes involving the addition of various roles. This process of characterization corresponds to the sociological theory of role dedifferentiation, by which persons respond to crisis through adding roles, including roles that would be socially inappropriate in normal times. This theory can assist the literary interpretation of the book of Ruth.

Role Dedifferentiation

Many sociological theories depend on notions of increasing distinctions between elements of a system, which is termed differentiation.[3] Through structural differentiation, social systems become increasingly complex. At the microsociological level, individuals' roles become more distinct from others. Modern bureaucracies evince the results of differentiation, both as a system and as a set of roles, since the system tends toward complexity and the roles of individuals toward specialization.

Recently, certain sociologists have focused their attention on the complementary process of dedifferentiation. Edward Tiryakian defined dedifferentiation as the undoing of prior patterns and role definitions, resulting in a condition of less structure.[4] He has argued that this process is not necessarily negative, but that societies undergo dedifferentiation

---

2. I develop more fully the social context of the book of Ruth in J.L. Berquist, *Judaism in Persia's Shadow: A Social and Historical Approach* (Minneapolis: Fortress Press, 1995), pp. 221-32.

3. For a classic discussion of differentiation, see T. Parsons, *Structure and Process in Modern Societies* (New York: Free Press, 1960).

4. E.A. Tiryakian, 'On the Significance of De-Differentiation', in S.N. Eisenstadt and H.J. Helle (eds.), *Macro-Sociological Theory: Perspectives on Sociological Theory* (London: Sage, 1985), I, pp. 118-34.

in order to release additional energy and to remobilize themselves for greater efficiency under new situations.

Jean Lipman-Blumen noticed a connection between dedifferentiation and times of social turmoil and uncertainty. During crises, roles merge, as each person assumes additional roles.[5] Her chief example concerned women in the United States during the Second World War. As a systemic response to crisis, there was a sharp increase in the number of women employed in jobs such as manufacturing. These positions, which had previously been male gender-specific, were suddenly dedifferentiated by the removal of the gender distinctions. Both men and women could attain these positions. This redefined job roles and gender roles, but after the crisis the roles partially redifferentiated. This temporary dedifferentiation responded to a crisis, during which the redefinition of social and sexual roles resulted in society's greater ability to adjust.[6]

Ruth's Dedifferentiation of Roles

Setting the Stage: Crisis and Role Death

In Lipman-Blumen's understanding of role dedifferentiation, crisis catalyzes role shifts. In the book of Ruth, famine represents the crisis that triggers dedifferentiation (1.1). As the characters react to the famine, roles lose their stability.

The first role shift involves Naomi, the Ephrathite matriarch of the small family that migrates from Judah to Moab in search of food. Famine motivates the move, but once there, Naomi's husband and sons

---

5.   J. Lipman-Blumen, 'Role De-Differentiation as a System Response to Crisis: Occupational and Political Roles of Women', *Sociological Inquiry* 43 (1973), pp. 105-29. For a general discussion of role theory, see R. Dahrendorf, '*Homo Sociologicus*: On the History, Significance, and Limits of the Category of Social Role', in *idem* (ed.), *Essays in the Theory of Society* (Stanford, CA: Stanford University Press, 1968), pp. 19-87; and T.R. Sarbin and V.L. Allen, 'Role Theory', in G. Lindzey and E. Aronson (eds.), *The Handbook of Social Psychology* (Reading, MA: Addison–Wesley, 2nd edn, 1968), I, pp. 488-567. A recent revisioning of role theory and social structure is J.S. Coleman, *The Asymmetric Society* (Syracuse, NY: Syracuse University Press, 1982).

6.   For recent work on the theory of sex roles and gender in society, see A.H. Eagly, *Sex Differences in Social Behavior: A Social-Role Interpretation* (Hillsdale, NJ: Lawrence Erlbaum, 1987); and J.M.C. Nielsen, *Sex and Gender in Society: Perspectives on Stratification* (Prospect Heights, IL: Waveland, 2nd edn, 1990).

die (1.1-5). For Naomi, this transition from 'wife' to 'bereft woman' (1.5) is not a case of dedifferentiation, because she loses her major roles. She is left without affiliation and with little connection to the larger institutions of society (1.21). She severs her remaining connections to her adopted country (1.6-7) and to her daughters-in-law (1.8-9, 11-12). The beginning crisis, then, is threefold: a famine of national or international scale, the death of three men and virtual role death for Naomi.[7] This crisis signals the possibility for the response of role dedifferentiation.

Ruth's Clinging

Ruth enters the story in 1.4, where she is named; she does not act until 1.14, when she and Orpah provide different responses to Naomi's role death. For ten verses, Ruth watches the crisis grow to overwhelming proportions. Whereas family relations define Ruth's role in 1.4, the death of the family gives birth to Ruth as actor. The crises of famine and death lead directly to her dedifferentiation.

Orpah accepts her role as bereaved daughter-in-law and obeys her mother-in-law, in accord with the norms of her stratified society. By returning to her previous family, Orpah fulfills her role expectations. Ruth, however, deviates from her mother-in-law's command and from standard expectations for young widows: she clings (דבקה) to Naomi (1.14). The Hebrew word 'cling, cleave' (דבק) is a moderately common term, occurring 40 times in the G stem. The most frequent Hebrew Bible use of this term is in the phrase 'to cling to God'.[8] However, there are only eight references to clinging between humans, and four of these appear in Ruth. Of the other references, perhaps the best known is Gen. 2.24: 'a man leaves his father and his mother and clings to his wife, and they become one flesh'. This clinging between a man and a woman relates to love, to marriage, and/or to intimate sexual relations.[9]

---

7. The end of 1.13 should be translated, 'it is more bitter for me [Naomi] than for you [Ruth and Orpah]'. See Fewell and Gunn, *Compromising Redemption*, p. 28 n. 12.

8. M. Weinfeld also notices the use of דבק in a Deuteronomistic phrase of religious disloyalty, 'cling to the nations' (Josh. 23.12; 1 Kgs 11.2), but he misconstrues this phrase, which refers more particularly to the practices of marrying women of other nations (*Deuteronomy and the Deuteronomic School* [Oxford: Clarendon Press, 1972], pp. 83, 333, 341).

9. Against Campbell, *Ruth*, p. 81, who sees דבק as covenant language. But the

Furthermore, דבק refers to the male role in initiating marriage. Outside of Ruth, the term 'cling' never describes a woman's act. This makes Ruth 1.14 all the more striking. When Ruth clings to Naomi, Ruth takes the male role in initiating a relationship of formal commitment, similar to marriage.[10]

Ruth responds to crisis with dedifferentiation by adding roles. She remains in the female role of daughter-in-law even though there is no longer any basis for that role, and she adds the male role of 'clinging' to Naomi as a husband. Ruth maintains both roles; she is still daughter-in-law (1.22) even *after* she clings (1.14). This is not role replacement, but role addition. Facing a crisis in which there are not enough men to fulfill typical male roles, Ruth adds a specifically non-female role, 'clinging'. This is an instance of role dedifferentiation.

Family Roles

Ruth's second chapter begins with a notice that Naomi has a relative (2.1). By the end of ch. 2, Naomi exclaims, 'The man is close to us; he is one of our redeemers (מגאלנו)!' (2.20). Thus, family connections provide an important set of roles, including the role of redeemer that would provide a possible solution to the crisis. Whereas the narrator unswervingly reports the precise familial relationship of mother-in-law and daughter-in-law (1.6, 7, 8, 14, 15, 22; 2.18, 19, 20, 22, 23), Naomi calls Ruth 'daughter' or 'my daughter' (2.2, 22).

Within this network of family relations, the reader finds an essential clue about the nature of the problem to be solved. Naomi attributes her initial role death to her lack of sons (1.11-14), agreeing with the narrator's definition of the problem (1.5). The issue is not the lack of

---

three other non-Ruth uses of דבק for intrahuman relationships also carry a sexual meaning. Shechem's infatuation with Dinah results in kidnapping and rape, but then his soul 'clings' to Dinah (the parallel verb is אהב, 'to love'); Shechem then desires marriage (Gen. 34.3). Josh. 23.12 explains 'clinging to the nations' as a reference to marrying (חתן) foreign women. Similarly, 1 Kgs 11.2 condemns Solomon for 'clinging' in love to foreign women, preceding an enumeration of Solomon's wives and concubines.

10. Fewell and Gunn (*Compromising Redemption*, pp. 97, 103) notice Ruth's caretaking of Naomi as represented in this term and they understand this as a husband image, but they do not further develop Ruth's taking of a specifically male role. As discussed below, the other uses of this term in Ruth carry different connotations, but the reader familiar with other texts would have likely used the standard marriage meaning to interpret Ruth's first use of the term in 1.14.

children or fertility *per se*, but specifically the lack of *sons*. Once Naomi sees Ruth taking the husband role of clinging, Naomi accepts Ruth as kin, in the form of a son. This restores a familial relationship, albeit a strange one, and Ruth begins to provide for Naomi, offering a short-term solution to the problem of bereavement.

A Plan for Role Development: Gleaner and Seducer
Ruth's dedifferentiation does not stop with these family roles of husband and son. In the larger society, Ruth adds non-family roles, beginning with the role of gleaner, in order to provide Naomi with food (2.2).[11] Levitical regulation specified that all landowners must allow the poor and the foreigner to enter the fields after the harvesting, in order to gather up whatever was missed or dropped by the field laborers (Lev. 19.9-10). The gleaners could keep what they gathered. The law required landowners and laborers to cooperate, but reluctance could well be expected. Gleaning provided subsistence for those lowest in social status. In Ruth's case, with two persons eating one's gleanings, even survival would be questionable. Ruth must find another solution to hunger and poverty.

The narrative immediately indicates another, more permanent solution. Ruth suggests more than gleaning when she says, 'I intend to go to the field, so that I may glean among the grain after anyone in whose eyes I find favor' (2.2). Since the law insists that all landowners allow gleaning, Ruth's intention seems more than finding kindness. The expression 'to find favor in one's eyes' (מצא חן בעיניו) typically refers to petitioning, but in Ruth 2.2 the phrase is a sexual innuendo.[12] Here finding favor cannot refer to a petition, since gleaning would not require permission from the landowner (Lev. 19.9-10), and since Ruth does not seek permission from anyone before she gleans (2.3).[13]

Ruth intends to use gleaning to attract a husband who would take the

---

11. Fewell and Gunn (*Compromising Redemption*, pp. 76, 98) refer aptly to Ruth as a breadwinner.

12. The expression occurs 48 times, of which 14 refer to a man's petitioning of God and 23 to a man's petitioning of a higher-status male. In fact, relative status is often a crucial point (Gen. 39.4; 39.21; 47.25, 29; 50.4). Of the 11 cases of women's use of the phrase, 7 are petitions, but 4 cases (Deut. 24.1; Ruth 2.2; Est. 2.15, 17) suggest the context of sexual attraction.

13. Campbell (*Ruth*, p. 94) argues that Ruth asks for permission in 2.7, but the text is missing.

role of provider. Thus, her statement announces both a short-term solution to hunger (gleaning) and a plan for a long-term solution (marriage). For the proposed long-term solution, Ruth adds another role: seducer.[14] Ruth's intention of sexual attraction allows a clearer understanding of her actions in the field (2.3-16):

> [3]So she walked and came and gleaned in the countryside after the field-workers, and happened across the portion of the countryside that belonged to Boaz, who was from the family of Elimelech.
> [4]Then Boaz came from Bethlehem, and he said to the fieldworkers, 'YHWH be with you'. They said to him, 'May YHWH bless you'. [5]Boaz said to his boy, who was in charge of the fieldworkers, 'Who is this girl?' [6]The boy who was in charge of the fieldworkers answered and said, 'She is the Moabite girl who returned with Naomi from the country of Moab. [7]She said, "I wish to glean and to gather among the ears of grain after the fieldworkers", and she came and stood from then in the morning until now. She stayed in the house only a little.'[15]

Ruth 2.3 tells of Ruth gleaning in fields and happening across Boaz's field, but the scene shifts in 2.4 to focus upon Boaz's entry into the field. In this new scene, Ruth's location remains unannounced. In fact, though the setting for the first part of this scene (2.3) is clearly the field, the setting of the rest (2.4-7) is ambiguous. Though the reader may presume the field, the last line (2.7b) forces a re-reading, especially as the next scene starts (2.8-13). Suddenly, Boaz's house seems the location! The narrative brings the scene into shocking clarity. Boaz entered his property and passed by the fieldworkers on the way to his house, where a surprise awaited him: his field supervisor with a foreign girl. With apt suspicion, Boaz challenged the supervisor, 'Who is this girl?' The supervisor's infelicitous speech betrayed the nervousness of his defense, insisting that Ruth intended gleaning and had hardly been inside long enough to do anything improper. In the context of Ruth's announced intentions to seduce some man (2.2), this scene seems clearly to be evoked: during a morning's gleaning, Ruth located the ranking man present and began her seduction.[16] Now an

---

14. In this role, Ruth parallels Tamar's actions toward Judah (Gen. 38), as recognized by Fewell and Gunn, *Compromising Redemption*, pp. 46-48.

15. This reading has the advantage of requiring no emendation of the MT.

16. Echoes of Potiphar's wife (Gen. 39) resound here: a woman's seduction leads a young man into trouble with his superior. In that story as well, the house (and the master's possession of all therein) is a key point.

even higher-ranking man catches her and uncovers her plot. Immediately, the supervisor exits from the narrative, and Ruth's designs focus solely on Boaz.

Boaz's references to Ruth are oddly ambiguous. He uses the term 'cling' (דבק), as discussed above, to describe Ruth's relationship to Boaz's female servants in the harvest, and he encourages her to stay away from the men in the field, suggesting a protected status (2.9). Not only should Ruth follow behind these women, but she should identify with them and become part of their association.[17]

This passage portrays the relationship between Boaz and Ruth. He forbids her contact with other males and gives her freedom to glean, which the law already granted. Ruth had worked to seduce the supervisor; Boaz counters that and sends Ruth back out into the field. Since Boaz understands this as an act of protection, Ruth capitalizes on his action and interprets it as 'finding favor' (2.10), referring to the beginnings of sexual attraction.[18] His pious blessings appear ironic: Ruth does not seek refuge in God, but in a man. Despite his protestations, Boaz now appears to be that man (2.12), and she seeks her reward under Boaz's 'wings' or skirt (3.9).[19]

At this point in the narrative, Ruth has attempted to take the role of Boaz's seductress, but Boaz has not accepted her advances. However, Ruth's role dedifferentiation continues to expand. At this point, the narrative breaks down. Boaz has blocked Ruth's seduction, while encouraging her role as gleaner. As gleaner, Ruth attains a short-term solution, but without her seduction she finds no role that leads to a permanent amelioration of the incipient crisis. Thus, the narrative must find another opportunity for the seduction to continue.

17. Note the rejection of parents in Ruth 2.11 and Gen. 2.24, both of which appear with clinging language. This strengthens the impression of a close relationship, similar to marriage. In another reference to the early narratives, Boaz credits Ruth with going to a previously unknown land, as Abram left Ur (Gen. 12.1).

18. Also, the phrase 'speak to the heart' has sexual connotations, according to Fewell and Gunn (*Compromising Redemption*, p. 102).

19. As fitting for someone in the process of role dedifferentiation, Ruth concerns herself with role labels. She rejects Boaz's title of female servant (2.13), but she accepts the title 'girl' (2.6), which parallels the title of the supervisor. She takes egalitarian role labels while rejecting subservient ones. Eventually, she receives the role label that she prefers: 'woman of strength' (3.11), parallel to Boaz, who is a 'man, a hero of strength' (2.1).

The Spreading of Dedifferentiation

Naomi as Matchmaker

The second chapter ends with a desperate situation. Ruth's short-term solution of gleaning would soon fail, since the harvest was approaching its end, and Boaz's rejection of Ruth's seduction blocked the marriage that would have provided the permanent solution. In the narrative's time frame, months pass in a single verse until the need for action is once again crucial (2.23).

Naomi then undertakes her second active role.[20] In 3.1-4, Naomi prods Ruth to act toward the permanent solution. Naomi assumes the role of the matchmaker who seeks rest for Ruth (3.1, אבקש־לך מנוח). The term for rest (מנוח) usually refers to a place in which one can rest, and thus some translations render the word as 'home'.[21] Along with this meaning can also reside the sense that Ruth should find a way to rest from the daily labor that has provided survival for her and her mother-in-law. Thus, Naomi directs the active search for a long-term solution, which is profitable marriage.

The addition of the matchmaker role is role dedifferentiation. In ancient Israel, fathers arranged marriages for their children.[22] Naomi's matchmaking is a male role. Once more, dedifferentiation sets the narrative into motion. When Naomi oversteps the roles acceptable for women, work toward the permanent solution restarts.

Boaz as Suitor

Boaz adopts the role of suitor when he acknowledges Ruth as seducer (3.8, 10). Boaz's response facilitates the solutions to the story's problems, since his wealth can save Ruth and Naomi from hunger and social isolation. Ruth's attempts at the seduction of a provider (2.2) and Naomi's prodding toward these ends (3.1-4) both advance the plot in anticipation of Boaz's reply. The plot's success requires not only that Boaz accept the sexual seduction, but also that he undertake the proper courting of Ruth. Appropriately, his response to Ruth's

---

20. See J.W.H. Bos, 'Out of the Shadows: Genesis 38; Judges 4.17-22; Ruth 3', *Semeia* 42 (1988), pp. 58-64.

21. Trible, *God and the Rhetoric of Sexuality*, p. 182.

22. See R. de Vaux, *Ancient Israel*. I. *Social Institutions* (New York: McGraw–Hill, 1961), p. 29. Rebekah initiates the search for a wife for Jacob (Gen. 27.46), but Isaac makes the arrangements (Gen. 28.1-5), and she has no further role.

unexpected presence on the threshing-floor moves from acceptance of her loyalty (3.10, חסד) to a proclamation of action (3.11). Thus, Boaz allows Ruth to perform her role of seducer successfully, and he responds with the appropriate parallel role of suitor.

Boaz as Redeemer

As Boaz acknowledges his added role as suitor, he also accepts the role label of redeemer (3.9, 12, גאל) that Ruth attributes to him.[23] Boaz's acquisition of this role violates social expectation, since he is *not* the closest of Elimelech's relatives. The sexual liaison could be fleeting, but the role of redeemer grounds their relationship in the wider network of social and familial obligations. When Boaz accepts this role of redeemer, he obligates himself to the purchase of the land once owned by Elimelech (4.3). The law requires a close relative to buy back real property sold because of debt (Lev. 25, 27).[24] Naomi does not currently own this land; Elimelech sold it to pay off debts, probably forcing the family's move away from Judah.

Boaz's pending redemption of the land would entail the purchase of the land from whomever currently owned it and the ensuing transfer of that land from Boaz to Naomi, as the representative of Elimelech, at no charge.[25] This would provide a one-time infusion of funds to Naomi and Ruth. Though such an action would discharge Boaz's responsibility, it does not solve the women's long-term problem. Two women could not farm to feed themselves, since they had no means to

23. The view of redemption presented herein is similar to that developed by R. Gordis, 'Love, Marriage, and Business in the Book of Ruth: A Chapter in Hebrew Customary Law', in H.N. Bream, R.D. Heim and C.A. Moore (eds.), *A Light unto My Path: Old Testament Studies in Honor of Jacob M. Myers* (Philadelphia: Temple University Press, 1974), pp. 241-64.

24. Cf. Exod. 6.6 and 15.13, where God redeems the enslaved people by buying them from their owners.

25. Ruth 4.3 indicates that Naomi owned the land outright, causing interpretive difficulties because there has been no mention of this property earlier in the story. But this problem can be solved through a close investigation of the redemption law. The redeemer would buy the land from the stranger and then give it to Naomi, who would sell it back to the redeemer. The redeemer would gain land (at twice its value, one presumes) and Naomi would gain some funds with which to live for a while. In 4.6, the closest relative refuses purchase because he could not afford to buy the land and the slave, Ruth, from Naomi, since that would be his second purchase of the property. For a more standard view, see E.W. Davies, 'Inheritance Rights and the Hebrew Levirate Marriage', *VT* 31 (1981), pp. 138-44, 257-68.

invest in seed or to survive the off-season. The role of redeemer did not obligate Boaz to long-term care, and ch. 3 does not refer to Boaz as potential husband, a role that does not necessarily follow upon that of redeemer.

Boaz does not lose his previous roles as he gains new ones. He maintains his role as provider (3.15, cf. 2.16) and as man of worth, as seen in his attribution of a parallel role label to Ruth (3.11). This gain without complementary role loss presents role dedifferentiation.

Boaz reluctantly agrees to function as redeemer in ch. 3, and then seeks the closest relative to be Naomi's redeemer.[26] The nameless relative accepts the challenge to buy back the land, but then Boaz springs a trap: there is also a slave to be repurchased with the land (4.5). Boaz, however, gives the other relative a chance to renege on the family duty by offering to serve as redeemer himself (4.4). Though the relative agrees to buy the land, he does not accept the idea of repurchasing the slave. The expense of purchasing and/or maintaining the slave would be too great, and such a purchase would deplete his funds that were available for inheritance (4.6).[27] Through the legal machinations in the gate, Boaz assumes the role of legal redeemer for Naomi and Ruth. He locates someone else to take responsibility, but then he uses trickery to bind himself with the enormous costs of redemption.

Boaz as Husband

Surprisingly, Boaz volunteers for the role of Ruth's husband (4.5, 10). This is a permanent legal role; Boaz the husband must provide for Ruth and Naomi for the rest of their lives, unless divorce should sever the relationship. Were Boaz only redeemer, then the one-time transfer of funds would have continued the marginal existence and social isolation of Naomi and Ruth. However, the new role of husband creates a long-term relationship between Boaz and the women that

---

26. Campbell (*Ruth*, pp. 109-10) emphasizes Boaz's willingness to help, but Fewell and Gunn (*Compromising Redemption*, pp. 87-92) realize his reluctance.

27. Though there would have been a need to pass Elimelech's redeemed wealth to Elimelech's son through Ruth, there is no evidence that redemption law required the child of a redeemed woman to receive *all* of a man's inheritance. Thus, the traditional argument that the relative fears his own sons receiving nothing with all of the family wealth going to Ruth's son is erroneous. The depletion of funds due to the expense of the repurchase seems a simpler explanation.

grants them society's greatest guarantees of economic and social security.[28]

Marriage provides an elegant solution to the economic interplay of the redemption process. By bringing his distant relatives into his own family, Boaz acquires Elimelech's property at cost. His machinations in the gate work to his own economic benefit, and so he becomes a fitting trickster hero within the traditions of the Hebrew Bible. Once Boaz considers marrying Ruth, he has a perfect plan to maximize his own wealth, if only he can trick his relative out of his rights to redeem the property. Apparently, the plan succeeds only because Boaz's opponent cannot envision marriage to a foreign woman. For Boaz, the entire narrative takes on a different character. He searches for ways to maximize his own advantage while maintaining his proper family honor; his solution bends the social rules about marriage while adhering to and exceeding the redemption law. Thus, the story ends in success for him because of his willingness to go beyond the role of redeemer and into the role of husband.[29]

The narrative emphasizes Boaz's final role dedifferentiation by depicting it in two stages. In ch. 3, Boaz functions only as potential redeemer, with no indication of the husband role. In 4.5, Boaz asserts the necessity of providing a child to Ruth to perpetuate Elimelech's legacy, but marriage *per se* does not yet appear; Ruth is 'the wife of the dead one' (4.5), not Boaz's future wife. Only in Boaz's concluding speech of the book does he state that he will take Ruth as wife (4.10); the narrator echoes this in 4.13. With this last action of role dedifferentiation, Boaz falls silent; his story has ended.

Role Restoration

At the end of the story, Ruth acquires her last role as she becomes mother (4.13), which leads to the popular proclamation that she is more than seven sons to Naomi (4.15). Naomi, whose bereavement begins the narrative, now ends the tale with a final role dedifferentiation. She becomes the mother of the child, Obed, even to the point of nursing him (4.16). The women's chorus agrees, asserting that this son has been born to Naomi (4.17). The barren (1.11) receives a

---

28. Sasson (*Ruth*, p. 91) also argues that redemption and marriage are separate acts.

29. For the trickery involved here, see Sasson, *Ruth*, pp. 168-69.

child. The cycle of the story finds its completion with Naomi's assumption of the role of mother.[30]

Social Deconstruction of Gender in the Book of Ruth

Though the social processes of the characters within the book of Ruth do not necessarily correspond to any social roles within historical Israel, the narrator presents characters who perform their roles in ways that ancient readers would comprehend. This social sensibility allows sociological analysis to join with literary study in the exegesis of this story. Attention to role dedifferentiation demonstrates that the plot depends upon Ruth's addition of roles and upon this tendency's spread to Naomi and Boaz. Once all of the characters are adding non-standard roles, the narrative's problems attain solutions.

From the start of the story, women deconstruct their gender by dedifferentiating their roles. Specifically, the women take a number of roles that, in their society, were exclusively or predominantly male roles. Naomi dedifferentiates her roles in ways that catalyze; Ruth's dedifferentiation is more active, leading directly to the solution of the story's problems. In terms of gender boundaries, Ruth operates as a man in a man's world, and thus she can affect the changes needed to assure her own survival in a male-dominated culture.

The crucial point in the narrative comes when Boaz adds the roles of suitor, redeemer and husband, thus undergoing role dedifferentiation. When the most prominent male in the story redefines his own roles in response to the story's dedifferentiating women, solutions to the story's problems become available. Boaz accepts the role reversals, including those of gender, even to the point of rescinding his right to the naming of his child.

In this way, the book of Ruth deconstructs gender. Problems attain solutions only when people transgress social conventions and take roles that society limits to the other gender. In the process, the actors reinvent their own social roles and perhaps even their own selves.[31] Certainly, the actions of the story's characters change the social reality

---

30. Bos ('Out of the Shadows', p. 58) clearly articulates the 'radical reversal' implied here, as does Trible (*God and the Rhetoric of Sexuality*, p. 196).

31. L.A. Zurcher, *Social Roles: Conformity, Conflict, and Creativity* (Beverly Hills, CA: Sage, 1983), pp. 211-37; and B.R. Schlenker (ed.), *The Self and Social Life* (New York: McGraw–Hill, 1985).

of their narrative world, so that gender no longer defines and limits potential and possibilities. The deconstructing of gender empowers and enables, eventually resulting in the solution of the story's original problems.

If one recognizes the book of Ruth as a deconstruction of gender, then the book may well have functioned as a rationale for social change.[32] Though the motives of its characters make sense within a framework of patriarchy,[33] their modes of action are explicitly non-sensical because they violate the norms that socially construct reality. This text moves to deconstruct the social-sexual reality of its narrative world, thereby offering a critique of the social-sexual role expectations of its implied audience.

Through a depiction of crisis-initiated dedifferentiation, the narrative deconstructs the gender boundaries of the narrative world in lasting ways. Even after marriage and birth re-establish the story's original state, the women continue to add men's roles, as the women of the community name the new child. The surprising end demonstrates the power of the story, in which people permanently destroy gender role boundaries in mutually profitable ways. Though this process began as a response to crisis, its continuation marks a permanent change within the narrative world. In that context, the story is subversive, focusing not on a redeemer's salvation of the needy through established social rules, but on a disadvantaged foreigner's deconstruction of gender boundaries in order to save herself and her woman.

32. A. LaCocque (*The Feminine Unconventional: Four Subversive Figures in Israel's Tradition* [OBT; Minneapolis: Fortress Press, 1990]) argues that Ruth protests the Ezra–Nehemiah marriage reforms.

33. For a recent discussion of the patriarchy implicit in biblical texts, see K.M. Craig and M.A. Kristjansson, 'Women Reading as Men/Women Reading as Women: A Structural Analysis for the Historical Project', *Semeia* 51 (1990), pp. 119-36.

JSOT 55 (1992), pp. 15-23

INCLUSION, EXCLUSION AND MARGINALITY
IN THE BOOK OF JOSHUA

Lori Rowlett

Times of turmoil tend to produce narratives of identity, requiring a set of axiomatic principles, usually unspoken, but inscribed in the text, which differentiate between 'us' and 'them' (the Other). The conquest narrative of the book of Joshua is such a narrative of identity. On one level, the story appears to be a simple national epic, a narrative of warfare, in which 'all Israel' marches into the land of Canaan by miraculously crossing the Jordan, which functions as a boundary to the promised land.[1] At first glance the division between Israel and the Others appears to be ethnic. The Canaanites are to be destroyed by military action with divine assistance so that 'all Israel' can possess the land. However, most of the episodes in Joshua are not simple battle stories. The focus throughout most of the book of Joshua is on the marginal cases, exploring the questions: who is included, who is excluded, what are the criteria for inclusion, and most importantly, why?

As 'New Historicist' literary critic Stephen Greenblatt has pointed out, a work of art will not only reflect the negotiations and exchanges of power taking place in the society which produced it, but will also be a part of the process.[2] Therefore, any text has an ideological function as an assertion of power. My interest is in the way that the text of Joshua interacts with its sociopolitical context, since the threat inherent in the tales of violence functions as an instrument of coercion, or at least

1. D. Jobling, 'The Jordan a Boundary', in *The Sense of Biblical Narrative* (JSOTSup, 39; Sheffield: JSOT Press, 1986), II, pp. 88-132.

2. S. Greenblatt, *Shakespearean Negotiations: The Circulation of Social Energy in Renaissance England* (Los Angeles: University of California Press, 1988).

encouragement, to submission. The message is that the punishment of Otherness is death, and that insiders can easily become outsiders (Others) by failure to submit to the central government asserting its authority.

Most scholars of the Hebrew Bible agree that the conquest narrative in Joshua, as part of the Deuteronomistic History, was composed in the wake of Assyrian domination, and subsequently re-edited by an exilic redactor or redactors. M. Fishbane,[3] M. Weinfeld,[4] B. Halpern,[5] F.M. Cross[6] and R.D. Nelson[7] see evidence of at least two layers of redaction (one Josianic, one exilic or post-exilic), on the basis of stylistic distinctions and of divergences in theological attitudes. Several German scholars, most notably W. Dietrich[8] and R. Smend,[9] have put forth the hypothesis that the exilic additions were made by two different hands: a nomistic redactor with legal interests, and a prophetic redactor. However, the number of later (exilic or post-exilic) editors (whether one or more) is irrelevant to my central point that the main body of the text took shape during the time of King Josiah, when the monarchy's control was far from secure, as the Assyrian Empire was crumbling and the Neo-Babylonian Empire had not yet risen to power. The values promulgated through the book of Joshua are the values being asserted in Josiah's attempt to consolidate his kingdom.

On the surface level, the book of Joshua tells the story of the people of Israel and how they conquered the land of Canaan. The story of their battles is gruesome but apparently simple. The deity Yahweh is giving Israel the land and enabling them to defeat the various groups

3. M. Fishbane, *Biblical Interpretation in Ancient Israel* (Oxford: Clarendon Press, 1985).

4. M. Weinfeld, *Deuteronomy and the Deuteronomic School* (Oxford: Clarendon Press, 1972).

5. B. Halpern, *The First Historians: The Hebrew Bible and History* (San Francisco: Harper & Row, 1988).

6. F.M. Cross, *Canaanite Myth and Hebrew Epic* (Cambridge, MA: Harvard University Press, 1973).

7. R.D. Nelson, *The Double Redaction of the Deuteronomistic History* (JSOTSup, 18; Sheffield: JSOT Press, 1981).

8. W. Dietrich, *Prophetie und Geschichte* (Göttingen: Vandenhoeck & Ruprecht, 1972).

9. R. Smend, 'Das Gesetz und die Völker: Ein Beitrag zur deuteronomistischen Redaktionsgeschichte', in H.W. Wolff (ed.), *Probleme Biblischer Theologie: Gerhard von Rad zum 70. Geburtstag* (Munich: Chr. Kaiser Verlag, 1971), pp. 494-509.

of Canaanites who are living there. Israel is 'us', the people with whom the reader is to identify. The Canaanites are the opponents, the 'Others'. The emphasis in the battle narratives is on *total* destruction:

> Joshua captured Makkedah...he utterly destroyed it and every person in it. He left no survivor (Josh. 10.28).

> And Yahweh gave it (Libnah) with its king into the hands of Israel, and he struck it and every person who was in it with the edge of the sword. He left no survivor (Josh. 10.30).

> And Joshua and all Israel with him passed on from Lachish to Eglon, and they camped by it and fought against it. And on that day they captured it and struck it with the edge of the sword, and utterly destroyed every person who was in it...(Josh. 10.34-35).

Time after time the same words are repeated: 'he utterly destroyed every person who was in it; he left no survivor'. The text makes its point absolutely clear: the punishment for Otherness is death.

However, the distinction between Israel and the Others based primarily on ethnic, cultural and religious difference begins to break down almost immediately. The surface ideology, in which the cohesive group 'all Israel' is to take complete control of the land inside the boundary of the Jordan and institute pure Yahweh worship there, is already undermined by the problem of the Transjordanian tribesmen in the first chapter. Therefore, the first set of negotiations and exchanges in the text has to do with the question of a marginal case. The Transjordanians have the right ethnicity, the right patriarchal lineage, but they receive their inheritance outside the symbolic boundary of purity, the Jordan—right ethnicity (qualified for insider status), but wrong geographical location (outside). They make an interesting case when compared with another group, the Gibeonites, who are exactly the obverse: wrong ethnicity, but inside the boundary of the 'pure' geographical location. In both marginal cases, the standard of demarcation turns out to be voluntary submission to the authority structure represented by Joshua and his military men; the alternative is the standard punishment for otherness: death.

The book of Joshua begins with a clear delineation of the lines of authority. Yahweh, as the national deity, is to be supreme commander of military affairs. Since Moses the servant of Yahweh is dead, Joshua the servant of Moses is elevated to second-in-command, representing Yahweh on earth. The people are represented as a cohesive entity under the central authority of Joshua. Although they are arranged hierarchically under tribal authority, the text continually reinforces the idea that the people are to find their primary identity as parts of the unified whole, 'all Israel'; tribal identity is to be secondary.

The military hierarchy continues to receive emphasis after Yahweh puts Joshua in charge. The first thing Joshua does, when the deity has finished giving him his orders to cross the Jordan and conquer the territory, is to command the officers of the people, telling them to pass through the camp, commanding (in turn) the people, with exactly the same orders:

> Pass through the midst of the camp and command the people, saying, 'Prepare provisions for yourselves. Within three days you are to cross this Jordan to go in and take possession of this land, which Yahweh your god is giving you to possess' (Josh. 1.11).

The repetitiousness underscores the hierarchical military values of the text.

Once the lines of authority have been established and commands given, Joshua turns to his first marginal case, the tribes of Reuben, Gad and the half-tribe of Manasseh. His words include them as part of the whole. He tells them to cross over with the rest and help them to take possession; afterwards, they may return to their own possessions on the other side of the Jordan. They willingly place themselves under Joshua's authority: 'all that you have commanded us we will do, and wherever you send us we will go' (Josh. 1.16). The lines of military hierarchy are once again reinforced when they promise to obey Joshua, just as they obeyed Moses 'in all things' (v. 17). The most telling part of their submission to authority, however, is their elaboration on their willingness both to obey and to enforce obedience in their own internal ranks (v. 18): 'Anyone who rebels against your command and does not obey your words in everything which you command us, he shall be put to death'. Anyone who steps outside the lines of authority incurs the same fate as the Others, the enemy troops: death.

The Gibeonites in ch. 9 also voluntarily submit to Joshua's central authority and take a place in the hierarchy. 'We are your servants', they announce to Joshua in v. 8. With elaborate trickery, they get Israel to make a covenant by presenting themselves as inhabitants of a land far away when they are actually ethnic outsiders living in the promised land. So their problem is the obverse of that of the Transjordanians: the Transjordanians were the right people on the wrong land, whereas the

Gibeonites are the wrong people on the right land. Their motive for submitting to Joshua is their fear of his, and Yahweh's, military prowess. They have heard of what Yahweh and Joshua did to destroy other opponents. Joshua makes a covenant with them, backed up by an oath sworn by the leaders of the congregation (v. 15): 'Joshua made peace with them and made a covenant with them, to let them live...' Then when their trickery is discovered, the congregation becomes annoyed because of the deception, but the leaders say,

> We have sworn by Yahweh, God of Israel, so we cannot touch them. This will we do for them: let them live, lest wrath be upon us for the oath which we swore to them. The leaders said, 'Let them live' (vv. 19-21).

In return for their deception, the Gibeonites are made into permanent slaves, to hew wood and draw water for Israel, which does not seem like a very appealing covenant from the Gibeonite point of view. The Gibeonites, however, seem to accept their lowly status with gratitude for their lives:

> ...we greatly feared for our lives because of you, and we have done this thing [meaning the deception]. Now, behold, we are in your hand. As it seems good and right in your eyes to do unto us, do it. So he did unto them. He delivered them out of the hand of the sons of Israel, so that they did not slay them (vv. 24-26).

Thus they are spared the usual punishment for Otherness, which is death, because of their voluntary submission to Joshua's and Yahweh's authority. They are allowed to live, and even to stay within the geographical boundaries of the promised land, but they have to take a lowly place in the hierarchy and remain in it forever.

Another pair of marginal cases which can be used to test the theory that voluntary submission to the central authority is the line of demarcation for Otherness is Achan and Rahab. Rahab seeks the protection of Joshua's men when she says to the spies:

> I know that Yahweh has given you the land, and the terror of you has fallen on us... (Josh. 2.9). For we have heard how Yahweh dried up the water of the Red Sea before you... and what you did to the two kings of the Amorites who were beyond the Jordan, Sihon and Og, whom you utterly destroyed (Josh. 2.10).

The men under Yahweh's military command receive homage from Rahab precisely because of their ability to destroy others (like Sihon and Og) in battle.

A key incident in the Joshua story, one which reveals who the real target of the threatened violence in the text is, can be found in the story of Achan. Achan (Josh. 7) is the obverse of Rahab (Josh. 2 and 6). Rahab, a woman and a prostitute as well as a Canaanite, was the ultimate 'Other' who became an insider by voluntarily submitting and pledging her allegiance to Yahweh's hierarchy, represented by Joshua's military machine. Achan was the exemplary insider (with the right lineage) who made himself 'Other' by his lack of submission to the hierarchical authority headed by Yahweh. In his confession to Joshua, Achan acknowledges the deity Yahweh as the one against whom he has ultimately committed his act of insubordination (Josh. 7.20). The hierarchy under Yahweh is further delineated by the repetition of Joshua's name in both the posing of the question and Achan's answer:

> Then *Joshua* said to Achan, 'My son I implore you, give glory to Yahweh the god of Israel, and give praise to him; and tell *me* now what you have done. Do not hide it from me.' So Achan answered *Joshua* and said, 'Truly I have sinned against Yahweh, the god of Israel, and this is what I did...' (Josh. 7.19-20, [italics mine]).

In the space of just a few lines, the text has told us not once, but twice, that Yahweh is the 'god of Israel' and that Joshua is his human representative to whom Achan is answerable. Central to M. Foucault's analysis of power relations is the issue of who has the right (power) to pose questions, and who is obligated to answer them.[10] The text here is highlighting Joshua's authority, second only to Yahweh's in the hierarchy.

Achan's initial insider status is emphasized in the text by the double citation of his parentage and affiliation in precise, patrilineal terms. Again a hierarchical order is given twice (forward and backward) within the space of a few lines:

> Joshua arose early in the morning and brought Israel near by tribes, and the tribe of Judah was taken. And he brought the families of Judah near and the family of the Zerahites was taken; and he brought the family of the Zerahites near, man by man, and Zabdi was taken. And he brought his household near, man by man, and Achan, son of Carmi, son of Zabdi, son of Zerah, from the tribe of Judah, was taken (Josh. 7.16-18).

The strong overcoding of the lines of authority in the text makes the power assertion inherent within it perfectly clear: individuals belong to households, which belong to families; the families are subordinate

10. M. Foucault, *Surveiller et Punir* (Paris: Gallimard, 1975).

to the patriarchal heads of the tribes, who, in turn, are to find their identity primarily as components of the entity 'Israel', whose god is Yahweh. The deity's chosen representative on earth, to whom Yahweh gives commands and to whom the people are answerable, is Joshua. Everyone has a particular place in the centralized system, and everyone ('all Israel') belongs firmly under Joshua's control. Achan, the individual who has tried to step out from under the lines of authority, is therefore subject to punishment not only by Joshua but by 'all Israel', the cohesive yet stratified entity:

> Joshua and all Israel with him took Achan the son of Zerah, the silver, the mantle, the bar of gold, his sons, his daughters, his oxen, his donkeys, his sheep, his tent and all that belonged to him; and they brought them up to the Valley of Achor. And Joshua said, 'Why have you troubled us? Yahweh will trouble you this day.' And all Israel stoned them with stones, and they burned them with fire after they had stoned them with stones (Josh. 7.24-25).

Everything which falls underneath Achan's control in the patriarchal system, namely his offspring and possessions, is destroyed along with him, which serves to emphasize further the hierarchical aspect of the political arrangement. The total destruction of Achan and everything under him is also reminiscent of the ban, which Achan had violated in his insubordination. By hoarding the booty from Jericho, he had infected the entire community with its presence among them. In order to restore purity, the source of the pollution—Achan himself, possessor of the banned items, and everyone in close proximity to him—had to be removed from the community. (The purity–impurity aspect of the ban is emphasized also in Deut. 7.22-26 and 13.13-17.) Impurity is usually projected onto the opponents in literature of violence in an attempt to justify the action taken against them.

Rahab's function as an obverse image of Achan is reinforced by her reappearance in the text (Josh. 6.22-25) immediately before the Achan incident of Joshua 7. According to the basic structure of the conquest narrative in Joshua, Israelites are insiders and Canaanites are outsiders (Others) to be utterly destroyed in battle. In the battle reports and war oracles, the lines are starkly drawn in ethnic terms. However, most of the book of Joshua consists of a series of what Greenblatt would call 'negotiations and exchanges',[11] which determine who will be accepted

11. Greenblatt, *Shakespearean Negotiations*, p. 12.